With love

from Dad.

1-6-72

THE MODERN LIBRARY
of the World's Best Books

≫≫≫

THE FLOWERING
OF NEW ENGLAND
1815-1865

THE FLOWERING
OF NEW ENGLAND
1815-1865

>>

BY

VAN WYCK BROOKS

>>

>>

THE MODERN LIBRARY
NEW YORK

#41472669

THE MODERN LIBRARY

IS PUBLISHED BY

RANDOM HOUSE, INC.

BENNETT A. CERF · DONALD S. KLOPFER · ROBERT K. HAAS

Manufactured in the United States of America
Printed by Parkway Printing Company   Paper by Richard Bauer & Co.
Bound by H. Wolff

VAN WYCK BROOKS

(1886–   )

A NOTE ON THE AUTHOR OF
"THE FLOWERING OF NEW ENGLAND"

Immediately after his graduation from Harvard in 1907, Van Wyck Brooks cultivated his interest in literary criticism by working on the editorial staff of Doubleday, Page and Company. At the end of two years of reading miscellaneous manuscripts he decided to abandon the search for a needle in a haystack to write his own first book, *The Wine of the Puritans*, a critical examination of American civilization and institutions. It was considered so brilliant that it led to an offer of a lectureship at Leland Stanford University from 1911 to 1913. During that time he wrote *The Malady of the Ideal*, a study of Obermann, Amiel and Maurice de Guerin, and he produced three critical works in the following three years: *John Addington Symonds*, *The World of H. G. Wells* and the still influential *America's Coming-of-Age*.

Because the attraction of publishing was too strong to resist, Brooks returned to an editorial post with the Century Company, and, in 1920, became associate editor of *The Freeman*, and, subsequently, of *The American Caravan*. In the meantime he created something of a literary sensation with his iconoclastic study, *The Ordeal of Mark Twain*, and added very considerably to his stature as a critic with *The Pilgrimage of Henry James*, *Emerson and Others*, *The Life of Emerson*, *Sketches in Criticism* and *Three Essays on America*. For these contributions to the art of criticism he was awarded the *Dial* prize of $2,000.

An indefatigable worker, Brooks has to his credit numerous translations. But all this labor was in preparation for the appearance, in 1936, of his masterpiece, *The Flowering of New England*, which has been accorded every honor that can be bestowed upon a book in the United States. His last published work, *New England: Indian Summer*, carries forward his study of American literature from the close of the Civil War to the time of the First World War.

To

MAXWELL EVARTS PERKINS

CONTENTS

CONTENTS

PREFACE

THIS is the first of a number of volumes in which I hope to sketch the literary history of the United States. It is an episode of a larger cycle, neither the first nor the last, and I have omitted various authors who might have been included but whose lives are more properly seen in other connections. Among these are Bryant and "Artemus Ward." Whether I can carry out the whole of this undertaking, I have no means of knowing at the moment. The present volume, at least, is complete in itself.

My subject is the New England mind, as it has found expression in the lives and works of writers. I have chosen the narrative form to present this subject, but I can assure the sceptical reader that I have not indulged in fiction. It has seemed to me unnecessary to resort to notes to support my own authority. I have therefore used them only to convey additional facts for which there was not room in the text. But I have taken pains with the documentation, and I can quote chapter and verse—in some trustworthy source of the time, some diary, memoir, letter or whatever—for every phrase that appears in the book. I raise the question here because the "fictional" method has become so common, in the writing of lives and histories, and because my work may have an air of fiction.

In dealing with separate authors, in several cases, I have incorporated in my text phrases directly taken from their writings. I have used this expedient elsewhere, in my books on Emerson and Henry James, to give an effect of immediacy in conveying the author's thoughts and feelings.

In a succeeding volume, I propose to continue the theme of the present volume, picturing the literary scene of New England from the Civil War to 1915. It is my plan, in this volume, while dealing with a new group of authors, to describe the later careers of the older group, relating the generations to one another. Among the younger authors I shall include a few like Francis Parkman, already known before the Civil War, whose work mainly belongs in the later setting.

THE FLOWERING
OF NEW ENGLAND
1815-1865

CHAPTER I

THE BOSTON OF GILBERT STUART

AT THE time of the Peace of Ghent, which brought to
a close the War of 1812, Gilbert Stuart, the portrait-
painter, was an old inhabitant of Boston. He had lived in
the town,—for it was still a town, not to become a city for
almost a decade,—nine good years. The son of a Rhode
Island snuff-grinder, he had made his way up in the world
of art until nobody questioned his eminence. He was
famous in London and Dublin, where he had been a rival
of Lawrence and Beechey. In all American circles, his
word was law. No one dared to praise an American poet
until the *Edinburgh Review* had done so, but Stuart was
the arbiter in painting. In his careless way, he had neglected to answer the letter from the Academy of Florence
asking for a portrait of himself. He did not need these
testimonials. In the capital of New England, whither he
had come to live and die, everyone praised and admired
him. Even John Adams, the patriarch of Quincy, who
said he would not give sixpence for a Raphael, yielded to
the spell of the genial artist. The old man had rejoiced,
with a Puritan's fervour, that the age of painting and sculpture had not arrived to corrupt his beloved country. But
Gilbert Stuart's witty anecdotes charmed away his prejudices. After his first sitting, he exclaimed that he would
be glad to sit to Stuart from one year's end to another.

Times had undoubtedly changed in the Christian
Sparta, as John Adams's cousin, Samuel Adams, had called
the town of Boston. Gilbert Stuart, who was a notable

wag, liked to begin his anecdotes by saying, "When I lived in the Athens of America." Everyone knew what he meant by the phrase: he was referring to Philadelphia. And every Bostonian knew that he was mistaken. William Penn's town had taken the lead in all these matters of enlightenment—thanks to a good Bostonian, Benjamin Franklin; but that was in days past. The real American Athens was the Christian Sparta. At least, it was advancing towards this position, with large and rapid strides; and Stuart knew it. He was only indulging a taste for mischief. In England, when people had asked him where he was born, he had said, by way of explaining Narragansett, "six miles from Pottawome and ten miles from Poppasquash." His sitters were little the wiser when he added that he had spent his early years at Newport, where, in some of the old merchants' houses, he had seen portraits by Van Dyck and Kneller, real or supposititious. And if he liked to tease the men of Boston, who suffered from no lack of self-esteem, it was not because he found them dull. He laughed at blue laws and blue noses, but so did many of his Boston sitters, those who had not lost their Tory ways and some of those who belonged to the younger circles. For the dominant Boston nose was far from blue: it was a Roman nose, flanked by a full-blown complexion. Stuart, with his lordly style, his fresh, ruddy face and downright manners,—not to mention his taste for the best Madeira, which he poured from a half-gallon ewer, throwing off tumblers like cider in haying-time,— was quite at home with the great East India merchants, whose ships had sometimes carried the Madeira twice round the Cape, to give it a good rocking. They liked the hearty freedom of a man who, when one of his sitters fell asleep, painted him with ass's ears. They liked a man who, if he used snuff, used half a pound of it a day. They liked his high spirits and his flowing talk, as well as the claret he seemed to mix with his paint. And they liked the uncanny skill with which he dived into their own thoughts, —for they were proud of their thoughts,—and made them live and speak on his eloquent canvas.

This was the golden age of portrait-painting. It was an age of public men. It was an age of family pride, nowhere more marked than in Boston. It was an age of modest wealth, which the recent war had checked but not extinguished. For three generations, since the days of Smibert, Boston had supported its portrait-painters, and Gilbert Stuart was another Copley. It was true that the town had little feeling for art. Stuart was to die as obscure and poor as any tippling poet in the gutter. The Boston people did not cherish him—much as they enjoyed his company—because they were proud that one of the world's artists had chosen to live in Boston. They cherished him, because he so greatly added to their own pride in themselves; and when they finally buried him in the Common, near the famous Julien of the "soup," they did not even mark his grave. Boston was torpid in aesthetic matters. Stuart had refused to exhibit his pictures because they had been hung so badly. Boston was congenitally obtuse in all that concerned the senses, except Madeira; and this was still to be true a century later, when, with little more aesthetic feeling, the town possessed so much aesthetic knowledge. It was always to look on the plastic arts, instinctively, as a clever woman said, in the days when New Yorkers liked to tease Bostonians, merely as branches of literature. There was something cold and dry in its perceptions. But the very elements in its social life that nourished the portrait-painters,—the family pride, the wealth, the public spirit,—were obviously creating a situation that fostered all its natural faculties. The merchant-patricians, like those of Holland and Flanders, in times gone by, wished to perpetuate their names and glorify their capital not only in the elegance of their mansions but also in churches, parks and public buildings, in professorial chairs at Harvard College, in schools and asylums and hospitals. Such were the desires and thoughts that Stuart caught in the faces of his sitters.

All the omens favoured these intentions. The recent war had cleared the atmosphere. For twenty years after the Revolution, Boston had been poor and apprehensive. The nation was torn with sectional dissensions. Everyone feared the interference of England. Napoleon was abroad like a wolf in the night. But Waterloo and Commodore Perry had quieted these anxieties. England had ceased to be a menace. The abhorrent career of Napoleon had broken the old connection with France. Europe had become engrossed in problems that had little meaning across the ocean. America, united and free at last, with all its problems solved, as it seemed at the moment, faced a future that was almost dazzling. The "era of good feeling" was beginning, and circumstances had been kind to Boston. The war, which had largely destroyed the commerce of the smaller New England ports, had had no lasting effect on the capital. Strong enough, in fact, to survive the crisis, it prospered with the ruin of so many rivals; and it was attracting more and more the younger merchants of the rural regions who had taken advantage of the decline of shipping, during the years of war, and the boycott of English goods that followed the war, to build up a manufacturing system and supply the American people with native products. Factory-towns were rising on every hand, in eastern Massachusetts and New Hampshire,—Lawrence, Lowell, Fitchburg, Manchester, Lynn. Every village with a waterfall set up a textile-mill or a paper-mill, a shoe-factory or an iron-foundry; and as Boston remained the financial centre, as well for manufacturing as for shipping, the mercantile fortunes of the inland counties were joined with those of the magnates of the seaboard.

Boston was rich, in short, as never before; and, having the means, the leading citizens could not imagine why their little town should not be the finest in the world. No one challenged this prepossession. New England was an isolated region, and Boston had some right to its self-esteem. It had taken the lead in the Revolution, with the statesmen of Virginia, and played a large part in both the wars in which the United States had defeated England. The boast of the Boston poet, —

> We have the guns,
> We have the ships,—

was justified by the British themselves. All their commentators had asserted that the American cruisers were the best and that the Yankee rifle in Yankee hands had set a new standard of marksmanship. No one could guess what happy fortunes lay before the valiant young republic, and Boston hoped for a special dispensation. The old dream of a Puritan commonwealth, a true city of God, lingered in the New England mind, and it seemed as if the appointed hour had come. Cotton Mather had foretold this hour. Jonathan Edwards, on his lonely rides over the forest hills of leafy Stockbridge, had seen the millennium approaching. Bishop Berkeley, on his farm at Newport, had prophesied the golden age. The hard conditions of life in earlier days had yielded to more propitious circumstances. The time was surely ripe; and what wealth was unable to compass might be left to piety and reason. The Boston people had only themselves to blame, or so, at least, they felt, if the kingdom of heaven, a sober New England kingdom,—not built of the gaudy materials that vulgarized the Book of Revelation,—were not, at last, at hand.

They meant to do their best. The Lowells, the Cabots, the Appletons, the Jacksons, the "codfish aristocracy" and the "Essex Junto,"—the members of which had wished to break the Union, in favour of their New England separatism,—the Perkinses, Higginsons, Cushings, the brothers Lawrence, who had made their fortunes on the sea, along with the Hong merchants of the Flowery Kingdom, or from the whirring of their wheels and spindles, united in a passion for the *genius loci*. Some of them suggested in their faces, faithfully painted by Stuart, the florid merchants of colonial times, their grand-sires and uncles, in velvet cap and flowered robe, flushed with wine and generosity. Others recalled the Puritan cast, the lean, shrewd, nervous Yankee type, cautious, with a turn for metaphysics, dried by the American atmosphere. All of them lived and moved, walked and spoke as if their little town were a holy city and Rome, Paris and London were their suburbs. For this there were certain reasons. Boston was only a regional capital, but a Boston man could say to himself, quite truly, that it was much more a capital than either New York or Philadelphia; for the people were more homogeneous. A visitor from New York, observing the crowd in the streets, exclaimed, "Why, all these people are of one race. They behave like members of one family, whereas with us a crowd is an assembly of all the nations upon earth." As one of the results of this homogeneity, the institutions of the town and country had a greater similarity than in other regions,—a fact that was full of meaning for the future. It favoured the growth of the region in all its parts. For, while Boston attracted the master-minds and took them away from the smaller towns, it rendered them more active and efficient; and, precisely because of this concentration of powers, it was able to send forth influences that were beneficial to the rural districts. It was able to do so and it wished to do so, more and more as the century advanced. The older patrician families, those that had come over in the "Arbella," and those of whom it was said that, at the time of the Deluge, they had a boat to themselves, possessed a sense of responsibility that sometimes seemed acute. The eminent men who had come from the country, or from the smaller ports and county-seats, and who mingled on equal terms with the patricians, were loyal to their rustic antecedents. One and all felt, as the Boston orators were always saying, in the old "cradle of liberty," Faneuil Hall, that they were the heirs of the Revolution. They were determined to carry out, in every sphere in which their interests lay, their duties as American citizens. They meant to make Boston a model town. They meant to make New England a model region.

Boston was another Edinburgh, with marked variations of its own. It resembled Edinburgh in many ways, as New England resembled Scotland. The bitter climate and the hard soil, the ice, the granite and the Calvinism, yielding to more gracious forms of faith, the common schools, the thrifty farmer-folk, the coast-line, with its ports and sailors' customs, the abundant lakes and mountains, the geological aspects of the region, all suggested the land of Sir Walter Scott, as well as the adjacent land of Wordsworth, whose bareness and simplicity, together with his loftiness and depth,—proofs, as Hazlitt said, that his work was written in a mountainous country,—commended him to the young New England mind; and if, in this mind, there was something cold and hard that recalled the ice and the granite, there were reserves of feeling and perception that were to find expression in the years to come. A well-known Scottish traveller * remarked of Boston, "I could scarcely believe I was not in Scotland." One found there, as in Edinburgh, the same wealth, similarly earned, the same regard for manners and decorum, the same respect for learning, the same religious point of view, alike in its antecedents and in its liberal modifications, the same scrupulous conscientious-

* Sir Charles Lyell,—some years later.

ness, the same punctiliousness and the same pride, even the same prudence. One found the same exactions in matters of taste, the same aristocratic prepossessions and the same democratic feeling underneath them. The golden calf the Bostonians worshipped was a mere pygmy, as Dickens said, a generation later, beside the giant effigies one found in the other American cities.

Not that the Boston people were other-worldly, for all their messianic expectations, except as compared with the profane New Yorkers. Some of them lived in magnificent style. Many of them were accomplished in the art of living. The Cushing house in Summer Street was surrounded with a wall of Chinese porcelain. Peacocks strutted about the garden. The Chinese servants wore their native dress. The older folk, sedate, a little complacent, dwelling in the solid garden-houses that stood about the Common, each with its flagged walk and spacious court-yard, filled with fragrant shrubs, shaded by its over-arching elms, were genial and pleasure-loving, as a rule. Here and there one found a Sybarite. Harrison Gray Otis, at the age of eighty, after forty years of gout, breakfasted every morning on *pâté de foie gras.* Every afternoon, at the Otis house, ten gallons of punch evaporated out of the Lowestoft bowl that was placed on the landing. One of the Perkins brothers, challenged by a rigorous pastor, who had come out for total abstinence, doubled his children's ration of Madeira. Even the young girls, in some of these houses, where they maintained the royalist traditions and sometimes toasted "the King," under the rose, read *Tom Jones,* Smollett and *Tristram Shandy,* as if they had never heard of a Pilgrim Father. In every house one found the standard authors, Hume, Gibbon, Shakespeare, Milton, Dryden, Addison, the *Arabian Nights, Don Quixote,* Sir William Temple's works in folio, a set of Hogarth's original plates, perhaps, or two or three first editions of Pope, books that were worthy of their calf bindings, on shelves that might have been carved by Grinling Gibbons, surmounted by marble busts. The children were brought up on Maria Edgeworth and the writings of Mrs. Barbauld and Fanny Burney. Sons who came home from abroad with too many airs were greeted with an almost crushing composure. The Boston people were willing to learn, but only if one recognized how much they knew already. Their minds were closed on certain lines, and they did not like "originality." But, as a generation that knew the world, they were prepared to humour their sons and daughters.

There were many strains in the Boston mind, a warm and chivalrous Tory strain, a passionate strain of rebelliousness, a strain of religious fervour, a marked and even general disposition,—despite the sybaritic Mr. Otis, who, for the rest, was public-spirited,—to sacrifice at other than mundane altars. The town abounded in quixotic souls, "unmanageable" Adamses, younger sons who refused the social uniform, visionaries, *exaltés,* nonconformists. The future was to provide them with their causes. It was true that these idealists, who spoke for "impossible loyalties," found Beacon Hill a mountain of ice. Principle was a reality in Boston. Conscience was a large reality. Everyone knew the story of the merchant who, when one of his ships was overdue, found that he was more anxious about his thoughts than about the money he was losing. Was it possible, he asked himself, that he had really grown to love his money more for itself than for its noble uses? To settle the point in his own mind, he reckoned the value of the ship and cargo and gave the sum to his favourite charity. The story was typical of the Boston merchants who, within a space of thirty years, from 1810 to 1840, established thirty benevolent institutions. And yet there were those who said

that Boston had a double intellect and only half a heart.
The prevailing mind was cautious, excessively formal,
singularly obsessed with its own importance, bigoted in
its fear of political change. The mother of "Athenæum"
Shaw enjoined upon him, during his early travels, the
virtues of silence, secrecy and circumspection, quoting the
counsel of an experienced father, that one should keep
one's countenance open but one's thoughts close. The
Puritans had learned this art in their days of persecu-
cion, and a trading community had found it useful. Moreover, the prevailing mind was legalistic. Burke—with Dr.
Johnson, its favourite author—noted that more than half
of the first edition of Blackstone's Commentaries found
its way to America. A large proportion had remained in
Boston, where it served as an arsenal of logic against the
Jacobins and their bob-tailed crew. For Boston was controlled by an oligarchy, an unofficial caste of leading men
for whom a "republic" and a "democracy" had next to
nothing in common. Hamiltonian Federalists to a man,
Whigs after the fall of Federalism, they had found that
the doctrines of Burke and Johnson admirably supported
their property-interests. For the rest, they had "looked
at France," as Fisher Ames had advised them to do, and
witnessed the results of a red revolution,—anarchy, in-
fidelity, just as Burke had prophesied, with a lord of mis-
rule, Napoleon, as the end of all things.

Stability at any price! They had had too many wars
and altercations. The first French Republic had gone to
the dogs. They could not believe that their own would
fare much better. In days of debt and disunitedness, it
was a natural assumption that power ought to go with
property. The theory had a special justification in days
when *not* to have property, if one wished it, was almost
a certain sign of shiftlessness. "Where are your poor?"
said Lafayette, when, a few years later, he scrutinized
the crowds in the Boston streets. The slum was a thing of

the future,* and most of the rich men had acquired their wealth by the superior exercise of traits that almost every Yankee shared and applauded. Besides, if their minds were closed in political matters, they were more than liberal in religion. They took a lenient view of human nature. Few traces of Puritanism were left among them. Most of them had seen the world, as supercargoes, merchants, statesmen, students. They had fought with Tripolitan pirates, visited Canton, India and Egypt, bought skins in Canada and sold them in China, carried ice from Labrador to Java, taken the grand tour to Rome and Naples and had themselves measured by London tailors, who continued to make their clothes when they had shrunk within the measurements. The fact that the clothes were made in London was more important than that they did not fit. If their views were not loose, like their clothes, at least they were enlarged, as people said. They no longer looked on their fellow-beings with the eyes of Puritan deacons. Indeed, the human nature they found about them, far from being totally depraved, seemed, in the light of these wider circumstances, compared with Chinese coolies and Italian beggars, singularly innocent and good. Who had measured its capacity? Boston boys believed in themselves. They grew up alert and self-reliant,† battling with the east winds, coasting over the frozen snow, convinced that they were able to "lick creation."‡ How could they accept the ancestral doctrine of

* There was, however, one region in Boston, on the Cambridge side of Beacon Hill, that is said to have been extremely squalid and vicious. It was filled with crowded, tumble-down tenements where crime ran riot. The population was largely black, with a worse white intermixture. This region greatly exercised the Boston and Cambridge humanitarians, notably the fathers of Lowell the poet and Charles Eliot Norton.

† A rule of the household of Wendell Phillips's father, the first mayor of the city of Boston: "Ask no man to do for you anything that you are not able and willing to do for yourself."

‡ All classes in New England shared this assurance. See Emerson's Journal, at sea, 1833: "The captain believes in the superiority of the American to every other countryman. 'You will see,' he says, 'when you get out here how they manage in Europe; they do everything by main strength and ignorance. Four truckmen and four stevedores at Long Wharf will load my brig quicker than a hundred men at any port in the Mediterranean.'"

the worthlessness of human efforts and motives? How could they hear themselves described as "vipers"? Were Boston boys "little fallen wretches," even worse than vipers? They were more ready to think that, having succeeded in so many things, they could succeed in everything. In short, they believed in perfectibility.

This change in their religious point of view, gradual, scarcely perceptible at first, signified an emotional revolution as marked as the events of '76. Absorbed as they were in politics and trade, the Boston folk were hardly aware that the old faith had vanished from their horizon. Twenty years before, the well-known wit, Robert Treat Paine, had cursed the "Vandal spirit of Puritanism,"— a levity of the fashionable circles, savouring of the colonial governor's court, that had grown to be a commonplace. In 1809, the most popular preacher in Boston, referring to the creed of the Pilgrim Fathers,—Calvinism, with its "revolting forms,"—spoke of Milton's eyes as having been "quenched in the service of a vulgar and usurping faction." A mild and tolerant Unitarianism, rationalistic, torpid, utilitarian, had been set up as the State Church. Known far and wide as the "Boston religion," it still possessed a frail dogmatic structure, of which it was only conscious when it was challenged. The ministers were graceful rhetoricians. Calling themselves Arminians or Arians, sometimes Moderate Calvinists, they still believed in the supernatural; and, having "disproved" the Trinitarian doctrine, with most of the other doctrines of their forbears, they clung to the Christian miracles, as the proper evidences of the faith.

Negative and pallid as it was, the new religion sprang from an atmosphere that was favourable to the flowering of the mind. The ministers, learned, cultivated men, lovers of music and eloquence, had introduced the literary sermon. Their models were Bossuet and Massillon. They had abandoned the older pulpit methods, the texts, the

arguments and the commentaries. Their sermons were
glowing essays, dealing with the interests of daily life.
Joseph Stevens Buckminster, the melodious preacher, the
"Chrysostom of America," as he was called, who had
read his Greek Testament at five, had prophesied the
birth of a great school of American letters. Poets and
historians, he had said, in one of his discourses at Harvard College, were soon to appear, to direct American
taste and mould the genius of the young republic, men
of whom posterity was to stand in awe. "You, my young
friends," he had exclaimed, "are destined to witness the
dawn of our Augustan age, and to contribute to its
glory,"—a very different note from Fisher Ames's, the
spokesman of the previous decade, who had never missed
a chance to say that the American genius was foredoomed
to fail. Buckminster's successor, William Ellery Channing, the great ethical leader of the future, equally san-
guine, was more critical. The impassioned little saint with
the burning heart, whose intellect was the conscience of
New England, felt that the hour had struck for American
thinkers. Mind, mind required all one's care! In his youth
he had had a sudden illumination, a vision of human
nature, which seemed to him a godhead in the making.
He ceaselessly preached the gospel of self-improvement.
"We want great minds," he said, "to be formed among
us. We want the human intellect to do its utmost here."

Boston corresponded to Plato's city, a population that
was not too large to hear the voice of a single orator.
The people were prepared for these stirring sermons.
With Faneuil Hall as their Acropolis, they were accustomed to public speaking, and oratory had filled them
with exalted thoughts. At school they learned to recite
the swelling strains of the *Life of William Tell:* "Friends
of liberty, sons of sensibility, ye who know how to die for
your independence!" Bombast, in a sense, but they believed it. Their fathers and uncles had fought in a sim-

ilar cause, swept along by a tide of eloquence. Moreover, Plutarch was their second Bible, together with Pope's Homer. Deep in their hearts they cherished the conviction that they could emulate these heroic models and reproduce the deeds of history. The sons of William Emerson, for instance, the former minister of the First Church, who had founded the Philosophical Society, were born with these convictions in their blood, and one of them, a boy of twelve named Ralph, a chubby little spouter of Scott and Campbell, who had recently trundled his hoop about the Common, where he pastured the family cow, was to express them later in his essays. The Emerson boys, "born to be educated,"—the object of a Boston childhood seemed to be to prepare for the Latin School,—were typical of a ministerial household, heirs of a long line of divines and scholars, one of whom had prayed every evening that none of his descendants might ever be rich. Their mother, like all the devout New England matrons, enjoyed her morning hour of meditation. Their aunt, the minister's sister, Mary Moody Emerson of Concord, who despised the new religion, poor, low, thin, as she thought it was, dwelt in the fiery depths of a Calvinism which, although she only half believed it, filled her with a sombre poetry. She prophesied that her nephews were to be called of men Rabbis and Fathers. Ralph already had a mind of his own. He carried the *Pensées* of Pascal to church, to read during the sermon. At night, in his cold upper chamber, covered with woollen blankets to the chin, he read his precious Dialogues of Plato. He associated Plato, ever after, with the smell of wool.

Under its placid surface, Boston tingled with a new ambition. Half the boys expected to go to sea. They hovered about the ships and the wharves, scenting the salt air, the ropes and the tar, listening to tales of Chinese pirates, greeting some cousin, home from Spanish Manila, in white trousers and jacket of sky-blue silk, marvelling over an older brother who, for a lark, on his way back from Cairo, had travelled the length of Italy, in his carriage, dressed as an Oriental potentate. As many others dreamed of a life of letters. Here and there, some poor young man, who could not go to the Latin School, bought his own Andrews and Stoddard's grammar, from which every proper Boston boy supposed the Latin language had been derived, and spent his nights over a commonplace-book, copying his favourite passages from Gibbon. Learning was endemic in the Boston mind, as befitted a town whose first inhabitant, the Cambridge scholar Blaxton,—who had built his thatched cottage, with a garden and spring, on the site of Louisburg Square,—had brought his library with him. There had been books on the slope of Beacon Hill when the wolves still howled on the summit. There had always been some Boston man who could address in Arabic or Persian a merchant or diplomat from the land of Xerxes; and now that the war was over, and the nation seemed to be on a solid footing, the intellectual life grew apace. The clever Frenchmen, with their godless notions, had made all thought suspicious for a while. The Boston people preferred to settle questions by thumping the table, or by whacks and blows,* in the manner of Dr. Johnson. But subtlety had grown with confidence. The argand lamp, improved by Jefferson, had furthered the habit of reading. It was observed at once that dinner-parties, formerly lighted by candles, ceased to be as brilliant as of old. Those who had excelled in talking took to their books and writing-desks. It was true that this intellectual life was timid, cautious and derivative. In short, it was still colonial,

---

* Not, however, delivered on the person. In spite of the downright ways of the old Bostonians, New England was noted for its mildness. Timothy Dwight reported that he had never heard of a New England man using arms in a private quarrel. Josiah Quincy said that only five duels were known to have taken place in New England up to 1820.

forty years after Bunker Hill. English culture had a right
of way that no one thought of challenging, and every
Boston boy was taught to regard Pope and Burke as unapproachable. The literary government of Europe was a
more potent yoke than the political government had been.
But the ferment of the rising generation might be expected to break it.

As if to provide the future with a proper setting, the
Boston people had rebuilt the town. The architect,
Charles Bulfinch, the son of a doctor, had appeared with
providential promptness. A man of sensibility, he had
been moved to tears, on a tour of Europe, when he had
entered St. Peter's at Rome. He had been obliged to
teach himself. Among so many carpenters and builders,
skilful, well-trained craftsmen, schooled in the styles of
Wren and Inigo Jones, there was not an architect in Boston when he returned in 1787; and, search as one might,
high and low, one could not find a book on architecture.
Bulfinch, who had bought some books in Europe and
found his taste and talent in demand, soon developed a
style,—an outgrowth of the prevailing style, more
delicate than the colonial Georgian, quite without the
English massiveness,—that caught the temper of the Boston people. It was modestly elegant, somewhat prim, but
dignified and simple. He had built the first theatre in the
town, as far back as 1793, where all Boston rejoiced in
The School for Scandal, disguised as a "moral lecture."
He had built the admirable State House, which was to
serve as a model for so many others. He had filled Boston
with his works, houses and blocks of houses, crescents,
churches, which, with their grace and propriety, struck
the note of an epoch, an outward and visible sign that the
new Boston mind had crystallized and found its appropriate form. Various institutions of learning followed in
rapid succession, a Library of Law in 1806, a Theological
Library in 1807,—in the same year, the Boston Athe-

næum. Modelled on the Liverpool Athenæum, this was largely the work of Buckminster, who had spent most of his little fortune buying books in Paris. He had sent three thousand volumes home, sets of the British essayists and poets, the Botanical Magazine, topographical works on Greece and Rome that brought the classical world before one's eyes, works in unknown realms, Roscoe's *Lorenzo de' Medici,* Duppa's *Life of Michael Angelo,* Italian and Spanish dictionaries. The first wistaria vine, the first mimosa was scarcely more of a novelty in Boston than some of these intellectual plants and vines that 'were to scatter their seeds across New England.

Two other institutions, the Handel and Haydn Society and the *North American Review*—founded, both, in 1815—marked the coming-of-age of the Boston mind. For music and for letters, these were of the future. The culture of the immediate past and present found expression through another organ. For several years there had existed, from 1803 to the outbreak of the war, a club devoted to literary interests. The Anthology Society, as it was called, numbered among its members Buckminster, Channing, William Emerson, Dr. Gardiner, the rector of Trinity Church, William Tudor, the merchant, President Kirkland of Harvard, John Lowell and other well-known men. The members met one evening every week to discuss the manuscripts for their magazine, the *Monthly Anthology,* over a modest supper of widgeons and teal, brants or a mongrel goose, with a little good claret. There was too little intercourse, they felt, among Americans who cared for letters. They even hoped that their review, the first of its kind in the country, which had succeeded many feebler efforts, might foster the growth of a national literature.

The members were not professional men of letters, a species that was still unknown in Boston. Moreover, their expectations were not excessive, or much beyond the

pleasures of their task. William Emerson was the editor.
William Tudor, who had established the club, had made a
small fortune, with his brother, shipping ice, cut from
their pond at Saugus, to Martinique and South America.
Indeed, the Tudors introduced, throughout the equatorial
world, even as far as Calcutta, the custom of using ice in
table-drinks.* Dr. Gardiner, an Episcopalian, conducted
a little school in his spacious study, instructing a chosen
handful in Latin and Greek, following the methods of his
master, the great English scholar, Samuel Parr. Among
the other contributors or members, some of them correspondents from a distance, were the rising Portsmouth
lawyer, Daniel Webster, who had not yet moved to Boston, the Reverend Aaron Bancroft, who lived in Worcester, a theologian of the older school, the father of a
son who was soon to be famous, Joseph Story of Salem,
the notable jurist, the greatest writer on the law since
Blackstone, as the Lord Chief Justice of England called
him later, and various younger men of ample promise,
Alexander Everett and George Ticknor. Judge Story, a
classmate of Dr. Channing, had published a poem, *The
Power of Solitude,* suggested by the writings of Zimmer-
mann. Although he had taken a "lawyer's farewell of the
muse," he often entertained himself in court by making
his notes of arguments in verse.

The magazine, though somewhat staid in manner, decidedly starched and impersonal, was yet an enterprise
that promised much, in days when "Who wrote Junius?"
was still an exciting topic of conversation. In style it resembled the British reviews, not yet irradiated by Lamb
and Hazlitt,—the English Unitarian minister's son who
had spent three years, as a boy, in Massachusetts, who
had seen Boston before he saw London and never forgot
the Yankee barberry-bushes. Far from calling a spade a

---

* It was to William Tudor, when he was presented to George the Fourth,
that the king remarked, "What, one of us?"

spade, it always called a name an appellation. Behind
these traits of Johnsonese, moreover, might have been
discerned the self-distrust that marks the colonial mind,
a mind that has no centre of its own and clings to the
well-tried ways of the mother-country after the mother-
country has thrown them off. It abounded in Addisonian
bric-a-brac, playful bits on toast and cranberry sauce,
worthy of a Grandison's hours of ease, accounts of visits
to Dr. Johnson's birthplace, continuations of Collins's
Ode to the Passions, reviews of *The Gamesters: or Ruins
of Innocence,* Beresford's *The Miseries of Human Life*
and *A Wreath for the Rev. Daniel Dow.* It defended
Pope against all comers, especially Coleridge's nonsense.
Even in Boston there were even lawyers who thought its
tone was pompous and said that Dr. Gardiner was a snob.
This was a little severe. The magazine was well-informed.
It reviewed the museums, the theatres, the social assemblies, and criticized the state of Harvard College.
It noticed the important publications, Washington Irving's *Knickerbocker,* Aaron Bancroft's *Washington,*
Madame de Staël's *Corinne,* Wilson's *American Orni-
thology.* It published intelligent essays on Erasmus, the
Carelessness of Dryden, Sir Walter Scott, whose poems
stirred the Boston breast and who was supposed to be
writing the Waverley novels: "Who writes the Waverley
novels?" was almost as thrilling a question as "Who
wrote Junius?" It attacked Blair's *Grave,* for the mortu-
ary vein was running out.* It printed papers on Italian
painters, Luca Giordano, the Carracci, and even a version
of the *Sakuntala,* the first Hindu work to appear in the

* "Sixty years ago," said Emerson, referring to this period, "the books
read, the sermons and prayers heard, the habits of thought of religious
persons were all directed on death. All were under the shadow of Calvinism, and of the Roman Catholic purgatory, and death was dreadful.
The emphasis of all the good books given to young people was on death.
We were all taught that we were born to die; and, over that, all the terrors that theology could gather from savage nations were added to in-
crease the gloom."—*Letters and Social Aims.*

country. It deplored the backward state of American letters, the servile imitation of England, the fruits of a
superficial education. Whatever the future might produce,
the writers of the review showed that the Boston of Gilbert Stuart had roused itself out of its ancient slumbers.
Some of these writers, in fact, prefigured the future.
Buckminster professed the daring notion that there was
a higher poetry than the "mere language of reason." He
had himself taken as much delight in the ragged splendours of a western sunset, rich, disorderly, indistinct in
shape, as in the seven colours of the rainbow, properly
disposed in a semicircle, as if a good Bostonian had arranged them. This was quite absurd, Dr. Gardiner said.
Heaven could only tell what it betokened, in a world that
persisted in moving and changing its mind.

CHAPTER II

HARVARD COLLEGE IN 1815

ALL ABOUT Boston, to the north, west and south, there still dwelt, in these days of Gilbert Stuart, many a veteran of the Revolution, protagonists, masterminds and lesser worthies. In Cambridge, in Concord, up and down the coast, in every port and village, one found survivors of the stirring hour, with their firelocks over their chimney-pieces. They recalled the brave days of the Roman republic, when the chief men of the State stayed on their farms, awaiting some summons for a public council to call them from their villas to the Senate.

At Pepperell, near the New Hampshire line, Colonel William Prescott had his farm, which he held by its original Indian title. The hero of Bunker Hill, like Cincinnatus, had taken up the plough again where he had left it standing in the furrow. Passing through Dorchester southward, or driving through the quiet lanes of Brookline, where the great East India merchants had their villas, with spreading lawns and airy parlours, filled with plaster casts and Italian paintings, and summer-houses in the Chinese style, one came at last to Quincy, where John Adams lived. There, like Thomas Jefferson at Monticello, with whom he had resumed his correspondence, on his ancient terms of good will,—since all passion was spent now,—the patriarch cheerfully sat for the painters and sculptors and studied the greater art of growing old. Once a year, together with his Bible, he read and pondered Cicero's *De Senectute*. He liked to talk with his friends on subjects suggested by his reading, such as the merits of Alexander the Great; and, as the years passed, he waited calmly for a better world, where he expected to meet all the great and good who had gone before him.

Close by, his kinsfolk, the Quincy family dwelt. Josiah Quincy, now in the prime of life, the ancient doge of later times whose mind had been formed in the stress of the previous age, also spent his leisure hours, those he could spare from active politics, either in Boston or Washington, or from the toils of his farm, reading his three editions of Cicero, one for the shelf, one for the table and one, in twenty volumes, for the pocket, along with his Plutarch and his well-conned Horace. For generations, on their ancestral acres, where, with his six servants, the first American forbear of the family had raised his honoured roof-tree, the Quincys had lived as magistrates and squires, loving their field-sports as they loved their country and poring over the Tusculan Disputations: for Cicero, the defender of liberty, stirred a responsive chord in the Quincy bosom, Cicero, the instructor of every profession, the friend of every age! If the present master of the house, a house as ample as those of the Brookline merchants, overflowing with cousins and friends and public men of half a dozen countries,—if the present Josiah Quincy was not himself a man of the Revolution, he might, equally well, have been his father, whose life he had seen mirrored in Pope's Homer. He was the happy warrior who, for a long generation to come, was to fight for all the Revolution had stood for. He was the *integer vitae* who, like the Romans, in his inmost heart, had built twin temples to virtue and honour, so joined that one could enter the temple of honour only by passing first through the temple of virtue. He knew and loved the ancients, as Harvard knew them, not so much because he cared for learning as for their noble patterns of behaviour.

The happiest moments of the Adams household, few as they were at present, snatched from the busiest life that America knew, were those that John Quincy Adams, the rising hope of the old President's heart, was able to spend with his aging father and mother. Already in train for the White House, Minister to England, Secretary of State, almost a popular hero, like Andrew Jackson, thanks to his work in concluding the recent war, he, too, was a man of the Revolution. At eight, he had watched the Battle of Bunker Hill; at nine, he had served as a little post-rider; at fourteen, he had entered public life as secretary to the Minister to Russia. He had known Washington, Franklin, Jefferson, Jay, as a younger member of their constellation, and had followed a proud, unmanageable course that had won him the hatred of his own party and the gratitude of the nation. Against the interests of his Federalist friends, for whom money counted more than country, he had fought for Jefferson's Embargo, as later, in the teeth of the cotton-interests, he was to fight the slave-power. For the selfish claims of his class and breed he cared no more than he cared for his own popularity; and yet, by the force of his intellect and will, he had carved for himself a career that every common politician envied. It was a career that his father understood and Abigail Adams rejoiced in, for he had never compromised his faith that statesmanship was the noblest of human callings. And if, at times, his methods were those of the hedgehog, at Quincy the quills were always folded in.

There, in the peaceful homestead, where later generations of Adamses were to sit in the old President's chair, in the quiet upstairs study, and write their memoirs and their histories, father and son, at these propitious moments, discussed the great problems of their country. John Quincy Adams, now turning fifty, short, stout and bald, less florid than his father,—for the English type was gradually dying out,—had passed his earliest years there, and there, in later years, still fighting, in the House at Washington, for justice, for improvement, justice for the negroes, justice for the outraged Indians, for science, for the Smithsonian Institution, with both feet planted on the Rock of Ages,—there he was to pass his long vacations, always writing, writing, with ink-spots on his fingers, notes on Plutarch, notes on the Book of Leviticus, speeches, essays, poems, nodding in his chair, wandering about the garden and the ragged orchard, with hatchet and saw in hand, pruning his pear and cherry-trees, hoeing and plucking weeds, bending over his plants in their pots and boxes or using his wife's best tumblers to cover the caterpillars that were supposed to turn into butterflies but—as his grandsons noticed—never did so. At Quincy, as a little boy, with his thoughts filled with birds' eggs and trifles, he had begun his famous Diary, enjoined thereto by his austere papa, so that he might later be able to note the stages by which he had advanced in taste, knowledge and judgment. There he had read his fairy-tales and revelled in the *Arabian Nights* and Shakespeare. In all the furious years he had passed in Holland, Prussia, Russia, France and England, as well as in Boston and Washington, since, as a boy, he had gone to school in Paris, in Amsterdam and Leyden, the charm of his life had been literature. Rising at four or five, lighting his fire and candle, reading his Bible first, with English, French and German commentaries, reading his Homer and his Latin authors, without whom he could not have endured existence, reading Evelyn's *Sylva* for his garden, reading all the new books on science, bent on his own improvement, bent on the improvement of his children before he undertook to improve his country, he had mastered Dutch and Russian as well as the tongues that other people knew. And the summit of his ambition was to write, to serve his country, at its feeblest point, by some enduring work of literature.

One work he was to write that served his country, the celebrated *Report on Weights and Measures*. But this was not the work he had in mind. Nor was the Pepysian Diary, incomparable in American letters, the living portrait of his wilful mind, with malice towards all, with charity for none, least of all himself. He had written a volume of *Letters on Silesia* that showed what gifts he had for observation. His *Lectures on Rhetoric and Oratory*, delivered at Harvard College in 1806, revealed his powers of organized reflection. He had heard the greatest orators of the previous age, Fox, Pitt and Burke, as well as their American contemporaries, and Harvard was prepared to hear the doctrine, sanctioned by Cicero and Demosthenes, that, while liberty was the parent of eloquence, eloquence was the stay of liberty. It was a doctrine that Harvard wished to hear, in an age when the art of the pulpit, the art of the forum, the art of the judge and the lawyer, soon to be followed by that of the lecture-platform,—all one art, in its several branches,—was the only literary art that performed a vital function; and Adams, with his experience and his learning, his gifts for perspicuity and order, was certainly the most competent instructor the college could have found. His lectures served as a textbook for the rising generation of public speakers.* But this was not the writing he had dreamed of, and dreamed of still, when, on a Christmas morning, he read Pope's *Messiah* to his household, or when he noted that an

---

* "When he read his first lectures in 1806, not only the students heard him with delight, but the hall was crowded by the professors and by unusual visitors. I remember when, long after, I entered college, hearing the story of the numbers of coaches in which his friends came from Boston to hear him. On his return in the winter to the Senate at Washington, he took such ground in the debates of the following session as to lose the sympathy of many of his constituents in Boston. When, on his return from Washington, he resumed his lectures in Cambridge, his class attended, but the coaches from Boston did not come."—Emerson, *Letters and Social Aims*.

actor's letter, asking for his analysis of *Othello,* pleased him more than all his political honours. Like his own grandson, Henry Adams, who, longing to think like Benvenuto, knew that his instinct was "blighted from babyhood," he longed to think and feel as Shakespeare felt, or as the Germans Wieland and Bürger felt, whom he had read so many years before, as far back as 1800, when he was living in Germany, the first of all Americans to do so. But his instinct also had been blighted by the long winter of Puritanism. The time had not yet come for New England poets.

The time had not yet come, but the time was coming, and Adams, in his pertinacity, represented the chill before the dawn. During those years in Germany, he had translated Wieland's *Oberon.* The poet, to whom his tutor sent the version, compared it with the English Sotheby's version. Adams's was more accurate, he said, but Sotheby's was more poetical. Alas, the more Adams had written since, the more he realized that, with poetry, there was a certain point that one might reach, by means of the virtues that New England knew, beyond which no vigils or vows would take one. But he was under a spell. What was he to do? Riding, walking, musing, he poured the verses forth, odes to Lucinda, Narcissa, Belinda, whose charms he could not refuse to acknowledge, translations of Juvenal's Satires, elegiac stanzas, versifications of La Fontaine's Fables, versions of the Psalms in rhyme, even a long poem, *Dermot McMorrogh,* a satire in the eighteenth-century mode that filled his mind for weeks and left him, at the end, like a pleasant dream, to dull and distressing realities. What could he do when the rhymes insisted on coming and he found he could sometimes hold in his mind fifty lines at once? Throw his poems behind the fire? Or suffer a few, at least, to appear in print? Certainly one of the greatest statesmen living, he was content to be known as one of the smallest poets of his country. Meanwhile, as a

searcher of the skies, who knew that there are many kinds
of stars and who liked to promote astronomy, he scanned
the horizon every day for other and better poets than
himself.

* *
*

Cambridge, across the Charles, was a quiet village, so
quiet that one could hear in Harvard Square the booming
of the guns in the navy-yard in Boston. One even heard
the murmur of the waves breaking on the far-away sea-
beaches. Cambridgeport was a huckleberry-pasture, with
a few wharves and houses. Thence the sloop "Harvard,"
moored to its dock, a Viking ship in the eyes of the village
boys, sailed once a year to the coast of Maine to bring
back wood for the college.

Through the port, as first through the village centre,
passed the white-topped wagons that brought to the Boston market the wares and products of the inland regions.
They filled the yards of the inns, the Porter House, for
one, beyond the village, and the shouts and oaths of the
teamsters rang through the tranquil air. Around the un-
garnished Common, where the dust and the snow blew
unchecked, a few old houses stood amid their ample gardens. One of them, a gambrel-roofed dwelling, General
Ward's headquarters in the Revolution, was the house of
the Reverend Abiel Holmes, the author of the *Annals of
America,* a work, sufficiently bald, that was yet the first
of its kind. The house next door was that of the Higginson
family. On Dana Hill stood the Dana mansion. The family
of Chief Justice Dana, the first American minister to Russia, had owned their Cambridge farm for six generations.
On Brattle Street stood the Craigie house, one of a line of
spacious Georgian villas that were known as Tory Row.
They had been built before the Revolution by opulent
loyalist families, who owned slave-plantations in the West
Indies. In the careless eighteenth-century days, the great

halls and chambers of these houses had echoed with the sounds of music and dancing. "Elmwood" stood a mile or so beyond, the last house in the row, formerly the home of Elbridge Gerry. It had been occupied for several years by the Reverend Charles Lowell and his household. Widespread lawns encircled these dwellings, covered with wineglass elms and willows, with orchards at the rear. The windows of the Craigie house overlooked the placid meadows to the river Charles.

From these Cambridge windows peered,—one saw them from the street,—the faces of aging women, now and then with turbans on their heads and massive silver spectacles, eyes that had witnessed and remembered the passing of guns and troops in the Revolution. Mrs. Craigie's head was often seen, as she sat at her parlour window. Her house had been Washington's headquarters, in the winter of '76, and there Mrs. Washington had come, with a coach and servants in scarlet livery, to celebrate her wedding-day. The late Mr. Craigie, the Boston merchant, had been famous for his entertainments; and among his guests, in this house, had been Talleyrand * and Queen Victoria's father. But the days of Queen Victoria had not arrived, nor the days of a Cambridge poet who was to make the house more famous still. Mrs. Craigie, once a well-known beauty, a widow now, much reduced in fortune, even to the point of taking lodgers, spent her days reading her favourite authors, Voltaire and the British reviewers. Her house was well-stocked with books, like all the other liberal Cambridge houses. Hume, Addison, Gibbon, Swift stood on every shelf, along with Milton and *Evelina,* Richardson, perhaps a polyglot Bible, Casaubon's Polybius, two or three Elzevirs. The library of the Reverend Charles Lowell, who had a church in Boston, numbered nearly four thousand volumes.

* Of whom Miss Mary Moody Emerson said, "I fear he is not organized for a future state."

Mr. Lowell had exiled to the attic the old prints that had
filled his grandfather's study, heads of the ancient wise
men, Plato, Pythagoras, Socrates, Cicero, Seneca; for,
without thinking less of the ancients, he thought more of
the moderns. He had studied his theology in Scotland
and had visited Southey and Wordsworth, the new English
poets, whose work he enjoyed discussing; and facing his
chair in the dining-room hung a portrait of Wilberforce,
the symbol of his humanitarian interests. The Reverend
Mr. Holmes, who also made the most of the art of living, had yet maintained the ancient faith. Indeed, he was
deposed for doing so, although he was only mildly Orthodox, for the Cambridge people were Unitarians. They
had settled this great question for good and all, along
with the Boston people. They were Unitarians as they
were Whigs. Here and there one found a Calvinist, as
here and there one found a Democrat, like Mr. Timothy
Fuller of Cambridgeport. But one had to be a personage,
a Member of Congress or a magistrate, a man who could
afford his coach and pair, to carry off these odious opinions. The Cambridge people knew what they believed,
and they did not propose to discuss it. But Mr. Holmes
had literary compensations. His house overflowed with
books. Amid the lumber in the attic, one found Erasmus's
Colloquies and queer old Latin works on alchemy. Sometimes, in the evening, Mr. and Mrs. Holmes and their
sons and daughters gathered about the London-made
piano, and one of the daughters, who was the family
minstrel, sang the *Irish Melodies* of Thomas Moore.

All of these ampler houses, those of the ministerial
and legal families, and some of the merchant families,
abounded in family portraits. They were the work of so
many journeyman painters, at ten, twenty or forty dollars a head, that they represented only a decent regard
for fathers and mothers who would have thought themselves passing rich on a thousand dollars a year. If one

had a Copley or a Stuart, one had the right to lift one's
chin a little. On the shelves of the closets lay bundles of
mint and catnip, lavender, sweet-marjoram, pennyroyal.
Apples were stored there, and peaches spread their fragrance on the darkness, as if waiting to inspire strains and
strophes. For little boys were growing up in Cambridge
who were to be known as "household poets," and often
as something better. Their parents even wished them to
be poets. The Cambridge fathers and mothers were not
poetic, but they respected poetry. Their gardens were
full of marigolds, hollyhocks, larkspurs, with the humbler
vegetables of the working kind, carrots, parsnips, beets,—
as if to remind the sons of the Revolution that classes
were provisional in republics, that a deserving carrot was
better than an undeserving lupin, that hollyhocks were
only hollyhocks when they were plucky enough to with-
stand the wind, each on its own stalk (which made them
pleasing vegetables indeed), and that the man who had
the family portraits must always prove himself on other
grounds. One of the "household poets" * was to make
this clear. The Cambridge flowers had a moral meaning,
as good New England flowers ought to have; but they
had a poetical meaning that was even more apparent. So
did the sounds one heard on summer evenings, the bells
of the cows ambling home at twilight, the lullaby of the
crickets in early autumn, the hymns of the frogs, in
spring, in some neighbouring swamp, not to speak of the
creaking of the winter wood-sleds, dragging their loads
of walnut over the complaining snow. Every sound and
odour had its value. One heard the carpenter smoothing
his knotty boards, and the whips of the four-horse
coaches rattling by; one heard the ticks in the joints of
the old bedsteads; one smelt the salt of the sea in the
summer breeze. What a store of allusions and similes,
drawn from the homely facts of his daily living, a Cam-

* Oliver Wendell Holmes.

bridge boy might pack into his poems! When it came to
associations and recollections, such as all New England
boys shared in common, buried under the leaves of many
summers, the Cambridge boys who were to write their
poems were to understand the meaning of Byron's line
about "striking the electric chain."

In Cambridge, other facts pressed themselves upon
one's attention. There was the village church-yard, where
one puzzled over the Latin inscriptions on the grave-
stones of old theologians and presidents of the college,
the diamond-shaped cavities in the stones from which the
leaden escutcheons had been removed to be used for
bullets in the Revolution, the graves of ancient scholars,
with virtues ending in *issimus* and *errimus*. One somehow
acquired the sense that learning was a very distinguished
object, which made the scholar a natural leader of men.
The spot where Washington took command of the army
was near the spot where President Langdon of Harvard
had offered prayers, before the assembled troops, and
sped them on their way to Bunker Hill. Learning might
indeed be quaint and queer, as, for instance, with those
living tutors who had so steeped themselves in Latin that
their English was a foreign babble, men who said "in-
tramural aestivation" when what they meant was town-life
in summer, men who might have written a poem beginning—

> In candent ire the solar splendour flames;
> The foles, languescent, pend from arid rames.*

But all the New England statesmen were also scholars,
and most of them had come to nurse in Cambridge. There
had been set up, in the year the town received its name,
the first printing-press in the commonwealth, brought from
England in 1638, the press that had produced for two-

* Holmes.

score years all the printing in the colonies, including Eliot's Bible and the *Freeman's Oath*. Learning was immemorial in Cambridge. Learning was omnipresent. In a population wholly derived from England, one counted the foreigners on a single hand: two Scotch gardeners, a hair-cutter of nebulous antecedents, one Irishman, the master of a spade. And the Irishman knew his Latin, like everyone else: he had learned his Horace at a hedge-school and was always ready to lean on his spade and test a boy's knowledge of the *Quo me, Bacche.* The shop-keepers around the square added tags of Latin to their signs. The janitor of the newly-established Law School was a notable spouter of Virgil. The height of wit in all the Cambridge circles was a thoroughly sound Latin-English pun.

The schoolmasters in Cambridge, as in Boston, were cut on the ancient pattern. They drove the boys with switch and ferule, and even drove the girls, all the more when the boys and girls were children of the learned families; for everyone in Cambridge was precocious, and only a dunce could fail to be ready for college at fourteen or fifteen. The best-known school, soon to be opened, for Greek and Latin only, was that of William Wells, an Englishman. It was he who had published in Boston the Cicero in twenty volumes. He had also edited Tacitus. His school was a Gehenna of blood and tears.* At Cambridgeport, there was another school where, in the process of flogging the Latin in, and pulling the boys about by the ears, the master almost pulled their ears off. One of the little Dana boys, the grandson of the old Chief Justice, never forgot how his ear had felt. He had his mind made up in regard to floggers, especially when he sailed before the mast and saw the sailors flogged; and in days to come he was to speak his mind. But the boys had pleasures,

---

* "My dears, it was hell," said Charles C. Perkins, the art-critic of later days.

too. They pitched hay with the hired men, and even with
their fathers, on occasion. They knew all the trees by
their bark and leaves, and all the birds by their notes and
manner of flying. They scoured the country in search of
flowers and insects; they fished for pouts and waded for
water-lilies; they searched for powder-mills and old re-
doubts, left from the Revolution. They lay and chattered
on the grassy slopes and fought the battles over again.
They haunted the Boston wharves, redolent of the ocean
and swarming with ear-ringed seamen. Moreover, they
had their parties with the Cambridge girls. Strangers who
came from less heroic regions sometimes found these
parties a little chilly. One of them said that, during the
quadrille, his partner touched his hand as if she were feeling for cucumbers in the dark.

Harvard College was the heart of Cambridge. Seven
generations before, every New England household had
given the college twelvepence, or a peck of corn, or its
value in unadulterated wampum peag. But those were
the good old days when the Orthodox faith reigned in
every mind. Established now on a Unitarian basis,—for
the founding of the Divinity School, with Dr. Henry
Ware as its chief professor, settled the character of the
new regime,—the college was considered, in the country
districts, dangerously lax and liberal. West of Worcester,
and up the Connecticut Valley, the clergy, Calvinist
almost to a man, united in condemning the Cambridge
collegians, in the very words of Whitefield, as "close
Pharisees, resting on head knowledge,"—the same collegians who had called Whitefield "low." But as for this
"head knowledge," no one denied that they possessed it.
More than a few of the Orthodox admitted that it was
what collegians ought to possess. Harvard still had an
exalted prestige. The patrician families of Boston and
Cambridge regarded it as more than a family affair. It
was a family responsibility. They sent their sons to the

college, as a matter of course. But they considered it a public duty, not only to endow and foster it, in the interests of the meritorious poor, but to maintain its standards and oversee it. They founded chairs that bore their names, the Boylston chair, the Eliot chair, the Smith professorship.* They watched and brooded over its progress and welfare. Who would have respected wealth in Boston if wealth had not, in turn, respected learning? And, if the professors' salaries were very small, everyone knew they were partly paid in honour.

It was true that the standard of learning was not too lofty. In this, as in certain other respects, the well-known "Harvard indifference" resembled that of Oxford and Madrid. Intellectual things took second place. The object of study was to form the mind, but this was to form the character; and Massachusetts knew what its character was and took a certain satisfaction in it. Everyone was aware of the best Boston and Cambridge type, the type that Josiah Quincy represented, or the late Chief Justice Dana, formed on the classic models. A clear, distinct mentality, a strong distaste for nonsense, steady composure, a calm and gentle demeanour, stability, good principles, intelligence, a habit of under-statement,† a slow and cautious way of reasoning, contempt for extravagance, vanity and affectation, kindness of heart, purity, decorum, profound affections, filial and paternal. A noble type, severely limited, which Boston celebrated in its marble busts. Comparing it, trait for trait, with half of Plutarch's characters, one might have felt that Boston

---

* The Boylston chair has been held, among others, by John Quincy Adams, Edward Tyrrel Channing and Charles Townsend Copeland. The line of the Smith professors is as follows: George Ticknor, Longfellow, Lowell, Bliss Perry. Of Adams, Emerson says: "I have heard that no man could read the Bible with such powerful effect." (*Letters and Social Aims*.) This has been a distinction also of Adams's successor, Mr. Copeland.

† See Jonathan Phillips's remark about his saintly friend, Dr. Channing: "I have known him long, I have studied his character, and I believe him capable of virtue."

deserved its busts. Moreover, beneath its cold and tranquil surface, burned, though the fires were low, the passions and convictions of the Revolution, ready to flame
forth on a fresh occasion. But would the occasion ever
recur? That was what a stranger might have asked, face
to face with the marble busts. The surface, at least,
seemed somewhat tame, suited for the merchant and the
lawyer, and the man of God after the Boston fashion.

This was the type, and almost the only type, the curriculum of Harvard contemplated. Whatever studies favoured its formation, whatever were the best ways to
form it, these were the ways and the studies that Harvard
knew. Whatever studies did not favour it, or favoured the
formation of other types that Boston did not like or had
never heard of, these were no concern of Harvard, or
its concern only to oppose them. Josiah Quincy was not
enthusiastic. Why should Harvard be? Mr. Dana was
eminently decorous. He had caused the arrest, for contempt of court, of a butcher who, appearing at the bar,
had left his coat behind him. Decorum was a Harvard
characteristic.* Neither Mr. Quincy nor Mr. Dana cared
a button for the German language, which had been spoken
by the Hessian troops, a half-barbarous tribe of Europeans who had been hired out to the British king. German, from the point of view of Harvard, always excepting John Quincy Adams, who, as everyone knew, was a
little queer,†—German was an outlandish dialect; and,
while it was not improper to speak French, the language
of Lafayette, which it was quite improper not to know,
more than a few felt that Bonaparte had destroyed its

* In time, it even became, with Irving Babbitt, one of the many Harvard
religions.

† Concerning the Adams family, the popular view remained unchanged
for four generations. "I think them all . . . exhibiting a combination of
talent and good moral character with passions and prejudices, etc. . . .
that would puzzle La Bruyère to describe and which has no prototype in
Shakespeare or Molière."—Harrison Gray Otis on Charles Francis Adams
the first.

respectability. Greek was esteemed as the tongue of a group of ancient republics that possessed some of the virtues of New England. Greece had produced a number of orators who were more eloquent even than Samuel Adams. Search as one might, however, in Massachusetts, one could not find a play of Euripides; besides, compared with Latin, which everyone drank in with his mother's milk, Greek was a little dubious. The Roman word "convivium" meant "living together." "Symposium" had a similar sense in Greek, but what did "symposium" imply? "Drinking together." Was not this alone enough to prove that the Romans were more respectable than the Greeks? Cicero had made the point, and everyone knew that Cicero must be right.

These were the days of the genial President Kirkland, who, after conducting an examination, regaled the boys with a fine dish of pears. He was an easy-going man, a Unitarian minister, like most of the professors, sympathetic and of the gentlest temper, naturally frank and cordial, with all the delicate feeling for human behaviour that characterized the best New Englanders. It was said that he threw his sermons into a barrel, as the farmers threw their corn into the silo, and that on Sunday morning he fished out enough for a discourse and patched the leaves together. The story had a symbolic truth, at least. It signified the president's "Harvard indifference," which was accompanied by the best intentions and a notably warm heart. He never took the narrow view. Hearing that the flip at the Porter House had proved to be too attractive to the students, he dropped in to see the proprietor. "And so, Mr. Porter," he said, "the young gentlemen come to drink your flip, do they?"—"Yes, sir," said Mr. Porter, "sometimes."—"Well, I should think they would," the president said. "Good day, Mr. Porter." Any sort of illumination, physical or spiritual, might have taken place under his eye. He was kind to the rich young men whose fathers, at their graduation, gave them dinners in a great marquee, with five hundred guests and dancing in the Yard. He was kinder to the poor young men whose black coats were turning green. He was not a man to oppose any important change in the system of studies; and before the end of his long reign, in fact, certain changes were to occur that were eventually to transform the college. But he could not see why changes should occur. He thought the old ways were good enough, and he played into the hands of firmer men who thought that all other ways were bad. Four hours a day for study and recitation were quite enough for anyone. A library of twenty thousand books was certainly large enough. In fact, the Harvard library was a wonder. No other American library was larger, except perhaps one. A young man with literary tastes could find Hakluyt's *Voyages* there, Cotton's Montaigne and Dodsley's *Old Plays,* as well as the books that he ought to have at home; and the window-sills were broad enough to sit on, if he was too fidgety to keep his chair. What more, in reason, could one ask for? For the rest, the teaching consisted of recitations. No nonsense on the part of the professors, no lectures, no unnecessary comments, no flowery illustrations. One ground in one's Latin and mathematics, under a pair of candles, and the next day one ground them out again. Professors were not nurses, neither were they dancing-masters. One did not go to Harvard to stimulate a dubious fancy. One went to learn to deserve a marble bust.

A few imaginative persons had their doubts. The college was dying of antiquated notions,—so, at least, they thought. Twenty years before, one of the students, who was known later as a writer,* had printed certain strictures on the college. He had called it "the death-bed of genius." How many immortals, he asked, had Harvard educated?—and how could it expect to produce immor-

* William Austin, author of *Peter Rugg, the Missing Man.*

tals? The delicate muse of belles-lettres could never be induced to visit Harvard. "No, she would recoil at the sight of our walls." And very properly, the professors thought. The college was not for ladies, neither was it meant for men of genius, or any other sort of extravagant creature. For a thorough Boston lawyer, a merchant who desired a well-trained mind, a minister who did not indulge in raptures, Harvard had proved to be an adequate nest. It fostered polite, if not beautiful letters, it sent one back to Plutarch for one's models, it sharpened the reasoning faculties, it settled one's grounds for accepting a Christian faith that always knew where to draw the line.

In short, the college was a little realm as fixed and final as a checker-board. The squares of the various studies were plainly marked, with straight lines and indisputable corners. All one had to do was to play the game. Dr. Popkin, "Pop," was Professor of Greek. Over his cocked hat he carried a circular canopy that Cambridge learned to know as an umbrella. The doctor was a sound grammarian. He found his poetry in the Greek roots; he did not need to seek it in the flowers. A second umbrella appeared in the Cambridge streets, in the hands of Professor Hedge, who had written a famous *Logic*. He had spent seventeen years composing this work, with the aid of the other members of his household. No Logic could have been better, and he hoped his students would learn it word for word. For logic was important. Unless one knew logic, one could not read Locke; and who that had not read Locke could ever be certain that his Christian faith had a solid bottom? Logic was the Golden Calf of Cambridge, the muse of Theology, the muse of Law. For Hebrew, one went to Professor Willard; for Latin, to Brazer or Otis; for Natural Religion, to Professor Frisbie, whose taste for the ethically severe was modified by his love of graceful ease. He enjoyed Maria Edgeworth as well as the rigours of Tacitus. Dr. Ware presided over

Divinity. Dr. Ware's favourite phrase was "on the one hand, on the other hand." He knew he possessed the truth, but he did not wish to slight its minor aspects. He was famous for the accuracy of his definitions. No one could distinguish better than he between "genuineness" and "authenticity"; and, although he had nineteen children, he never used the rod. He punished infractions of the household law by the hydropathic treatment.

Towering modestly over the other professors, Andrews Norton symbolized the *zeitgeist,* a word that he would have deprecated. It savoured of those antic tricks which the young men were beginning to play with language (or were so soon to begin to play),—German barbarisms, exclamations, inversions, coarse and violent metaphors, innovations which, to Mr. Norton, seemed both *outré* and *bizarre,* much as he disliked to use two foreign words in a single sentence. His own greatest days had not arrived, but Cambridge was prepared for his fortunate marriage. The heir of John Norton, who had proclaimed his line a "royal priesthood," not himself ordained, was yet a potent theologian, the Dexter Professor of Sacred Literature. He was more than a match for the daughter of a Boston merchant who kept a variety-store on Dock Square and who, after sending his son to Europe, to make the grand tour in his own carriage, wished his daughter to live in becoming style. Mr. Norton's father-in-law purchased "Shady Hill" for the promising couple, made a gentleman's house of it and bought the fifty acres of "Norton's Woods," as the domain was henceforth to be called, an elegant park, unrivalled in homely Cambridge, where, in time, were to blossom, along with little Charles Eliot Norton, the handsome daughters whom the college knew as the "Evidences of Christianity," a reference to their father's famous book. "Shady Hill" was to have a notable history long after its first lord, the "Unitarian Pope," as Carlyle was to call him, who, for a generation, was to fight, on behalf of Harvard and common sense, against the Germanizing radicals, the Transcendentalists and their noxious crew, metaphysicians of the wilder sort, —long after the great Andrews Norton had laid his cold head in the colder tomb.

These days were still remote. Professor Norton was not married yet. He was not yet the "tyrant of the Cambridge Parnassus," nor was there an Emerson to call him so. He had not yet edited Mrs. Hemans, although he had written his own devotional poems. He had not visited his English readers; nor had he produced his commanding work, the *Evidences of the Genuineness of the Gospels,* which proved, to the satisfaction of honest men,—whatever the Germans might say, in their so-called higher criticism,—that Matthew, Mark, Luke and John had really written the books that bore their names, a demonstration as clear as Hedge's *Logic.* The four great volumes were still unborn, but Mr. Norton had won his spurs already. His head was long, his head was firm, his mind never wavered or misgave him. In Cambridge, *chiaroscuro,* a word unknown, would have been thought to savour of corruption; and the man who had put the Calvinists to rout, by sheer force of reasoning, was not the man to be upset by any other appeal to the vulgar "feelings," that of the pantheist Schleiermacher, for instance, with his notion that the verities of religion rested, not on the letter of the Scriptures, but on "the soul's sense of things divine." Odious phrase, how German! Mr. Norton's lectures had spread his fame. There was not a lawyer in Boston or Cambridge who could find a crack in his chain of logic. No one could prove that he was mistaken; and, inasmuch as a lawyer-proof religion was exactly what Boston wished for, Mr. Norton's eminence was uncontested. Was he a little petulant and vain? That was beside the point. And if he was called a Pharisee by certain ill-bred persons, that was wholly a matter of definition. Mr. Norton, like Professor Ware, was a master of definition. He was benevolent, he was conscientious. Moreover, he was the only professor,—or he was soon to be,—who had his private carriage. One saw it every Sunday, drawn up beside the president's carriage at the entrance of the college chapel.

Such was Harvard College, as it might have appeared in the eyes of a travelling Persian. It resembled Paley's watch. One found the watch on the seashore and instantly inferred that some intelligent mind must have designed it. One found Harvard College in the village of Cambridge: the evidences of design were also there, the wheels and all the parts in perfect order. The mainspring was useful common sense, based on a thrifty view of Christian ethics; and, if it resembled the watch in other ways, if it was small, cold and mechanical, was it more mechanical than Oxford, where they also put the Apostles in the witness-box and drowsed over their bottles of port? Oxford was torpid also, droning along in its eighteenth-century grooves, waiting for its great awakening. Harvard was only a more provincial Oxford, as the travelling Persian would have seen at once. A sympathetic stranger, an aspiring student, especially one who had been born in Cambridge, would have seen it in a rosier light. The Cambridge boy would have known the "Cambridge elm," with its suggestions of the Revolution, the old houses with their charming customs, the gracious lawns, the birds, the luxuriant flowers, stuff for a dozen poets, especially when the naturalist Thomas Nuttall became curator of the Botanic Garden and wrote his books on birds and plants, drawn largely from observations of the local scene. The Cambridge folk were intelligent and kind; and, if it was one of their foibles to put other people in their places, this was an indication, after all, that other people's places were not Cambridge. They were serious, devout, cultivated, stable. They were not given to excesses, even on the side of righteousness. The "ministers' sons" who became proverbial were the sons of the brimstone God of the inland regions. The ministers' sons of Cambridge never knew repression and therefore had no wild oats to sow. Neither in its action nor in its reaction was the Cambridge mind marked by a waste of force. Its only danger was a certain smugness. Its only excess was an excess of caution.

Harvard, moreover, was on the brink of change. Woe to the student, woe to the youthful tutor who counted overmuch on the signs of the times, who interlarded his speech with foreign phrases, sported embroidered waistcoats or even thought that modern languages ought to be included in the course of studies. Harvard was intellectually sound, and the sound intellect makes its changes slowly. But the changes were plainly imminent. President Kirkland might have been indifferent, but he was also liberal in temper. The ethics that Professor Frisbie taught might have been cold and dry, but the warmth with which he taught it,—he was a poet himself, in a modest way,—gave his pupils an impulse to study ethics instead of accepting it on authority. The Harvard philosophy was not exciting,—Locke, Paley, Reid,—but one became excited over it. One acquired a taste for philosophy. One acquired a sceptical attitude that opened the way for other points of view. Even Andrews Norton promoted this sceptical attitude. He had no sympathy with the new ideas that were dawning in people's minds, but he had demolished the old ideas. One could not, after hearing Mr. Norton, revert to the Calvinist view; and if one had disposed of Nortonism, to one's own satisfaction, at least, one was obliged to go forward to something else. And Mr. Norton's positive tone aroused the desire for combat in his pupils. They learned to fight, in the world of the mind. Their intellectual life was filled with zest.

In a word, the students learned to think. Moreover,

they learned to write. Whatever might have been said of
the Harvard professors, their taste could not have been
impugned. Their taste was as refined as their ethical instincts. Their standards were severe. Their students might
have certain limitations, but certain others they could
hardly have. Their style was almost sure to be marked by
grace and, as often as not, by force. Their scholarship
was sure to be exacting, especially when Edward Tyrrel
Channing, the younger brother of Dr. Channing, became
professor of Rhetoric,—two years after the birth of a
Concord boy, Henry Thoreau by name, who was to acknowledge, in later years, that he had learned to write as
Channing's pupil. In fact, the whole New England "renaissance" was to spring so largely from Channing's pupils,
Emerson, Holmes, Dana, Motley, Parkman, to name only
a few, that the question might have been asked, Did
Channing cause it?—

> Channing, with his bland, superior look,
> Cold as a moonbeam on a frozen brook,
> While the pale student, shivering in his shoes,
> Sees from his theme the turgid rhetoric ooze.*

That the rhetoric oozed from his pupils' themes, under
his bland eye,—that is to say, the "turgid" rhetoric,—
was one of the secrets of his influence; for turgid rhetoric
was the bane of letters in the days of the Boston orators,
the orators whom every boy adored. He had a remorseless
eye for the high-falutin, the swelling period, the em-
phatic word, morbid tissue to this ruthless surgeon whose
Puritan instincts had been clarified by a sensible classical
culture. None of his pupils grew the sort of feathers that
required the ministrations of Artemus Ward.

One of these pupils † kept his college themes, and a

* Holmes.
† Thoreau.

list of some of the subjects that Channing set might go
as far as any other fact to explain why his pupils were to
go so far. Bearing in mind the careers of his pupils, poets,
historians, essayists or whatever, one asks oneself what
must have been the effect, on adolescent minds, prepared
and eager, of questions like the following,—on which
they were obliged to write, and to write with perspicuity,
whether they shivered in their shoes or not: on keeping
a private journal, the anxieties and delights of a discov-
erer, the cultivation of the imagination, the pleasures and
privileges of a literary man, the duty and dangers of conformity, the superior and the common man. These were
the subjects that Channing discussed and urged his little
classes to discuss, these and the topics of his brilliant
*Lectures,** a writer's preparation, a writer's habits, permanent literary fame. The literary life, as he described
it, seemed very important and very exciting. Moreover,
he spoke of its problems in a way that brought it home
to the rising generation. He referred to the confident freedom of thought and style that comes from a writer's
pride in his own people and gives him a fine "bravery and
indifference to foreign doubts and censure." He showed
how the world in general values most the writers who
bear the unmistakable stamp, the pungency and native
sincerity, of their own time and place. The early Roman
writers—like the American writers of the past—depended
on foreign examples and supplies. In Rome, at least, this
question had found an answer in the praise the Romans
bestowed upon their writers for turning home at last for
their themes and their style.

Judging by the fruits of his instruction, one might
almost say that Channing sowed more of the seeds that
make a man of letters—when the seeds fall on a fortunate
soil—than all the other teachers of composition and all
the writers of ingenious text-books that have ever taught

* Edited by Richard Henry Dana, author of *Two Years Before the Mast*.

a much-taught country. A Harvard student of his generation had certain advantages of an inward kind that were not likely to be soon repeated. One of them was that, reading Plutarch, in this sympathetic atmosphere, he might have understood Cicero's youth,—how, consulting the Delphic oracle, he listened to the pythoness who advised him not to regard the opinion of other people, but to make his own genius the guide of his life.

CHAPTER III

THE COAST AND THE HINTERLAND

IN EVERY corner of this New England country, where the ways of the eighteenth century lingered on, a fresh and more vigorous spirit was plainly astir. On the granite ledges of New Hampshire, along the Merrimac River, in Essex and Middlesex counties, where the spindles whirred, or westward, on the lovely Housatonic, life was filled with a kind of electric excitement. The air resounded with the saw and hammer, the blows of the forge, the bells in the factory-towers. In all directions the people were building turnpikes, hundreds of miles of straight lines that cut athwart the old winding roads. The Green Mountain boys had erected their State House. Dwellings were going up in clearings and meadows, or, being up, were carted bodily off to better sites. Churches grew like snowdrops in early March. Villages, towns sprang from the fields. A current of ambition had galvanized New England. The "era of good feeling" was on its way.

As yet there were no signs of a similar movement in the intellectual life of this buzzing region. No poets, no historians had arisen, none or few, feeble as they were few, to celebrate and record men's thoughts and feelings. The mind of the country, torn, since the Revolution, with other anxieties and preoccupations, was tired and too busy with the present. It had no use for its own imagination. The ways of the folk, the deeds of the past, of the notable sires and grandsires of New England, if surely not unhonoured, were unsung. The seaports, like the inland villages, bristled with their legendary lore, tales of the wars, tales of Indian fights, of painted Indian faces at the farmhouse window, of the war-dance, the pow-wow and the forest, of great snows in which men had lost their lives, of haunted bridges, buccaneers and redcoats, of Yankee maidens and their Tory lovers, of shipwrecks and battles,—themes for a New England Scott or Byron. One heard of the "screeching woman" of Marblehead. One heard of "witches' hollows," groves of beech and hemlock, where the Indians had held their demon-worship and burning crosses appeared in a greenish light. There were popular ballads and folk-songs,— "Skipper Ireson's Ride," for one,—sailors' chanties along the coast, ballads of village murders, rockaby songs, sugar-makers' songs, sung by weavers and carpenters, by farm-wives and wandering fiddlers, by hunters, trappers, guides and lumbermen, snatches and refrains and longer pieces, brought from the old world or natural outgrowths of the American soil. But the rhymesters, for there were plenty of these,—the rural colleges and academies were turning them out in hundreds,—the rhymesters, unmindful of Burns, whom they imitated, ignored these rude materials of their art, as they were unaware of the greater themes the history of their country offered them.

They felt, these rhymesters, one and all, as later writers felt,—as Hawthorne was to feel, in his earlier days, —that the American scene was too prosaic. How could one write poems and romances about a world that seemed so spick-and-span?—a country that had no shadow, no picturesqueness, no mystery, no pageantry of the past, none of those romantic associations that gathered like moss about every roof and tree, about every hill and valley of the older countries? A land where everything sprawled on the same dull level, in the broad, simple,

garish light of day? It required a vision that no one as
yet possessed to detect the stores of poetic interest that
lay beneath this commonplace appearance. Among these
living poetasters, whose style and tone were so flat and
thin, whose only thought was to follow the current fashion, or who were busy translating Horace's Odes, or giving new twists to the Psalms, there was not one who had
the diviner's eye. But for two hundred years the New
England people had been actively working their minds.
They had been striving to educate themselves, thinking,
brooding, keeping their journals, reading their Bibles,
their classics, their books of sermons; and all this life
was preparing to bear its fruit. In the country schools, no
doubt, in the grammar schools, even in Boston, Cambridge and New Haven, the masters droned along in
their ancient ruts. No business of theirs to produce Vir-
gils and Livys! They made the scholars spell aloud in
chorus. One learned, at the rod's end, the longest words
in the language, learned them to the last sad syllable, a
method which, if it failed to rouse one's mind, taught one
that every error meant a rap. One saw the schoolmarm,
with her willow switch, pinning the boys and girls to her
terrible apron, when they were restless and unruly. One
found, in many a village, the methods of some old
"Ma'am Betty," who kept school in her bedroom and
chewed tobacco and drank from the nose of her tea-
kettle. But other, more promising methods were rapidly
growing, in the Latin schools about the capital, as well as
in the towns along the seaboard.

At Newport, Salem, Portsmouth, where the great
square mansions faced the sea or lined the stately streets,
with their beautiful gardens, cultivated by Scotch and
Irish gardeners, there were notable scholars in charge of
the young, Harvard men or Englishmen, French tutors,
Italian dancing-masters, the dim dawn of a cosmopolitan
culture. There were public reading-rooms in Newport

and Portsmouth. Salem, like Boston, had its Athenæum and a Philosophical Library, one of the prizes of the late war, second to that of Philadelphia. In Portland, in the cultivated circles, where many spoke French and a few Italian, they were beginning to criticize Dr. Johnson, whom no one had ever criticized before and who had been so unjust to the poet Gray. Music, so long the symbol of the ne'er-do-well, began to be heard on summer nights. The strains of the harp and the flute had ceased to suggest the danger of a drunkard's grave. Here and there some carver of figureheads, or of pumpheads and wooden urns for gate-posts, some young whittler, fired by a book on Rome, which he had found in the reading-room, dreamed of a sculptor's life. If he could carve these eagles for McIntire doorways, these heads of Galen for the apothecaries, why should he not create a marble group that would fill the portico of the county court-house?

In all these bustling ports, or ports that had recently bustled, where the forests of masts rose at the wharves and Portuguese sailors sauntered through the streets, the wide world was omnipresent. Everyone talked about voyages "up the Straits," or to Hong Kong and Calcutta, towns that seemed closer to Salem or Portsmouth than Hartford or New York had ever seemed. The lofty chambers of the great dwellings, hung with French or English tapestry, adorned with arches and columns and carved Italian mantel-pieces, were papered with bold designs, brilliantly coloured birds and tropical flowers and scenes from the Mediterranean lands. The massive bedsteads in the upper rooms were draped with curious curtains of India linen, covered with quaint pagodas and figures in turbans. Canton shawls and Smyrna silks were as common as linsey-woolsey. There were parrots and pet monkeys in half the houses. The children played with cocoanuts and coral and spent their pennies for tamarinds and ginger, or spent their Russian kopeks and their British coppers, which circulated as freely as American coins. The men wore Chinese gowns at the Salem assemblies, and the horn-pipe was taught in the dancing-schools. At the great merchants' houses there were formal parties, where the heads of the Federal government came to dine, with ambassadors from the European countries. One of the Salem magnates of the previous decade was the largest shipowner in the world.

All these towns abounded in interesting persons, sometimes droll and quaint, often witty, almost always learned. At Salem, the most imposing of the seaports, dwelt a circle of distinguished men who were to leave their mark in American history. One of them was Joseph Story, already Mr. Justice Story, who wrote for the *Monthly Anthology* in Boston. Judge William Prescott was another, the son of the old hero of Bunker Hill, who lived on his farm at Pepperell. Both these worthies were men of renown and both the fathers of sons who were famous later. Another was John Pickering, the son of Timothy Pickering, who had learned Arabic in his youth, while travelling with his father, and had mastered twenty other tongues. He had refused, as a busy lawyer, the chairs of Greek and Hebrew at Harvard and was at work on a philological project, for the spelling of the American Indian tongues, that was to lead to a worldwide movement for the study of all the primitive languages.* Presently, Rufus Choate joined the circle, the great Boston orator of the future, a weirdly exotic creature in appearance who might have come over in one of the ships from Java. All the members of this Salem group,—like Daniel Webster of Portsmouth, Choate's more famous fellow-orator, who had already made his mark in Congress,—were soon to move to Boston, as the

---

* John Pickering, the first president of the American Oriental Society, was the author, among other works, of a pioneer book on Americanisms.

fortunes of Salem waned and the capital spread its tentacles through New England.

So was the most illustrious of the Salem worthies, the great mathematician, Nathaniel Bowditch, the author of *The Practical Navigator,* a little, nimble man with burning eyes, with silky hair prematurely white, who darted about, rubbing his hands with excitement. This second Benjamin Franklin, the son of a poor cooper and mechanic, who had learned his Latin as a boy in order to read Newton's *Principia*—in which he found an error— had found eight thousand errors in the best English book on navigation. The book he had written himself, the *Navigator,* had saved countless lives and made the American ships the swiftest that had ever sailed. Everyone knew that, as a supercargo, bound for Sumatra and Manila, Bowditch had mastered astronomy so well—between the stars that he watched from the deck and the books he carried with him in his berth—that he was able to revise Laplace. Everyone knew how, on a Christmas night, in the midst of a blinding snow-storm, when he was captain of his own ship and there was not a landmark to be seen, Bowditch had sailed straight to his Salem wharf, as if it had been a sunny day in June. He had taught all his sailors navigation, and every one of them became a captain. And what a work was this *Practical Navigator,* a work that was still to be in active use a century after his death. The literary circles in Boston and Cambridge blushed over the taunts of the British reviewers, the clever men in London who were always asking, "Who reads an American book?" They felt so helplessly mortified. But here was an American book that every British seaman had to read if he hoped to get ahead of the Yankee skippers. It was a classic in its realm, as stoutly built as one of the clipper-ships for which Dr. Bowditch had prepared the way. If the Yankee mind could produce a work like this, what could not the Yankee mind produce when it turned its faculties in other directions? Even here in Salem, where the Prescotts lived, where a little boy, also called Nathaniel, the son of another skipper, was reading his *Pilgrim's Progress*.

In all these centres of the seaboard life, there had arisen a buffer generation that lay between the hard old Puritan ways and the minds of the younger people. Alive itself to literature and thought, prosperous, interested in a larger world, creative, though only, or mainly, in practical spheres, it was a kind of *cordon sanitaire* against the repressive habits of the past. The lawyers, merchants, ministers and scholars who formed the society of these towns preserved the faith in discipline and standards that had marked the older culture, and yet they encouraged in their sons and daughters a free mind, a knowledge of mundane things, the study of languages, music, drawing, dancing, an education of the eye and ear which, from the point of view of the inland regions, savoured of the frankest paganism. The Unitarian cause had won the day all along the sea-line. The leading families professed the "Boston religion." Their intercourse with other lands and peoples had mollified their mental habits; indeed, almost as much as their wide-flung commerce, a little good Madeira softened the old rigidities. They smiled at the faith of their forbears, when they were not shocked by its consequences. For which of them had not seen, in some neighbouring farmhouse, or even in one of the mansions or beside the wharves, some poor crazy woman, chained to a bed, or held by a staple in the floor, driven mad by some hysterical sermon about some unpardonable sin? Wherever one turned, in these prosperous ports, far more in the towns of the hinterland, one seemed to encounter simpletons, and worse, idiots and harmless lunatics, freely walking about, as if the supply of chains were insufficient; and the young people drew their own conclusions. They respected the old ways and the old religion. But they felt there was something unwholesome in this life from which their own minds had been liberated.

For among the younger folk of all these towns, on the sunny side of this buffer generation, these lawyers and merchants and scholars and experienced skippers, there were boys, growing up in dozens, who were to thrive on these new influences. Newport was already reaping its harvest, for there the Channing family lived. William Ellery Channing, the Boston preacher, had spent half the hours of his childhood wandering about the beach and the towering rocks, listening to the music of the waves, with the wide ocean before him, filled with a sense of awe and rapture; and there he spent all his vacations now, in the house surrounded by the charming garden, which had been laid out by the son of Gilpin, the famous writer on the picturesque. At Newport, on winter days, the air was soft and springlike, tempered by the Gulf Stream. There the northern blizzard seldom came, and the English ivy grew on the old stone walls and covered the well-known Mill. Legends throve in the languid atmosphere, and the British arms still hung in Trinity Church, near Bishop Berkeley's organ. And there, in a setting half rustic, half cosmopolitan, the Southern planters brought their families and mingled with the New York and Boston merchants. One could almost see in imagination the Brighton or Baden-Baden of the future. On the promenade, as if it were Europe, the men took off their hats to one another; and the ships set sail from the strange little wharves for Mozambique, Fayal or Zanzibar. The sailors talked of the East and the West Cape and a voyage to the Indian Ocean, perhaps in some fishing-smack of fifty tons.

Newport, the "American Eden," so like the Isle of Wight, had fostered in Channing a feeling for Wordsworth and Byron, those two romantic poets who had shared his moods. There, as a boy, after some sulphurous sermon, dealing with infant damnation, he had heard his father whistle. That was the end of the old faith for Channing. If his father did not believe in it, life was not so dismal, after all. Mingling with the Southern families, he had come to dislike what he called the avarice of the North, the selfish prudence of his fellow-Yankees. He loved the spontaneous ways of the Southern folk, who took no thought for the morrow, ways that fostered poetry and art. He had spent a year as a tutor in Virginia, and it was the Jeffersonians there who had weaned him away from his Federalist prepossessions, strong enough, at first, in a Newport boy whose father had entertained, as he well remembered, Washington, Jay and the other Federalist leaders. In the South, he had read the French philosophers, Godwin's books and Mary Wollstonecraft, and first conceived those dreams of social justice that were to find a voice in his later years. His health had never been strong since those early days when, with a stoic desire for self-improvement, he had slept on the bare floor, subjected himself to a rigid system of diet and prolonged his studies till two or three in the morning. But the slender, pallid, nervous little man, grave, reflective, fond of lonely rambles, teemed with the new ideas that were slowly coming to birth along the seacoast. All thanks to Newport!—where the South and Europe seemed so close at hand. And if Newport had also sheltered the great, grim author of the *System of Doctrines,* Dr. Samuel Hopkins's views had gradually melted away from people's minds. They were no longer "willing to be damned." All that the Newport people wished to recall was the doctor's prediction that the millennium was bound to occur within two hundred years.

In this little corner of New England, Roger Williams too had lived and toiled for the cause of religious liberty. Channing's brother, Edward Tyrrel Channing, had also spent his childhood there. So had the cousin of the Channing brothers, Richard Henry Dana, the poet and critic, the son of the old Chief Justice. So had Washington Allston, the painter and poet, the child of one of the South Carolina families who flocked to Newport for the summer season. His father and mother, distressed by his early talent, and fearing that he would disgrace a planter's household, had sent him North to cure him of his folly; and at Newport he had fallen in with Malbone, the unrivalled painter of miniatures. Allston, whose first wife was Channing's sister and who was later to marry the sister of Dana, had played as a boy with both of his brothers-in-law, both his friends at Harvard and both the inseparable friends of his Boston years. At Newport, Gilbert Stuart had lived, and there the great Berkeley had dwelt for a while. In his house, "Whitehall," near the sea, he had planned his new-world university. He had written his *Minute Philosopher* among the rocks where the Channings, Allston and Dana had dreamed and wandered. One might have imagined that Berkeley's benign spirit still lingered in the gracious Newport air.*

Other writers and poets were to draw from Newport the themes of poems and stories. There were themes enough,—the writers had only to pluck them,—in the burying-ground of the Portuguese Jews who had settled there after the Lisbon earthquake, in the Mill, which, as people supposed, the Norsemen had built, in the old black houses and rough-stone mansions, in the anomalous figures, vaguely savouring of the great world, whom one saw on the promenade or behind the curtained windows, one the reputed sister of an English queen, one the heroine of a strange romance, an impoverished lady of title who paid her washerwoman with costly lace. There were

* Most, if not all of the fashionable American watering-places were first "found" and colonized by writers and artists,—Newport, Bar Harbour, Southampton, East Hampton, Monterey, etc.

themes near by on the Providence Plantations, where lingered, and were to linger for many years, the great feudal dwellings of the rural magnates, households of seventy, eighty, ninety persons, where the master of his twelve thousand acres, his fox-hounds and his four thousand sheep kept twelve dairy-maids at work, each with another girl to wait upon her, and two dozen cheeses, as big as cart-wheels, vanished into the void every day. There were stories enough to the north and west, in the valleys and plains of Connecticut, on the green hill-slopes of Vermont, where the Scottish ballads, on the lips of immigrant weavers and shepherds, bloomed again as in their native air, and the farmers and hunters were building a commonwealth. Themes enough for the novels and the poems, waiting for the novelists and the poets.

But still, or more than ever, in these inland regions, not poetry, or history, or romance, but a more sombre form of exercise possessed the people's minds. They did not care for stories. They thought that fiction was a fraud, and worse. Religion was their only poetry. The cultivated few, the "mansion people," those who had seen something of the world, or knew at least Boston or New York, the families of the rural magistrates, the squires, the village notables who had connections in the capitals, made an exception of Scott, whose Waverley novels were in every house. They read Scott for his moral tone, just as they read Richardson's *Clarissa* and the tales of Maria Edgeworth, which all the leading families enjoyed and discussed,—often with the families of the Boston merchants, who, in their travelling-carriages, constantly made tours across New England, to Stafford Springs, through the Berkshire hills, to Round Hill, Mount Holyoke or Graylock, perhaps on their way to Niagara or Trenton Falls, for a little holiday outing, stopping to see their cousins on the way. These novels, so moderate and so elevating, served them as patterns of manners. Scott, who adorned and beautified all that was growing old and passing away, appealed to their conservative feelings, and Richardson's Grandison was their beau ideal. Many a girl said she would never marry until she found his like. Novels like these were hardly "fiction." One read them without loss of self-respect, as one read the works of Hannah More, or Mrs. Chapone on the bringing-up of girls.

This was only in the mansion-houses. The mansion people formed an invisible chain, stretching across the country, through which the currents of the great world passed. Outside, the village life continued in its primal innocence. Even the rural aristocracy, touched as it was by foreign influences, retained its strong indigenous character. America was the only land it knew, or that its forbears had known for seven generations. In towns near the seaboard, one found a loyalist family here and there. A few old ladies lingered on who spoke of themselves as "eating the King's bread," because their father had fought on the Tory side and they still received a British pension. Miss Debby Barker of Hingham, a town that was much like "Cranford,"—as everyone saw at once when the book came out,—went into mourning, donned a purple dress, at the death of George the Fourth. There were many Miss Debby Barkers in Boston and Newport, but most of the country aristocracy had always opposed the crown. The village folk in general, mainly of the purest English stock, carried on their ancient village ways, not in a spirit of Anglophobia, but rather as if England had never existed.* They formed a self-sufficing

---

* Anglomania, in all its forms, social or poetic, was confined to the fashionable urban classes. The British, from the rural point of view, were as foreign as any other foreigners, and most of the country-people, high and low, deprecated intermarriage with them. Miss Fortune, in *The Wide, Wide World,* undoubtedly expressed their attitude: "I wish Morgan could have had the gumption to marry in his own country; but he must go running after a Scotchwoman! A Yankee would have brought up his child to be worth something. Give me Yankees!"

Yankee world, separated by a pathless ocean from the ways of the mother-country. They were farmers almost to a man, aside from a few mechanics. Most of the ministers tilled their own soil. Each village had its Indian population, a cluster of huts on the outskirts, a few negroes who had once been slaves, sometimes two or three Irishmen and one or two beggars and paupers. The larger towns had public reading-rooms, possibly a Franklin Institute, where a few odd volumes of Shakespeare, Hume and Milton, Young's *Night Thoughts,* Thomson's *Seasons,* Rollin's *Ancient History,* filled the shelves with old books of sermons, Owen on Sin or *An Arrow Against Profane and Promiscuous Dancing.*

Every village had its squire and parson, a Deacon Hart, living on the turnpike, where he raised the golden squashes, the full-orbed pumpkins, the rustling Indian corn and the crimson currants that straggled by the painted picket fence. Further on, dwelt some Abihu Peters. An Ebenezer Camp contrived the shoes. A Patience Mosely made the village bonnets, hard by Comfort Scran's general store. There were always two or three hired men, a handy-andy, usually a fiddler, who had made his violin from the bole of a maple and strung his bow from the tail of the family horse. Now and then one found a village drunkard, who might have been a poet, perhaps some scalawag of a Stephen Burroughs, the worst boy in the town, who was often kept in chains in the county jail. There were a few Yankees of the swindling kind who found their proper sphere in the peddling business. Sometimes they were caught as counterfeiters. The Yankee mind was quick and sharp, but mainly it was singularly honest,—as honest as the men of Maine a hundred years later. Everyone who travelled through the country marvelled that the New England farmers' doors were seldom locked or barred, even at night; and, while

the land flowed with rum, and even overflowed,* the
great popular drink was homely cider. The cider-barrel
was never empty at weddings and ordinations, on train-
ing-days, at huskings, at Thanksgiving, when the sounds
of chopping and pounding and baking and brewing rose
from the smoke-browned walls of the farmhouse kitchen.
Those who grew up in these inland regions, looking back
on the old village life, saw it in the light of Goldsmith's
Auburn, abounding in mild virtues, faithful swains, rural
virgins, peace and innocence. The goodman's daughters
made his shirts and stockings; his garments were provided by his flocks and herds. So were those of the
women-folk, who, as they spun and knitted, discussed the
weekly sermon.

For religion filled the horizon of the village people, all
that was left by politics and law. On Sunday morning, in
the church, one heard the Psalms repeated, in Sternhold
and Hopkins's version, which some of the old women
believed were the very strains King David had sung to
his harp,—"The Lord will come, and he will not," and,
after a pause, another line, which most of the children
thought was another idea, "Keep silence, but speak out."
The old-fashioned polemical sermon followed, fortified
with texts and garnished with quotations in Greek and
Hebrew, for most of the clergy were still learned men.
Perhaps only the week before, the minister had driven
in his one-horse chaise twenty or thirty miles across the
country to meet some reverend brother and settle some
nice point in theology on which he was writing a treatise:
he could not agree with Dr. Stern that God had created
sin deliberately, and he wished to lay his case before his
flock. Many of the village ministers, whose cocked hats
and gold-headed canes were symbols of their unques-

* When the Reverend John Pierpont made his pilgrimage to the Holy
Land, the first object he saw, on the wharf at Beirut, was a hogshead of
New England rum.

tioned authority, as shepherds and judges of the people, devoted their lives to writing these treatises. The farmers discussed them over their ploughs, and the farm-wives over their spinning-wheels. For religion was their romance. They named their children after the biblical heroes, **and the Bible places,** Chittim and the Isles, Dan and Beersheba, Kedar and Tarshish were stations on the map of their El Dorado. The congregations followed the web of the sermons with a keen and anxious watchfulness, eager to learn the terms of their damnation. And they talked about fate and freedom and how evil came, and what death is, and the life to come, as familiarly as they talked of their crops and the weather.

All New England seethed with these discussions. One heard about "potential presence" and "representative presence" and "representative identity," and Dr. Bancroft's sermon on the fourth commandment. Blacksmiths and farriers, youths and maidens argued about free will and predestination, about "natural ability" and "moral ability" and "God's efficiency" and "man's agency." Sometimes it was a morbid interest, when the children sat on "anxious seats" and wept over their wicked little hearts. The conscience of New England was precocious. Even Cotton Mather had observed that "splenetic maladies" throve among the people, maladies that were scarcely allayed by some of the more emotional preachers. One heard of "sweating" sermons and "fainting" sermons, followed by "convulsion-fit" sermons, in the best tradition of Whitefield.* Sometimes, in the frontier settlements, on the borders of the wilderness, in the forests of New Hampshire and Vermont, where men almost forgot that they had voices, and only the axe and the hammer broke the silence, where, on the frozen slopes, the snow fell for days together, strange and terrible thoughts rose in the mind. A Green Mountain boy with

* See the Reverend Mr. Stoker, in Holmes's *The Guardian Angel.*

an axe in his hand might sing his happy songs in the busy
summer, rejoicing in the Alpine air, scented with fir and
hemlock, for the Green Mountain boys had their mountain freedom. But when the snow began to fall, and he
sat brooding beside the stove, over his calfskin Bible, in
the close, foul air of the farmhouse kitchen, digesting
food that was never meant for man, then, as he conned
the mystical Revelations and the savage mythology of the
ancient Jews, visions of blood-atonement swept his brain.
Among the native ballads of the Vermonters, bloodshed
was an omnipresent theme. They felt the presence of the
God of Vengeance. They heard voices that were not
benign. From them was to spring, a few years hence, the
cult of Joseph Smith and Brigham Young,* where flourished now, as foretastes of the Mormons, the quiet murder and the loud revival.

Sometimes, on the other hand, these wrestlings over
sublime abstractions rose, in some lonely soul, to the
loftiest heights, where the mind was lost in mystical raptures over the universe and its great Architect, and men
conversed with angels. Here and there, in the woods of
Maine or among the hills of western Massachusetts,
some spinster or some godly man, like Benedict in his
solitary cell, seated on the mount of transfiguration, kept
his days of appointment with the Eternal. What hopes,
what rhapsodies possessed his soul, what meditations on
a time and space in which all transient ills were engulfed
or muted! He saw the whirling of the puppet-world with
the eye of the mounting eagle that faces the sun. What
mattered this changing planet with its petty cares, lost
in the unfading light of moons and stars? † There was a
fire in the New England heart, in the intellectual depths
of Calvinism, which the cold minds of Unitarian Cambridge possessed no knowledge of, a hunger for right-

* Both born in Vermont.
† See the journals and letters of Mary Moody Emerson.

eousness and a thirst for truth, a passionate dream of perfection. Concord knew this dream, and Concord was to express it. Not for nothing had this vigorous race invested in its flaming ancient faith all the treasures of its thought and feeling. Deep in its mental caverns lingered still the spiritual passions of the Middle Ages. Deep in its mental caverns lingered the passions of the Roundheads, who had suffered and fought for freedom and human rights. Let the trumpet sound again, let the God of Hosts unfurl his banners! New England was prepared, when the time was ripe, for another holy war.

At the moment, the state of mind of these inland regions,—even Connecticut, which faced the sea,— seemed hardly auspicious for the man of letters. It was not quickened by the mental currents that brought new light to the towns of the Eastern seaboard. It was wrapped in an atmosphere of gloom; and its doctrines of total depravity and the utter vanity of human effort paralyzed the literary sense. Whatever mobility this mind possessed was all but confined to the theological sphere.

One could only say that in this sphere its mobility was surprising. The great New England schism had broken out, thirty years later than in Boston. The theocratic Church was giving way. Many of the farmers were moving westward; others were in revolt against the blue laws. The Church had been forced to yield in its main positions, as the democratic movement grew apace, for the democratic movement, with its faith in equality, could and would no longer tolerate the aristocratic doctrine of "election"; and, breaking at the centre, it had begun to branch at the outer edges into forms that were often fantastic. Many of the congregations were held together by the prestige of some ancient minister, who still ruled the village as of old. But as these ministers vanished, one by one, the congregations fell apart in factions, and hundreds of conventicles arose,—poor little ugly scraps of wooden Gothic,—in the shadows of the village churches. The mansion people, up and down the country, had begun to be touched by the Unitarian movement. Some of them, as in Boston, were Episcopalians. All of them had lost their taste for the Orthodox phraseology; and to please them, or to express their own views, which were also rapidly changing, numbers of the Orthodox clergy let down the bars of the old religion. Their sermons wandered from the ancestral standards. The humbler folk, meanwhile, who were breaking away, the farmers, mechanics, factory-hands, were offered a wide choice of isms, some of them brand-new, an assortment as appetizing and variegated as that of any Connecticut pedlar's pack. The more emotional sects, the Methodists, throve on the sudden reaction against the logical sermons of the past. The Universalists promised salvation to all. For the Adventists, Christ was coming at once: they did not have to wait for a far-away judgment. Perfectionism captured some; Restorationism captured others. According to the Come-outers of Cape Cod, the word was written in the human heart, a doctrine that pleased the unlettered who had heard too many texts in Greek and Hebrew. As for the question of punishment after death, one could choose between No Punishment, Eternal Punishment, good for most of one's neighbours, or a strictly limited punishment that stopped after the first million years.

All this represented a movement of mind that was to find expression in other spheres, the practical sphere, the scientific sphere,—for it promoted enquiry and the feeling for action,—but whether in the sphere of literature was rather open to question. At present, the intellect of the rural regions was largely confined to two of these factions: the mansion people, with their broader leanings, and the still potent Orthodox party. The sects, appealing to the simpler-minded, contributed to the Abolition movement, which was to make its appearance presently; but they had little to give to thought or letters. The Unitarians were still few and scattered. There remained the Orthodox leaders who, to regain their power, as the dissolution of the Church advanced, redoubled their ancient threats of hell-fire. To stop the Unitarian movement, the "icy system," as Lyman Beecher called it, they founded the Andover Seminary and built the Park Street Church in the centre of Boston, fortresses of the old faith, in the heart of the enemy's country, from which to pelt the enemy with their sermons,—"each one fresh, like bullets from a mould." * They denounced the "vandal spirit of innovation," as Robert Treat Paine had denounced the "vandal spirit of Puritanism." They reaffirmed the glory of the Pilgrim Fathers. As far back as New England history went, the "Connecticut school" had had its own tone, distinct from that of the "Massachusetts school"; and now more than ever, with Lyman Beecher,—as erstwhile with "old Pope Dwight," Timothy Dwight, the president of Yale, who died in 1817,— the Connecticut school was conscious of its strength. Its efforts were futile to capture the stronghold of Boston, but on its own ground it stood firm. The ancient Puritan faith had been revived in a new and powerful cult.

This energy seemed to promise an abundant life in various other realms. At Yale, for instance, the great centre of learning, the second capital of the New England mind, a notable school of science had arisen, with Benjamin Silliman as its presiding spirit. Harvard, with all its literary prospects, had nothing to show as yet, or for years to come, beside this genius of the laboratory, who formed for Yale its collection of minerals and its physical and chemical apparatus, along with the *American Journal of Science*. Silliman's pioneer work in science might have been expected to offset the obscurantist the-

* Lyman Beecher.

ology of the college, for Yale, like the other and lesser
centres of learning, Williams, Amherst, Bowdoin, Brown
and Dartmouth, those minor Paley's watches, continued
to be stoutly Orthodox. Through Silliman's *Journal,* the
science of the world passed into the mind of the nation;
and Yale was in other respects nationally-minded, with
broader political sympathies than Harvard and a much
more all-American student-body. But it was isolated from
the great-world interests, outside the field of science, that
were so soon to stir Boston and Cambridge; and this, in
addition to its religious thinking and the relative poverty
of the institution, portended little good for literature.
Certainly there was little enough at present. Timothy
Dwight, the "last of the Puritans,"—as people had
called him once, before they became aware of Lyman
Beecher,—Timothy Dwight, Jonathan Edwards's grandson, a mighty man, a prodigy of learning, even a poet
himself in earlier times, had frowned on "song" and the
"arts of the pencil and chisel." He had made every effort
to restore the Puritan modes and methods. Of the New
Haven poets of the hour, James A. Hillhouse was symptomatic. The son of a well-known senator, a college-mate
of the novelist Cooper, he wrote long poems, correct but
decidedly dismal, on biblical themes.*

At Hartford, the political capital, the second New
England seat of the Federalists, which had grown in
about the same proportion as Boston, the literary scene
was scarcely brighter. A few of the "Hartford Wits"
lingered on. Humphreys, Barlow and Lemuel Hopkins
were gone, but Theodore Dwight remained, the "old
Pope's" brother. One saw him strolling about the Hart-

* "Yale has never put its football relish into letters or followers of letters. All that related to rhetoric or composition in my day was most shab-
bily pursued or methodized; nor, indeed, has Yale ever put its foot strongly
in that direction."—Note by "Ik Marvel," in Dunn's *Life of Donald G.
Mitchell,* page 71. See also President Hadley's remarks in *Four American
Universities.* Naturally, all this was changed later.

ford streets, filled to the brim with anecdote and learning, Dwight who had once pursued the Jacobins with the vigilance of a beagle in the brush. John Trumbull still lived in Hartford, the once-famous author of *MacFingal,* old, small, emaciated, bent, tottering on his cane, his fine little face alive with Erasmian humour. One could not forget that the Hartford Wits, whatever their faults and limitations were, had laughed away the popular taste for bombast, at least for a generation. They had had a vigorous interest in poetry which the Boston of their day could only match in the bilious rhymes of Robert Treat Paine. But their day was already remote. Hartford had lost its tincture of intellectual life, and Mrs. Sigourney and her little *salon* still belonged to the future. A youthful poet * who, at this moment, oscillated between Hartford and New Haven, cried to the empty air for someone with whom he could talk. A mere author had no place here. The only society that he could find was a handful of indolent and dyspeptic tutors, one or two lawyers without ambition and the illiterate mistress of a boarding-house.

The Connecticut mind, as travellers often noted, was keen, strong and witty, but usually narrow, educated rather than cultivated. It abounded in prejudices that were often small, like most of the "Yankee notions." It lacked, as a rule, the power of generalizing, which had been marked in New York, in Virginia and in Boston. It was a village mind, in short, that had never breathed a larger atmosphere. It bore few of the fruits that spring from an intercourse and collision with other minds from other mental regions. The only important Connecticut man of letters, a man of great importance, a symbol of his world in many ways, was the famous lexicographer,

---

* James Gates Percival. It was characteristic of these years at Yale that Percival, whose failure as a poet almost became proverbial, was eminently successful as a man of science.

Noah Webster, who was more concerned with "education" than he was ever concerned with "cultivation," but who was doing more with his education than all the American pedagogues put together. A tall, lean, black-coated man, with black small-clothes and black silk stockings, with the oddest, quaintest, old-fashioned air,—if you had met him in China, you would have known that he hailed from Connecticut,—always a farmer's son in his heart of hearts, a busy-body, self-important, vain, but upright and honest, aggressive, enterprising, pertinacious, a schoolmaster, lawyer, journalist, who had written on banking, medicine and statistics, and yet, for all these multifarious interests, possessed a vast and accurate fund of learning, he was at work, at New Haven, writing his Dictionary, for which his Spelling-book had prepared the way,—a new Declaration of Independence. His object was to establish a national language as a bond of "national union," for Webster, with his democratic tastes, was an old-school Federalist in politics. Already an elderly man, he had lived through the Revolution; and, filled as he was with patriotic fervour, he had not failed to note that, while the Americans boasted of their freedom, nevertheless their arts, their dress, their customs still aped the ways of the mother-country. Why should they receive, in this supine way, everything that came from a foreign press? A spirit of the blindest imitation stifled all American enquiry, benumbed the intellectual faculties. During the years of war, when the intercourse with England was interrupted and American school-books had to be improvised, he had supplanted Dilworth's Spelling-book with his own popular speller. He saw no reason why American children should learn that the letters "Ast. P. G. C." meant "Astronomy Professor of Gresham College," on the other side of the ocean. He had worked up his own vernacular word-book, based on the common usage of New England. The store-keepers, up and down the country, laid in supplies of Webster's Speller, along with their hogsheads of rum and their kegs of molasses. The pedlars carried it from door to door, until, as the decades passed, fifty million copies had been sold. It had given the population a uniform spelling.

The irrepressible Cobbett, in his will, bequeathed five pounds to Noah Webster to pay for a new engraving of his portrait, so that the children who used his speller might no longer be frightened out of their wits by the grim Websterian visage. But the visage had its work to do. Webster was a fighter. He had fought for an author's copyright law, travelling through the South and the Middle States, working on the minds of the legislatures. He spoke in terms that farmers understood. The copyright, he said, was the "author's soil." Only the products belonged to the purchaser; the soil should be vested in the owner. He fought for his mother-tongue in a similar fashion. He toiled along the road from village to village, visiting every country printing-house, handing the compositor a printed slip, saying, as he did so, "My lad, when you use these words, oblige me by spelling them as here," —*theater, center, honor,* etc. He had such a passion for detail, for the fruits and even the process of enumeration, that he often counted the houses in the village, counting up one side of a street and down the other side. For the rest, he saw no reason why the language should not be spelled as the average man pronounced it, even,—he had his little crotchets,—dropping the final *e* in *fugitive;* for he had no use for the formal grammarians. As a patriotic gesture of a wholesome kind, he used, as illustrations in his work, quotations from the American fathers, Hancock, Barlow, Livingston, along with Burke and Johnson. It happened that all his own affiliations, in spite of his prodigious store of learning, had been with the plain people: a fact which, accounting for his success, also indicated his limitations. For he had little literary feeling; he had no sense, or only a primitive sense, of the flavour and the history of words, well as he knew his etymology. He had a somewhat arid emotional nature, and the relatively thin, pale speech that had come to prevail among the Yankee farmers, who had lost, in the dry American air, much of their ancestral heartiness,* sounded as rich and full in Webster's ears as the deep chest-notes of the men of old, whose tones were maintained in cultivated usage. His temper, as befitted a man of Yale, was rather scientific than humanistic; and his influence, as a result of this, was very far from happy. When it came to the niceties of language, whether in spelling or pronunciation, Webster's work was always to be challenged. But he did his task so well, within his limits, adding his thousands of words, adding his tens of thousands of definitions, which no previous book had ever contained, that "Webster," with its countless modifications, was destined to remain a standard work for the English-speaking peoples of the world.

In short, the great Connecticut Dictionary stood, as a monument of New England learning, beside Bowditch's *Practical Navigator*. Only by courtesy works of literature, these two solid books rose like a pair of imposing gate-posts at the opening of an epoch. Indeed, the lonely scholar, Noah Webster, who, for a generation, prowled round and round his study-table, shaped in a hollow circle and piled with dictionaries of Greek and Latin, Hebrew, Arabic, twenty other tongues, was a highly symbolic figure; for learning, at this moment in New

---

* Emerson often remarked on this phenomenon, in its various aspects, e.g., "In America I grieve to miss the strong black blood of the English race; ours is a pale, diluted stream . . . Our American lives are somewhat poor and pallid, no fiery grain; staid men, like our pale and timid flora . . . The Englishman speaks with all his body. His elocution is stomachic,—as the American's is labial."

England, was in a very active state. The new sects paid
less attention to it, but there were many country ministers like Mr. Taylor of Westfield, who took such delight
in Origen's works that, not being able to purchase them,
he copied them out in four quarto volumes. One heard of
ministers who, rebuked for heresy by a group of others,
defended themselves in Latin, Greek and Hebrew, and,
when they were cornered in all these tongues, retreated
into Arabic, where they were safe from pursuit. Here and
there, some secular scholar, dressed in his decent black
coat,—old but not untidy, neatly bound at the cuffs,—
conned his Christian fathers and his Cave and Stanley
while he composed his work on the Universe. The children of the ministerial households, whose mother, as
often as not, read Virgil aloud in the afternoon, talked
about Homer and the ancient myths while they were
milking or learning to bake, or, in New Hampshire and
Vermont, sugaring-off in the spring. Serving-women were
not unknown who read their Latin with the boys and
girls and heard them recite, after washing the dishes.
Young girls, who rose at five and asked themselves,
"What hard good work have I to do today?" began
with two or three books of *Paradise Lost,* to give them
the proper tone. They talked about Dugald Stewart and
Alison on Taste, or perhaps about the *Life of Sir William Jones,* which was spreading an interest in Oriental
studies. Older sisters advised their younger sisters, who
were filled with the *furor scribendi,* to discipline their
minds by studying Butler's *Analogy.* One little girl of
seven, who had read a book on the ancient gods, telling
how much they had been loved and honoured, they whom
no one worshipped any more, felt her heart fill with pity.
Entering the woods near by, she built a little altar of
stones, decked it with flowers and shells and laid her
favourite toys on the summit. Then she apostrophized
the god of gods: "Poor old Jupiter, I love you! Nobody

else worships you, but I will, dear old god. You shall have my doll, and I will bring you flowers every day."

All over New England, not only in the "Literary Emporium," as Boston was called far and wide, there was a passionate interest in self-culture. Countless households followed Miss Edgeworth's theories, or some other theory of education, and practised on their friends and youthful cousins. All the sons and daughters of the well-to-do were sent to the "literary institutions," the colleges and academies. Children of the poorer families, who could not afford to buy paper and ink, made their own, or used chalk or charcoal, and learned to write on the kitchen floor; and here and there some group of boys and girls, who had read Washington Irving's *Salmagundi,* edited a family magazine. This interest in reading and study, in books and authors, laid trains of feeling in the general mind that were about to burst into expression. Throughout the region, as throughout the nation, there was a widely spread presentiment that a great native American literature was about to make its appearance. Everyone read English books, histories, poems, essays, in which people found the moulds of their minds and manners; but they already felt that these English authors described a world that had ceased to be their own. They read about beggars, in the British novels, just as they read about kings, but few had seen a beggar, no one had seen a king. They read about skylarks and nightingales, but a skylark was as rare as a "pampered menial." Who had seen a pampered menial? Most of the distinctions and conventions which they found in the European writers were foreign to their own experience. They were ready to welcome tales and poems without the kings, the menials and the beggars,—with bobolinks instead of larks, with the blue-bird and the wood-thrush where the nightingale had been, and fresh American flowers instead of the far-away verdure of the British poets,—whenever the authors appeared who were able to write them.* They were ready for historians and poets who might prove to be as independent as their statesmen had already been.

Of this frame of mind it was symptomatic that a New England author of the future, describing the generation that preceded his own, wrote a story about a valley in which the people cared so much for greatness that they were watching for the man to come, the child born in the valley, who was to be the greatest of his time. The story of *The Great Stone Face* had its prophetic element. It also had a foundation in fact, which it could not have had a century later; for it was true that the New England air was filled with a sense of expectation.

* Within a few years, almost all Americans felt as Hosea Biglow felt:
"Why, I'd give more for one live bobolink
Than a square mile o' larks in printer's ink."

CHAPTER IV

GEORGE TICKNOR'S WANDERJAHRE

IN THE spring of 1815, two young Boston men had embarked on a voyage of discovery. Not content with the state of affairs at Harvard, they had made up their minds to go to Germany and investigate the reports that had come to Boston about the prodigious progress of the German scholars. Was the German tongue obscure and artificial, as everyone supposed in Massachusetts? Were the Germans merely a race of barbarous pedants, as almost everyone thought in England also? George Ticknor, a lawyer, a Dartmouth man with a great respect for Harvard, had serious doubts about it. So did Edward Everett, a brilliant young minister of twenty, with whom and two or three other friends, Everett's older brother Alexander, Edward Tyrrel Channing and Nathan Hale,* who had married Everett's sister, Ticknor had formed a reading club. At the meetings, they shared their Latin compositions, largely aimed at one another's foibles, and ended up with a hasty-pudding frolic.

These two enquiring spirits had sailed for Liverpool, the first stage for Germany, along with a party of other Boston friends and two sons of John Quincy Adams. George Ticknor was a rich young man, with very engaging manners, vivacious, with a melodious voice, with large, dark, velvety eyes and hair that curled and might have been romantic. He was positive, self-assured in the Boston way, not by any means a man of genius, or

* The father of Edward Everett Hale.

he would not have been so self-assured,—that is to say, at twenty-three, but certainly a man of remarkable talents, and talents of a useful kind. The son of a notable merchant who, before he acquired his wealth, had written an English grammar and who shared his son's scholarly aspirations, the young man was favourably known in Boston, as a member of the Anthology Club and the editor of Buckminster's posthumous papers. Everett was even better known. He was an intellectual prodigy. At twenty, he had already preached for a year in the most fashionable of the Boston pulpits. The son of another minister who had composed a famous "Eulogy on Washington," which Everett was to repeat for fifty years, with variations and modulations,—or so his enemies said,—he had been highly praised for his school orations. He was the prize boy as a speaker of pieces and had once interrogated the listening air with a question that was soon to have an answer. Why were there no American poets? Why was not New England what it should be, a "nest of singing birds"? Everett sang in prose. His florid and affluent fancy was greatly admired. He was compared to Massillon.* John Adams called him "our most celebrated youth." Moreover, Everett really knew his classics; and, when he was asked to become Professor of Greek,—one of those Harvard chairs that were almost as important

---

* See the comment of John Quincy Adams on a sermon of Edward Everett's: "It was without comparison the most splendid composition as a sermon that I ever heard delivered. . . . His composition is more rich, more varied, more copious, more magnificent, than was that of Buckminster. There were passages that reminded me perhaps too much of Massillon, but the whole sermon was equal to any of the best that Massillon ever wrote. It abounded in splendid imagery, in deep pathos, in cutting satire, in profound reflections of morals, in coruscations of wit, in thunderbolts of feeling."—J. Q. Adams's *Diary,* February 13, 1820.

It may be said of Adams that, while he shared the taste for the rococo that was common among his contemporaries, he knew, by comparison with the best in the world, what oratory was. Boston abounded in connoisseurs of sermons. They knew all the points of oratory, as Haydn's audience knew a fine concerto. They enjoyed it so luxuriously for itself that they were glad to overlook its frequent emptiness of content.

as a seat in the Senate,—he accepted the nomination without reluctance, on one condition only, that he might prepare himself in Europe.

The two friends had much in common. Both were model students. Both had an ample share of the Boston sense of responsibility. Everett was considered the brightest student who had ever passed through Harvard. Ticknor had had less opportunity to show what he was made of; but anyone could see that he was solid, whatever his limitations were, while there were several persons who suspected that Everett might be hollow. This was quite unjust. Everett was a little spoiled, perhaps. How could he not have been spoiled when President Kirkland said that he resembled the bust of Apollo? He was a little vain, but he was unquestionably gifted. He was a little ambitious, in every sense of the word; but he had his own way to make in the world, while Ticknor had been born on the upper crust. If he had abandoned, with little scruple, the career of the man of God, everyone knew that half the ministers were only men of God because the pulpit, which was highly honoured, also gave them time to read and write. No one denied that he was conscientious. He was a helpful friend. Besides, his Greek was really something to boast of; it could only have been more surprising if he had studied in Germany. So, at least, Everett surmised. That was why he had sailed away with Ticknor.

But how had it all happened? Who had put the notion of Germany into the heads of these two exemplary students? Madame de Staël, of course, the lady who owned the land in upper New York, bordering on Lake Ontario. They had read her famous book, *De l'Allemagne,* which had just appeared in an English version. They were predisposed to like the book, since everyone knew that Napoleon did not like it. He had suppressed the book and driven Madame de Staël out of France. Moreover, they had read a remarkable pamphlet defending the University of Göttingen against the evil intentions of Napoleon's brother, the ill-famed King of Westphalia. Everyone knew that a thing must be good, whether a university or a book, if the Bonapartes disliked it. The University of Göttingen was plainly good, almost too good to be true, Ticknor thought, when a travelling Englishman who had actually seen it,—he must have been one of the first,— described the library to one of his friends. Ticknor, having time to spare, set to work to learn the German language. But where was he to find the books he needed? Several young men in Boston had heard of a Mr. Goethe, who was said to have written a few respectable pages. They had even heard of Dante, the Italian bard, who had been almost forgotten even in England.* But of either tongue, German or Italian, who possessed a grammar? Everett's clever brother, Alexander, produced a German grammar from his desk, and Ticknor remembered that one of his friends in New Hampshire had spoken of a German dictionary. Then he found that John Quincy Adams had bought and kept a copy of *The Sorrows of Werther*. He puzzled it out and made a translation of it.†

Whatever Ticknor did was sure to be thorough. Everett was thorough, too, in all these scholarly matters. Much as he might have been thought a Laodicean, in

---

* The popular knowledge of Dante, among the English-speaking peoples, dates from the publication of Cary's translation at about this moment, 1814.

† Carlyle's experience in Scotland, at just this moment,—as related by him to Charles Eliot Norton,—was a parallel case. Having become aware of German thought through Madame de Staël's book, he could find only two persons in Edinburgh who had any knowledge of the German language. There was not a German book to be bought in the city. He finally procured a set of Schiller through the skipper of a trading-ship at Leith. This was about 1815.—See *Letters of Charles Eliot Norton*, I, 480-481.

Although German was so little known in Boston, there were a few students of the language elsewhere in New England. Dr. Bentley of Salem and Professor Moses Stuart of Andover both owned collections of German books.

certain aspects of his later life, he was bent on the welfare of Boston and Harvard, as afterwards, no doubt, of a larger world. He was convinced that the scholar had a mission. Going to Germany was not a lark, for such a mind as his; it was a novitiate, to be taken strictly. Ticknor felt this even more profoundly, or had the time and means to appear to do so. His country, he felt, would never lack good lawyers, but it was in urgent need of scholars, not the musty theologues of old but well-trained teachers and men of letters. In this capacity he could be more useful, especially if he had seen the world. And he was well-equipped for seeing the world. In fact, he was a man of the world already, with a shrewd eye for the traits of human nature. He could recognize at sight a man of genius, or, if not genius, animated talent. Real genius might be another matter: the fact that one is actually in its presence "dawns slowly on a Boston mind," as one of the Adamses remarked later. To this rule, Ticknor was no exception. He was to meet several men of genius, both in his own country and in Europe, who never dawned on his mind at all, unless they were his friends or men of high breeding.* But his eye for talent served him well. When the famous Francis Jeffrey came to Boston,—the editor of the *Edinburgh Review,* —in pursuit of a young lady of New York whom he had met in Scotland, most of the Bostonians disliked him. They did not know what to make of the stout, little, red-faced man who seemed to have none of the dignity for which his magazine was so respected. They thought he was a merry-andrew, frivolous, vain, far too free and familiar, who had obviously not grown up in a well-bred circle. But Ticknor liked him thoroughly. Why expect from a foreigner the decorum that could only spring

---

* See the remarks in his *Journal* about Lamb, Hazlitt and other English "bohemians," together with his marked indifference to the later movement of mind in Boston and Concord.

from an early discipline,—that is to say, a Boston discipline? Jeffrey's impatience and abruptness, which
wounded the self-esteem of the Boston people, seemed to
him rapidity of mind. It was prodigious. It was wholly
pleasing. If this was the sort of torrential eloquence, torrential and yet logical and compact, that characterized
the foreign intellect, Ticknor was prepared to see it
twice.

Not, however, before he had taken pains to see what
the American intellect yielded. The American mind had
produced the Revolution; and everyone knew, not in
Boston only, that there was no event in modern times
with which to compare the American Revolution. The
French Revolution, perhaps, but in Boston one did not
dwell on this fiasco. Besides, everyone knew, even in
France, that the French would never have had a revolution unless the Americans had had óne first. The men
who made the American Revolution were world-heroes
of the first order. Even in London, nobody questioned
this; and as two or three of these men were still alive,
Ticknor proposed to see them. Adams and Jefferson were
a pair of yardsticks with which to measure any man in
Europe,—for Jefferson had risen in the Boston mind,
now that he had abandoned politics and found his Horace
and his Tacitus much more interesting than the daily papers. A journey through the other American cities would
surely give a young Bostonian that proper notion of his
own country which Dr. Johnson said a man should have
before he travelled abroad.* Moreover, he might encounter a few persons who, having been to Europe,
could give him a little useful information about the
universities and means of study. With a number of

* It was the rule, at this period, for young Americans, e.g., Josiah
Quincy, to make the grand tour of the United States, through Virginia and
the Carolinas to Charleston, and sometimes Savannah, before they went
abroad. This sensible classical custom was later indicated in the well-
known tag, "See America first."

letters that Adams placed in his hand, Ticknor had set out for New York and the South; and before many months or weeks had passed, he could almost have said, —he would not have said it,—that he knew John Randolph, Madison and Marshall. The old philosopher of Monticello was more than pleased with this ardent neophyte, who offered to purchase books for him in Europe,—the new German editions of the classics,—and who was so ready to discuss his plans for the education of the Southern people. Not since his own years abroad had Jefferson seen such an eager student; and, seated in his beautiful study, surrounded by his seven thousand books, he talked of the days when, on his foreign missions, he had escaped, when he could, from his public business to spend his time with the continental scholars. Twice, a few years later, he was to invite the young Bostonian to teach in the university he had founded, offering him an unheard-of salary. And he gave Ticknor letters to his friends in Europe, scholars and men of affairs, that almost conferred on him the rank of an unofficial ambassador.

Everett, too, had made the American tour and called on President Madison. He, too, was equipped with letters that opened every European door. In fact, amid all the adventures that lay before them, the heads of these two young men might well have been turned. For what young men of any other country,—during this year that followed the Peace of Ghent,—could have had quite their opportunities, as the first young scholars, with attractive manners, or, rather, the first after Washington Irving, representing the new American nation, upon which so many hopes of humanity rested, at a time when humanity was full of hopes, a nation that interested every sentient being, not least, because, for the second time, it was the victor in a war with England? What were they to say and feel when Madame de Staël remarked to them, "You are the advance-guard of the human race," when Lafayette, Chateaubriand, Benjamin Constant greeted them in the same soul-stirring fashion? They were to find that in Germany all the great writers of the previous age, Lessing, Herder, Klopstock, had sympathized with the American Revolution,—which they themselves were felt to represent,—that even the old courtier-poet Goethe, whose name had reached their friends at home, recollected the Boston Tea-Party as one of the symbolic events that had stamped itself on his mind as a child. What was a young man to say when the Pope told him that in a few years the new world would dictate to the old? However it might have been with Everett, Ticknor's head was not to be turned; and he quite agreed with those who praised his country. When the Grand Duke of Tuscany asked him where, among all the nations, he thought a man could live most happily, and Ticknor replied, "In America," he did not spare the Grand Duke's blushes, which became visible as he explained—as only a Bostonian can explain such matters—that America was more elevating than other countries.

These were the fortunate days of the youthful republic, when the good old Anglo-American sang-froid had solid facts to base itself upon,—when young men, heirs of the Great Event, knew that they had beaten England twice, although they were too well-bred to mention it, and felt, if they were students and men of letters, that they were volunteers in a nobler war, as builders of a great new civilization. If Ticknor, and even Everett, in his way, stood so calmly in their own shoes, and used their heads so shrewdly, during a four-years' tour of observation that might have flattered a diplomat,—as Ticknor's *Journal* was to prove in time, a picture of the Europe of these years that could hardly have been more full or more discerning,—it was because, with the Revolution behind them, they were engaged, and they knew it, and everyone knew it, in serving the purposes of the Revolution.

They were serving the cause in their studies and travels, a fact they were not likely to forget, with Washington Irving on the ground before them. For wherever they went, they were to meet Irving, who never seemed to weary of discoursing on the prospects and the duties of their country: he liked to tell his young compatriots that, at their time of life, they ought to set aside all other cares and lay up a solid stock of knowledge. Follow their ends, at any cost; scramble, if they had to scramble; buy books, whatever else they lacked. Learning,—this was the sense of Irving's counsel,—was the first of patriotic duties. The touching letters of Ticknor's merchant-father breathed the same spirit. The old man, who had fitted his son for college, longed to see him in a professor's chair. And how would any son have wished to respond to such a letter as the following, so filled with everything that was good in Boston?—

I can look forward and see you, every week, and every month, employed in some part of Europe, in acquiring something which will be useful and pleasant to you in after life. So long as you continue to be the kind, discreet, wise and dutiful son . . . so long I shall . . . continue, even to the end of my life, to aid and assist you, and make the path of life easy and pleasant to you . . . The great object of your journey I am sure you will keep in mind, and never turn to the right hand nor to the left, viz., to improve in solid science, the arts, and literature, and in the knowledge of men . . . You have not left your home for the sole purpose of describing the lawns, the hills, the valleys, the tops of mountains, the columns of smoke, the villages,—except for amusement, and as shades to ornament your other improvements, which may be often and happily interspersed; but you have left your father to grow wiser and better,—to learn how to be more useful to yourself, your friends and your country.*

With a letter like this in his pocket, a letter worthy of a Roman parent, a young man knows how to behave when

* *Life, Letters and Journals of George Ticknor.* II, 410.

he meets Lord Byron and Sir Humphry Davy, when Byron tells him about his love-affairs, tells him the story of his life,—as Englishmen are prone to do, in the presence of a sympathetic stranger,—gives him a beautiful copy of his poems, gives him a letter to Ali Pasha, in case he wishes to go to Greece, and a splendidly mounted pistol with which to defend himself there. And when Sir Humphry Davy presented Ticknor with another handful of letters, one to Canova, one to Madame de Staël,— to whom he already had two letters,—he might have felt that he was fairly launched. The young men were quite at home in England, which was only a larger and livelier Massachusetts. Indeed, their first celebrity, Mr. Roscoe, the Liverpool banker-scholar, a sound Whig and patron of learning who had been the smith of his own fortunes, had been exactly like a Boston man, one of the founders of the Athenæum. Southey also had a Puritan conscience and the same laborious habits one knew at home; and the grand old Dr. Parr, Dr. Johnson's ancient friend and the master of Ticknor's master, Dr. Gardiner, received the young men as if they had had a volume of introductions. He said he had turned on his heel, in the days of the Revolution, when he heard the Americans described as rebels. He added, in his hearty way, "I was always glad that you beat us."

But Ticknor and Everett had not crossed the ocean to find another Boston, with improvements. As for the English universities, Oxford was only a larger and livelier Harvard, far from having had its own reforms. In Germany they were soon to meet a scholar who had put the English Latinists to the blush. He had pointed out several grammatical errors in the Latin notes of a posthumous work of Porson, the pride of the Cambridge scholars. In fact, these German professors were something new under the sun, as formidable in the field of studies as Frederick the Great had been in the field of arms; and

Ticknor and Everett, once in Göttingen, found themselves on their mettle. What a mortification, the grievous distance between an American and a German scholar! America had never known, not only what a Greek scholar was, but even the process by which a man became one. At Harvard, they thought they knew how to work, heirs of the Puritans as they were, but it was plain enough that, beside these Germans, they cared for nothing but their own convenience. They were more indolent than the English scholars. They thought two years sufficient to make a Grecian, and here was little Dissen of Göttingen who had spent no less than eighteen years, at sixteen hours a day, on Greek and nothing but Greek, and who said that even now he could not read Æschylus without a dictionary. It all depended on what one meant by "knowing." No one who had ever seen a German could ever again call a man a scholar unless he was willing to follow Eichhorn's programme: 5 A.M. to 9 P.M., with half-hour intervals for meals. As for the poor little Harvard library, it was a good half-century behind the times.

All this became painfully evident as Ticknor and Everett pegged away, for twenty solid months, at a typical Göttingen schedule: 5-8, Greek, 8-9, German, 9-10, exegesis, 10-12, Greek, 1½-4, Latin and French, 4-5, philology, 5-7, Greek, 7-8, the drill-sergeant, 9-11, résumé of lectures, varied, perhaps, by Hebrew and Syriac, a little natural history and a four-mile walk. No man ever died of study, Eichhorn often said, though he thought that perhaps for soft young Yankees twelve hours a day might answer, at first. Harvard was a school for ministers, and Harvard men could hardly be expected to know what a scholar was. Who had ever seen an American scholar? While everyone knew that the Yankees were enterprising, the wonder was, not that they studied badly, but that they studied at all. And Ticknor and Everett did not study badly. Full-grown as they were, they were glad to go to school again, with their big portfolios under their arms, just like two boys who fear the birch. So was their friend, Joseph Green Cogswell, another Harvard man who joined them shortly, and who was also to play a historic role: for as Ticknor was to become, in America later, the father of modern-language studies, as Everett was to give an unparalleled impulse to the study of Greek mythology and letters, so Cogswell was destined to become, as head of the Astor Library in New York, a founder of the modern library-system. Cogswell, who was thirty, had already had a varied life. His work as a lawyer had taken him to Marseilles, where he had found himself regarded as an authority on books. In the length and breadth of this great commercial city, one looked in vain for a book that was not connected with trade; and, whenever a stray volume in Latin or Hebrew turned up in the hands of the dealers, Cogswell was asked to examine it. The town was more benighted than New York. It was dangerous to be thought a savant there, as the president of the Marseilles Academy told him, and he might well have died of ennui if he had not happened to fall in with two or three learned Spanish exiles. In Göttingen, along with his other studies, Cogswell pursued his bibliographical work, going over the shelves and catalogues of the university library. On their walking-tours, in vacation-time, the three young men visited and examined the great German libraries and several universities. At Weimar, at various times, they called upon Goethe, who gave them fresh sheaves of letters. The old poet was living much alone. He was glad to hear their news from America and eager for their recent impressions of Byron. Cogswell especially touched him. He thanked the young man for taking an interest in his old age and kissed him with affection. He sent Cogswell several presents after he had returned to his own country. *

As for Edward Everett, Cousin said, before he set out for home, that, for Greek, he had never seen Everett's equal. He was at least so competent in German that Eichhorn asked him for contributions to the Göttingen magazine. Before his visit to Greece, he had spent several days with Sir Walter Scott, who had neglected his old German studies and was glad to talk them over again. He had given the little Scotts a lesson in Tasso. He had heard Moore and Béranger sing their songs, passed a day with Ugo Foscolo and dined with the Bonaparte family, assembled in Rome. He had taken the first steps of his later life as a diplomat; and, when he went to Greece, with Byron's letters,—for he wished, in his way, to consult the oracle, too,—he was received and passed on, from one official to another, as if he had been a diplomat already.

Ticknor's studies, after Göttingen, still lay before him. He had been appointed, in his absence, the Smith Professor of Belles-Lettres at Harvard. He was expected to teach Popular Latin, Old French, Provençal, Spanish and Portuguese. For this he had to prepare in the southern countries. He had formed certain habits as a student that were to make his teaching influential. One of them was to choose, for his private instructors, in Germany first, then elsewhere, in France, Italy, Spain and even Scotland, scholars who were typical of their nations, men with round, full, musical voices who could direct his reading and share it with him, and give him, along with the grammar and the literary history, the overtones and the intimacies of feeling, a sense of the popular spirit from which each literature had sprung. The scholar Conde, who, for all his fame, was dying of starvation at Madrid, —for Spain was in a sad state, and most of the men of letters were so wretched that they were ashamed to re-

* It was through Cogswell that Goethe presented to Harvard College a set of his works in twenty volumes.

ceive a stranger,—Conde was one of these instructors.*
With him, during a spring and summer, Ticknor spent
several hours a day, reading the old Castilian authors.
In Rome, for four months, a well-known archæologist
was his cicerone. In Edinburgh, he read the Scottish poets
with Robert Jamieson. Scott, who was glad to give him
several days, walking with him about the countryside and
telling him stories of the Scottish border, spoke of him
to Southey in a letter as a "wonderful fellow for romantic
lore."

All this was to have its effect on the rising generation
of American poets, so many of whom were to study under him. For Ticknor was not only to sow at Harvard,
in a ground already prepared, the seeds of the modern
literatures of Europe; he was to stimulate, in some of his
pupils,—by opening up these veins of popular legend, the
balladry of Spain, Provence and Scotland,—a feeling
that was already half awake for the legendary lore of
their own country. Scott had renewed the literature of
his people by building on this ancient balladry; and Scott
had conceived his idea of doing so by reading Bürger's
Lenore, which had had the same effect in Germany. Why
should not America follow Scott, as Scott had followed
Bürger? Washington Irving had already done so. He
had shaped, in charming prose, the legends of the Hudson River; and every river-valley in New England
teemed with similar legends, waiting for other Irvings,
in prose or verse. Ticknor did not need to make the point.
Boys who had grown up among the ballads of the Revolution, the folk-tales of Marblehead and Portsmouth, could
hardly fail to draw the inference, especially when Ticknor was able to tell them how interesting Southey had

---

* Ticknor visited Spain at a moment when, under the despot, Ferdinand
VII, the country, ravaged by the Peninsular War, had sunk to the depths
of poverty. It was the depressed condition of Spanish letters that gave
Ticknor,—as later his friend Prescott,—an opportunity to make himself a
world-authority in things Spanish.

found the New England legends. For, to Southey, Mather's *Magnalia* was enthralling; he knew more about Roger Williams than anyone in Boston cared to remember; he had written a long poem on King Philip's War. This was to mean as much to renascent Harvard, with its instinctive respect for an English poet, even a dull poet, as if New England had produced a Shakespeare. And it was to come with force from Ticknor because of his gift for lecturing. Not for nothing had he observed, in the midst of his other studies, the world-famous lecturers of Paris, Cousin and Lacretelle, with all their art and grace of execution.

In fact, as one followed Ticknor on his travels, one could imagine already how he was destined to stir his Harvard class-room. Although his main concerns were prosaic enough, philological data, sober facts of literary history, still the lives that he was to talk about, Cervantes, Lope de Vega, Dante, Petrarch, Froissart, Calderon, the old explorers and soldier and sailor poets, were quite enough to excite a roomful of boys who were able to do their own embroidering. They opened up vistas of adventure, unheard-of prospects for a poet's life. And if, without wishing to spread the peacock's feathers, he dropped, in those years to come, into reminiscence, he could unfold a world-panorama such as few in Cambridge had ever dreamed of. He seemed to have met, and more than met, every famous living personage. He had pleased Byron, on a later encounter, by telling him how Goethe admired his work. He had spent three days at La Grange with Lafayette, and Humboldt had read to him from his book of travels. Chateaubriand had told him again and again about his wanderings in the United States, through the unbroken forests.* He had known Canova and

* Chateaubriand remarked to Ticknor that, in a hundred years, when all the legitimate sovereigns had vanished, Europe would be full of despotisms. He knew what happens after world-wars.

Thorwaldsen, the sculptors, and Bunsen and Niebuhr in Rome, as well as he knew Sismondi and Madame de Staël, with whom he had often talked beside her death-bed. He had met the Countess of Albany many times, the wife of the last Pretender, who had liked his frankness when he said that England was better off without the Stuarts. He had travelled about Spain with a band of smugglers. At Naples, he had spent all his evenings at the *salon* of the old archbishop, where a group of Italian cognoscenti read Alfieri and Poliziano, in the Attic fashion of the Renaissance. With Washington Irving he had gone to Windsor: his pupils had read of this excursion if they knew *The Sketch Book*. He had met, among a hundred others, Lord Brougham's "bare, bold, bullion talent,"—for Ticknor was a master of the phrase, when it came to judging character. He had spent an evening with Godwin's circle, Hazlitt, Lamb and Hunt, and had never seen Sydney Smith's equal,—this was at Lord Holland's house, where he felt more at home,—for floating down the stream of conversation, and, without seeming to influence it, giving it all his own hue and charm.

In days to come, the young men at Harvard were to reap the fruits of Ticknor's *wanderjahre*. Here and there, as they followed his lectures, they were to catch a phrase or an allusion that opened up the picture. What patterns of the literary life the great professor, cold as he was, and distant, was able to place before them!—Humboldt, with his fifteen hours of study, pursued in the midst of all his social duties; Schlegel, who spent his evenings in the drawing-rooms, but rose at four and worked again till midnight; Madame de Staël, whose pen, lifted against Napoleon, was almost mightier than Wellington's sword. Never before, in America, had anyone invested with such glamour the life of the poet and the man of letters; and Harvard was ready for the new evangel.

CHAPTER V

THE NEW AGE IN BOSTON AND CAMBRIDGE

IT WAS 1819 when Ticknor returned to America, a youthful master of the grand style. Safe in his father's house, he felt rewarded for all these years he had spent away from Boston. He unpacked his collections of books, acquired at such expense, with the aid of half the booksellers in Europe, especially the Spanish collection, which was later to become so famous. There was no room in his mind for that malaise which, in after times, was to affect so many Americans, newly returned from the old world. The sense of an enthralling purpose dominated all his other thoughts.

It was a fortunate moment. "We are living," said the great Dr. Bowditch, who had come to live in Boston, "in the best days of the republic." He said this in his most impressive manner, and Dr. Bowditch was always impressive, partly because he was Dr. Bowditch and partly because of his reputation, which was already international. He felt obliged to add, as one who was accustomed to calculation, that worse days were bound to follow. But that worse days were to follow, even remotely, few Bostonians were prepared to think.* The nation was on the march, moving with equal tread towards unknown splendours; and a young man with a ruling passion, that of reforming Harvard College and making it worthy of

* Josiah Quincy was one of the few. Always cheerful and hopeful,—insomuch that at eighty-two, in 1854, unable to agree with most of his friends, who thought the world was going to the dogs, he said, "Almost everything at the present time seems to me to be better," even religion and morals,—he yet foresaw, through the "era of good feeling," the great convulsion coming, the Civil War.

the new day, had some reason to be happy. With Daniel Webster as one of his intimate circle,—for Webster, too, had settled in Boston,—with Bowditch as another, and Dr. Channing, with the Prescotts, father and son, Judge Prescott and William Hickling Prescott, Ticknor's younger friend, with Edward and Alexander Everett, recently the Minister to Spain, he could watch the wheels of progress turning and even give the wheels a push himself; for all these men, whatever their interests were, had a touch of the statesman in their composition. So did the great East India and China merchants and the men who were building up the factory-system and believed they were building up the country. Their public aims and their known distinction, which carried them into diplomatic posts, attracted to the little capital,—larger in its littleness than it was to be when it was big,—every traveller from the old world; and at their tables one met, from week to week, members of the German and Russian legations, Spanish grandees and Danish princes, Chancellor Kent from New York and Lafayette, scientists and historians from England. The Liverpool packets discharged their passengers in Boston, which, for a while, with the Cunard Line, became the main American port of entry.

Boston was more than ever like Edinburgh, the Edinburgh of the last few decades, when the Scottish metropolis was in its heyday. Later, these days of renown were to pass, or to pass, at least, in a measure, when London overshadowed Edinburgh and much of the glory of Boston passed to New York. But the social world of Scott, Gifford and Jeffrey, of the Waverley novels, *Blackwood's* and the great *Review,* was reproduced, and more than reproduced, in the New England capital, for a generation. The intellectual life was the fashion there, just as it had been in Edinburgh, where university professors and men of letters, judges and learned lawyers, lowland lairds and Highland chieftains gathered for evening

routs in the winter season. Chalmers had his counterpart
in Channing, the shepherd of the Boston flock; nor was
there any lack of superior women, cultivated, witty and
devout, enough to meet the exactions of Abigail Adams.*
The greatest mind that was ever born in Boston was able
to feel that the town, in its spirit of emulation, suggested
Florence. Everyone with talent was impelled to struggle.
Everyone laboured to be foremost.†

"I meet in London occasionally," Stuart Newton, the
painter, wrote, "such society as I meet all the time in Boston." There were many people in Boston who took this
for granted. They did not give the British capital the
benefit of a doubt, whether their correspondent had met
all London. "The true Bostonian," Henry Adams said,
"always knelt in self-abasement before the majesty of
English standards"; but this was less the case at the present time than at any time earlier or later. No doubt, in
the Boston soul, politically American, there was a sub-
stratum of Anglicism that was never to be eradicated; and
this grew stronger, rather than weaker, as New England
lost its control in politics. The more the centre of gravity
of the nation shifted towards the West, the more the Boston mind, thrown back upon itself, resumed its old colonial allegiance. Boston, at present, was dominant and
potent. It was not Persepolis, of course: one did not find
there, or wish to find, the "courts where Jamshyd gloried
and drank deep." What one did find, or what the Bostonians found, was a singular situation, together with the
will to cope with it. They had received a nation from

* "If we mean to have heroes, statesmen and philosophers, we should have
learned women."—Abigail Adams.

† "What Vasari said, three hundred years ago, of the republican city
of Florence might be said of Boston: 'that the desire for glory and honour
is powerfully generated by the air of that place, in the men of every profession; whereby all who possess talent are impelled to struggle that they
may not remain in the same grade with those whom they perceive to be
only men like themselves, even though they may acknowledge such indeed
to be masters; but all labour by every means to be foremost.'"—Emerson
Natural History of Intellect.

their fathers, and they proposed to make it a great nation. This was a notable school of self-respect,* even of the self-sufficiency for which the Boston people were celebrated; † and, if there were many Pharisees among them, others deserved the phrase, uttered by Benjamin Constant,—they had all the virtues they affected. No one spoke of provinciality. The word had not yet come into use; there was even no occasion for it.‡ The word provinciality implies a centre, and nations that are in process of building themselves are always self-centred. That "the mind is its own place" no one doubts when people are occupied with important matters. The Bostonians were absorbed in public interests, and they had another centre in the classics, which they shared with all Western Europe. Moreover, having known great things at home, they knew a great thing when they saw it elsewhere.§

* Ticknor, to whom Metternich said that he found the present state of Europe "disgusting" and who discovered everywhere abroad the seeds of decay and "moral degradation," expressed the feeling of all his contemporaries in writing, "A man is much more truly a *man* with us than he is elsewhere . . . It is much more gratifying and satisfying to the mind, the affections, the soul, to live in our state of society."

† See the remark of President Eliot's mother, addressed to a friend who had joined the Episcopal Church: "Eliza, do you kneel down in church and call yourself a miserable sinner? Neither I nor any of my family will ever do that."—Henry James, *Charles W. Eliot*, I, 33.

‡ "Americans of that generation hadn't that snobbish shamefacedness about their country,—and especially if they were well-born as you represent Wentworth to have been. It is a vice of the *nuova gente* altogether. The older men took their country as naturally as they did a sunrise. There was no question . . . as to whether their country were the best in the world or no—they *knew* it was."—Letter of Lowell to Henry James, 1878, apropos of the latter's novel, *The Europeans*.

§ "A noble school," wrote Channing, in one of his note-books, "is profitable only to noble spirits. The learner must have something great in order to receive great lessons." Today, in many large American cities, a man may enjoy every material advantage, and even the advantages of travel, yet still remain as unconscious of the great currents of contemporary thought as any European peasant. But when, a hundred years ago, the *zeitgeist* penetrated New England, with its train of world-ideas, it found a sensibility prepared for it; and a man like Thoreau, who scarcely stirred out of his little Concord, instinctively understood Mazzini and Kossuth,—the Gandhis and the Trotskys of his time. Those who have in their minds the pattern of greatness recognize this pattern wherever they find it. They belong to the freemasonry of the enlightened, whatever their condition may be or wherever they live.

The republic had proved to be a triumphant success, for
the clouds had not yet risen in the Southern sky; the
wealth and population of the country were growing at a
prodigious rate, most of all, perhaps, in Massachusetts.
By virtue of their experience and cultivation, the Boston
people saw themselves as leaders in a great forward
movement of the race.* No wonder their portrait-
painters throve. "How rages the Harding fever?" asked
Gilbert Stuart, in 1823, referring to Chester Harding, the
admirable backwoods artist, who was luring away his own
clients. Harding was to know as well as Stuart what Boston was willing to pay for its *amour-propre*. He had so
many orders that he could not fill them. The Boston people thronged his studio, sometimes fifty in an afternoon.
He had to book them like a racing-tout.†

Of this little statesmanly world, of which Ticknor was
to be *pars magna*, Webster was the great political figure.
A demon of a man, a full-blooded, exuberant Philistine,
with a demiurgic brain and a bull's body, a Philistine in
all but his devotion to the welfare of the State, his deep
strain of racial piety,—this was the grand thing in Webster,—with an all-subduing personal force, an eye as
black as death and a look like a lion's, as the farmers in
his native New Hampshire said, almost a foreigner, with
his rustic manners, among these Boston lovers of ele-

* Emerson expressed the general feeling when, some years later, he wrote:
"I do not speak with any fondness, but the language of coldest history,
when I say that Boston commands attention as the town which was appointed in the destiny of nations to lead the civilization of North America."
—*Natural History of Intellect.*

† One readily understands how Ticknor, who had been received as an
honoured junior by Humboldt, Madame de Staël and so many others,
asked for nothing better than an opportunity to address the hard benches
of a Cambridge class-room. Similarly, John Quincy Adams, aged eighteen,
after having served abroad as Secretary of Legation, had been only too
happy to resume his place as a Harvard sophomore. These facts imply a
variety of conditions that make the place and time unique. They are certainly not remarkable, from the point of view of a sensible man. But few
professors and students in the great universities of our day are sensible in
quite this fashion.

gance, he was fighting, in and out of Congress, first for
the Constitution, for the Union, imperilled by so many
factions, and secondly for the manufacturing interests
that lay behind New England's rising fortunes. With an
oratorical gift as great as Burke's, in learning, in unction,
if not in cultivation,—for, while Webster had a feeling
for the sublime, he had little feeling for the beautiful,—
he fought for the solid facts of property and the good old
Yankee motive of self-interest. His politics, his economic
doctrines were those of any sound New Hampshire
farmer who owned a dam and a mill and turned his dollars over to the Boston bankers. These doctrines naturally pleased the Boston bankers. As a lawyer, he was
unapproachable. When he talked about other lawyers, he
made them seem like characters in Plutarch. He could
invest a common murder-case with the atmosphere of an
Æschylean drama.

A hunter, fisherman, farmer, who gloried in his rural
avocations, in which the traits of the backwoods pioneer
were mingled with those of an old border baron, Webster
was to become, as the years went by, a legendary figure
in New England. In Boston, he was the rock of the Constitution, as kings had been defenders of the faith.
Throughout the country districts, he was "Dan'l," whose
every word, as a farmer remarked, seemed to weigh a
pound. People said that Dan'l was made of granite, and
they knew he had learned his American history from old
Captain Webster of the minute-men, who had guarded
Washington's tent on the battle-field and for whom Liberty and the Union, far from being phrases, were facts
that represented blood and steel. Everyone knew the
great squire of Marshfield, where he had a farm as large
as half a county. Everyone had heard him on the platform, every boy and girl had seen his picture, the dark
brow that looked like Mount Monadnock, the wide-
brimmed hat and the knee-high boots, the linsey-woolsey

coat and the flowing necktie, the walking-stick that was said to be ten feet long. There was something elemental in his composition, something large and lavish. Even his faults were ample. Webster despised the traditional virtues.* He spent money in a grand way, borrowing and lending with equal freedom. He was far from sober, or would have been if two tumblers of brandy had been enough to put him under the table. He could be surly enough, when he had his moods of God-Almightiness, or when he wished to insult some sycophant. The thunder-clouds would gather on his brow and the lightning flash from his eye, and he would tell a committee that their town was the dullest place on earth. No one could be more truculent, especially in the hay-fever season; but he was always good-natured with the farmers, who liked to think of him as their man. They knew what Webster meant when he said that his oxen were better company than the men in the Senate. They knew all his ways and the names of his guns and animals, as the Jews of old knew the weapons of Nimrod, or Abraham's flocks and herds,—his great ram Goliath, his shot-guns, "Mrs. Patrick" and "Wilmot Proviso," his trout-rod, "Old Killall." They knew he had written the Bunker Hill oration, composed it word by word, with Old Killall in his hand, wading in the Marshfield River. They had heard of his tens of thousands of swine and sheep, his herds of Peruvian llamas and blooded cattle, the hundreds of thousands of trees he had raised from seed. They knew that while his guests were still asleep,—the scores of guests who were always visiting Marshfield,—he rose at four o'clock and lighted the fires, roused the cocks with his early-morning

---

* "Thirty years ago, when Mr. Webster at the bar or in the Senate filled the eyes and minds of young men, you might often hear cited as Mr. Webster's three rules: first, never to do today what he could defer till tomorrow; secondly, never to do himself what he could make another do for him; and, thirdly, never to pay any debt today."—Emerson, *Letters and Social Aims.*

candles, milked and fed the stock and chatted in the kitchen with his farm-hands, quoting Mr. Virgil, the Roman farmer. And at Marshfield, as everyone knew, his horses were buried in a special graveyard, with all the honours of war, standing upright, with their shoes and halters.

From Boston, across New England, across the nation, Webster's fame spread, as the years advanced. Boston men who had seen Garrick and Foote and heard Burke and Sheridan, the masters of the spoken word, were satisfied that Webster was their equal. Countless thousands, bankers, lawyers, farmers, read his orations aloud by the evening fire. They felt as if the woods and the fields and the ocean had found a worthy voice in Webster's words; and Captain Thomas, his neighbour, was not the only man who longed for death when Webster met defeat. This faithful follower, fearing that all was lost, after Senator Hayne's second speech, cast away his boots, saying he would never want them more, and took to his bed for days. New England had never known a public man with such a Jovian personality,* whose words, when he chose to deploy them in a diplomatic encounter, had the force of a fleet of battle-ships. He could make the United States appear the mightiest of all historic empires. Who knew better than he, or could say it better, that America was the hope of liberty, as those who had visited Europe could see for themselves, as Ticknor and Everett had already seen, when the old regime had been restored in force, in Italy, France and Germany, when liberal ideas, even in England, were still in doubtful debate? Who was more the symbol of his country? Were the Boston people, with all their self-possession, still, in a measure, tinged with colonialism? Were they prone to ask the

---

* "There was the monument, and there was Webster," Emerson wrote, referring to the Bunker Hill oration. Sydney Smith exclaimed, when he saw Webster in London, in 1839, "Good heavens, he is a small cathedral by himself."

visiting European what he thought of American institutions? Were the countryfolk too ready to protest that they had whipped the redcoats? Were the gentry still English in their customs? Webster was the universal answer. Noah Webster, with his dictionary,—whether for better or worse,—had established American usage in the matter of words. Daniel Webster was equally potent in matters of personality. All his traits, his references, his habits bore witness to the national character and buttressed it with the kind of authority that could not be gainsaid. When he spoke of the Bay State and Bunker Hill, of Plymouth Rock, Lexington and Concord, one felt that to belong to Massachusetts was the noblest privilege of history. *Civis Romanus sum.* "Thank God, I also am an American!"

With Webster as the great political figure, Channing was the great religious figure, another member of Ticknor's circle,—for Channing had not yet embarked on his later career as a social reformer, which was to divide the Boston household. As Webster spoke for the outer life of the town, its property-sense and a kind of patriotism that largely represented its mundane pride, Channing spoke for the inner life of Boston, with a charm and glow of intellectual goodness that triumphed over its prejudices. Although he was a Unitarian, the only man of genius in the movement, who had defined the faith and even defended it in controversy, when the Orthodox party attacked the "Boston religion," he was a poet in his theology, for whom a creed was only a vestibule. He was not at home with the Cambridge logic-choppers, whose ways he found repelient. His fluid mind, suspicious of every dogma, wished to live "under the open sky." The adoration of goodness was his religion. He hungered and thirsted for it; and the great, wide, ingenuous eyes that beamed under his broad-brimmed hat and lighted up the little figure, wasted by so many sufferings, proclaimed his inextinguishable faith in the natural possibilities of men. He detested the jealous caution of New England, the insane love of money that pervaded the trading world, the coldness of the calculating mind, the dullness and timidity of provincial manners. Oh, for a Burns to shock the Boston burghers out of their staid decorum! Under the crust of American life, so frigid on the surface, was to be found, he thought, if one looked for it, the simple, wild stock of human nature, with all its natural feelings and social instincts, the seeds of every noble attribute. It required stimulus, it required affection. Channing was always young for liberty,* not the mere terrestrial liberty that Webster represented, but a liberty of the intellect and spirit that tended to form a superior race of men.

In days to come, Channing's ideas, which had their own logic, were to be expressed in certain ways that Ticknor and his circle did not like. These were the days,—one saw them in advance,—when Ticknor, with Everett as his only rival, was the great intellectual and social figure, as potent as Webster and Channing in their spheres, the host of every visitor to Boston, the one man who had seen all the world, where others had seen only portions of it, and numbered among his countless correspondents the preëminent minds of half a dozen countries. These were the days after he had married one of the daughters of the well-known merchant whose other daughter had married Andrews Norton, and people spoke of him with bated breath; for wealth united with learning, and learning with prestige, and prestige crowned with conscientiousness,—

* George S. Hillard recalled that, at the time of his graduation from Harvard, Channing, to whom he was introduced, remarked: "I see that you young gentlemen of Cambridge were quite too wise to be thrown out of your accustomed serenity by the new revolution in France! I was in college in the days of the first French Republic, and at every crisis of its history our dignity was wholly upset. We were rushing to meetings of sympathy, or kindling bonfires of congratulation, and walking in torch-light processions. But now the young American has come to years of discretion and may not give way to such unseemly excitements." Channing, in spite of his early Federalism, always felt at heart as he had felt in college.

all these formed a constellation that would have dazzled any other town. By virtue of a similar constellation, Andrews Norton reigned over Cambridge; and Ticknor's great house at the head of Park Street, dominating the Common from Beacon Hill, soon became the symbol of his renown. There he kept his famous library, the amplest private library in Boston, housed in the largest and most elegant room, approached through a marble hall by a marble stairway, about which the butler discreetly hovered. Over the mantel hung the Leslie portrait for which Sir Walter had sat at Abbotsford, and the walls of the stately apartment were covered with books, methodically arranged and richly bound. And there, with his air of the scholar-nobleman, gracious but somewhat marmoreal, like his hall and mantel, Ticknor dispensed his counsels to aspiring students. He was ready to give advice about the various versions of Cervantes, if someone wished to make a new translation. He was happy to lend his books, as many as two or three hundred, to any qualified applicant, even in Maine or New Hampshire, or the South. Everyone knew that, where books were concerned, he knew, as no one else, all the resources of Europe, from Naples and Spain to Scotland, from Holland House in London to the cabinet of Prince John of Saxony, where his own portrait hung in later years. He had seen all the books, even the lumber-rooms of the Escorial, even the Medical Library at Madrid, where he had been the first enquiring student for three-and-twenty years to break the rust on the locks and the wire nettings. He knew, or was to know, even the little bookcase that stood near the window in Tieck's parlour; and if, as befitted one whose knowledge of Spanish literature was greater than that of any man in Spain, he was especially rich in Spanish works, he was a great collector in other fields. Under the mantel, beside the fire, he held frequent classes for young ladies, the daughters of his friends, in Dante, Milton and Shakespeare.

This was a type that Boston understood, the magnani‐ mous man who passed its peculiar tests. Correct himself, and willing to diffuse correctness, he was able to correct a duchess, when the case called for correction, without disturbing the poise of a drawing-room. Moreover, in addition to his wealth and learning, he was a faithful adherent of Dr. Channing, as long as Channing did not go too far. His pamphlet on Lafayette passed through three editions in the French translation. But in his teach‐ ing he was most the statesman; for, although he con‐ tinued to live in his Boston house, he had at once assumed his post at Harvard. Jefferson, as everyone knew, had tried to induce him to go to Charlottesville: all he desired was that God might send him two or three Ticknors. But Ticknor was not to be drawn aside. The Harvard library, which had seemed so large, seemed to him now a closet‐ ful of books. The college could scarcely be called a respectable high school. To turn it into a university, one that could bear the name and deserve the name, and set the intellectual pace of the country, was the Jeffersonian task that lay before him.

Meanwhile, Everett and Cogswell had also returned to Cambridge. Cogswell, the master-bibliographer, took the college library in hand and rearranged the books on the Göttingen plan. Everett began his career as Profes‐ sor of Greek, a notable career, alas, too brief. The old grammarians, who had taught the classics, might have had warmer hearts than Everett, but they had colder minds. They had no feeling for the Greek myths, no feel‐ ing for the poetry of Homer, and Everett was another Abélard, or so the Harvard students were convinced. But there were other irons in Everett's fire, as time was soon to show. On his arrival from Europe, he had preached a sermon in Washington, where no one had ever heard such magical words. Senators, justices, cabinet members praised him as the prince of orators and asked him to remain as the chaplain of Congress. He had come back to Cambridge with a halo, but with his mind torn with a new ambition. The incident had unsettled him for life. As the years passed and he carried on his lectures, he watched the rising star of his friend Webster. Webster had risen by oratory, and he was as good an orator as Webster. Why should not he too enter Congress and meet his college classes between the sessions? Why should he not be Minister to Greece, as his brother had been Minister to Spain?—especially when, like Ticknor and Andrews Norton, he had formed a fortunate marital alliance, with the daughter of the richest man in Boston? Not that he craved the splendid burdens of office! But were not the splendid burdens of office, painful as they were, more in the line of a man's public duty than teaching a roomful of boys? Others who have been known to ask this question have answered it as Everett answered it. He complained, in a letter to Justice Story, which he asked Story to burn, that he found the life and duties of a professor far too humble for him. They were not, he said, respectable enough.

The roomful of boys at Harvard knew nothing of the professor's doubts and dilemmas. That he was discontented never entered the head of one of these boys, Ralph Waldo Emerson, who thought of Everett as "our Cicero" and took it for granted that, like his prototype, Everett scorned the opinion of the vulgar, those that held a man in low esteem who, side by side with the politicians, was known merely as a "Greek and scholar." Everett held the students spellbound. He was severe and precise in his college class-rooms, eager to impart, in detail, the wealth of the new German learning, Wolf's theory of the Homeric writings, the exegesis of Voss and Ruhaker, the criticism

of the ante-Homeric remains.* Outside, in his public lectures and speeches, to which the students flocked, he let
his fancy soar. His Greek brought back the days of
Pericles, his imagery was opulently Persian. That he was
magniloquent they did not know. That he was theatrical
they did not care, for oratory was their theatre. His
elegance, his confidence, his ease stirred their imagination.
What pictures he could present of Scott and Byron, the
reigning British poets, whose Harolds and Manfreds and
Marmions were on every lip, of Humboldt, Madame de
Staël and Lafayette! Standing before the panorama of
Athens, which had been presented to the college, he discoursed on Greece as one who had seen it. His multifarious quotations were so apt, his style so fluent and graceful, he uttered such inspiring reflections on the future of
American literature! The fame of his foreign training,
the glamour of his adventures attracted students from
the remotest parts, from Georgia and Tennessee.

It was a triumph of style and fantasy. In later years,
some of Everett's pupils, seeing how vacuous his career
had been, wondered that he had so beguiled their minds.
Too tender-minded for a statesman,—as they perceived,
looking back,—he had followed Webster as an under-
study. He had been Governor of the Commonwealth,
Secretary of State and Senator, but always, as one of
these pupils said, a "dangler;" and the more he elaborated
his outward graces, the more he became a shaken reed
within.† And yet he had not really beguiled the students.

* "During the present century, I believe that Harvard received and welcomed the new learning from Germany . . . before it had been accepted by
the more conservative universities of the Old Home. Everett's translation
of Buttmann's Greek Grammar was reprinted in England, with the 'Massachusetts' omitted after 'Cambridge,' at the end of the preface, to conceal
its American origin."—Lowell, *Literary and Political Addresses.*

† Emerson said of Everett, in his journal: "Webster has done him incalculable harm by Everett's too much admiration of his iron nature;
warped him from his true bias all these twenty years, and sent him cloud-

Empty as so much of his rhetoric was, it stirred the adolescent imagination. False, or largely false, it communicated an impulse that was true. A student who imitated Everett's style was sure to be corrected by Edward Channing, who hated a purple patch as he hated the devil; and meanwhile Everett waved a wand that opened up the magical world of Homer. Some of the boys who saw the wand waving were always to have a foothold in that world, with all its wild beauty, even while the dour Professor Channing kept their other foot in Yankee-land. And with Ticknor busy, with unsleeping eye, over his new department, that of the modern languages, and lecturing, with all of Everett's verve, on French and Spanish literature, a student might well have found himself alert. For Ticknor was a scholar born, as Webster was a statesman born and Dr. Channing was a born priest, never tempted to stray from his natural sphere. He fought for his reforms. He did his best to substitute thorough teaching for the old sing-song ways the college loved. There was a brief flutter. Then the old system was resumed, except in Ticknor's own field. There he had his way. He gath-

hunting at Washington and London, to the ruin of his solid scholarship, and fatal diversion from the pursuit of his right prizes."

In later times, Everett, in contradistinction to Webster,—the oratorical "Michael Angelo," as Everett was the "Raphael," so called,—became the classic example of all that was bad in American oratory. One marvelled over the bursts of applause that followed his apostrophe to Stuart's portrait of Washington in Faneuil Hall: "Speak, glorious Washington! Break the long silence of that votive canvas!" But Everett's style was the style of his age in all but the greatest men. Italy, France and Ireland, in the eighteen-twenties, afforded similar examples. Even Victor Hugo, and even a generation later, abounded in this vein. Everett was a master of calculation. John Bartlett of Cambridge,—"Familiar Quotations" Bartlett,—saw him drilling a group of old Revolutionary soldiers who were to sit on the platform during his Concord oration. The poor old souls were expected to rise when Everett exclaimed, "Noble men!" and bob up and down in their seats at various other points in the oration. He was once observed in a country book-store asking for a pocket Bible, which he wished to produce dramatically during a speech. As the Bible was not forthcoming, he took a copy of Hoyle's *Games* instead. It served just as well, and nobody knew the difference. In fact, there was so much "theatre" in Everett's speeches that people soon wondered whether there had ever been anything else.

ered together a staff of foreign instructors, French, Italian, German. And there he established a path for the university to follow later.

During these years of change and growth at Harvard, Dr. Channing's mind was also growing. Shortly after Ticknor's return, he too had reappeared in Boston, after a year of travel and rest in Europe, charged with fresh life. In England, he had found many admirers, for the great Boston preacher's reputation had spread beyond the sea; but the doctor, ill and depressed, had fled from all these kindly ministrations and sought the solitude of the English lakes and the conversation of Wordsworth. He had read the poet's *Excursion* again and again; indeed, he had never read anything but Shakespeare more. Ever since his early youth at Newport, he had shared this mystical sense of the universe as the outer garment of God; and the landscape of New England had prepared him for the charms of the Cumberland country. For Channing was a lover of lakes and mountains. He had studied their contours under various skies; he knew all the effects of atmosphere, of mist and cloud and dry and watery sunlight. The grandeur of New Hampshire, the gentle, pastoral beauty of Vermont had swayed and attuned his feelings. He could form a friendship with a mountain; and he knew the interminable depths of the virgin forests as well as he knew the ocean, beside whose crashing waves he had leaped for joy. These temperamental sympathies had drawn him to the new German *Naturphilosophie*. Through Madame de Staël, at first,—whom he had read with different eyes from Ticknor's,—and then through Wordsworth's friend, the poet Coleridge, he had been introduced to the writings of Schelling, in whose intimations of a divine life, manifested in nature and the soul, he had found his mental home. He had been roused as well by Fichte's heroic stoicism, which spoke of the grandeur of the human will. These prophets seemed to him to corroborate the great hopes of the French Revolution, which he had shared in his youth. In deference to the feelings of his congregation, the richest and most respectable in Massachusetts, practically-minded Whigs, with little taste for nonsense, he had suppressed his natural sympathies. But he belonged to the race of the older and bolder. He looked askance at the reigning thoughts of Boston, with its "scared and petrified" conservatism.

His year in Europe, spent with congenial friends, in England, among the Alps, in Rome and Florence, had quickened all his apostolic instincts. Wordsworth had read to him passages from *The Prelude*. He had communed with Coleridge, who described him later as the "very rarest character" he had known. He had formed the friendship with Lucy Aiken that was to result in so many relations between the old world and the new; and it was observed, on his return, that a change had taken place in his mental horizon. The preacher who had delighted everyone with his penetrating discourses on ethical questions, dear to the Boston heart, seemed at once more literary and more social. Not that he ceased to be a moralist, one of those rare artists of human behaviour,—like his own Fénelon, for instance,—who, by virtue of some inward grace, constantly flowing through the intellect, purge the mind of cant and win the imagination of untold thousands to the beauty of their own unworldly goodness. Channing was a poet and a saint; and he shared and led, as no one else could lead them, the deeply devout religious conversations that occupied so many Boston minds. He did not care to discuss theological matters, the question of Particular Providence, the Evidences of Christianity, the Genuineness of the Gospels, all those special, textual, technical problems that exercised the learned men of Cambridge. But he was often present at those reading parties where they talked over a chapter of *Rasselas,* or a passage from Plato or Milton, and the topic set for the evening was the distinction between natural and moral happiness. Whether the performance of one's duty should have any connection with one's self-regard. Whether the moral nature was immortal or would be swallowed up in the divine. Gratitude, personal obligation. If one saw two persons in grave danger, which should one save first, one's benefactor and private friend or the person of most use to humanity? In these Boston parlour-conversations, carried on by scholarly casuists, blue-stockings and others, Miss C. defending Paley, Mrs. S. taking the side of Kant, Channing was a frequent arbitrator.

But the focus of his mind had been gradually shifting, along with the general focus of the Boston mind. The serious atmosphere of these discussions,—so like the discussions of similar circles in England, those that surrounded Macaulay, Mill and Ruskin, the rising generation of British authors,*—assumed another aspect as the years advanced. The great problems of the factory-system, which was so rapidly growing, the problems of the poor forced themselves on these conscientious minds. They could no longer ignore the social questions that complicated the ethical point of view. What was the effect of an occupation with wholly mechanical things? What was the moral difference between workers in mills and those who worked by themselves? How much taste and judgment were involved in making a handsome shoe? What were the obligations of the rich in regard to the education of the poor? Unitarianism, it was noted, had always been accompanied by radical movements. Even in far-away Poland, the Unitarians had been non-resistants

---

* Also the discussions of the Jansenist circles of seventeenth-century France. The atmosphere of Geneva, in the eighteen-thirties and forties, as reflected in Amiel's *Journal Intime,* was strikingly similar to that of Boston.

For this aspect of the New England mind, see *Memoir of W. E. Channing,* by W. H. Channing, the *Memoir of Mary L. Ware,* by E. B. Hall, and *The Life of Charles Follen,* by E. L. Follen.

and pacifists, conscientious objectors, communists, trouble-
makers for the powers that be. The Boston Unitarians,
as a group, cared for none of these things. They had
made a State Church of their religion, and, with their
shrewd sense of the interests of trade and their temperamental self-complacency, they were opposed to any further changes. But the Unitarian leaven that worked in
Channing was of a much more fundamental kind. He
pondered all these questions in his heart, and, as the years
passed and his fame grew, the rift grew wider and wider
between the doctor and the respectable classes he represented. Living in his beautiful house, the property of his
wife, he slept in a cold and cheerless attic, struggling to
solve the problems that weighed upon him. How to
destroy the worship of money. How to elevate the
depressed classes. How to remove the evils of competition. How to convince human beings that they were parts
of a great whole, bound to work for the welfare of this
whole. The union of labour and culture. Slavery in the
South. He could not please the Abolitionists, for he saw
things in too complex a light; nor could he please his
parishioners, who began to cut him on the street. Only
his fame and his saintly character kept for him the respect
of the practically-minded.

This was in the future, when his name had travelled
round the world and he had readers in India.* Now
already, in these early twenties, he had begun to play the
part of a leader in the renaissance that was evidently at
hand. Were there not seasons of spring in the moral
world, and was not the present age such a season? Could
one fail to see on every side the signs of an unparalleled
energy? And yet the mind of the nation was still asleep.
As a boy, Channing had been a famous wrestler. He had
loved adventurous sports and had borne well the name

---

* It was Channing's secular essays, on **Milton**, Fénelon and Napoleon,
that gave him, at first, this larger reputation.

of "little King Pepin." He had climbed the mastheads of all the ships at Newport. For twenty years he had wrestled with himself; and who was better prepared than he to wrestle, in the name of enlightened reason, with all the dark forces, inward and outward, that cramped the spirit of his countrymen? Had not theology laboured without ceasing to cover human nature with infamy, to crush its energy and confidence, so that men had almost ceased to believe in their mental and moral powers? They idolized wealth because they did not know what other and greater goods they were capable of. They looked to what was profitable first and only on second thoughts to what was right, for their natural feelings were masked and petrified by caution, policy, prudence. Their lives were needlessly joyless. For himself, he thought the ancients were too solemn in calling the earth Mother, the earth, so youthful, so exuberant, so living and rejoicing. The first of all the wonder-signs of Jesus was that in which he blessed a wedding-feast and heightened all its pleasures, even its pleasures of sense. Was not the intemperance of New England a signal judgment on the Puritans, who had tried to banish pleasure from the world? To rid society of its sordid vices, music should be taught in the common schools. Dancing should be encouraged and festivals fostered, so that old and young might share in sports and pastimes. There should be picture-galleries and halls of sculpture. Boston should develop the sense of beauty by creating beauty.

Such were the luminous thoughts of the climber of mastheads. Every Sunday morning, he mounted his pulpit and poured into the ears of his congregation, willing or unwilling, large draughts of intellectual day. His eyes grew wider and wider as he spoke, and the little figure seemed to grow taller and taller. One saw him in the streets, at public meetings, ubiquitous, alert, robed in his blue camlet cloak, a shawl about his neck, with his drawn, ethereal face almost lost under the enormous hat; or at Newport, at his summer home, "Oakland," surrounded by its gracious lawns and gardens. There, like Lamennais in his retreat,—for Channing, too, had written his *Paroles d'un Croyant,* even his *Essai sur l'Indifférence,*— he gathered his younger followers about him, discussed and read philosophy and history, in the summer-house or on the wide verandahs, Plato's *Timæus,* perhaps, or Coleridge's *Biographia Literaria,* Schiller, Wordsworth, Shelley, *Wilhelm Meister,* or led them to some seat among the rocks, where Berkeley had also talked with his disciples. He rose at Newport earlier than ever. One heard his quick step on the gravel walk, as he strolled among the shrubs, with the dogs gambolling beside him, or in and out of the green-house, where he studied the plants and flowers. Often the children joined him, trooping along the paths, for Channing was a friend of all the children. "A child's little plan should be respected," he wrote in one of his note-books. To say of a child or a man, as they often said in Boston, "There is a great deal of human nature in him," did not mean to Channing what it meant to so many others. He had a large opinion of human nature,—so large that people thought he was romantic,—even when its powers were in eclipse. Every day, for years, it was known in Boston, he fed with his own hands two poor old women who fancied that people wished to poison them and would accept their food from him alone.

Everyone could see, in after times, that Channing had been the great awakener. By raising the general estimate of human nature, which the old religion had despised, he gave the creative life a prodigious impulse; for, if human nature was a thing so precious,—however enslaved, insane, depraved, degraded,—how could one hesitate to emancipate it? How could one fail to fly to its assistance? How could one fail to offer it the means by which to achieve the beauty that was proper to it? Channing was the father of half the reforms that characterized the Boston of his age.* Moreover, he harrowed the ground for literature, first by his harrowing of the ground for life, and also by his intuitive understanding of the function of art and letters. He knew his country and he knew the poets, and he knew what his country and the poets needed. Independence, he was well aware,—the basis of all enduring greatness,—was something that had to be earned, and that could be earned. It was for the poets and thinkers to earn it. "A people," he wrote in one of his essays, "into whose minds the thoughts of foreigners are poured perpetually, needs an energy within itself to resist, to modify this mighty influence . . . It were better to have no literature, than form ourselves unresistingly on a foreign one . . . A country, like an individual, has dignity and power only in proportion as it is self-formed." † That the true sovereigns of a country are those who determine its mind, its modes of thinking, that writers are the originators of all those currents of thought by which nations and peoples are carried forward,—this was Channing's constant theme and vision. Mind, mind required all one's care.

* Among the many well-known reformers who drew their impulse largely from Channing were Dorothea L. Dix, once a governess in Channing's household, who devoted herself to improving conditions in the prisons and asylums, Elizabeth Eaton, founder of a society to help the poor foreigners who were appearing in Boston, 1830–1840; Elizabeth Peabody, the "grandmother of the kindergarten," etc.

† *On National Literature.*

CHAPTER VI

THE NORTH AMERICAN REVIEW:
SPARKS, BANCROFT

THE LITERARY mind was astir in Boston. Not like thunder, not with a roll of drums, but with a little chirrup here and there, the dawn had slowly broken. In Channing, in William Tudor's books of essays, in the *Travels of Ali Bey,* modelled on the *Lettres persanes,* Boston had become self-critical. Dozens of minds were asking themselves the questions that had found words in the *Monthly Anthology.* Hundreds issued the summons, —which was to be repeated for a hundred years, on each new frontier of the American mind,—for a literature that was really American, "redolent of the soil," "purged of old-world influences." In later years, when people spoke of the "renaissance" in New England, they spoke with a measure of reason; for in Boston, as in Florence, four hundred years before, there was a morning freshness and a thrill of conscious activity. The New England imagination had been roused by the tales of travellers and the gains of commerce, the revival of ancient learning, the introduction of modern learning, the excitements of religious controversy. After the long winter of Puritanism, spring had come at last, and the earth reappeared in its beauty.

Ever since 1817, the little circle of the cognoscenti knew that something important was in the air. There had been decisive proofs of this. Professor Edward Channing and his cousin, Richard Henry Dana, had been driving from Cambridge into Boston. Channing was the editor-in-chief of the new *North American Review,* and Dana was his assistant. As they drove along, side by side, Channing read to Dana two poems that had just come into his hands by a young man named William Cullen Bryant, who lived in a village in the Berkshires. One of them was entitled *Thanatopsis.* As Channing continued to read, Dana exclaimed, "That was never written on this side of the water!" His excitement, he said later, was natural, considering what American poetry had been up to that moment. The day before, a middle-aged country doctor had appeared at the office of the review and drawn from his voluminous pocket-book these poems by his son, which he had brought clandestinely to Boston and eagerly showed the editor. Dana, hearing that Dr. Bryant was making a speech before the Legislature, went at once to the State House, to have a glimpse of the father of such a poet. The American world had moved a step forward when village poets could produce such verses and country doctors could be proud and happy to know that their sons were men of genius.

All the circumstances of this event were typical of the moment. First of all, the excited recognition that something had really happened: the time and the place were ready for the poet. The feeling of Bryant's father was typical also, for most of the writers of the coming age were actively encouraged by their fathers and mothers, for whom the career of letters seemed as normal as that of the pulpit or public affairs. Not even in Catholic countries, where almost every peasant family aspired to produce a priest, was there a keener wish, in the poorest household, that a brilliant son might have "advantages" and follow the line of his intellectual interests. Still more symbolic was another fact: a magazine existed,—after so many abortive attempts,—that could provide an outlet for the writers who were appearing on every hand. Edward Channing and Dana, at this moment, with George Ticknor, also of their circle, were probably, of all American readers, the best informed on English poetry, from Chaucer to the new Romantic School. The rest of the group who wrote the new review, and followed one another as editor,—Edward and Alexander Everett, Jared Sparks and John Gorham Palfrey, two young students of history, Greenwood, Dr. Gardiner, together with Bowditch, Webster and Andrews Norton,—were all men of the world, more or less, who had kept up with the literary current and knew what living writers really counted. They proposed to meet the sneers of the British reviewers in a tone that was neither provincial nor chauvinistic. They were greatly obliged to Scott, the first of living writers, in their opinion, who had said, in his kindly way, that when people once possessed a three-legged stool they would soon contrive to make an easy-chair.

The new review was the easy-chair in question. It was a little angular, perhaps, but no one could have called it a three-legged stool. Its tone was almost as cold and tame as that of the *Monthly Anthology*. It had the dry simplicity, the hard strength, the timid correctness and those other traits that Goethe said so naturally belonged to the early period of every art. It was like the old New England furniture, re-expressed in words. Modelled on the British reviews, still the foundation of all American thought, it imitated their magisterial air. The editors seemed to be on their best behaviour. But the British reviews also were cold and formal, even when they "stripped and whipped" their victims. The great Romantic critics had not appeared, to take the starch out of their pompous manners; and the *North American* had many virtues. It was aware of all the important writers in England, France and Germany. It noticed all the American writers, Cooper, Irving, the poet Bryant, who was soon to settle in New York, the centre of his future life and work. It was on guard against the colonial note: one of the writers condemned a Canadian author on the ground that no colonial government had ever evoked the nobility of mind that was essential to greatness. Its standard was severe and thorough: some of its reviews represented five months of study, during which the reviewer went behind the author, read all the works that he had read and verified all his citations. In short, with a firmer hand and greater resources, it carried on the task of the *Monthly Anthology;* and, as the years passed and it grew in strength,—until its conservative policy sapped its strength,—the public became aware that it had at last a genuine organ of criticism, one that deserved to rank with the best reviews in the world.

There was no doubt about its conservatism. If it was clear, orderly and well-informed, if it possessed all the scholarly virtues, it was hostile to the forms of feeling, literary, political, philosophic, that were to characterize the coming age. It was a Unitarian-Whig review, with all the temperamental limitations that marked Webster's class of "solid men." In politics, its aim, as time advanced, was to keep the tariff up, to keep the Whigs in power for the sake of the tariff, and to keep on good terms with the Southern magnates, whose cotton fed the Northern factories, so that the tariff might serve the Boston bankers. All very simple, like the old curriculum at Harvard. In literature, it had a marked aversion for the notes of the new age, enthusiasm, mysticism, rapture. Although it felt obliged to accept the English Romantic poets, if only because they were English, it still preferred the eighteenth-century modes. For this reason, the tender-minded Dana soon broke with his fellow-editors. A Whig, even a Tory in politics,—in the current American sense of the words,—a lover of old customs and associations, who wrote Addisonian "Letters from Town," he was a professional man of letters, the first of his kind in New England, and the only one of the group, for the *North American* followed the principle of "all gentlemen and no pay." In him, the old idea of "polite letters" had given place to something more profound. He did not think of poetry as a recreation, for he had taken Wordsworth in sober earnest; and he thought there were truths beyond the "understanding" that could not be reached in the usual Boston way. In fact, he preached the high Romantic doctrine. He had written a series of papers on the British poets, defending the Lake School.* He had said that Pope was not a poet at all.† This was too much for his friends, and much too much for Boston. A furious hubbub resounded through the town. Out Dana went, and out went with him any hope that the *North American* would ever understand the new generation.

Alas for Dana, born too soon, not strong enough to break his own path and yet the symbol of a rising world where other poets of a tougher grain were to find their audience waiting. A sensitive dreamer, diffident, selfdistrustful, with all the shy and solitary ways that marked the romantic poet as a type, he was to become an ancient Nestor, the only man living, decades hence, when even the Civil War was growing dim, who could still remember Washington's death. As he strolled through the Boston streets, a forgotten ghost, or basked in the sunshine of his Cape Ann garden, his silvery curls reaching to his

* In the opinion of Professor John Nichol, these essays were the best that had appeared, up to that time, on the Lake School, either in America or in England.

† The division of feeling in regard to Pope marked the new age more clearly than anything else. See Parson Wilbur's comment, in *The Biglow Papers,* on the youthful Hosea Biglow's view of Pope's verse: "He affirmed that it was to him like writing in a foreign tongue,—that Mr. Pope's versification was like the regular ticking of one of Willard's clocks, in which one could fancy, after long 'listening, a certain kind of rhythm or tune, but which yet was only a poverty-stricken *tick, tick,* after all,—and that he had never seen a sweet-water on a trellis growing so fairly, or in forms so pleasing to the eye, as a fox-grape over a scrub-oak in a swamp."

shoulders, he would speak of the British essayists of old and the charm that lingered round their memory; but he had lived his life as a recluse, sending forth shoots of prose and verse that had very rarely grown or flowered. He had written a long poem, *The Buccaneer*, the fruit of his early rambles on the Newport beaches, poems modelled on Coleridge and Byron, verses that were not as good as Bryant's, tales of the "darker passions," after the manner of Brockden Brown, *Tom Thornton*, *Paul Felton*,—young men doomed to live in a world that cannot comprehend their aberrations. Not one of his poems or tales could have been called conclusive. He had started a magazine, *The Idle Man*, filled with his own musings and his friends' verses, and lapsed into an unembittered silence, hoping that perhaps the day might come when an American author would be valued as much as an argand lamp. Thirty years of writing as a profession had brought him less than four hundred dollars. No man, he said, could go on forever without some little response from the world about him.

The circle of the *North American* could hardly have been described as sympathetic. These positive minds, however, had other qualifications. Their interests were historical and political, their gifts of a purely critical order. Dana's ablest work was his criticism, and many essays in the magazine were as good as the best in the foreign reviews of their time. One might mention, as an instance, the essays of Alexander Everett, whose mind was livelier and more vigorous than that of his more famous younger brother.* Criticism, oratory, history,—

* As Minister to Spain, Alexander Everett had studied the South American republics, which were revolting against the mother-country. In his surveys of America and Europe, translated into German, French and Spanish, he showed a remarkable understanding of the post-Napoleonic political era. His literary papers on *Gil Blas*, Voltaire, Mme. de Sévigné, Chinese manners, etc., lucid, learned, often witty, revealed the *North American* at its best. He translated Theocritus and Goethe and passages from the *Brahma Purana*, among the first examples of Oriental studies in oratory, the statesman's instrument, and history, the record of his achievements,—these were the forms of literary expression in which, at the moment, America most rejoiced. In the early days of Rome, with which New England had so much in common, the orators had come before the poets, the chroniclers before the dramatists. To the little statesmanly world of the Boston patricians, of which the *North American* was a spokesman, the noblest, the most honourable career, after making history, was to write it. Or, better still, to speak it. Had not Luther said: "Whoso can speak well is a man"? *

In fact, all over the country, in the Middle States, in the South, as well as New England, during these opening decades of the century, the historical mind was extraordinarily busy. Old men who had fought in '76 gathered the children about their hearths and told them tales of Lexington and Concord. People thronged to Plymouth Rock, which Webster had signalized in his great oration. The neglected chronicles came to light. Growing boys and girls rediscovered Mather's *Magnalia,* wonderful stories about their country that made them feel the very ground they trod on was consecrated by Providence. Hundreds of local histories, histories of states and counties, histories of towns and villages, proud of the parts they had played in the recent wars, poured from the rural printing-presses. It was a symptom of a world-wide movement, for everywhere Napoleon's campaigns had roused the sense of nationality. In England, Macaulay, Grote, Carlyle and Milman, in France, Thiers and Guizot, in Germany, Niebuhr and Ranke were only a few of the notable men who were immersing themselves in historical studies. The archives

America. Among the early *North American* writers, one might also mention Caleb Cushing, the statesman who coined the phrase "man on horseback." Cushing's *Reminiscences of Spain* compare well with Washington Irving's writings.

* "If ever a woman feels proud of her lover, it is when she sees him as a successful public speaker."—Harriet Beecher Stowe, *Dred.*

in the European capitals were searched and brought to
light, and tens of thousands of dusty documents were
scrutinized and passed from hand to hand, even from
country to country. The historians formed a princely
brotherhood, forwarding one another's investigations,—
like the men of science of the future. Niebuhr had set an
example and a standard for critical scholarship in historical writing, first in the search for materials and secondly
in the examination of them; and there had never been a
time when a new and distinguished contribution to history
received such universal appreciation. England, like America, stirred by the great continental scholars, had awakened from its age-old isolation and begun to study the
history of other peoples, and the English historians were
developing, thanks to the recent revival of classical
studies,—at Oxford, as at Harvard,—a new and fresh
feeling for composition, for the artistic virtues of the
ancients. Upon all the English-speaking historians, Sir
Walter Scott had a profound effect. He gave them a
sense of local colour. He taught them to reproduce, in
their narrations, the atmosphere of the times with which
they were dealing.

The American school of history, established in New
York by Washington Irving, was one of the phases of this
world-movement. For its culmination in Boston there were
various reasons. The first large library in the town, that
of the Massachusetts Historical Society, founded in 1791
by Jeremy Belknap and others, was almost exclusively
stocked with historical works. The Athenæum and the
Harvard Library were both especially strong on the side
of history. Young men with literary tastes were drawn into historical research largely for want of other choices.
There was little else for them to read. This was the "accident," as Palfrey called it, that gave rise to the New England school, soon to fulfil the prophecy of Horace Wal-
pole that Boston was to produce a Thucydides. But the

circumstance was not an accident. Everything had prepared the Boston mind to centre its thoughts on history, as it had chosen theology in the past; and the general interest that filled the libraries with all this apparatus of research animated the young historians and gave their works a sympathetic welcome.

The accumulation of private wealth in Boston, thriftily guarded by the canny Whigs, also served the historians. Prescott, Motley and Parkman were men of large means. So was George Ticknor. Bancroft, who was relatively poor, found himself obliged, and contrived to spend, in the preparation of his earlier volumes, almost three times as much as the President's salary. Ticknor's *History of Spanish Literature* cost as much to produce as a public building. In these formidable bills of expense, the assembling of books and documents was the largest item; for the public and semi-public libraries grew very slowly. Prescott, as late as 1839, said that an American historical writer had to create a library of his own if he wished to write even on American themes, much more if his theme were Spain or Holland. In another twenty years, all this had changed, and the wealth that had made it possible for a few scholars to command the means of study provided the means also for the poor. In 1857, the German, Kohl, describing the private libraries of Boston, which were largely open to students, spoke of the American "author-princes" who flourished side by side with the merchant-princes. Even in London he had scarcely found such splendid collections of books or studies that were arranged so picturesquely, with busts, paintings and curiosities, spaciously illumined from above. Many of the merchants were bibliophiles. One of them owned twelve hundred Bibles, including several that were very rare. Another collected engravings, hundreds of fine examples of every school. Another had a collection of Americana, first editions of every known work relating to the early history of the country. Thomas Dowse, a journeyman leather-dresser who, in the days of his poverty, when he did not own a pair of boots, possessed "six hundred books, well bound," bequeathed a great collection to the public. There were many rivals for the distinction of owning the finest library in Boston. No doubt, George Ticknor's outshone them all; but by some the honour was claimed for Theodore Parker, the great preacher of the eighteen-fifties, whose library was a river of books that flooded his house from attic to cellar. The libraries of Everett and Prescott were re-,nowned. The books of Rufus Choate, the Salem lawyer, who settled in Boston in 1834, filled his large house from floor to floor, in spite of all the efforts of his wife to stem the appalling tide.

With all these new facilities, the studies of the histori- ans made rapid progress. For a number of quiet readers, more or less in Boston and more or less in touch with one another, were preparing a series of monumental works, George Bancroft, the son of Aaron Bancroft, the well- known minister of Worcester, Jared Sparks, William Hickling Prescott, J. G. Palfrey * and Richard Hildreth, editor of the Boston *Atlas.* Rufus Choate's friends thought he was better fitted for history than any of these professional historians. The dream of Choate's life was to write a history of Greece; and, in preparation for this, he made a translation of Thucydides, never choosing a word,—or so he said,—until he had thought of at least six synonyms. But the busy lawyer, whose mind dwelt in Athens, had no margin of time for meditation. There were plenty of others to take his place. Half the men of letters in New England were spreading out their notes and documents in emulation of Robertson and Gibbon. To

* Palfrey, the author of the *History of New England,* published, in 1821, an article in the *North American Review,* pointing out the use that writers of fiction might make of early American history. The first New England historical novel, Lydia M. Child's *Hobomok,* was written in response to this article.

be sure, they were few at first. Jared Sparks, even in 1840, wrote home from the British Museum, where he was examining manuscripts, "In the reading-rooms are daily congregated more than a hundred readers and transcribers, of all nations and tongues, plodding scholars, literary ladies and grave old gentlemen with mysterious looks. When shall we see the like in the Athenæum?"

Boston was not London; but at least in the Athenæum one might have seen, even years before, the well-known Hannah Adams, working on her history of the Jews, the lady of whom one heard so many stories, as that they were obliged to lock her in, because it was not polite to lock her out. Living, Miss Adams was the only female who ventured to claim her statutory right to browse in these, to her, celestial pastures. Dead, as she was soon to be, she was the "first tenant" of Mount Auburn, or so her gravestone said, though a Boston lawyer, pondering the inscription, remarked, "She cannot properly be called a tenant." One had seen Miss Adams at the Athenæum; one saw the Everetts, Ticknor, Palfrey, Sparks, the pillars of the *North American*. One saw Richard Hildreth, a little later, a tall, thin, aging man in black, deaf, absorbed, sitting at his table in one of the alcoves, with his books and papers before him, rising from his chair only to consult some work of reference. The vogue of historical writing increased day by day, in this still air of delightful studies; and the regular Boston dinner-hour, three or four o'clock, lent itself to long, laborious mornings. In 1840, Charles Francis Adams, the famous diplomat of years to come, brought out the *Letters of Mrs. Adams*. John Quincy Adams, Abigail's son, expressed the feeling of a thousand readers when he said that his mother's letters affected him till the tears streamed down his face; and the editor of the book, Abigail's grandson, already touched to tears by these old papers, exclaimed, "Happy are those who pass through

this valley with so much of innocence!" * The new generation was engrossed in history, not in American history
alone, and not exclusively on the highest level. J. S. C.
Abbott, the brother of Jacob Abbott of the Rollo Books,
represented an army of popular writers. Of his *Life of
Napoleon,* Emerson said later, "It seems to teach that
Napoleon's great object was to establish in benighted Europe our New England system of Sunday schools." †

In Cambridge, in the middle thirties, the boys and girls
of the university circle were permitted to dive and delve,
with well-washed fingers, into the great boxes, eight in
number, where lay the unpublished letters of Washington.
There were forty thousand of these letters, which the
great man had written or received, many of them in
the spacious study where they were now assembled, in the
Craigie house on Brattle Street, Washington's study during a long winter. Jared Sparks had moved out from Boston, bringing with him the famous correspondence, which
he was preparing for the press, and had rented a suite of
rooms from Mrs. Craigie. Sparks, the "American Plutarch," was working on his "lives," the *Library of American Biography,* a series of twenty-five volumes, written by
various hands, including his own, describing a whole Pan-
theon of American heroes. He was soon to be more widely
known as the "patriarch of American history." ‡ He was
already engaged in his great campaign, along with George
Bancroft and Peter Force, to collect, preserve and publish the documents of the period of the Revolution.

His writings, however useful, were hardly exciting, at

* Charles Francis Adams maintained the literary habits of the most artic-
ulate of American families. Brought up in the White House as a boy, he
kept an Adams diary, like his father, for more than fifty years. He contributed seventeen articles to the *North American Review,* on Aaron Burr,
Lord Chesterfield, etc.

† E. P. Whipple, *Recollections of Eminent Men.*

‡ After his appointment, in 1838, as the first Professor of History at
Harvard,—at any American college,—a date that marked an era in historical studies.

least, to later readers; and yet they represented a life as exciting as that of an Arctic explorer. Indeed, Sparks had wished to be an explorer, like the hero of his first "life," —the best of all his lives,—John Ledyard, the old Connecticut Yankee, Captain Cook's corporal of marines. He had risen from the ranks, the poorest of the Connecticut poor, supported himself as a carpenter, walked three hundred miles through northern New York, trying to find a school where he could teach. He had battled his way through Exeter, where he had written an essay on the subject, "Intense application to study not detrimental to health." He had battled his way into Harvard at twenty-two and found a position as tutor at Havre de Grace. His Harvard friends protested. How could a man endure existence hundreds of miles from Boston?—considering that, from the point of view of Boston, civilization came to an end at Worcester. But Maryland was the making of him. The inn where he lived was on the post-road, and half the notabilities of the nation stopped there on their way to Washington.* At the time of the War of 1812, he saw the British sack Havre de Grace. They burned the great houses where he worked as a tutor, and the British admiral commandeered the finest coach in the town and sent it aboard his ship. Sparks was prepared to write with feeling when he came to consider the days of '76.

In this wider American world, he soon lost his New England particularism. He was appointed chaplain of Congress, and, with an interest already aroused in history, found himself surrounded with those who make it. Reading Mungo Park, he dreamed of exploring Africa. The plan came to nothing, or, rather, it led him to discover

---

* Josiah Quincy, who was then in Congress, stopped at the inn one day with Dr. Channing, who had also been a tutor in the South. Quincy and Channing liked the young man and remembered and helped him later. It was Quincy who, as president of the college, called him back to Harvard, and Channing preached at Sparks's ordination, when he became a minister, at Baltimore, the sermon on "Unitarian Christianity" on which his own fame as a theologian was so largely based.

Ledyard's papers and remains, including parts of the journal that Ledyard kept, describing Cook's death in the Sandwich Islands. Then, having followed Ledyard in imagination, he turned to the exploration of another world, almost as dark as central Africa, the world of American history. He had had enough experience of public life to know where his materials were to be found. He visited all the Southern States, examining the papers in the archives and those in private hands, as often as not in the old family dwellings of the men he had met in Washington. Then he went abroad, to England, Holland, Germany and France, searching the public offices, with Lafayette's assistance, arranging with Guizot and others to publish translations of his *Washington*. One of his aides was Henry Stevens, the "Green Mountain boy," a bibliophile in London, who introduced into Europe thousands of American books and made the British Museum a world-centre for American historical research.

Now, in his Cambridge study, in Washington's own chambers at the Craigie house, he was engaged in the great work of his life. About his standing desk, on every side, heaps of papers lay, not only Washington's letters but the letters of Jay, John Adams, Gouverneur Morris, the statesmen and diplomats of the great war-years. Simple as a child, with his gentle, winning voice and grave smile, he was the boast and delight of scholarly Cambridge. Everyone knew the story of Washington's letters, how Sparks, having found them at Mount Vernon, had arranged to carry them up by ship to Boston. Everyone knew the story of the other letters, Gouverneur Morris's, Franklin's. Some of them Sparks had been just in time to save. He had found two large trunks of Franklin's letters in a Pennsylvania garret, where they had been lying for forty years. Another mass of Franklin's letters and papers turned up in a London tailor's shop, on a shelf, in loose bundles. One of the manuscripts had already been cut in the form of a sleeve-pattern. One shuddered to think what might have happened if Sparks had not possessed the explorer's eye. Two or three years more, and it might have become forever impossible to write a correct history of the Revolution.

It was true that he "embellished" all these papers. He could not let the father of his country speak of "old Put": he changed the phrase to "General Putnam." He could not allow Washington to speak of a sum of money as a "flea-bite." The sum was "totally inadequate to our demands." In short, he bowdlerized the political fathers, in the spirit of a neo-classic age. He had in mind the marble bust, after the timid fashion of Canova, the bust that later times, too cynical, were to find little better than plaster. For this there were certain excuses. Science had not regulated history. No settled standards existed anywhere in regard to documentation. Quotation-marks had no precise value, and the greatest historians did not hesitate to revise their quotations without comment. There were other local excuses that were not so sound. In the days of Andrew Jackson, those who cherished manners, grace and form had some reason to feel, as the Romans felt in the days of the Gothic invasions, that all the amenities of life were threatened. The amenities received a double sanction, all the more because, in America, there was no prescriptive class to defend them. The famous "genteel tradition," of which one was to hear so much later,—so very much too much, when the phrase ceased to be used with any discretion,—largely dates from these days of Jackson, who brought the Wild West into the White House; and the high-minded Sparks, who, for the rest, had made his own way in a world that worshipped manners, could hardly have been expected to underrate them. The wonder was that he remained so candid. His Washington had to be a correct example, in harmony with the feelings of the thirties and forties; but he took pains to see that the causes of evil fell on the right heads.*

As for the nature and value of his writings, they were excellent *mémoires pour servir*. Sparks preserved the materials for later writers and placed them in a position to correct himself; and those who, in days to come, visited the library at Harvard looked with respect at the carved mahogany chest, modelled after the tomb of Scipio, in which reposed the Jared Sparks papers. The fame of his work showed what an audience awaited the coming historians, and what a social function they fulfilled, a function as vital as that of the orators, the ministers, the scholars and the portrait-painters.† For the twelve volumes of his *Washington,* orders came from the remotest hamlets in Georgia, Alabama, Illinois. Two hundred sets were sent to the Red River. The *Franklin* was translated presently into one of the dialects of Hindustani.‡ But Sparks's vogue was slight beside that of Bancroft, whose *History of the United States* began to appear in 1834. Never before had anyone attempted to tell the whole story of the nation, and the poor little dry chronicles and annals, Dr. Abiel Holmes's and so many others, that stood for American history were swept from the shelves by Bancroft's enterprise. There were reasons for Bancroft's renown. He was a conscientious student, laborious, open-minded, enquiring, zealous, with the strong will of an old Puritan

* Sparks, in his bowdlerizations, followed a general practice of the time. Similar cases can be found in every European literature. The heroes of the early eighteen-hundreds, conceived by readers of Plutarch, had to be heroes at any price.

† The first necessity of a new nation is to believe in itself. To create this self-confidence was the function of the early American orators and historians. "The only nations which ever come to be called historic are those which recognize the importance and worth of their own institutions." —Tolstoy, *Anna Karenina.*

‡ This was the greatest period of Franklin's universal fame. "The Greeks admire the character of Franklin. His name is far more familiar to them than that of any other American, not excepting Washington. Many of the 'sayings' of the philosopher are in the mouths of their instructed men." —Samuel G. Howe, *Historical Sketch of the Greek Revolution,* page 264.

settler. He had the imagination to see and present the life of the South and the West, as well as New England. He was learned enough to place American history in the main stream of historical events. His style was often picturesque and moving, irradiated with a solemn glow. It was true that, in the first editions, before Bancroft "slaughtered the adjectives," the book was like a Fourth of July oration, like one of Everett's speeches long drawn out, with the Stars and Stripes streaming from the author's hands.* This was the note of the nation in Jackson's time, when, with little reflection or criticism, the "giant of the West," rejoicing in size and numbers, growing, mounting in wealth and population, building its turnpikes, railroads and canals, heaping up its factories, bounded towards its "manifest destiny." For Bancroft, God was visible in history, and history culminated in the United States. No wonder his "epic of liberty," with its solid merits, was also acclaimed for other reasons.

He was well prepared for his task. He had grown up in a scholarly circle, and, when he was six years old, his father, Aaron Bancroft, referred to him a question in Roman history which two friends of the house, one of them Chief Justice Theophilus Parsons, found themselves unable to settle. He had known Sparks at Exeter. At Harvard, Edward Everett and Andrews Norton had taken him under their wing. The college had sent him to Germany. Another grand tour, like that of his predecessors. Wherever he went, in England, Italy, France, the first question that everyone asked was "Do you know Everett and Ticknor?"—who had been so diligent and so attractive. Bancroft was prouder than ever of his country; and he was en-

---

* "Come, children of sorrow! You on whom the Old World frowns; crowd fearlessly to the forests; plant your homes in confidence, for the country watches over you; your children grow around you as hostages, and the wilderness, at your bidding, surrenders its grandeur of useless luxuriance to the beauty and loveliness of culture."

The pruning of these unnecessary feathers of the newly-fledged American eagle was Artemus Ward's special joy and task.

gaging, too, with his black hair and firmly cut features, his eager air and obvious earnestness. Humboldt wrote to a friend, "He belongs to that noble race of young Americans for whom the true happiness of man consists in the culture of the intelligence." With all his exciting adventures, his meetings and visits with Byron and Benjamin Constant, Manzoni, the Princess Borghese, Lafayette, whose house was hung with engravings of American scenes, he never lost sight of his object. At Göttingen, along with his Latin and Greek, he studied Hebrew and Syriac. He met students from every country, Poles, Hungarians, Netherlanders. He learned to waltz, he learned to ride on horseback: one saw in him already the little sprightly man with the Santa Claus beard who, at eighty-eight, two generations later, pranced about the roads at Washington, with a big red rose in his buttonhole. At the same time, as a Christian devotee, a more than passive Unitarian,—in short, as that species of minister, sometimes ordained, sometimes not, under the guise of which so many young New England men of letters made their first appearance before the public,—he preached to the country congregations about the town of Göttingen, always speaking in the German language. He spent much of his time with Schleiermacher, the great court preacher at Berlin, listening to his lectures on education,* and made a study of the German schools.

Bancroft's heart, however, was far from simple. Still less simple was his outward manner. Returning home, as tutor in Greek at Harvard, who wished as much as Everett and Ticknor to introduce the German thoroughness, he found himself thwarted at every turn. This was not merely because of the Harvard indifference that also thwarted Ticknor. Bancroft was a vain young man and even more ambitious than Everett, in the less engaging

* The influence of Schleiermacher was apparent in the mystically religious passages in Bancroft's history.

sense of the term. He had neglected to observe Bacon's admonition in regard to travel, which all good Americans regarded as sound, that one should not change one's country manners for those of foreign parts, but only prick in some flowers of that which one has learned abroad into the customs of one's own country.* He had half forgotten the English language. French, German, soft Italian phrases blossomed on his lips, a flaunting of the dulcet strain that was much too much for Brattle Street. Bancroft's apparel and gestures were a scandal. He greeted his old protector Andrews Norton by planting a large kiss on each of his cheeks. There was a Cambridge tableau! It was the beginning of the end for Bancroft. But this young instructor was resourceful. He took himself off to Northampton and founded the Round Hill School with Cogswell, another peacock in the eyes of Cambridge. Indeed, there were anchors on every side of Bancroft's little ship. A diligent scholar, who worked for his school, he worked still harder for his own advancement; and the good Sparks, who welcomed his contributions to the *North American Review,* felt obliged to chide him for his foibles. He urged him not to use too many words like "emotions, love, affection, sensation, feeling," which carried him sometimes "into more soft abstractions." This was the counsel of a severe student with an eye for the rigours of language, who knew, as Bancroft did not know, the perils of a turgid rhetoric. And Sparks, with even greater penetration, told him frankly that he was too greedy after the treasures that the moths enjoy. "After what else, pray, should a man be greedy?" Bancroft had replied, with equal frankness. It was all very well to talk about "filthy lucre." A young man, the son of aged parents, had to be up and doing. "The only way," as the young man said, "to show you are fit for a better world is to show yourself not unfit for this." And

---

* This useful piece of wisdom was sadly misplaced in later American epochs.

Bancroft made the most of all his opportunities. No "musing with unseen spirits" for him, no folding his hands in contemplative indolence. He was ready to risk the chance that this was the way to rival Tacitus.

In short, with motives that his friends suspected, he had joined the Democratic party. He had little to fear from censorious Cambridge and Boston, when he had the growing will of the nation behind him. A Democrat in Boston was a social outcast; * but Bancroft had allied himself with powers which, as he well knew, and as Boston surmised, had the future with them. He had transcended the sectional mind of New England. From an equally obvious point of view, he had placed himself in the practical line of advancement; for the Democrats of New England were so few that any distinguished member of the party was sure to be rewarded in the end.† This prospect was certain in the case of Bancroft, a practical man with a gift for administration, almost the only scholar in the party, a learned Harvard man who had had the courage to smite the Boston Whigs with his scorn,—the Whigs who had smitten him, in the person of Andrews Norton,—even one who found in the people's hero, Jackson, the "nursling of the wilds," the hand of God himself. Bancroft, visiting Washington, drew his chair "close up" to the powers that were, as he said in one of his letters. Jackson and Martin Van Buren liked a man who could shape their political views in eloquent words, who was "easily first in literary improvements," as the "kitchen cabinet" called him. Bancroft's career in politics followed as a matter of course.

* William Henry Channing recorded later that, as a boy, he had heard with utter amazement,—as if such a thing could scarcely be conceived,—the remark of an old Bostonian, "A Democrat may be honest in his convictions."

† "A Massachusetts man has little chance of success in public life unless he starts a Federalist; and he has no chance of rising above a certain low point unless, when he reaches that point, he makes a transition into Democracy."—Harriet Martineau, *Society in America*.

No doubt, his association with politics was useful to a writer of history. Who, moreover, could impugn a man for taking sides against the Whigs? The party that Jefferson founded and Jackson maintained was grounded in the welfare of the nation, as some of the best Whigs had begun to see; and the Adamses had always agreed with Bancroft that Hamilton's aristocratic policy, shaped in the interests of the few, had no base in principle and morals. Bancroft's sympathy with the popular will was honest, beyond all question. Aside from his political associations, most of his European associations confirmed him in his faith that the Democrats represented the all-American cause for which the Revolution had been fought. Byron had sided with the Democrats. The Democratic party upheld the convictions that Lessing, Herder and Klopstock had in mind when they spoke of the "lodge of humanity" in the West; and yet, alike in Bancroft's life and mind, there was that element of self-deception which often dogs the spokesman of popular interests. The sentimentalist was marked in Bancroft. The conservative Prescott detested the Mexican War,* as a travesty of American principles. It was the Democrat Bancroft, the voice of the people, by no means including the Mexican people, who, as acting Secretary of War, ordered Taylor to march into Texas and gave the command to seize California,—in order to extend the "area of freedom" for those who did not rightfully own the country. Literary men indulge in humbug only at a price, and Bancroft abounded in humbug. "Did he believe what he was saying?" Anthony Trollope remarked in later years, after one of Bancroft's swelling speeches. Emerson had asked the same question when he said that Bancroft was a "soldier of fortune" who would "take any side and defend

---

* "The impolitic and iniquitous war in Mexico . . . mad and unprincipled . . . The patriot would rather see us go ahead by the arts of peace than war, as better suited to the permanent prosperity of the republic." —Prescott, *Correspondence*, 648, 658, 668.

it." Who can say how much a man believes, when he has an actor's temperament and a demagogue's faith in numbers? *

And yet Bancroft's work was impressive and made him "one of us," as Ranke said. All too keen for the cloud of witnesses, very imperfectly a man of letters,† insomuch that, after revising his work, pruning its highly-coloured feathers, he gave it an effect of truncation and bareness, he was an indefatigable student, with a grandiosity that was sometimes grand. He had first conceived the enormous task during his years at Göttingen and had exercised himself, to prepare for it, in a series of shorter studies, most of them on historical themes, the Economy of Athens, the Decline of the Roman People, the Wars of Russia and Turkey, some of them on German literature.‡ Meanwhile, he had steeped his mind in the legendry of the country, and, as the years went on,—the fifty years during which he was occupied with his twelve volumes, each one emblazoned on the back with the well-known phrase of Berkeley, which summed up the note of the days of Jackson, "Westward the course of empire takes its way,"—he mastered every corner of his field, as far as a

* "Bancroft talked of the foolish *Globe* newspaper. It has a circulation of 30,000, and, as he said, each copy is read by ten persons, so that an editorial article is read by three hundred thousand persons, which he pronounced with all deep-mouthed elocution. I only told him that I wished they would write better if they wrote for so many. I ought to have said what utter nonsense to name in *my* ear this *number,* as if that were anything. Three million such people as can read the *Globe* with interest are as yet in too crude a state of nonage to deserve any regard. I ought to have expressed a sincere contempt for the Scramble newspaper."—Emerson's Journals, IV, 410.

† His later writings, *The Life of Martin Van Buren* and *The Life and Character of Lincoln,* are always either commonplace or tumid, sometimes ridiculously so.

‡ Printed in the *North American Review.* Jared Sparks, as editor, had spoken up for nationalism in Italy, Greece and South America, and the magazine was widely read abroad. A dozen copies a month were sold in Calcutta, and the Bourbon king, Louis XVIII, caused to be prohibited in France this tribune of popular liberties. Bancroft's essays on Goethe, Herder and Schiller were among the first in America on these subjects. Goethe thanked him heartily for the paper he had devoted to himself.

contemporary could have done so. He had laid out a plan on the scale of Gibbon. He carried on a voluminous correspondence with every man and woman he could reach, north, south, east and west, who was able to give him any information or any unpublished letters. He opened up veins of tradition, collected half-forgotten anecdotes, travelled up and down the Mississippi, set his agents to work in London and Paris, searching the archives for him. After his first volume had been published, the whole world of scholars was ready to help him; the libraries and manuscript collections of almost every family in Europe that had had associations with America were freely opened to him. No one questioned his thoroughness. After forty years, he was still alert for any new material that he could use in some fresh revision of his work. The hardy old man, at eighty-five, still rose in the night, lighted his fire and candles and read his Gibbon and sometimes toiled for fourteen hours on end.

This was the great life-pattern of New England,* and Bancroft's work was not unworthy of it. One still recaptures, as one turns its pages, the pride that thrilled the bosoms of the forbears for whom the glowing historian first unrolled the panorama of the national epos. The forbears shared Bancroft's fervour. The young republic shared it; and the republic saw itself reflected in Bancroft's flattering mirror. There, like a river-system seen from a lofty mountain, the whole American story stretched its length, down to the adoption of the Constitution: the founding of the colonies, the struggles with the European peoples, the Puritans, the Cavaliers, the Quakers, the red men and their ways, the slave-trade, the early wars, the wonders of the Western wilderness,—the elk, the stag, the bear and Daniel Boone, pausing to rest in the golden thickets,—the savage forests and the great planta-

* "For fifty years he rose before the sun," as President Kirkland of Harvard said of John Adams.

tions, the gathering of the forces in the Revolution, the nation rejoicing in its strength, all in connection and relation, God the cause, Progress the effect. Happy days when Plancus was the consul, remote as Rome itself, when the young republic delighted the soul of Tocqueville and every American morning was a Fourth of July! Who would smile, in the sweep of such a vision, at the touchy, self-important little man who served as its rhapsodist and its hierophant, the little leader with his buttonhole who called the steps in the barn-dance of Progress?

CHAPTER VII

PRESCOTT'S
FERDINAND AND ISABELLA

SUDDENLY, in 1837, out of this throng of historical studies, honest and laborious, some of them fervent, none of them august, a great work appeared, like a wonder of nature, as it seemed to American readers,—*The Reign of Ferdinand and Isabella*. It was a brilliant performance, as any child could see and no scholar was ever to deny. Its limitations were obvious enough. It was not a philosophical history. The author had no great leading views, nor any profound feeling for human motives. There were depths upon depths behind and beneath the story that he had never plumbed. But, as a work of art, a great historical narrative, grounded at every point in historical fact, and with all the glow and colour of Livy and Froissart, it was a magnificent success. Its outlines were as firm as those of a cartoon of Raphael, and its pageantry of picturesque detail was calculated to feed as never before the starved imagination of the country. The book had been planned like a battle and built as stoutly as a Salem clipper, destined to sail through many enchanted minds for generations to come.

It was the work of William Hickling Prescott, Ticknor's young friend, the charming, amusing son of Judge Prescott, who lived in his ample house in Bedford Street, overlooking a beautiful garden. Prescott?—who could believe it? He was partly blind, and he had an extravagant love of jolly parties. He talked with a joyous abandon,

running over with animal spirits, laughing at his own in-
consequences, with always some new joke or witty sally.
He could be happy in more ways, in spite of his defective
eyes, and happier in every one of them, than anyone else
his friends had ever seen. One met him in the street, with
his rosy air, with his gay blue satin waistcoat, tall, graceful, with light brown hair and a clear and ruddy complexion. He seemed to look younger every day. It was known
that, for twenty years, he and a group of his friends,—writers in the *North American,*—had carried on a literary club,
reading their papers over a merry supper. He had printed
a few essays in the review. But this was in a dilettantish
spirit, everyone supposed. One of his relatives, meeting
him on the street, not long before his book appeared,
urged him to undertake some serious task. It would be so
good for him. It would be more respectable than leading
this unprofitable life.

Every evening the light from his study-window glimmered through the pear-trees in the garden. But only
George Ticknor, outside the household, knew that, for at
least ten years, Prescott had been hard at work, harder,
perhaps, than any Boston merchant. And, if everyone
bought his book for a Christmas present, it was only because the author was so attractive. One of his cronies, who
was not a reader, rose before dawn, on the day it was published, to buy the first copy; but, while everyone saw at once
that it was good, no one was aware how good it was. There
were scarcely twelve men living who were able to know.
Within a year or two, the electoral returns came rolling
in, from England, France and Spain. The book had been
born a classic.

It was a conquest of personality. Prescott was a first-
rate human being, exuberant, gallant, wilful, firm, devoted, far removed from the clerkly sort of scholar, pains-
taking but wanting in vigour and sinew, who, in a world
in which the most virile types adopted careers of enter-

prising action, ruled over the sphere of books. He was an artist-cavalier. His temperament fitted him to understand an age of courageous exploits, and yet—as if in his veins flowed in equal parts the blood of the old colonel of Bunker Hill and that of the mild and philosophical judge, his father and his grandfather—he was a just and sensitive referee, whose verdicts could be trusted. Whatever he did was sure to be decisive. For the rest, he was happiest on horseback and might have been a soldier.* He did not like to get up in the morning and had to instruct his servant, the faithful Nathan, to pull away his bed-clothes. He did not like to work. He had to make bets with his secretary that he would write a certain number of pages or carry out some other resolution. He was always making resolutions, never too old to make them; and he was never old enough to keep them. He had formed this habit at Harvard: resolutions about the number of hours he was going to spend in study, about the number of times a week he was going, or not going, to balls and theatres. When he broke too many resolutions, he introduced into his reckoning sets of fixed exceptions, amendments on amendments; then he scored them all off and opened a new account. By this means, and others, he made himself a casuist, able to comprehend the Spanish mind.

The refractory horse makes the most mettlesome charger. Prescott had a formidable will, and his gay inconsequence gave it buoyancy. Underneath his mock self-scrutiny, he formed the habit of self-examination; and he had bridled and harnessed his indolent nature. Every morning, in the dead of winter, to wind himself up for the day, he mounted his horse and rode to Jamaica Plain, to see the sun rise from a certain hill. As for his blindness,

---

* Several of the New England authors, Bancroft, Longfellow, Parkman, etc., were, like Prescott, excellent horsemen.

"The absolute tyranny of a human will over a noble and powerful beast develops the instinct of personal prevalence and dominion . . . It makes men imperious to sit a horse."—Holmes, *Elsie Venner.*

which was never total, he made an advantage of it. One might have thought that blindness was a blessing. He could not read for more than ten minutes,—an hour or two a day at the best of times. And how could a blind man write a history, based on unpublished documents, in two or three foreign languages?—for Prescott, who was unable to study law, had fixed his mind on history. Dr. Johnson had said it could not be done, a very good reason to prove that it could, as two of Prescott's later friends, two of the great historians of Europe, Thierry and Capponi, were to prove as well. He made his ears do the work of his eyes, with the aid of a friend and a sister and later of a competent secretary. Blindness had always favoured contemplative habits. Had not Malebranche closed his shutters in order to drive the sunlight out? Had not Democritus, as the legend said, blinded himself deliberately to stimulate his thinking? Saunderson, Euler, Huber all were blind. The blind town-crier of Salem, where Prescott had spent his earliest years, had performed most of the functions of a daily paper. Blindness was good for invention, as many poets proved, from Homer to Milton. The blind were famous for their patience, especially for their feats of memory. One dwelt on passages that were read aloud.

Prescott, who was no fatuous optimist, summed up these thoughts in one of his essays. He taught himself to use a noctograph, by means of which, with the aid of an ivory stylus, pressing on a sheet of carbon-paper, he took his notes and wrote his manuscripts. The secretary copied the notes in a large, round hand, which Prescott was sometimes able to read. Meanwhile, he had learned to memorize, composing in his memory to such an extent that he could often carry in his mind as many as three chapters of one of his books, seventy-two pages of printed text. He could hold it there for several days, turning it over and over, remodelling every sentence. One chapter he thus remodelled sixteen times, before committing a word to paper. His blindness had another effect. No reader of his histories ever imagined that, however he dealt, perforce, in a wholesale fashion, with the butcheries of the Spaniards,—"the Inquisition dogs and the devildoms of Spain,"—Prescott was an impassive man. He had sat at the feet of Channing, for whom no sparrow fell to the ground in vain. His blindness increased the sensitivity that lay behind the judgments he conveyed—as an artist ought to convey them—by subtle modulations of tone and style. He spoke of the careless indifference with which men who would never abuse a dog crushed, without a thought, insects whose bodily agonies were imperceptible to the naked eye.

He had first acquired these mental habits when, as a young man with failing eyesight,—the victim of an accident in college,—he had been sent abroad, to London and Paris, to consult the doctors there, and had spent a quiet winter in the Azores, where his mother's father, Mr. Hickling, was consul at Saint Michael's. People were surprised, in later years, that Prescott, who had never visited Spain, or Mexico or Peru, knew so much about these tropical scenes and was able to fill his books with such glowing pictures,—Spanish gardens, myrtles, laurels, lemons, the box-tree and the rose, mountain vistas, wildly picturesque, the Cordilleras and the Sierra Nevada, with convent-bells ringing in the valleys. Through his writings, to the very last, even to the final portrait of Charles the Fifth, dying in his garden-monastery, breathed the fragrance of the orange-trees, flowering in the southern sunshine. A young man who had grown up in Boston, under cloudy skies, lashed by the east wind, would have had little imagination if he had not received vivid impressions during these June-like months at "Yankee Hall," on the outskirts of Ponta Delgada, with a grand old patriarch like Mr. Hickling, as warm-hearted and merry as his grandson, and a gay brood of half-Portuguese cousins. And sup-

pose this young man, surrounded by so many marvels,—
castellated country-houses, gorgeous churches, crumbling
nunneries,—passing enchanted hours in mule-back rides
over the volcanic mountains, had yet been obliged, in his
blindness, to spend half his time in a dark room, walking
scores of miles from corner to corner, throwing out his
elbows to feel the walls till he wore away the plaster, till
he knew what a dungeon felt like and might have been
himself, even he, one of the victims of the Inquisition,—
would he not have preserved these impressions of what
his eyes had beheld? One takes a good look when, for all
one knows, it may be a last look. One takes two looks at a
tropical scene when one has lived in New England. It was
in this dark chamber, singing as he walked, to keep his
courage up, that Prescott learned the art of memorizing.
He composed a long poem for one of his friends.

The rest of this European journey also had its consequences. A young historical student, one who is going to
write about soldiers and statesmen, cannot see too soon,
at close range, a few good specimens in the flesh, not to
speak of the scenes of which the Romans had written.
In Italy, with his Livy and his Horace in the net of his
travelling-carriage, he crossed the great battle-fields, those
of the Gran Capitan, which he was to describe in *Philip II*.
In Paris, he paid his respects to Lafayette, like all the
other good Americans, some of whom, alas, were eating their hero out of house and home.* There, in his dark-
ened room, where, at a crisis of his illness, he seemed to
be at the point of death, he renewed the friendship with
Ticknor that was never to lapse for forty years. And in
London, face to face with the Elgin Marbles, images of
classical form that left long traces in his mind,—traces
a little too long, perhaps, for there was too much marble

* Lafayette collected a fund to restore to their own country various penni-
less Americans who overran La Grange. Thus early the new world began
to turn the tables on the old. See John Neal, *Wandering Recollections*.

in Boston already,—he spent his days with John Quincy
Adams, who was acting there as minister. It was in
Adams's private library, the great collection of books
which he had deposited in the Athenæum, that Prescott
had browsed as a boy, the turbulent boy who could not
control his laughter and who had infected one of his sober
professors, insomuch that, when the professor rebuked
him, the more he looked at Prescott the more he laughed,
till the class dissolved in tears. In those earlier days, Prescott, who had the run of the Athenæum, had spent half his
time reading books of adventure and romances, like
Southey's *Amadis of Gaul,* wishing that he could have
been a knight-errant. He read French, Spanish and Italian ;
and he and a friend played at mimic battles, first with
bits of paper and then dressed up in old fragments of
armour, which were kept as relics in the Athenæum. On
their way to school, they told each other stories, impro-
vising epics of adventure, in the manner of Ariosto. Prescott's head was full of the wildest fancies.

At that time, the Peninsular War had been raging over
Spain. The newspapers were full of it; and Prescott, as a
grown man, could not recall a day when feats of arms
amid Spanish scenes had not filled the foreground of his
mind. Now, restored to Boston, after his taste of the
Azores, and with his feeling for history quickened and
sharpened, he was to find another stimulus to follow up
this interest of his boyhood. His friends rallied about him in
his blindness and read to him aloud, six or eight hours at
a time, especially the inseparable Ticknor, absorbed in the
study of Spanish literature, on which he was lecturing at
Harvard. Ticknor, to amuse him, read his lectures to him,
three or four afternoons every week, along with his favourite classics and historical works and the old English
romances; and, together with an exiled Italian scholar,
who was spending a year in Boston, they read the Italian
poets. The friends wrote to each other in Spanish. On a

snowy day, when they could not meet, Prescott defended his belief that Petrarch's Laura was a real woman. Ticknor was more sceptical, much as he loved Petrarch, whom he had read at Vaucluse, on a spring day beside the fountain. Ticknor was almost the only friend one had, in this bustling, money-getting American world, who, having the means, had the time, as well as the passionate zest, for these enchanting studies.

Prescott was reading for pleasure, with Ticknor's Spanish library as his hunting-ground. He had in mind no scheme for a composition, but he was planning a literary career, after the manner of Gibbon, for which he proposed to lay a firm foundation. This was one of the solid Boston customs. As John Quincy Adams had laid a foundation for the statesman's life, based on blocks of good political granite, so Prescott put his blocks together, first clearing the ground with a thorough study of the English tongue. Let the suitable subject find him ready, even the suitable field of concentration. He had made up his mind that the age of thirty-five was soon enough to put pen to paper. English grammar first, as if he had never gone to school or college. For style, Sidney, Bacon, Browne and Milton. One hour a day for the Latin classics, Tacitus and Livy for elevation: he knew them by heart already, but this was a different matter. A year devoted to French, from Froissart to Chateaubriand. A year for Italian, another year for Spanish. There he paused, there he felt at home, too much at home to carry on with German. His eyes were not equal to the Gothic script.

Meanwhile, for practice in composition, he wrote an annual essay for the great review. On one of these papers, *The Arabs in Spain,* which he decided to save for his first book, he spent seven months of close work: two hundred and fifty foolscap pages of notes, all carefully indexed. The review had set a pace for scholars. These essays, which he continued to write and later collected in his *Mis-*

cellanies, dealt with themes suggested by his reading, Molière, Cervantes, Scott, Irving, Bancroft, Scottish Song, Italian Narrative Poetry, the Poetry and Romance of the Italians. It amused him to note that Corneille's friends, like his own friends in Boston, had sat with him for six months at table without suspecting that he was at work on a *Cid.* He wrote a short biography of Charles Brockden Brown, who had found so much of poetical interest under the prosaic surface of American life. Brown had attracted him, perhaps, because he had planned to write two epics on the conquests of Mexico and Peru. As for the general quality of these essays, they were such as one found in all the reviews, the "Old North," as it was called already, as in those of England, Scotland and France, neither better nor worse than Southey's or Lockhart's. They were scholarly books in miniature, learned, lucid, rather like Macaulay's, without the prejudices and without the genius,—for Prescott's genius was for story-telling. They showed his temperamental limitations, those of the Boston Whig point of view, in its most attractive form,—positive, somewhat obtuse, clear, just, full of romantic feeling, with scarcely a shred of intuition.* He did not like the idea of looking for mystical meanings in *Don Quixote;* and for him, as for all his school, the French Revolution had been fought in vain. His essays were best when they touched upon Scott, and Ariosto and Tasso. Prescott understood, no one better, these poet-story-tellers of chivalrous times. He belonged to the same family of minds.

Out of these related studies, his great theme rose with a sort of inevitability. For a while, he thought of writing a history of Italian literature. But, no, an Italian subject

---

* Prescott remarked, however, in one of his letters: "I don't know how it is, but our critics, though not pedantic, have not the business-like air, or the air of the man of the world, which gives manliness and significance to criticism . . . They twaddle out their humour as if they were afraid of its biting too hard, or else they deliver axioms with a sort of smart, dapper conceit" (Ticknor's *Life of Prescott,* page 255)—phrases that might have been uttered a century later.

would not be new: Sismondi had covered the ground too well. He wished for a theme that was new as well as great, for he was not planning a history to please un-lettered readers who had not kept up with the progress of research. He meant to write for the world, for the guild of historians, first of all, who formed a super-nation, just as he wrote for the pure love of letters. If one pleased Irving, Southey, Thierry, and conquered, for literature and science, a realm that no other mind had conquered, one's work would be good enough for the popular taste; and Spanish history, if it was not unknown, had not been explored at its most vital point, the reign of Ferdinand and Isabella. Theirs was the momentous reign during which the scattered kingdoms had been brought together, —the age of the conquest of Naples, the age of the sub-version of the Spanish Arabs, the founding of the Spanish Inquisition, the opening of the Western hemisphere. It was an age of great men, Ximenes, Gonsalvo de Córdoba, Columbus, an epoch that contained, for better or worse, the germs of the modern political system; and, thanks to the present government of Spain, call it liberal, call it anarchistic, the archives had been thrown open to Spanish scholars. They were busily publishing documents, chron-icles, memoirs. But the decrepit kingdom, humbled by the loss of its foreign empire, rising from its ancient lethargy, was yet in too chaotic a state to foster any vigour of ex-pression. Spain, with all its historiographers, had not pro-duced a master-mind who could assimilate for a greater purpose all these documents that had come to light.

The great theme was at Prescott's disposal. For the books and manuscripts that he required, he could count upon Alexander Everett, the minister at Madrid, who had aroused Irving's interest in Spain. In order to feel sure-footed in the language, he went over his Spanish gram-mar again. Then he began to read all round the subject, beginning with the general laws of nations, the constitutional history of England, the histories of the continental countries, France, Italy, Germany, Portugal, the general history of Spain, before he settled on his special field. For a few weeks, each summer, he went to Nahant, where his father had a cottage, "Fitful Head," perched on a wild sea-cliff. Strolling under the chestnut groves, and among the silver poplars that throve in the salt sea-breezes, he often met the Muse of History there. But this old resort of Boston fashion, about which Willis had written his sparkling stories, was full of mundane souls. He worked better at Pepperell, in the plain old salt-box farmhouse, the home of his Prescott forbears. There he had always spent his best summers, close to the "Fairy Grove," with its woodland streams. Behind the house, looking towards Monadnock, a shady path wound beside a pond, where he composed many of his chapters, sauntering back and forth. Sometimes he composed on horseback, especially when he wished to describe a battle, shouting his favourite ballad along the wood-paths, to rally his impressions,—"O give me but my Arab steed." He felt as he had felt, years before, dressed in fragments of armour at the Athenæum.

Many were the bets he had to make, and the forfeits he had to give, to keep his wits screwed up to the proper pitch. The book was a ten-years' task: * three and a half years of study before he wrote the opening sentence, three months for chapter one, seven months for the final chapter, two years for condensing and abridging. He had the text set up in type and caused four copies to be printed, for his friends to correct and criticize. But who would have dreamed that a book on such a subject could have been received with such hosannas? Not Prescott, who, as he painfully scrawled his chapters, writing the lines twice over in his blindness, never guessed how hungry his coun-

* "If you wish to be happy, always have ten years' work laid out before you,"—a phrase of Prescott's father that Ticknor was fond of quoting to his classes. No doubt, the phrase had its effect in the lives of many of Ticknor's pupils.

trymen were for the brilliant glow and colour that he gave them, the pageantry of kings and queens and battles. This was the romance that America longed for, as if the tapestry-makers of Bayeux had suddenly reappeared in sober Boston. Nor had Prescott guessed how eagerly the English, who had won the Peninsular War and were keenly interested in Spain, welcomed tales of soldiers and empire-builders.

The book was a universal triumph, one that even grew, as the years advanced, as the progress of historical research proved that Prescott's skill and documentation had left him the master of his field. The freshness and the freedom of the descriptions, the unity and proportion of the structure, the quiet and modest authority of the apparatus, the lustre of the language were new notes in American history-writing, different indeed from Jared Sparks's bareness and Bancroft's grandiosity. As for the author's style, a little over-formal, in the good old Boston way, Prescott presently took it in hand. He knew that American writing was archaic, like all colonial and provincial writing; he knew that the style of the new generation in England had grown more personal and more familiar. He wished to write the "prose of the centre," of which one was to hear in later days; and, in preparation for his future work, he searched and reviewed his own prose, to make it the natural vehicle of his mind. The sympathy with which he presented his heroes, always judging the action, not the actor, was even more of an innovation, although he had certainly pictured Isabella somewhat in the guise of a Boston lady, in whom a Boston man could find no blemish. Or, rather, a Boston boy, for whom a lady could not be a bigot. For Prescott was a boy, from first to last, a charming, virile and romantic boy, with a scholar's conscience and an artist's genius. One might well ask for different things, but one could scarcely ask for anything better.

CHAPTER VIII

LONGFELLOW IN CAMBRIDGE

THE CRAIGIE house in Cambridge had grown accustomed to distinguished lodgers when, in the summer of 1837, a young man of thirty, Henry Wadsworth Longfellow, the new professor of modern languages, applied at the door for chambers. Jared Sparks had lived there, Edward Everett had brought his bride there. Dr. Joseph Worcester, the lexicographer, was living there at present, working on his *American Dictionary*. Dr. Worcester had recently moved from Salem, where he had been a schoolmaster and had had among his evening pupils the new professor's friend and Bowdoin classmate, the young Nathaniel Hawthorne. The dictionary on which he was working now was a counterblast to Webster, his fellow Yale-man, who had removed from the language, in the interest of American independence, so many of its ancestral elegances. In matters of quantity, numbers of words and the like, together with the excellence of his definitions, the utilitarian Webster had won the day, even against the English dictionaries. In matters of quality, he was much at fault. Dr. Worcester saw no reason why the speech of his countrymen should lose its inherited succulence and fullness. In the name of Massachusetts, he wished to protest against the Connecticut school, with its thin and calculated rigours.*

* Worcester remained for a generation the dictionary of the best New England writers. See Holmes, *The Poet at the Breakfast Table:* "Mr. Worcester's Dictionary, on which, as is well known, the literary men of this metropolis are by special statute allowed to be sworn in place of the Bible."

Early as one rose in Brattle Street, Dr. Worcester was up and out already. One saw him on his black horse, jogging along in the shadows of dawn. Then he vanished into his cave of notes. The new professor was equally unobtrusive. It was true that he had a rakish air. With his rosy cheeks and china-blue eyes, he wore his hair in curls. He was fond of colour in his raiment. His neckties and his waistcoats were open to question; so were his gloves and his cane. Mrs. Craigie, much as she loved Voltaire, regarded him with suspicion. But she had read the extravagant *Sorrows of Werther;* moreover, she had read a recent book, *Outre-Mer* by name, the work of the young professor, a sort of all-European continuation of Washington Irving's *Sketch Book.* She liked the book, she liked the young man. It was plainly another case, like Bancroft's, of having studied abroad, and the new professor, unlike Bancroft, was willing to live it down. He got his own tea and toast for breakfast, quietly went about his college duties and buried himself in his rooms. And he soon exchanged the garments of his heart for a broad-brimmed black hat, a black frock-coat and a black cane.

Change his skin as he might, the young professor could not change his spots. He was a romantic soul. He was a born poet whose every fancy clothed itself in images and rhymes as naturally as an apple-tree in May clothes itself with blossoms. He was a poet like those Troubadours, those early-morning "finders" of poetry, who found it on every bush and sang as the vireo sings in summer, about whom he was lecturing to his classes. For he was also a scholar, the man in all America best fitted to fill Professor Ticknor's vacant chair. Ticknor, who wished to resign, in order to visit Europe again and write his history of Spanish literature, had virtually appointed his successor. He had seen some of the young man's translations; and eleven years before, when Longfellow had set out for Europe to

fit himself to teach at Bowdoin College, he had given him
letters to Southey and Washington Irving, advising him
to study at Göttingen. Longfellow had spent three years
wandering over the continent, taught at Bowdoin six years
more and gone back to Europe for another year, in Germany and Scandinavia, in preparation for his new position. He had shown the practical sense that makes the professor, worthy of the son of a Portland lawyer who had
been Dr. Channing's Harvard class-mate. He had formed
an acquaintance with various eminent men in every corner
of Europe, Lafayette in Paris, who remembered his family pleasantly in Portland, the Swedish poet Nicander,
whom he met at Naples, Thomas Carlyle in London,
Grillparzer at Salzburg, Bryant, who was already known
as the "father of American poetry," with whom he shared
long walks at Heidelberg. He had taken a leaf from Sir
William Jones's letters and learned not only the usual
languages, all that Ticknor knew, but also Finnish and
Swedish, and had published several text-books, French
and Italian grammars, and a Spanish reader. But he was
a poet all the time. As a boy, he had written ballads of
the Revolution, songs of the Maine woods, elegiac verses
about Indian hunters whose race was falling like the
withered leaves when autumn strips the forest. He had
planned a series of poetic sketches dealing with aspects
of New England life, the taverns, the village customs,
the parson, the squire, the husking-frolics and the Indian
dances, the French-Canadian peasants. And in Europe,
where others were to be so conscious of all that America
lacked,—the castles and cathedrals and ivied ruins,—he
had recalled the corn-fields of New England, garnished
with yellow pumpkins, the green trees and orchards by
the roadside, the bursting barns, the fences and the well-
poles, the piles of winter firewood, the fresh, cheerful,
breezy scenes of home. Everywhere, the Europe that he
witnessed,—the Europe of the "Romantic Reaction,"—

had gone back to its national origins, and the poet had become the skald again, the bard, the singer and the story-teller, the moulder and hierophant of the national life, the people's aspirations. Longfellow had felt this world-impulse.

Settled now in Cambridge, in the gracious mansion, so like an Italian villa, the young professor, who was always ready to draw forth some scrap of song or story to entertain some fair Angélique, found willing ears also in his classes. Beside the round mahogany table in University Hall, he sat among his pupils, discoursing with a silvery courtesy,—how different from the harsh, monastic fashion of most of the older professors,—in a style that was far too flowery, the older professors thought, but with a feeling for the romance of letters that was much more intimate than Ticknor's. In Ticknor one felt the glow of a marble surface. This lecturer was a painter and a poet. All the tones of his voice were soft and warm. He was a master of the pastel shades, whose mind was suffused with the light of Claude Lorrain. The facts, the details, the philology he left to his large corps of young instructors,—for the university, having abandoned itself to these degenerate modern languages, wished to do it handsomely. His task was to provide the general outlines, to give the aroma, the bouquet; and in what corner of the house of song was there a chamber where he had not lived? From the mouldering walls of the Anglo-Saxon bards, weather-stained and ruined, he passed to the courts and gardens of the French Trouvères, *en route* for the Minnesingers and the Mastersingers. (One had to use these French words now and then, silly as they seemed in Cambridge ears.) He told again the ancient Frankish legends, the Chansons de Geste, the story of Reynard the Fox, souvenirs of far-off springs and summers that seemed to have a sort of occult relation to these early-morning days of the young republic. One heard the New

England birds in the old French gardens, the songs like cherry-blossoms, drifting through an air of dawn, notes of expectation. Were some of the ballads rather grim and ghostly for a bright May morning in the college yard? The lecturer knew how to win his pupils . . . How joyously this ballad opens! It is the Feast of Pentecost. The crimson banners wave on the castle walls. You see how well-arranged the contrast is. The knight appears in his black mail, the mighty shadow trembles in the dance, the faded flowers drop. However, this ballad tells its own story. It needs no explanation. Here is something in a different vein, *The Castle by the Sea*. A somewhat sombre piece. Would you like me to read it? . . . Grim as the poem might be, it was inviting beside the Paley, the Locke or the mathematics one heard in the other class-rooms.

Warmly, too, with what a gift for colour, the young professor spoke of his life in Europe. This was not the cold, old classical Europe that everybody knew or had read about, the Europe that one crossed in a travelling-carriage, on grand tours, with letters of introduction. It was a garden of memories, songs and tears, softly bright as a spring bouquet, tinted with rose and apple-green, pale canary-yellow and the palest blue. One followed the professor on his travels, whether one had read his book or not, shared his pipe in homely Flemish inns, floated with him in a Dutch canal-boat, through meadows laden with tulips, played on his flute, like Goldsmith, on the Loire, among the peasants busy in the fields. One stopped for a month or two in a Spanish village, ambled through Tyrolese valleys, over the blossoming carpet, lay beside him on a flowery ledge, drenched with a summer silence that was broken only by the sound of evening bells. One walked through the still Swedish forests, heard the hemlocks murmuring, watched the sunlight on the waterfalls; one saw the yellow leaves drifting over Denmark. One called upon old Dannecker, Goethe's friend, the great

Canova's pupil, the sculptor of the charming "Ariadne," and shared the young man's thoughts on his homeward stroll,—whether he too might not accomplish something, bring something permanent out of this fleeting life, and then, serenely old, seat himself in his garden, like the artist, wrapped in a flowered morning-gown, and fold his hands in silence.

The young professor often spoke of Goethe. Once he dreamed that Goethe came to Cambridge. The professor gave him a dinner at Willard's Tavern and told him he thought Clärchen's song in *Egmont* was one of his best lyrics. The god smiled. He liked to speak of Heidelberg, where, to the music of the nightingales that flooded the castle garden, he had filled his heart with the old German lore. His friends there dwelt in a land of fancy where brooklets gushed and hemlock-trees were faithful, where maidens' bosoms were not always faithless, where graves were the footprints of angels and all things that lived sang together, the roses, the tulips, the birds, the storms, the fountains. The flowers melodiously kissed one another, keeping time with the music of the moonbeams. Many were the talks the young men had about fame and the lives of authors. Where should the poet and the scholar live, in solitude or in society, in the green stillness of the country or in the grey town?—urgent problems to be passed along to the young men at Harvard. There were admirable examples at Heidelberg, students with their sixteen hours a day and men of letters with retired habits: Thibaut, poring over his Pandects, and that wild mystic who spent his nights reading Schubert's *History of the Soul,* while his own soul dwelt in the Middle Ages. There, with his German Minna, lived the French poet, Edgar Quinet, who, having helped to revive the long-forgotten Chansons de Geste, had written his fantastic *Ahasvérus,* with its Holy Roods and Galilee-steeples, its arabesques and roses, hoping to do in words what Strasbourg Cathedral had done in stone. Lives of great men to remind one . . . toiling upward in the night. One had to learn patience, especially in the world that surrounded Harvard, where the pulse of life beat with such feverish throbs. At Heidelberg, one heard tales of Richter, of Goethe, Hoffmann, Schiller, who loved to write by candle-light, with the Rhine-wine always on his table. What more could a professor do, for his aspiring pupils, —and who was not aspiring at Harvard?—than to picture all these French and German scholars, toiling, in want, in pain, sickness, sorrow, familiar with the weeping walls of dungeons, to carry out their noble purposes? But for them, who would have kept alight the undying lamp of thought? But for them, the flapping of some conqueror's banner would have blown it out forever.

Thus the professor discoursed, beside the mahogany table, while the shadows of the elm-trees in the Yard danced on the white pilasters of the class-room. His mind was like a music-box, charged with all the poetry of the world.* Ballads that rippled with the River Neckar. Ballads of summer mornings and golden corn, blossoms, red and blue, leafy lanes and hedge-rows. Spanish, Swedish, Danish ballads. Epics and fragments of epics, like *Frithiof's Saga,* by the mad Scandinavian bishop, Esaias Tegnér, half pagan Viking, half Lutheran priest, who had revived the chants of the ancient skalds in the pastoral setting of a Swedish Wakefield. Sagas of ships and sea-craft and laughing Saxons, dashing their beards with wine. Songs of Norwegian chieftains, proud of their flowing locks, night-songs, songs of childhood, Christmas carols, stately Italian sonnets. The music-box unrolled its coloured stream; but the lecturer was not an antiquary. He was a poet and teacher of poets who spoke with a mildly apostolic fervour. He had published an essay de-

---

* For the range of Longfellow's knowledge of poetry, see his prodigious collection, *The Poets and Poetry of Europe,* 1845.

fending his vocation. Poetry did not enervate the mind or unfit the mind for the practical duties of life. He hoped that poets would rise to convince the nation that, properly understood, "utility" embraces whatever contributes to make men happy. What had retarded American poetry? What but the want of exclusive cultivation? American poetry had been a pastime, beguiling the idle moments of merchants and lawyers. American scholarship had existed solely to serve the interests of theology. Neither had been a self-sufficient cause for lofty self-devotion. Henceforth, let it be understood that he who, in the solitude of his chamber, quickened the inner life of his countrymen, lived not for himself or lived in vain. The hour had struck for poets. Let them be more national and more natural, but only national as they were natural. Eschew the skylark and the nightingale, birds that Audubon had never found. A national literature ought to be built, as the robin builds its nest, out of the twigs and straws of one's native meadows. But seek not the great in the gigantic! Leave Niagara to its own voices! Let the American poets go back to the olden time, studying not the individual bard but the whole body of the world's song. They could only escape from their colonial heritage in this all-human testament of beauty.

Sufficiently mild words with which to announce an era. Twenty other poets and orators were saying the same things. Longfellow spoke for them all and only spoke with more authority because, with his chair at Harvard, he had an ampler sounding-board behind him. He represented the new school. But what was the older school? Who were the living poets of New England, most of whom were destined to fade and vanish within a score of years? Who were those poor "self-deluded" creatures, pictured by the disappointed Dana, "seated, harping, on some weedy knoll, and fancying it the mount of all the Muses"? Self-deluded or not, their name was legion. The bolder talents, Bryant, Halleck, Willis, had gathered round Washington Irving in New York, but enough remained in New England to constitute a timid air of springtime. Pale, shy little books of poems blossomed on every hand, like the anemones of an April woodland. Connecticut had most to show, for the best-known Boston poet, after Dana, Charles Sprague, author of the "odes,"—odes in the marmoreal style, which he produced for every Boston "occasion,"—was a survivor of the days when Pope and Dryden were the reigning writers.* Connecticut had its little school, with Lydia Huntley Sigourney at Hartford and James Gates Percival at New Haven. John Quincy Adams, watching the skies, wrote in his famous Diary: "It would take nine such poets to make a Tate."

In fact, there was not a poet in New England, except perhaps Maria Gowan Brooks, who could have written a stanza of the translation with which the Cambridge professor had shown his mettle. Longfellow, in days to come, might have been thought, by some, tame and faded; but the beautiful tone of the *Coplas of Manrique,* the old Spanish funeral ode,—an act of high talent, if there ever was one,—sounded like full summer, in its music, beside the pallid poems of the thirties. Mrs. Brooks, who had lived in Boston, although she had, decidedly, not been read there, had written with this bell-like depth of tone.†
It was true that her poem, *Zophiël,* partly composed in Cuba, where, on her coffee-plantation, Mrs. Brooks had built a Grecian temple, over-abounded in the female vein. This lady's personal charms, as the reader gathered,—as the reader, in fact, was virtually told in Mrs. Brooks's story, *Idomen,*—had not been appreciated by her Boston

---

* Sprague had the luck to see one of his odes published in Calcutta, a few years later, with its American names cleverly altered, and afterwards reprinted and praised in London, as the work of a British officer.

† So well that Charles Lamb, when Southey showed him a copy of *Zophiël,* said that there had never lived a woman capable of anything so fine.

husband, a cold-blooded merchant. She had redoubled the
spell, in consequence, ransacking half the libraries of
Paris, plunging into the Talmud and a Persian grammar
for perfumes, precious stones and passion-flowers, for the
irritated comments of monks and saints on the secrets of
the toilet, on women's hair, lutes and bridal bowers, serpents and fallen angels. Her notes were an armoury of
exotic learning. Her fancy, like a Cuban jungle, rioted
with Byron and Thomas Moore. But Mrs. Brooks possessed an energy that triumphed over all these fripperies.
The good-hearted Southey, who gave her a lift—and
opened himself to the vulgar levity that always pursues
relations of sentiment—never wearied of quoting the
lines that began, "And as the dove from far Palmyra
flying." Of *Egla's Song,* he said again and again that it
was "far superior" to Sappho. The poem as a whole had
a glow and movement that made it one of the best of a
short-lived school, on either side of the ocean. The song
was destined for a longer life.

Energy was the one desideratum of all this poetry of
the New England thirties. Longfellow's *Coplas* possessed
it, Mrs. Brooks's *Egla's Song* possessed it. Where could
one find it in the other poets, especially in the other
"female poets"? For these were the days of the female
poets, that soft and sprightly brood. These were the days
of "Peter Parley" Goodrich, the Jack who built the house
of the female poets, the Tokens and Ladies' Portfolios,
the Souvenirs, Albums, Pearls and Caskets of Gems, a
family of magazines more fecund, as one of the critics
said, than any of the animal tribes. Connecticut knew
them well, the annuals and the female poets, almost as
well as New York, better than Boston, the home of
Katherine Ware's "Bower of Taste;" for none of the
brood mildly raged to the tune of Mrs. Sigourney, whose
writings filled fifty-seven volumes. Mrs. Sigourney's little coterie abounded in the balmier mental graces, soft

as the breath of gazelles; but among the virtues of their "moral pieces" energy was not preëminent. Mrs. Sigourney's poems, as a critic said, were "more like the dew than the lightning;" and Sarah Edgarton, Hannah Gould, Sarah J. Hale,* and Eliza Townsend, shadows and shades of shadows, blossomed in other corners as if to prove that "annuals" were not perennials. Nor was Percival's masculine vigour of a hardier kind. This man of prodigious learning, who versified in thirteen languages and who thought that he might have been happy if he had got a cell in Tasso's mad-house, whose life and personal attributes, like Poe's, fulfilled the romantic pattern, wrote as if to prove another fact, that masculine vigour is not energy. If the pattern, not the poems, made the poet, Percival, like Poe, would have been immortal; but all his vigour ran to commonplace.† Fluent commonplace engulfed the rest, John Pierpont,‡ John Neal,§ who was so desperately anxious to "show" the British.

---

* Author of "Mary had a little lamb."

† Percival is the classic American example of the almost-good in poetry. A typical "manic-depressive," whose life was a mass of pathetic oddities, he was an admirable geologist and died as State Geologist of Wisconsin. He was one of the most remarkable American philologists of his time, and, as a linguist, a rival of George Borrow and Burritt, the "learned blacksmith." He wrote a report on the Basque tongue and spoke and read Sanskrit, Gaelic and six of the Slavonic languages. He made interesting experiments in Greek and German metres. The small house he built for himself at New Haven had no door or windows at the front.

‡ The grandfather of John Pierpont Morgan, a Connecticut man, a minister in Boston, an admirable reformer, who pawned his family spoons to pay the printer of his well-known *Airs of Palestine.*

§ The Portland "Down-Easter," John Pierpont's partner for a while in business, a shop-keeper, clerk, teacher of drawing and fencing, auctioneer, merchant, editor, lawyer,—in short, a typical Yankee handy-andy,—a journalist in England, for a time, who tried to show the British what the Americans were made of by talking about the "charter of greatness" written on our cataracts and mountains. Neal was a good-hearted soldier of fortune who "bounded" with the bounding years of Jackson. His once well-known poem, *Niagara,* was described as a "swash of magnificence." He wrote many slapdash novels, one of them, *Seventy-Six,* in three volumes, which he composed in twenty-seven days. His only book of value, *Wandering Recollections,* contains amusing glimpses of the American Grub Street of his time, together with a description of Jeremy Bentham, with whom he lived for three years in London, 1824–1827.

Pierpont's odes and songs, in the manner of Moore and Campbell, shouted and stamped by schoolboys,—

> Stand! The ground's your own, my braves!
> Will ye give it up to slaves?—

filled the air at public ceremonies with a sound as of horns and trumpets. But these poets came and went as the orators came and went: not one of them left an enduring line.* It was their unconsidered dash and go that carried them all into the void together.

What they needed was not praise, alas, but a more stringent kind of criticism, a lack which the Boston mind had begun to repair. They were overpraised, as a rule, as Poe remarked. Many of them passed through three editions, and the magazines that published their work rose like the waves of the sea.† The good "Peter Parley" befriended them all.‡ Pierpont's *Airs of Palestine* had

* Some of Pierpont's lines lasted as long as the nineteenth century. There were schoolboys in 1898 who knew *Warren's Address to His Soldiers at Bunker Hill,* although they never guessed who wrote the poem.

† One student has counted 137 periodicals "of a literary character"—and he knows of others—established in the United States within two decades of the War of 1812.—W. B. Cairns, *On the Development of American Literature from 1815 to 1833.*

‡ "Peter Parley," Samuel Griswold Goodrich, the tireless book-purveyor, the reformer of juvenile literature, an honest, courageous, simple-minded man, has left, in his *Recollections of a Lifetime,* the best account of many of these early minor writers. He was kind to Percival and Brainard; he published Trumbull's *Poems* and paid the author $1,000 for them, about the sum of his own ultimate loss. While his other books have no intrinsic value, the *Travels, Voyages and Adventures of Gilbert Go-Ahead*—who "wasn't made a Yankee for nothing"—reflects the Connecticut popular mind of the time. The hero, a pedlar of clocks in China, Java, Siam, etc., suggests Mark Twain's "Connecticut Yankee." His adventures enable the author to unfold an "educational" panorama of travel like that of the Rollo Books. In his *Sketches from a Student's Window,* Goodrich enumerates, as the works in demand, in a typical book-store of the eighteen-thirties, *Thaddeus of Warsaw, The Scottish Chiefs, Young's Night Thoughts* (of which thirty editions were published, in a generation, in the United States), *Sandford and Merton, Paradise Lost, The Mysteries of Udolpho, Caleb Williams, The Lady of the Lake, Cœlebs in Search of a Wife,* and *The Castle of Otranto,* along with Webster's Spelling-book and a large assortment of hymn-books and Bibles.

an honest vogue among the devout. Numberless readers looked for Percival's "P" in the newspapers and magazines. Brainard's *Niagara,* written in twenty minutes, sped through the country. If there was nothing decisive in their work, nothing or so little,—Brainard's *Connecticut River* was a good poem,—what was to blame but a national frame of mind that rather welcomed hasty composition, the strained voice, the high key, the midnight fervours of the adolescent? Even in Boston itself, where the angel of intellect had stirred the waters, criticism was only half awake. One found cases in point on every side, in Cambridgeport, for instance, across the river, where Washington Allston wrote his poems and nursed his dreams of Titian under a cold and distant sky. Allston was idolized as a human being. Everyone loved the silvery old man in the red-lined velvet robe. He was a charming talker, with his great, soft, luminous, dreamy eyes and the white curls that clustered about his neck, so vehement, so gracious, so refined,—for the rest, so well-bred and well-connected. The Boston people liked to stop and see him, in his painting-room at the port, an awkward-looking house with a great north window. They read his poems, they sometimes bought his pictures, usually hanging them in a cramped back-parlour between a deadly cross-fire of lights; they marvelled over the dust on his studio floor, thick as a heavy snow-fall, just as it ought to be in an artist's den! They never came back from Europe without a higher opinion of his genius, they were to lecture about him when he was dead. But anyone might have seen with half an eye that Allston's great talent had run to seed. Cambridge was a depressing place for painters.* Even more to the point was the want of criticism, or rather the quality of the criticism, along with various other deprivations. The people who adored poor

---

* "Cambridge is like Kaulbach's pictures. It is all literature."—William Morris Hunt.

Allston's genius said that he made his women much too plump. These intimations of carnality disturbed their quiet minds. They did not like their limbs to be flesh and blood, they liked their limbs to be metaphysical, though how one was to be another Titian *without* the carnal reminder,—and they wished to think that Allston was another Titian, they wished to think that Boston had produced the last great man of the Renaissance,—might have puzzled even the metaphysicians. This would have mattered less if Boston had given Allston a few carnal models; but, wherever he turned for a model, he only found another metaphysician. Everyone talked metaphysics, everyone praised the artist because his work was metaphysical,—"etherealized and sublimed by religious fervour." * His mind, bathed in the fluid mist, grew thinner and thinner every day.

Allston was the case in point that later generations best remembered. A painter, a man of letters,—a man of energy, beyond a doubt,—he had planted himself at the cross-roads, midway between Boston and Cambridge, where everyone was aware of his existence. Hundreds of young men passed his door, drank the enchantments of his conversation, took him for a symbol. He was the "eagle tied to the roost," over whom Horatio Greenough mourned. That he was an eagle no one questioned. The only question was about the roost, and this question loomed as the years advanced. He was a man of high talent. His portrait of Coleridge was enough to prove it, aside from his beautiful drawings. His prestige and his legend were imposing. The first enquiry every foreigner made—unless he asked for Channing—was, Where is Allston's studio? All the friends of his European years, Irving and Fenimore Cooper, Thorwaldsen, Vanderlyn, Leslie, Turner, Coleridge, whom he had known in Rome, —walked with them under the pines of the Villa

* James Russell Lowell.

Borghese, talked out the nights at the Caffè Greco, the haunt of the northern barbarians,—cherished and honoured his name and his work. He had praised the greatness of Turner when everyone in England laughed it down. He had taught Leslie to see Titian's colour, when people laughed at Titian as they laughed at Turner. The traits which the American mind revealed, at the very first encounter, in Allston, as in Bulfinch and Washington Irving, were a congenital sense of style and form, refinement and elevation. But something had gone amiss, the young men gathered. He had never ceased to paint and write,—fine sonnets on the Old Masters, grand letters to his brother-artists. His talk was enough to fire anyone's brain. And yet he had spent twenty long years trying to paint a picture he could not finish, the baleful "Belshazzar's Feast," the nightmare of his life. He had brought the picture back from London, in the far-off days of his youth, thinking it needed only a few touches; and Gilbert Stuart had shown him, all too plainly, that his perspective was not right. He had never outgrown those first misgivings. The picture had been bought in advance, he had mortgaged his life to finish it, and he had grown feeble with his doubts and fears. All the fault of the roost, the young men thought. All Boston's fault. A generation later, Henry James, puzzling over the unfinished masterpiece, "the mask of some impenetrable inward strain," was to draw his own deductions from the painter's nostalgia, "the grim synthetic fact of Cambridgeport." William Wetmore Story drew them first, the young poet, the sculptor of the future, Justice Story's son, a student of law in Cambridge, who, as he watched the eagle moulting, made up his own mind to fly to Europe. Allston had been starved, he wrote in one of his letters,—the rich and beautiful nature, he in whose veins the South had run so warm, born to have grown and spread such fragrancy. With nothing congenial outside him, he had been forced to feed upon himself. He had drained his memory dry. At Longfellow's very door! Times had changed when tragedies like this pressed themselves on one's attention. The younger generation was making demands which the older generation had never dreamed of. What were the right conditions for artists and writers? The portrait-painters, the orators, the historians had had no occasion to ask such questions. The young republic had given them their conditions, given them freely and fully, in the very fact of its existence. It wished for oratory, it wished for history. The statesmen wished to have their portraits painted. Oratory, history, portrait-painting were all connected with statesmanship; they had a *raison d'être* in politics and throve in an age of nation-building. But art and letters of an absolute kind, the kind that has no mass-demand behind it, had always given birth to the subtlest problems, problems of the artist's life, influence, environment, education. In two thousand years, the human mind had scarcely attacked or begun to solve these problems; and now they had risen before the American mind, portentous, all but insoluble, alarming. Young men who could see that Allston's failure had aspects that applied to painters only, or workers in the plastic arts, asked themselves if writers were not involved. For if Allston had gone astray, as the young men saw, how about the poets? —Allston himself as a poet, Neal, who had scattered his talents beyond redemption, Brainard and Carlos Wilcox, broken reeds, Percival, the walking suicide, feasting on his Connecticut moonshine, "brooding over the wrecks of celestial longings"?* No doubt, they had natural disabilities. They were victims of persecution-mania, Percival, at least, Brainard and Wilcox in a less degree. Were they not also victims of a social order that was still too immature for poets? Was not even Dana such a victim, Allston's brother-in-law and special crony, always an‹

* Preface to Percival's collected poems.

nouncing projects, even planning the famous book on Allston, after Allston's death, which, like all his plans, came to nothing? Dana had lost heart. For years his mind had been dying of inanition. Were writers and painters in the same plight? Allston's friends in England had besought him not to return to America, where there was no "antagonism of talent" to make him toe the mark; and what American artist had ever lived, aside from the portrait-painters, to prove that their advice had been mistaken? But Bryant, Irving and Cooper seemed to show that writers were in a different case, with human nature everywhere to study, with books as aids in the study of human nature, books, the only instructors in style and form. The question rested on a few examples.*

Great talents largely create their own conditions. At least, they may be said to crystallize tendencies that exist in the air about them,—tendencies that have gradually come to exist,—of which lesser talents have been unaware. Cambridge, like all New England, like New York, was ready for its poets and its tellers of tales. Cambridge was ready for literature, and Cambridge men were ready to provide it. The world had flowed their way. Allston's disabilities were as nothing,—the metaphysics and the want of models, the poverty under the pressure of which, he said, his pictures crumbled away,—beside the fact that he had lost the world, his world, the world-current of painters and painting. He had followed the wrong tune, as Stuart might have told him, Stuart who saw the dangers of "elevation" and ridiculed Benjamin West's "ten-acre pictures," filled with apostles and prophets. A painter's business, Stuart always said, was to paint what he saw with his eyes and leave the elevation to the poets; and Allston had followed West, against his eyes. No one doubted his elevation. It was his painting that had gone

---

* These doubts and dilemmas of the younger generation are indicated in several passages of Emerson's early *Addresses*.

to pieces, and anyone in Paris could have told him why.* *There* was the fault of the famous "provincial condi-tions" of which the future was to hear so much. In painting, Cambridge and Boston were out of the world. In literature, they were in the world, even a little too much, it might have been thought, by those who disliked the world of the thirties and forties. Whether or not one liked this world, the world of Alfred Tennyson and Tegnér, of Lamartine and Ferdinand Freiligrath, was a matter of time and taste. Whether one liked or rejected all its poets was a matter of time and taste. But no one was able to doubt beyond a decade that Cambridge and Boston wrote for the world, or that the world was repre-sented in Cambridge as it was represented in Rome and Oxford.

For Cambridge had ripened, in these few short years, as a well-tended garden ripens in June. All in a mist of birds and honeysuckle, the literary mind had put forth shoots. Thoughts were growing, books were growing under the quiet boughs of the ancient elm-trees, in the fragrant shadows of the locusts, the perfume of the daphne and the lilac. Robins darted down the leafy paths, orioles swung on their nests; one heard the murmur of bees and doves and the bobolink's song in the meadows along the river. The scent of the syringa filled the air. These were the scholastic shades that poets had always loved; and books, whether in verse or prose, were spring-ing from the Cambridge mind, thick and fast as the grass in the Cambridge door-yards. The old guard clung to its chimney-corner. Allston and Dana put their heads to-gether and talked about the Waverley novels. Allston

* Even Delacroix, who continued to paint historical canvases but who knew that the time for this *genre* had long passed. See his comments on the case of Gros, so strangely parallel to that of Allston. (Delacroix, *Œuvres Littéraires,* II, 195 *et seq.*) Gros, like Benjamin Robert Haydon, the English painter of "ten-acre pictures," tried to carry on the grand style in a world that had ceased to be "grand," and both, in despair, committed suicide.

had written a novel of his own, *Monaldi,* full of Italian souvenirs,—artists, bravos, convents, jealous husbands,—with a few charming pages of description. The hero was a painter, like himself, whose mission was to revive the grand style, in its Raphaelesque roundness. Allston had pencilled on his studio-walls various "texts for reflection." * At "Shady Hill," the redoubtable Andrews Norton rejoiced in his gladiatorial Indian summer, playing out his game of "evidences," which left him leisure for a little whist. One saw Dr. Popkin in the square, with his great caped coat and his ruddy visage, looking like an eighteenth-century beadle. Dr. Popkin's historic umbrella was a symbol of the old regime, the Harvard whose severity and simplicity seemed to be rapidly passing.

Everyone in Cambridge appeared to be writing a book. The Holmeses, the Lowells, the Channings, the Wares, the Danas were turning into literary families, expanding like rivers as they advanced. Dana's young son, Richard Henry II, who had spent two years before the mast, was assisting Edward Channing as instructor in English. Jared Sparks and his friends of the *North American* trudged back and forth between Cambridge and Boston, with bags under their arms stuffed with papers. Henry Cleveland was editing Sallust and writing a life of Hendrik Hudson. George S. Hillard was editing Spenser, with elaborate annotations. Cornelius Conway Felton, the jolly giant, the new Professor of Greek, who had edited Homer, with Flaxman's line-drawings, was making a translation of Menzel's *History of German Literature.* Felton was one of Longfellow's special friends. Another

---

* These sentences were preserved by Anna Jameson, who called upon Allston in 1838 and copied them, with the painter's permission. Some of them deserve to be remembered, e.g.:

"The most common disguise of envy is in the praise of what is subordinate."

"Fame . . . is only known to exist by the echo of its footsteps through congenial minds."

"The only competition worthy of a wise man is with himself."

was Charles Sumner, Hillard's partner, a lecturer at the Law School. The all-attractive Sumner,—the son of the grim old sheriff who hanged his murderers with his own hands "because it was disagreeable,"—dazzled even Boston with his legal learning. Only the other day, on a visit to England, invited to sit with the judges in Westminster Hall, he had settled a point that arose in the course of the trial. The Lord Chief Justice, at a loss for a precedent, had asked him if any American decision bore on the point in question. Sumner had answered that he knew of none, but that the point had been settled in his lordship's court, and he had given the citation. The incident had echoed through the world of lawyers.

With Sumner stretched on the sofa at Craigie House, reading Poliziano or Bossuet, the Funeral Orations that he loved,—for Sumner, like Hillard, was an orator,— with Felton to discuss the German poets, with Dr. Beck and Roelker, the young instructors, to sing German songs and share his hock, Longfellow had his Heidelberg in Cambridge. Sometimes, on a sunny morning, Prescott rode up on his horse to the door, handsome, gay, a little over forty, astonished to find himself so famous. Sometimes, Longfellow walked into town, to stop at Ticknor's house or stroll on the Common, lingering on the bridge to talk with Prescott and watch the kelp and the seaweed floating by. But the great event of the week was Saturday evening, when his rooms beheld a gaudy, worthy of a parcel of good-natured monks. Much as the young professor dreamed of Europe,—villas by the margins of lakes, city-casements looking on sun-swept squares, when the perfume, streaming in at his open window, brought Switzerland back, Italy, the Tyrol,—his mind rode quietly at anchor. He had his own name for the malcontents who, having tasted the old world, talked of nothing else. They were Frondeurs, difficult as the Fronde of Louis XIV. Even while he shared their homesick feelings, he was immune to the virus. He had a shield and buckler in the doctrine that Europe itself had taught him: a poet was the poet of his country. Easy to believe in this pleasant Cambridge, with the city across the bridge and the village about him, tokens of Europe on every hand, ample chambers, filled with books and pictures, with all the sights and sounds of the young republic, the cheerful hammer and the hopeful saw, a population that was up and doing. And when a poet had friends like Samuel Ward, his old Heidelberg crony, who greeted him with a German kiss,—for Cambridge was losing its rigours,—drew a bottle from each of his pockets, gave him all the gossip of New York and carried off his poems to Fitz-Greene Halleck, who liked to see him "resplendently coruscate" in Park Benjamin's paper, how could he not rejoice in his native land? His native land rejoiced in him, and, if it liked his poems all the more, the more they suggested Europe, that was the most "native" thing about it. "Europeans" never thought of "Europe." And anyone could see that Longfellow's poems, whatever their subjects were, expressed the young American state of mind.

For softly, without effort, as he sat in the vast shadow at his open window, the poems rose in his mind, like exhalations,—*Voices of the Night.* The black hulks of the trees rode at their moorings on the billowy sea of grass. The stars glistened through the heaving branches, the silver Charles gleamed across the meadow. Stanza by stanza, the poems came, sometimes all at once, songs, reveries, echoes of German verses, mingling with the whispers of the summer wind,—youthful regrets, youthful aspirations, psalms of a life which, on such an evening, might well appear a dream, though far from empty: *Footsteps of Angels, The Light of Stars, The Reaper and the Flowers, Hymn to the Night.* On these very evenings, at their open windows, thousands of young men in Hollis Hall, at Bowdoin, Yale, Princeton, in Cincinnati, up and down the Hudson and the Mississippi, in England, Scotland, Holland, in far-off Russia, beside the Neva as beside the Danube, heard the trailing garments of the night, shared these reveries of the New England springtime that Longfellow was putting into words, with such a lucid, natural, velvety sweetness,—verses drifting through the poet's mind as the yellow leaves drift from the trees in autumn and silently fall to the ground.

In later days, when other fashions came, when the great wheel of time had passed beyond them, one saw these poems in another light. They seemed to lack finality and distinction, whether in thought or phrase. But no one could quite forget their dreamy music, their shadowy languor, their melodious charm, their burden of youthful nostalgia; and the world of the Age of Revolutions, which knew the Romantic poets, shared this poet's mood of exaltation. A day was to come when a Chinese mandarin transcribed *The Psalm of Life* on an ivory fan, and a dying soldier at Sebastopol repeated the stirring lines. When *Excelsior* appeared in a German version, the students of Innsbruck, meeting the translator, thronged about him and embraced and kissed him, with such joy and transport, as he said, that he always looked upon that moment as the happiest of his life. These were the days when to be "up and doing, with a heart for any fate," seemed, after the drought of Calvinism, the drought of monarchism and reaction, in the continental Europe of '48, when people had thought they were powerless, a miracle and a sudden inspiration; and Longfellow spoke for the youth of all the world. He spoke for the young in his verses, even in his prose *Hyperion,* the romance of the American student who looked like Harold the Fair-hair and bore the name of an old German poet. This was his own romance, more or less, in the high-flown style of Richter. Many and many a reader, as the

years went by, readers in English, Swedish, Dutch and
French, followed in the footsteps of the hero, sought out
the inns where Paul had slept, the Star at Salzig, the
White Horse at Bingen, turned aside for a Sunday at
St. Gilgen, lingered, book in hand, under the lindens and
wept over the night at Heidelberg when the lovely star,
ι Emma, fell from heaven.

Such were the "voices of the night." The voices of the
day were firmer and clearer. On these summer mornings
at Craigie House, when the birds were carolling in the
trees, when insects chirped in the grass and the sunlight
and the perfume of the flowers poured through his open
windows, Longfellow's mind went back to Sweden, to the
still Scandinavian woodlands, carpeted with blossoms at
this balmy season, where, in a simple, primeval world,
like that of his own Maine, the leaves and ribbons
streamed from the lofty May-poles, and the old pagan
gods awoke once more, and one heard the hammers of
the Vikings, so like the hammers that one heard in Portland, building their oak-ribbed ships. That was his great
discovery, after all, that was the brightest feather in his
cap: other American writers and scholars were rediscov-
ering Italy and Spain, recapturing France and Germany.
He was the first who had visited, amply, at least, with a
living imagination, the lands of the skalds and the sagas,
where one found traces of one's forbears, in the days of
the Danish invasions, forests like one's own New England forests, builders of boats with masts of the lordly
pine, the Baltic dashing on the northern strand, desolate
as one's own North Shore, village ways like the New
England ways, houses of hewn timber, white-painted
churches, maidens with flaxen hair, brown ale worthy of
King Olaf, apples such as a village blacksmith loved,
poets, too, like the mad Esaias, scarcely concealing under
his bishop's gown the robe of the chanting gleeman,
chanting now not the deeds of blood but the wild freedom

of the days of old. There, in those northern lands, the ballad, like the ancient yeoman's life,—the life that was fit for free men and simple, fishermen, farmers, sailors, fit for Nantucket men and Portland men, as for the men of Gottland and Malmö,—there the epic and the story-poem still played living parts in human lives, not as mere survivals and revivals, as they were in the rest of Europe. One of the best of Longfellow's translations,—perhaps, like that of the Spanish funeral hymn, it could not have been better,—was *The Children of the Lord's Supper,* in which Tegnér had revived for Swedish ears, as Goethe had revived it for German ears, in *Hermann und Doro-thea,* the metre that Homer had used and Longfellow was to use in *Evangeline.* He had passed into this north-ern mind by such a line of sympathy that the old poet-bishop found his versions of *Frithiof's Saga* the only ones that fully satisfied him.

In Sweden, or in Scandinavia,—for he found in the Finnish *Kalevala* the form he was to use in *Hiawatha,*— he had gone to school to better purpose than elsewhere in his multi-coloured Europe. Before his eyes waved, and were to wave, the mingled shapes and figures of the past, the myths and scenes of European legend, "like a faded tapestry," faded then, how much more faded later. The Scandinavian world had given him something far more vital, rhythms that signified a secret kinship, deeper than a student's acquisitions, between the pastoral children of the Vikings and the child of Maine for whom the sea and the forest possessed an unfailing magic. The Scandina-vians had given him a feeling for the value of the forms, —the ballad, the folk-poem, the epic fragment, vehicles of the national sentiment that had come to life in Amer-ica, as it had come to a second life in the North,—through which his mind was to flow with its greatest vigour. All his evocations of feudal Europe, of the mediæval world that haunted him, of the biblical world and the world of the Renaissance, what were they ever to mean,—these incidents of an endless panorama, which the patient and facile showman unrolled for a generation before the eyes of his enraptured public, a Panorama of Athens, such as they had set up in Cambridge, extended over the history of the world's culture,—beside a handful of ballads and two or three narrative poems, redolent of the vast American woodlands, the prairies, the prodigious Mississippi, the sylvan solitudes of Canada, the gusty New England sea-coast, poems fragrant still with hemlock, spruce and balsam, the salt breeze of the rocky shore, the wild-brier, the rose and the syringa, breathing a tonic piety, as of paternal altars and forest gods?

Such were the voices of the day, which the poet heard, with a soft excitement, as he took his morning walk at sunrise, or, when evening came, lighted the long candles on his upright desk.

CHAPTER IX

THE YOUNGER GENERATION OF 1840

THESE WERE the days of the "march of intellect." The movement started in England by Lord Brougham "to promote useful knowledge" found the tracks laid for it in Boston. In a comedy produced at the Tremont Theatre, Master Burke, the "Irish Roscius," played the part of a professor who taught every subject known to man. The comedy was meant to satirize the much-talked-of march of intellect, and the Boston people saw the point and smiled. But, if their hearts had been opened, there would have been found, engraved within, the talisman Education. Education was the word in Boston, as a generation later the word was Culture.*

Whatever could be done by education, Boston proposed to do; for this was the age of "internal development," mental as well as commercial. The merchants had largely relinquished the maritime commerce that had created so much of the city's wealth and turned their energies to manufacture; and the effort of the Southern and Western magnates to build up what they called the "American system," at the expense of New England, drove the Boston mind all the harder. The wheels of the cotton-factories revolved at a furious pace, and the Southern slave-drivers plied their whips to feed the Yan-

---

* "We are all becoming cultivated up to the eyes . . . *tiers état* and all. A daughter of an old servant of ours, whose father is an Irish bogtrotter that works on the roads, told me yesterday, 'she had nearly completed her English education, was very well in her French, and should only give one quarter more to her music and drawing.' "—Prescott, 1840, *Correspondence,* 121.

kee mills with Southern cotton. The more the prosperity of New England came to depend on cotton, the closer the propertied classes drew to the Southern planters, with whom they felt obliged to ally themselves, yielding to them in all political matters. At the same time, to compete with the South and the West, they developed a system of closer communication between the capital and the hinterland. A network of railroads spread over New England, binding the six States together.*

This material growth was reproduced in the intellectual sphere. The rise of the Lyceum lecturing system, in 1826,—the work of the enthusiast, Josiah Holbrook, who went about the country lecturing on geology and natural history, urging the villages to form collections,—was only one of the educational movements that brought Boston and the rural centres into closer touch with one another. Webster, Edward Everett and Nathan Hale established the Useful Knowledge Society. Various other institutions followed. The Natural History Society, the Mercantile Library Association, the Mechanics' Apprentices' Association, the Lowell Institute diffused their currents of intellectual impulse. New England soon acquired the lecture-habit, the fruit of Edward Everett's enterprise, for Everett's public lectures on Greek antiquities were the first of their kind in America. There were constant courses in every town and village,—where Rollo and Lucy sat at the feet of Jonas,—on chemistry, botany, history, on literature and philosophy; and almost every eminent man in New England joined in the general effort to propagate knowledge.† A season-ticket for a course, ten to fifteen lectures, usually cost two dollars. In Boston,

---

* This development came quite suddenly. About 1831, Nathan Hale, the father of Edward Everett Hale, was considered a fanatic as a railroad-prophet. He suggested in a speech at Faneuil Hall that, if people could come from Springfield to Boston in five hours, an average of nine people would come every day. This was regarded as a preposterous statement.

† It was a practice of Dr. Holmes, after an evening lecture, to write a poem that was suggested by it.

all the boys and girls went to the Lowell lectures. As many as five hundred at a time learned that acids were not alkalis and that Homer did not write the Iliad.* It was quite the rage. The boys invited the girls, and after the lecture they walked home together, ending the evening with an oyster-supper.

Boston, all New England respected learning. No New England boy was allowed to question that he was destined to succeed in life, provided he knew enough; and Boston was determined that the boys and girls, and the blind and insane as well, should have an opportunity to know enough,—schools based on the best current theories, reform-schools that really worked reform, schools for the blind that caused the blind to see. Was not Dr. Howe's famous pupil, the blind, deaf and dumb Laura Bridgman, a proof that education was the mother of wonders? Boston had taken Channing at his word and really believed in perfectibility. It was true that at first the Boston pedagogues resented the assaults of Horace Mann, who had no use for their old-fashioned ways. But no one could resist this human cyclone, the tall, humourless man in the long frock-coat, so anxious, so exacting, so dogmatic, with the will of a battering-ram, who founded the State Board of Education in 1837. Having closed his law-office with the reflection, "Let the next generation be my client," Horace Mann found Boston thoroughly roused to a sense of the vital importance of public instruction. But what could be done with the country common schools, the merest "dormitories," as he called them, at least in comparison with the Scottish schools, which he had visited on a tour of study? The administrative features of the Prussian system seemed to him the best, and he adopted them largely, much as he detested,

* The "Wolfian theory," long since exploded. "Poor old Homer was relegated to the world of myth. As a schoolboy, I used to hear the belief in the existence of such a poet derided as 'uncritical' and 'unscholarly'."—John Fiske, *A Century of Science.*

in the Prussians, the "blind acquiescence" that enslaved the mind. For eleven years he travelled night and day, stopping in every hamlet in Massachusetts, forming conventions of teachers and school-committees. To make an impression on Berkshire County, he said, was like battering down Gibraltar with one's fist, and the Cape Cod mind was solid sand. Nothing new would grow there. But he knew how to deal with sand and granite, having so much of both in his own composition. He counted on the instinct of a people who thought there was nothing odd in asking a stranger if he was "learned in roses."

A Boston man had to be learned in something, and the passion for learning on the upper levels soon spread through all the other strata. Harvard set the pace. Thomas Wentworth Higginson was not unique as one who, at the time of his graduation, read French, Spanish, Italian, Latin and Greek, who later acquired German and Portuguese, Hebrew, a little Swedish, and always hoped for a chance to study Russian. Theodore Parker, the minister, somewhat older, the Roxbury Friar Tuck, the Lexington farmer's son who was able to carry a full barrel of cider, read Dutch, Danish and Russian, along with the others, Coptic, Chaldaic, Arabic, Ethiopic, and was found by one of his friends deep in a grammar of Mpongwe.* Here and there, some workman followed suit. Elihu Burritt of Worcester, the "learned blacksmith," was a typical figure of the moment. This well-known self-taught linguist who, as an apprentice, had kept a Greek grammar in the crown of his hat to study

* Theodore Parker's learning was famous in New England. T. W. Higginson related that he wished to find a certain reference in the Salic, Burgundian and Ripuarian codes before the codification of Charlemagne. Neither Sumner, Justice Gray nor Chief Justice Shaw could assist him on this occasion, but Sumner said, "Try Parker." Parker said at once, "Go to the Harvard Library, and on the fifth shelf in the fourth left-hand alcove you will find a small, thick quarto entitled 'Potgeiser: de Statu Servorum,' which will give you all the information you want." Higginson found his question answered there.—Chadwick, *Theodore Parker.*

while he was casting brass cow-bells, who made a version
of Longfellow in Sanskrit and mastered more than forty
other tongues, toiling at the forge or in the evening, after
a full day's work, affected no singularity, as he said. His
aim was "to stand in the ranks of the workingmen of
New England and beckon them onward and upward to
the full stature of intellectual men." The noble-hearted
Burritt * was not the only man of his kind. Many a boy
walked thirty miles to Cambridge to feast his eyes on the
sight of the college; and many a farmer's son, like
Burritt, might have walked to Boston, a hundred and
twenty miles, from New Britain, with two or three dollars and a silver watch tucked away in a handkerchief,
hoping to catch a ship for India, where he could study
Sanskrit. Sir Charles Lyell and Agassiz were surprised,
when they arrived in Boston in the forties, by the universal interest in education. Lyell had never seen such
crowds of workmen listening on winter nights to learned
lectures on geology and zoology, Shakespeare and Milton. Agassiz was present at an assembly of three thousand mechanics, brought together to form a library and
listening for two hours with rapt attention to a lecture on
the advantages of reading. Dickens was impressed by the
interests of the factory-girls of Lowell, a public that he
knew so well in England. There were joint-stock pianos
in their boarding-houses; the walls of the mills were covered with their poems; they subscribed to the British
reviews; they had classes in German; they all seemed to
know *Paradise Lost* by heart and talked about Wordsworth, Coleridge and Macaulay in the intervals of

* A passage from Elihu Burritt's diary, 1837: "*Monday,* June 18, head-
ache; forty pages Cuvier's Theory of the Earth, sixty-four pages French,
eleven hours forging. *Tuesday,* sixty-five lines of Hebrew, thirty pages
of French, ten pages Cuvier's Theory, eight lines Syriac, ten ditto Danish,
ten ditto Bohemian, nine ditto Polish, fifteen names of stars, ten hours
forging. *Wednesday,* twenty-five lines Hebrew, fifty pages of astronomy,
eleven hours forging. *Thursday,* fifty-five lines Hebrew, eight ditto Syriac,
eleven hours forging. *Friday,* unwell, twelve hours forging," etc.

changing bobbins on the looms. Flocks of these serious girls, described by Lucy Larcom in her *Idyl of Work,* afterwards went West as school-teachers and founded "Improvement Circles" on the prairies. The fame of the *Lowell Offering,* which contained their writings,—humorous and pathetic tales, fairy-stories, poems,—travelled round the world. A volume of selections, *Mind Among the Spindles,* was later published in London, and lectures were given at the Sorbonne on this portent of the times.*

In Cambridge, nobody was surprised to hear that the youthful Dana,—before the mast,—had kept his crew of sailors from going ashore, on the California coast, by reading aloud all day from Scott's *Woodstock.* Rough as the sailors were, most of them were Massachusetts sailors, and everyone took it for granted that in Massachusetts reading had a sovereign right of way. At Harvard, the young men read too much, or so it seemed to those who had frugal minds. They were hatching very strange ideas. They sat at their open windows on New Year's Eve and spouted the *Midnight Mass for the Dying Year.* Thomas Wentworth Higginson, the bursar's son, took a vow of poverty: he spoke of putting himself on equal terms with the vast army of the hand-workers. Marston Watson talked of raising pears, a better occupation than raising dollars. George P. Bradford, a brilliant scholar, a descendant of Governor Bradford, was bent on setting up a market-garden and trundling his own wheel-barrow through the streets. William Ellery Channing, the doctor's nephew and namesake, refused to go to chapel. Determined to be a poet at any price, he absconded from

---

* These lectures were given by Philarète Chasles. Recent writers on the Lowell mill-girls, tending to slight their accomplishments, dwell solely on the pitifulness of their wages. Their wages were pitiful indeed,—about three dollars a week. It is to be noted, however, that these wages were more than three times higher than the average corresponding wages in Europe.

college with his clothes and took refuge in a lonely farmhouse. All these notions were very disturbing. The young men said that terrestrial love was only a reflection of celestial love. They spoke of "bathing in a sea of thought." They went off mooning in the woods. They refused to talk about railroads, banks and cotton. They had no use for Blackstone and Justice Story. They were unwilling to be "mere" lawyers,—heaven save the codfish in the State House! They laughed when their fathers quoted Dr. Johnson. They smiled when their uncles quoted Burke, who had become a very old story. Goldsmith and Pope, to them, were as flat as stale beer. They spoke of the president of the college as President Littlego of Triflecut and referred to Cambridge as "Doughnut." They sneered at Doctor Phosphorus and Lawyer Smealmin and Swippens's Wholesale Grocery concern. They remarked that "the great art of being a merchant is to look wise and ride in a carriage." * Poetry was the only life for them, or painting, or contemplation, if they had to starve in a garret or a hut. And if all this was not the result of reading, where, pray, had they acquired their notions? The mothers and aunts and cousins of young New England,—not to speak of the fathers, who carried on the wholesale grocery business, the cotton-factory and the firm in State Street,—were filled with alarm and dismay.

Not that the fathers and mothers and aunts and cousins were opposed to books and reading. Many of the Boston merchants were authors themselves.† The solid men believed in education. They heartily favoured the great educational movement. It fitted the young men, their sons and nephews, not to forget the meritorious poor, to make the most of all the dazzling chances, legal, technological,

---

* See W. Ellery Channing, *The Youth of the Poet and the Painter,* in *The Dial.*

† See Nathan Appleton on *Original Sin,* and the miscellaneous writings of Thomas Handasyd Perkins, Abbott Lawrence, William Sturgis, Robert Bennet Forbes, etc.

commercial, which the expanding republic offered them. But books of a new kind had begun to appear, French and especially German books, even books by Englishmen and Scotchmen, who should have known better, filled with the wildest sort of metaphysics. These were the books that addled the minds of their sons, as Everett and Ticknor quite agreed,—for Everett and Ticknor, who knew the Germans, shared the opinions of the men of State Street regarding all these "follies of form and style." * The young men who read the new writers,—Thomas Carlyle, George Sand, Richter, Schleiermacher,—saw the matter in another light. If they were drawn to these writers, who spoke of the inner life, it was because the outer world repelled them. They could not share the current of ambition that galvanized the tougher-minded spirits,—the "forth-putting" types, as they said in New England, those that had "faculty," those that knew how to "take hold." What if trade and politics were advancing? Even if they had cared for politics, was it not evident that, with Jacksonism, the noble type of the trained statesman had yielded to the tricky politician? Politics had certainly lost the glamour which the great age of the statesmen had given it.† And commerce, too, had lost its grand role. The old China trade was a statesman's business. The factory was dull and small beside it. And who could ignore the abuses of modern business?— the fraud and perjury at the custom-house, the bribing of

* The *North American* group as a whole was invincibly opposed to the new school, the Transcendentalists and all their works. See Prescott's remarks on Carlyle's *French Revolution*,—"a shower of twaddle . . . new-fangled words . . . ridiculous affectations . . . perfectly contemptible . . . both as to *forme* and to *fond*."—Ticknor's *Life of Prescott*, 363.

† This was the standing complaint of Henry Adams, a generation later. Many fine minds anticipated Adams. Josiah Quincy wrote in 1834 that the new race of politicians "steer the ship of state by the winds of popular favour, before which they run, which they never seek to stem, which they dare not resist."—Edmund Quincy's *Life of Josiah Quincy*.

The *Letters of Major Jack Downing*, popular in the thirties and forties, added to the general disillusion. That American politics had returned to the Stone Age was a very natural deduction from this picture of Jackson's "husking frolic" around the Washington "crib."

foreign officials, the sweating of the workers in the mills, the hideous oppression of the sailors? Worst of all, slavery. Was not half the wealth of the Northern mills drawn from the whips of the Southern overseers? Was it not true that in Cuba one slave out of every ten died every year in order to give the Americans their sugar? The ways of trade were unfit for a chivalrous man, unless he could reverse the whole system.

In short, the more sensitive minds of the younger generation, the imaginative, the impressionable, the perceptive, those who characterize a generation,—for the practical people never change, except in the cut of their clothes,—were thoroughly disaffected. The shape of the outward world had ceased to please them. The Fourth of July orations had ceased to convince them that "freedom" had any connection with freedom of mind or that "liberality" in religion had any connection with religious feeling. The aristocrats of trade were essentially vulgar, the "rational" Unitarians were materialistic. The young people were radicals and mystics. They had no interest in size, numbers and dollars. They had begun to explore the inner life, the depths of thought and sentiment. They had returned, on another level, to the mental habits of their Pilgrim forbears. Those who were socially-minded allied themselves with the various cults and movements that were breaking out all over the country, the temperance and non-resistance societies, the vegetarian movement, the no-money movement, the Abolition movement, which was rapidly rising, the Socialist movement, which had come to stay. The Chardon Street Convention gave them a platform.* They sympathized with "Wandering

* The Convention of Friends of Universal Reform, 1840. The Chardon Street Chapel, the haunt of the reformers, was remodelled from the Parkman family's barn. Dr. Parkman, Francis Parkman's father, who did not like reformers,—although, as one of his eulogists said, he was "particularly kind to the unattractive,"—always referred to the chapel as "my mother's barn."

Jew" Taylor, who roamed about the roads and country
lanes and whom one saw, at street-corners in Boston,
standing, bare-headed, offering prayers for the city. They
sympathized with old Father Lamson, with his long beard
and white habiliments. They sympathized even with Abby
Folsom, the well-known "flea of conventions," who ended
each remark with the shrill refrain, "It's the capitalists!"
Those whom a dream had possessed!—mad, no doubt,
but God-intoxicated. The young people whose interests
were social wished to "do good," they wished to be "of
use,"—like the young people in Germany and Russia, in
England, Italy, Hungary and France. For in these late
thirties and early forties, at Harvard, as at Oxford, as
at Warsaw, at Heidelberg, Toulouse and Salamanca, the
young people spoke the same language. And not at Harvard only. At Yale, Princeton, Williams, in New York,
they grieved over the sorrowful disproportion between
their faculties and the importunate work which the state
of the world so patently placed before them.

For, whether their minds were social or poetic, they
all agreed regarding the state of the world. It was a cold,
unfeeling civilization, bred by commercial interests and
isolation, a negative moderation, an excess of prudence,
compromise, provincial good taste. It cast a censorious
eye on human nature, on all the free flights of the picturesque, the goodly growths of fancy. It offered employ-
ment to no one but the decorous and the complacent. It
was timid, imitative, tame; worse, it was mean and cruel.
It taught the mind of the young to aim at low objects,—
and never had the young been so unsubmissive. They did
not care a button for common sense. They were bored by
the ideal of the marble statue as a pattern of social behaviour. They did not wish to "get," they wished to
"have." They did not wish to "do," they wished to "be."
As one of them said, in a burst that amused their elders,

> Greatly to Be
> Is enough for me,
> Is enough for thee.

To reaffirm the senses and the soul. To exist, expand, feel, to possess their own uniqueness.* To have, when it came to "having," a flute, perhaps, a little telescope with which to study the tree-tops from Wachusett, a book of Tennyson's poems to sing and recite on long walks over the Andover hills. For Tennyson had just appeared in Boston, a little later than Keats, who represented the purest cult of beauty. If one parted one's hair in the middle and let the locks flow down over one's shoulders, if one wore a blouse or a frock on fitting occasions, one could forget, at least for a day or two, the brutal, monkish regimen of the college.

Here was a "newness" for the New England fathers. They had known ten younger generations who had accepted without sighs or murmurs the yoke of the farm and the counting-house and gladly sought the pulpit and the Senate. All of them had been stable and well-tethered. These boys and girls of the new age were as distinct from their predecessors as young Italians were from the people of Iceland. They had a mania for the "natural." They detested conventional ways. They chose to wander alone, like so many madmen. Stearns Wheeler, one of the tutors in Greek, built a hut in the woods and went to live there. Two young clerks in Boston counting-houses also spent a winter in the woods, reading and writing in their cabin, in imminent peril of an Arctic death. Jones Very, the poet, another Greek tutor, the son of a Salem skipper, lost his mind for a time and had to be placed in the McLean Asylum. A few fled frantically to Europe,

---

* "I want my place, my own place, my true place in the world, my proper sphere, my thing which Nature intended me to perform when she fashioned me thus awry, and which I have vainly sought all my life-time."
—Hawthorne, *The Intelligence-Office.*

where they could lose for a while their sense of oppression. Others committed suicide. Young women indulged in fantasies, one of them about a *femme fatale* who ran through the woods half-naked, bathed under the moon in icy pools, enticing men in order to repel them. The *mal du siècle* was in full career, though it usually assumed the most innocent forms. A "band" of aesthetic youths and maidens gathered in Cambridge and Watertown. They read Keats and Tennyson together, copied their own poems in manuscript-books, which they passed from hand to hand, and talked about women's rights and Socialism. The girls composed flower-pieces and painted in water-colours. The young men read Saint Augustine and Plato, traversed the cycle of religious faiths and thought they would like to join the Catholic Church; and, between a winter in Rome and a summer in Paris, they echoed the Plymouth tutor, Robert Bartlett, who said that they should make their own country "classic to themselves": the American mind should cease to replenish itself with the mighty wonders of Europe and find its fire within. When they could not meet, they corresponded, enclosing an anemone or a mallow-blossom. How swiftly, like magic, the spring was advancing!—every dry twig bursting forth, covering itself with beauty! Why should not the dry hearts of men burst forth in a similar way? Some new and hidden fount of life was about to revivify existence. The young girls read the young men's characters by holding the young men's letters against their foreheads. It was all rather bashful and indirect, as if they were a little ashamed to confess that they were interested in these mundane matters. They marvelled over their sensibility. One of them read character by the form of the letters, another by the merest "contact with a person." They made all sorts of discoveries, as that sometimes words came into one's mind that had a deep meaning for oneself, although they conveyed nothing to anyone else. Their thoughts seemed to come too fast for expression. They asked one another questions: "Has your impressibility returned?"—with a sort of breathless virginality, as if they were on the brink of some great secret. The strange, dire planet called Human Nature, hitherto so dark and almost baleful, had swum into their ken. It seemed to portend an age of novel-writing.

In Boston, these new feelings had a focus in the various institutions of art and music that were appearing now on every hand. The C-Minor Symphony of Beethoven was played in the Odeon in 1840, a flowering of the Handel and Haydn Society, which had put to rout the old psalms and glee-tunes. The young men walked in from Cambridge, in parties of three or four, deliciously thrilled by the darkness of the road and the chance of meeting a footpad. The Athenæum displayed its collection of casts, the gift of Colonel Perkins, the Brimmer collection of Italian drawings, collections of gems and engravings, Stuart's florid merchants, Allston's dreamy women, Copley's grim ladies, clad in satin, landscapes by Cole and West, an Annibale Carracci, a Murillo, a few half-fabulous Raphaels and Luinis. The galleries became a rendezvous, where art and love blossomed under the skylights. One could almost feel, in the tranquil air, that one had embarked for Italy, with a best-beloved companion. Sometimes in a single day a little group of youthful amateurs enjoyed a double wonder, a glimpse of "Belshazzar's Feast" and an hour of Mozart. Sometimes they met at the rooms of the *cognoscente* who had upon his door a blazing sun, with gilded rays running in all directions, bearing the motto, "Universal Unity,"—for the young man was a Fourierist,—and underneath the black-and-white inscription, to bring one's mind back to Massachusetts, "Please wipe your feet." Sometimes they found aid and comfort at Dr. Channing's "Club of the Jacobins," in Jonathan Phillips's rooms at the Tremont House, where the two old friends liked nothing better than to greet a Harvard man who was not "indifferent." Or they spent an afternoon of early summer on the spreading lawns of one of the Brookline merchants, with music and a game of battledore, a punch-bowl and a bowl of plum-like cherries, a Reynolds and a Ruysdael to look at, and possibly Prescott in the middle distance, or Daniel Webster sitting under an elm-tree. At night, beside their argand lamps, they pored over albums of engravings, Piranesi, Raphael Morghen, discussed the German poets and read the springtide writers, Chaucer, Boccaccio, Dante. They talked about spiritualism and mesmerism, phrenology and animal magnetism, all the dark problems of the human mind over which the sun of hope seemed to be rising.

Across the hinterland, through the rural centres, the new mood spread like the flowers of May. One heard the flute in the fields. Farmers and village tailors stopped to watch the birds building their nests. They went on woodland walks. They recorded the days when the wild-flowers opened. They observed the little tragedies of nature that no one had noticed before, a cat springing on an oriole and marching proudly off with her golden booty projecting in all directions from her mouth. They gathered the first hepaticas, the trailing arbutus that had bled unseen under the boots of their fathers. In hundreds of hamlets the neighbours assembled awe-struck while the night-blooming cereus opened its petals, standing hushed in the presence of the marvel, as the connoisseurs of Florence had stood in the presence of a new Botticelli. It filled them with romantic associations to think of these splendid flowers opening in the night of the Mexican jungle, where there were no eyes to look at them but the agate eyes of lizards and serpents. The cereus was their Boston Athenæum, and all the airs of Mozart sang in its petals; and the young men and women, like those of Boston, graduates of the female seminaries, of Middle-bury College, Dartmouth, Williams,—where Mark Hop-kins sat on the end of his log,—also wrote their poems and their meditations. It was true that the country minis-ters still preached on the Dangers of Beauty. Hiram Powers, the sculptor of the future, attracted crowds with the panorama of hell which he exhibited in the villages, an orgy of sulphuric flames, the livid faces of children and devils with pitchforks,—a sermon such as one might have heard in Rome. The old faith survived in force, and here and there some youthful minister, seduced by the Boston Unitarians, felt like a Hindu who has lost his caste and moaned through his house, "Oh, where shall rest be found?" He found his rest by "aiming at the stars" or writing a parable about the boy who climbed the Natural Bridge. For the old faith, like the new, con-tributed to the mood of exaltation. Life ought to be con-secration, labour, worship! All the young aspired who had read *The Psalm of Life* and knew the meaning of the "strange device" that Longfellow might have invented for Ibsen's Brand.

Poetry spread like fox-fire through the woodlands. Every village had its Gifted Hopkins, author of *To Myrtle Awaking* and *To Myrtle Retiring* or *Contempla-tions in Autumn,* after Pollock. Many a village had its youthful sculptor, who modelled figures of "Innocence" in snow, and a Pantasophian Society that served as a medium of exchange for minds that would otherwise have blushed unseen. Over his native Connecticut hills and meadows scudded the haggard Percival, the poet, with a wild glitter in his eye, startled at the approach of a fellow-creature, wrapping his rusty camlet cloak about him, silent, never smiling, the "old rock-smasher," as he was called by the farmers; for the poor rhymester-vagrant, with his sinister air, had taken to studying minerals and was to do in geology, in the end, what he had failed to do in poetry. Other and younger poets, destined for a happier flowering, or a happier life, at least, dreamed under the stars, perhaps in a hammock, swung between two elm-trees,—a boy who longed to be a Marcus Curtius and leap into a gulf to save his country, a girl, born in India, on a voyage, in the midst of tropical scenes that returned to her with the breeze of her sandal-wood fan. They were to have their say, they were to have their hour at the Tourney of Poets, when New England began to reveal its "portfolio" writings, the Thoughts on Art and Thoughts on the Scholar's Calling, the Musings of a Recluse, the "rapture-feelings" that were to fill *The Dial.* Here and there, a judge or a factory-owner, the great man of the village, touched by the note of a beauty-loving day,—a little confused as regards the fundamentals, though not more confused than the city-people,—built the Greek temple with the green shutters that was to be known as the "house on the hill."

For this, already for a generation, was the day of the Greek revival. Grecian dwellings rose on every Main Street, Parthenons of painted wood, churches and banks vaguely suggesting Athens, with variations in the Egyptian vein. Everett's lectures had borne fruit at Harvard, Byron had contributed a strain. The Greek struggle for independence had caught the imagination of the people, and Dr. Howe's romantic adventures in Greece,—whence he had returned with Byron's helmet,—appealed to the general mind.* The casts in the Athenæum played their part; so did the writings of Walter Savage Landor. A school of American sculptors had appeared and found a home at Florence, where they carried on the tradition of Canova: Horatio Greenough, who, as a boy, had learned to cut his chalk in the Athenæum, soon to be followed by Thomas Crawford, the carver of mantel-pieces in New

* See *Historical Sketch of the Greek Revolution,* by Samuel Gridley Howe, 1828, a vigorous and memorable book.

York, and Powers, who came from Vermont, where the ridges of the hills were of solid marble and marble pigsties rose on lonely farms. The children, brought up on Flaxman's outlines, knew their mythology as they knew the Bible; they were prepared for Emerson's Platonism and the *Wonder-book* and *Tanglewood Tales* of Hawthorne. Everyone talked mythology, as everyone had begun to discuss the history of religion; and the best New England novels, at the turn of the forties, those of William Ware, *Zenobia, Probus, Julian, or Scenes in Judea,* presupposed a feeling for ancient Greece, as they also took for granted a circle of readers who were steeped in the Bible and the Latin authors. Classical stories ran side by side with the realistic stories of New England life that Catherine M. Sedgwick was writing at Stockbridge, *Hope Leslie, Redwood, A New England Tale,* truthful, simple, sometimes too-too simple, after the fashion of Maria Edgeworth, in praise of the duties of home and the virtuous poor. Miss Sedgwick was a highly intelligent woman, a friend and correspondent of Sismondi; she was cultivated, bountiful and good, and her household was the centre of the Berkshires. The naturalness of her style was a kind of triumph, and she prepared the way for the writers who followed by stimulating the interest of her readers in their own landscape and manners; but no one could have supposed that her work would live. Her fellow-philanthropist, Lydia Maria Child, the editor of a magazine for children, the author of a novel of Puritan times, of the first important antislavery book, of *The Progress of Religious Ideas,* of lives of Madame de Staël and Madame Roland, produced a classical novel among the rest. *Philothea* followed *The Frugal Housewife,* a feminine *Poor Richard's Almanac,* a treasury of New England household lore that showed, with an abundance of quaint detail, how one could live on less than a dollar a day. *Philothea* was a dream of Greece, of Pericles, Plato and Phidias, in which a New England maiden in a peplus tries to reform Aspasia. It was a virginal vision, like Powers's "Greek Slave." But William Ware's novels were well-wrought and solid. This Unitarian minister, the son of Dr. Henry Ware of Cambridge, who had visited Greece and the Holy Land, well knew the world of which he wrote, the Roman Empire of the early Christians, and had the imagination to relive it. If his heroes and heroines savoured a little too much of Dr. Channing's circle, Ware was an artist notwithstanding. His novels were to remain for those who enjoy a style that reproduces, with their scenes and subjects, the enchanting rhythms of the ancient authors.

The interest in modern languages, meanwhile, had thriven under the influence of Coleridge. Professor James Marsh of Vermont had published editions of Coleridge's prose writings, but long before this the poet Dana had introduced his critical ideas, and the increasing numbers of American students who flocked to the German universities were spreading them far and wide. The doctrine of "following nature in variety of kinds" had led to an intellectual revolution; for, if nature was inexhaustible in variety, so were the possible forms of the human mind. This key had opened the worlds of letters that lay behind the modern languages. It had destroyed the "rules" that measured everything by the classical standards. The critic was no longer in a position to sit on a lofty throne and send to Gehenna authors who did not conform to these obsolete rules. He had to yield to times and circumstances. He was obliged to submit to other tests than the tests of the "savage and tartarly" Jeffrey and Gifford and the strip-and-whip school of the previous age, with its arrogant insularity. The critic had to "characterize" the author, to understand him and interpret him, asking, From what point does he look at life?

These catholic and supple views of Coleridge, derived from the writings of A. W. Schlegel, whom Ticknor had known in Paris, marked the new era in criticism. All the American writers of the future who had any claim to be considered central shared these views as a matter of course; and the writers of the *North American* group, learned but narrow in their range of feeling, dry, mechanical, timid, subservient to the abstract laws that had governed the eighteenth century, children of Burke and Johnson, gradually lost influence as they spread. In the dialect that Coleridge propagated,—also the fruit of his German studies,—the old school was the school of the "understanding," the new school was the school of "reason." These were the Transcendentalist categories for which the New England mind was so well prepared, for they corresponded with the generations, the older and the younger generations, or, rather, the temperaments of these generations, which were at open war with one another. The "understanding" was the faculty that observed, inferred, argued, drew conclusions. It was the Lockian faculty; it assumed that everything in the mind was drawn from the experience of the senses. Exactly! It was the lawyer's point of view that governed conservative Boston, the cold, external, practical notion of life that guided the merchants in their counting-houses and the Unitarian ministers in their pulpits. The "reason" was the faculty of intuition, warm, perceptive, immediate, that represented the mind of young New England. It assumed, it actually *knew*, that the mind contained powers of its own, not derived from the senses. In the theological sphere, Transcendentalism was a reaction against both Unitarianism and Trinitarianism, neither of which possessed any belief in the self-sufficiency of the human mind outside of revelation. It spoke for an order of truth that transcended, by immediate perception, all external evidence. "God becomes conscious in man," as Fichte said.

"the philosopher man, the man of reason, in whom the absolute being recognizes himself. The reason gazes immediately on the eternal realities." This was the gist of Schleiermacher's teachings, which shocked Andrews Norton,—the phrase, "the soul's sense of things divine." Herder, in the *Spirit of Hebrew Poetry,* translated by Dr. James Marsh, had extended the conception to literature. Writing of the Jewish prophets, he had abolished the distinction between the sacred and the secular, transferring to the credit of human genius all that had been ascribed to the divine. In the bards of Israel, all bards were glorified, a notion which, to the candid mind, far from drawing angels down, raised mortals to the skies. It recognized the creative powers of man. Coleridge had prophesied that a golden age, in letters, art, religion, social ethics, would follow the spread of Transcendentalism; and from various German thinkers, Jacobi and Fichte, the new generation in New England was receiving special impulsions, towards heroism and towards mysticism, that appealed to the youthful mind.

For the influence of Germany grew apace. It had passed quite out of the hands of the earlier students, Everett and Ticknor, Longfellow even, who scarcely shared the Transcendental impulse. It raged through other students and translators, some of whom, like Frederick Henry Hedge, the Unitarian minister in Bangor, the son of Dr. Hedge who had written the *Logic,* had studied in the land of Kant and Herder. To the hesitant *North American,* Bancroft contributed essays on the German writers. He also helped to popularize the sympathetic writings of Victor Cousin, the French eclectic philosopher, for whom all systems were true in what they affirmed, false in what they denied.* Felton, the anti-

---

* In the earlier volumes of his history, Bancroft appeared as a champion of the new philosophy, which he identified with Quakerism, the gospel of the Inner Light. See his discussion of Locke and William Penn.

Transcendentalist, translated Menzel's history. Mrs. Lee of Brookline wrote a life of Richter. Charles T. Brooks, the minister of Newport, began the long series of German translations that was to include, as time went on, works by Goethe, Schiller, Richter, Rückert. A collection of minor poems by Goethe and Schiller, in the version of John Sullivan Dwight, appeared as one of a number of similar works. All the young men and maidens read the German authors. They echoed Schiller's great command, "Keep true to the dream of thy youth." They pondered Novalis's *Heinrich von Ofterdingen:* several Harvard students spent a summer rendering this "apotheosis of poetry" into the language of their own hearts. They "longed for Italy" after Wackenroder. They believed in the gospel of *Lucinde* that poetry and life should be one and the same, and shared the despair of the heroine over the discord which they could by no means harmonize. They read the tales of Tieck, Musæus, Hoffmann. They yearned for the "blue flower." They dreamed of Jean Paul's Titan, Roquairol, who longed for an enterprise for his idle valour, the hero, torn by passions and hopes deferred, who did not possess the power to mould his world. They felt within, like Manfred,—

> an awful chaos—light and darkness—
> And mind and dust—and passions and pure thought
> Mix'd, and contending without end or order.

They felt that men should be true and wise, beautiful, pure and aspiring. They worshipped heroism, they worshipped genius. And they believed,—the thought was in the air,—that the way to greatness was through books, not battles. Thomas Wentworth Higginson, who seldom yielded even to moral excesses, said of Mrs. Lee's *Life of Richter* that it set before him, just at the right time, the attractions of a literary life, carried on in an unworldly spirit. "From that moment," he added, "poverty, or at least extreme economy, had no terrors for me, and I could not bear the thought of devoting my life to Blackstone."

Much of this German influence reached New England through the medium of a greater man than Coleridge, greater, at least, in energy, greater as a moral force, Carlyle. The readers of the British reviews,—and every well-instructed student read them,—had long been aware of the author of *Characteristics,* the essay entitled *The Signs of the Times* and the series of papers on the German writers. Carlyle,—the name began to emerge from a Scottish mist of anonymity,—Carlyle, the "Germanic new-light writer," was, in fact, the perfect middleman for this new movement of ideas. One thought of New England and Scotland as almost interchangeable terms. There was an occult relation between these regions, with their immemorial Calvinist past and their instinct for the heroic.* The greatest foreign influence in New England had been, for a generation, Scott, who had also been stirred by the German poets; and Carlyle was to find in New England his first large circle of readers, even a publisher for *Sartor Resartus* before the book appeared in his own country. He represented the romantic spirit on its ethical and religious side, where the New England mind was most at home; and for twenty years, down to the Civil War, his influence was to remain almost despotic. This was before the brutality of his later years grew upon him with his indigestion, till the splendid dreams of his youth were all but lost in the spoiled peasant's worship of lordship and power.

Over the rising school of New England writers, even

---

* New Englanders have often felt more at home in Scotland than in England. It is significant that little Ellen, in *The Wide, Wide World,* when she inherits her paradise, inherits it in Scotland, not in England, though the paradise is properly qualified as a "Scottish discipline" and she returns to America, with equal propriety, in the end.

over the toughest-grained, Carlyle and Carlylese were to leave their traces. Even the style of Thoreau was to be tinged faintly here and there with the rhythms and locutions of a writer whom lesser minds could not resist. Lowell was deeply affected by them. The eighteenth-century style of his Homer Wilbur, the intransigent parson of *The Biglow Papers,* was wrenched, by Carlyle's influence, even to the extent of whole pages, out of its normal channel.* Margaret Fuller wrote Carlylean essays. Theodore Parker's *Historic Americans* might almost have been written by the man whom Thackeray, Dickens and Ruskin called their master. Sylvester Judd's *Margaret* bristled with the dialect.† The picturesque historical style of Motley was almost as much affected by Carlyle as Dickens's *Tale of Two Cities.* This was the greatest magnetic force of an age that was much concerned with animal magnetism; and writers who seldom wrote greatly rose above themselves when they wrote of Carlyle.‡ He vindicated, they felt, their celestial birthright, showed them that the current ideals were shams, ridiculed the respectable, the "gigmen," the heroes of a mechanical age; he taught the "science of Dynamics," the "primary, unmodified forces and energies of men, the mysterious springs of love and fear and wonder." He gave them faith in their own endeavours. He told them to quit their paper formulas and know that they were alive and that God was alive. "Did the upholsterers

* "On whirls the restless globe through unsounded time, with its cities and its silences," etc.—Lowell, *The Biglow Papers.* See also Mr. Wilbur's sermon, First Series, No. VI.

† See the exclamations of Margaret, in the scene after the trial: "My poor murdered brother! Fades the cloud-girt, star-flowering universe to my eye! I hear the screaming of hope, in wild Merganser flight to the regions of endless cold!"

‡ See Bronson Alcott's description of the "British Taurus" in *R. W. Emerson: His Character and Genius:* "Curious to see him, his chin aloft, the pent thunders rolling, lightnings darting from under the bold brows, words that tell of the wail within, accents not meant for music, yet made lyrical in the cadences of his Caledonian refrain, his mirth mad as Lear's, his humour as wilful as the wind."

make this universe? Were you created by the tailor?"
The old ideal of manhood had been forgotten. To young
valour and the thirst for action, a calculating age of
profit-seekers was deaf, dumb and blind; and yet the
Invisible still existed, and opened itself to the inward
eye, and fought on the side of the seeker of it! That
every man had his own task, his own peculiar inlet into
the sea of Divinity, which, once found, destroyed the
canker of doubt: this was an open-sesame for young New
England. According to the Arab saying, "Every people
has its own prophet." Was Thomas Carlyle this prophet?
So it appeared, for a while. Then it became apparent that
Carlyle was only a part of the atmosphere. The real New
England prophet was another man who dwelt in the little
town of Concord.

CHAPTER X

EMERSON IN CONCORD

RALPH WALDO EMERSON had lived in Concord since 1834. The former pastor of a Boston church and a son of the Reverend William Emerson, he had withdrawn from the ministry. Having a little income, he had bought a house on the Boston turnpike, surrounded with pine and fir-trees. There was a garden by the brook, filled with roses and tulips. In the western window of his study, he placed an Æolian harp. It sang in the spring and summer breezes, mingling with the voices of the birds, fitfully bringing to mind the ballads that he loved, the wild, melodious notes of the old bards and minstrels.

He had been writing essays and giving addresses that grieved and vexed most of his older hearers. Dozens, even hundreds of the younger people, thinking of him, thought of Burns's phrase,

> Wi' sic as he, where'er he be,
> May I be saved or damned.

But, although he had his followers in Boston, he was anathema to the pundits there. Everett sneered at Emerson's "conceited, laborious nonsense." John Quincy Adams and Andrews Norton thought he was an atheist and worse. The Cambridge theologians reviled him: he was a pantheist and a German mystic, and his style was a kind of neo-Platonic moonshine. The Concord prophet smiled at these accusations. He had the temerity to think

that the great Cambridge guns were merely popguns.
There was nothing explosive in his own discourse. He
was a flute-player, one who plucked his reeds in the Concord river. But when he began to play, one saw a beautiful portico, standing in a lovely scene of nature, covered
with blossoms and vine-leaves; and, at the strains of the
flute, one felt impelled to enter the portico and explore
the unknown region that lay beyond. It was an irresistible
invitation. As for the smiling musician, he was a mystery
still. One thought of him as the man in Plutarch's story
who conversed with men one day only in the year and
spent the rest of his days with the nymphs and demons.

Everyone had heard of him in Boston, where he was
giving lectures. His birthplace there was a kitestring's
distance from the house where Franklin was born and the
house where Edgar Allan Poe was born. But, although
he belonged to one of the oldest scholarly families, with
countless names in the college catalogues, most of the
signs had been against him. Tall, excessively thin, so thin
that, as Heine said of Wellington, his full face looked
like a profile, pale, with a tomahawk nose, blond, with
blue eyes and smiling, curved lips, he had none of the
traits, aggressive or brilliant, that marked his brothers in
various ways. At moments, on the platform, he spoke
with a tranquil authority, but his usual demeanour was
almost girlishly passive. He had not acquired the majes-
tic air, as of a wise old eagle or Indian sachem, that
marked his later years. He appeared to be easily discon-
certed, for his self-reliance was a gradual conquest. He
had drifted through many misfortunes, drifted into and
out of tuberculosis, drifted into teaching and out of the
Church, maturing very slowly. He had known dark hours,
poverty, pain, fear, disease. His first wife had died; so
had two of his brothers. The trouble with him was, his
elders thought, that he seemed to like to drift. He had no
sort of record as a student. At Harvard, even three gen-

erations later, when people spoke of Emerson's "education," they put the word in quotation-marks,*—it was not
that he did not know his Greek and Latin, but that he
was never systematic. He had read, both then and later,
for "lustres" mainly. He had drifted first to Florida and
then to Europe, and finally settled at Concord, the home
of his forbears, where he had often visited at the Manse.
The minister there, Dr. Ezra Ripley, who was Emerson's
step-grandfather and very fond of the young man, felt
that he was obliged to warn the people against this leader
of the Egomites, those who "sent themselves" on the
Lord's errands, without any proper calling. As for the
lectures that Emerson was giving in Boston, on great
men, history, the present age, the famous lawyer,
Jeremiah Mason, when he was asked if he could understand them, replied, "No, but my daughters can."

To the outer eye, at least, Emerson's life was an aim-
less jumble. He had ignored all the obvious chances, rejected the palpable prizes, followed none of the rules of
common sense. Was he pursuing some star of his own?
No one else could see it. In later years, looking back,
Emerson's friends, remembering him, thought of those
quiet brown colts, unrecognized even by the trainers, that
out-strip all the others on the race-course. He had had
few doubts himself. He had edged along sideways
towards everything that was good in his life, but he felt
that he was born for victory. He had not chosen his
course. It had sprung from a necessity of his nature, an
inner logic that he scarcely questioned. In college, he had
consulted the *Sortes Virgilianæ,* opening at the line in
Dryden's version,—

Go, let the gods and temples claim thy care.

* See President Eliot's *Harvard Memories.* The true Cambridge mind
could never accept such cavalier remarks of Emerson's as that "books are
for the scholar's idle times."

It seemed to suggest the ministry, and he had followed the suggestion, as his fathers had followed it before him. But Unitarianism could not hold him. The walls of this temple, he thought, were wasted and thin, and at last nothing was left but a film of whitewash. Then, gradually, another faith possessed him. Channing, who had helped him with his studies, had mentioned some recent writer who said there were two souls in the human body, one the vulgar, waking, practical soul, the other a soul that never suspended its action and guided the involuntary motions. This hint of German Transcendentalism, savouring of the Neo-Platonists and the Sacred Books of the East, with which his Aunt Mary was familiar, lingered and grew in his mind. What was this involuntary soul, this "absolute being" of the German thinkers, but the "inner light" of the Quakers, with whom he had talked at New Bedford, that indescribable presence, dwelling in every being and common to all, which the contradiction of all men could not shake and which the consent of all could not confirm? Every religion had known it, the Holy Ghost, the Comforter, the Dæmon, the still, small voice, the light, the seed, Channing's moral sentiment, the One of Plato and Plotinus, the Universal Mind of the Yogis and Sufis. One felt this presence at moments only,—Emerson had felt it a thousand times, in the woods and fields at Concord; but there was a depth in these brief moments that gave them a strange authority. He felt a sudden influx of power; the currents of the universal being seemed to circulate through him. Was not all nature saturated with deity, and was he not himself a part of nature? He seemed to see in a flash the laws of life, justice, truth, love and freedom. Why should he not explore these wonderful realms? Why should he not proclaim this Joyous Science?

It was to confirm these intuitions that he had visited Europe. He wished to escape from theological problems, which seemed to him the soul's mumps and measles, and meet the living writers, Carlyle, Coleridge, Wordsworth, Landor, who, having nourished his own vigour, seemed to say that men were of tunable metal. He spent a few weeks at Rome and Naples and studied for a while at the Collège de France. In the zoological gardens in Paris, he underwent a strange experience that was the greatest lesson of his journey. Observing the rocks, the grasses, the fishes, the insects, the lions, vultures and elephants, he felt a conviction stirring in him that all these forms of life expressed some property in himself. He felt the zoöphyte in him, the centipede, the fox. He was moved by mysterious sympathies, such as he had felt in the woods at home. Was he not one with all these creatures? Nature was indeed a living whole, a spiral ever ascending. He had been struck by Lamarck's ideas. What Plotinus said, that all beings, even the plants, even the soil that bore them aspired to attain conscious knowledge, seemed to be confirmed by modern science. He had conceived, in his way, the theory of evolution, which he was to express in all his writings; and he felt that the new age of science represented a further ascent. Men would rise above their conventional notions, emerge from their belief in mere prescription, their blind and ignorant following of custom, as science more and more increased their insight into the laws of nature. They would learn to trust themselves, the universal soul within themselves, casting off their "old clothes," walking the earth at last as supermen,—for this was Emerson's notion before it was Nietzsche's. It was Carlyle's belief as well, and Emerson had visited Carlyle. He had spent a day and a night at Craigenputtock. He was "the one of all the sons of Adam" who, as Carlyle wrote later, "completely understood what I was saying and answered with a truly human voice."

In no haste to publish his reflections, Emerson, settled

in Concord, "put his ear close by himself," as Montaigne had done before him, and held his breath and listened. He liked the phrase of Simonides, "Give me twice the time, for the more I think the more it enlarges." Was not America full of puny scholars, clamorous place-hunters and village brawlers, whose talents were only for contention? Was it not a country of small adventures, short plans and daring risks? For patience, for great combinations, for long, persistent, close-woven schemes, where could one look in all this fuss and bustle? Was it not true that Americans lived on the surface, a poor, thin, plausible existence? Their vice, their national vice was imitation; they copied foreign forms in their manners and writing, forms that were merely capricious, as if these were permanent forms of nature. The scholars and the thinkers and the writers, as shallow and as frivolous as the rest,—able as they might be in special tasks, —had no advice to give in vital matters, and the public disregarded them. For the public had its own public wisdom: what it asked of the thinker was something else, the private, the universal wisdom of which it had been defrauded by its own dwelling in the street. Was it not time to be dumb for a while, to sit with one's hand on one's mouth, a long, austere, Pythagorean lustrum? Inner independence was what the thinker needed, and the life of the cottage and the woods,—insulation of place,—only had value as an aid to this. But in solitude, Emerson found, his faculties rose fair and full within, like the forest trees and the field flowers. He did not wish to print his thoughts until he had something to say that men would be obliged to attend and hear.

He knew and would know no such thing as haste in composition; and he was determined to keep his freedom, even at the risk of uselessness. A course in which clear faith could not go might well be worse than none. Besides, although he did not know his way, he felt that the current knew it. There was a pilot within him, and, when he did not know how to steer, and dared not hoist a sail, he had only to drift. He lectured here and there, in Boston, in the neighbouring towns, in Concord, in order to supplement his little income. He travelled further and further from home, until he was known as a lecturer throughout the West. He joined in the village life and served on local committees, and he gave the memorial address when Concord celebrated its second centennial. In the village Social Circle he found a suggestion of the well-known society in *Wilhelm Meister,* in which every member was a master of one of the arts of life, mechanics, agriculture, medicine, law. He liked to talk with farmers, millers, tailors, with carpenters and coopers at their work, horse-trainers, geologists, physicists, chemists, whom he visited in their laboratories, astonished by their feats of skill, their powers of observation and endurance. He watched with awe the life of his farmer-neighbours. Were not the men in the cities who were the centres of energy, the driving wheels of trade and the practical arts, the sons and the grandsons of farmers? And were they not spending the energies their fathers had accumulated in poverty, necessity and darkness, in their hardy, silent existence, in their frosty furrows? He looked to life for his dictionary. He wished to master in all these facts a language by which to embody and illustrate his own perceptions; for the thinker was a man for whom all men worked,—geologist, mechanic, merchant, chemist, king, painter, composer,—and a thousand men looked through his eyes. And why should he travel for his illustrations? Was it not the secret of the gods that they came in low disguises? Real kings hid away their crowns and affected a plain exterior, as Odin dwelt in a fisherman's hut and Apollo served Admetus as a slave. In the legends of fairy lore, the fairies largest in power were the least in size. It was the magic of genius to lift the curtain from the common, showing us the divinities that were all about us, disguised as gypsies and pedlars, as farm-hands and clerks.

With all this active social life, Emerson guarded his solitude. He bought a woodlot by Walden Pond, a wild, rocky ledge, with a grove of chestnuts, oaks, maples and hemlocks sweeping down to the shore. He trimmed the old path around the pond that had been worn by the feet of Indian hunters. He cut vistas over the water, where he bathed on summer afternoons; and there he strolled and lingered, sitting on the bank, reading Plato or Goethe, writing in his journal. There he was "adjacent to the One." He had always felt like a king in the woods, walking through tents of gold and bowers of crimson, garlanded with flowers, vines and sunbeams, surrounded with incense and music. An active enchantment seemed to reach his dust there, as if he had the keeping of a secret that was too great to be told, as if a god dwelt near him in a hollow tree. Every light from the sky, every shadow ministered to his pleasure. He seemed to dilate with the wind. He felt the blood of thousands in his body, and his heart seemed to pump through his veins the sap of all this forest vegetation. It was as if he had left behind all his human relations and become one with carbon, lime and granite. The frogs piped, the leaves hissed, the far-off waters tinkled, the grass bent and rustled, and he seemed to die out of the human world and enter another existence, a life of water, air, earth and ether. He passed into the trances of the Yogis and Sufis, the mystical state of Samadhi, in which the mind works without desire, objectless and bodiless, superconscious, and one feels free, omnipotent, immortal. In this state of elevation, elation and joy, shared by all the mystics, one feels that one belongs to another species, and the vision of a superhuman race becomes more real than reality. Nietzsche felt so at Sils-Maria, and so

Emerson felt in the woods at Walden. There was a god in man, an angel in disguise that played the fool! The millions that called themselves men were not yet men. They were half-engaged in the soil, pawing to get free, and they needed all the music that one could bring in order to disengage them. They seemed to be on the verge of all that was great, and so they were, indeed, were they only aware of the faculties that slumbered within them. Emerson's own path lay clear before him. It was to look within himself and report his own perceptions and reveal the powers that lay in the soul of man.

He had brought out a little book called *Nature,* the germ of his later essays; but he seemed to be more eager to further his friends than his own interests and ventures. He arranged with Stearns Wheeler, the Harvard tutor, who had built the hut in the woods and had edited Herodotus with notes, to copy out from *Fraser's Magazine* the pages of *Sartor Resartus,* which no British publisher would issue; and he had the first edition published in Boston. Far from shrewd in financial matters, he gathered money shrewdly for Carlyle.* He also edited Jones Very's sonnets. This excellent Greek scholar, a tall, spindling ghost of a man, was one of the new group of Harvard mystics. As a boy, he had voyaged in his father's ships, outward bound from Salem, and he had taken flight, in after years, to realms that Salem ships had never reached. In the McLean Asylum, where he dwelt for a while, he had written an essay on Shakespeare, which had been "told" him by the Holy Ghost. He believed that he had risen from the dead, that he had ceased to live in the physical world and had passed beyond earthly realities; and indeed his voice seemed to come from the

---

* Emerson told Edward Everett Hale that the first money he received from any of his own books was a cheque, in 1850, for *Representative Men.* He called on his publishers, Phillips and Sampson, and asked them if he was free to use the cheque. Mr. Phillips showed him how to endorse it.— E. E. Hale, *Memories of a Hundred Years.*

tombs, and his face with its web of skin suggested a
skull. He valued his sonnets not because they were his,
but precisely because they were not, because, as he supposed, God spoke through him. Emerson selected and
revised these sonnets, among them *The Stranger's Gift*
and *The Barberry Bush*. There was little magic in them.
Monotones in silver-grey, sober as a dove's breast, they
were true poems, none the less. They had a sort of
solemn incandescence. They were like frosted orbs of
electric light. One caught their dim glow of religious feeling three generations later, partly thanks to Emerson's
revisions; for no one knew better than he the importance
of skill. He had a passion himself for rhetorical studies.
He had aped the styles of various authors, Chateaubriand,
Montaigne, Bacon, Browne, during his years in college,
and had been drawn to the styles that were "rammed with
life," in Ben Jonson's phrase, those that were pregnant
and laconic, unlike the starched or flowing styles that were
popular and current in his youth. His own prose diction
suggested the seventeenth-century authors who had never
stooped to explain their thoughts. In his verse he avoided
the conventional forms, drawn from English poetry, which
all the other American poets accepted, the sonnet, the
romantic tale, the song. He liked to write gnomic lines,
epigrams and rules of life, conveyed in a lively image,
after the Greek or Persian fashion, sometimes contained
in a single stanza,—

> Though love repine, and reason chafe,
> There came a voice without reply,—
> ' 'Tis man's perdition to be safe,
> When for the truth he ought to die.'

Occasionally he wrote some longer poem,—the magical
Give All to Love and *Bacchus*,—in a free-verse style of
his own invention. But most of his poems were composed

in the couplets of Milton's *L'Allegro,* which he filled with a sunny sublimity.

The poet Very was one of the neophytes who felt the fascination of the Concord prophet. Emerson's address, *The American Scholar,* followed by his *Literary Ethics, The Method of Nature, Man the Reformer* and others, appealed to the younger generation more intimately than Carlyle and the German writers. These speeches and Emerson's essays, appearing at the same time,—*History, Self-Reliance, Compensation,*—were filled with their problems and dilemmas, which Emerson seemed to have shared. Unlike the professional orators, he addressed himself to the thinking classes, especially to students and beginners in life; and, instead of preaching the popular virtues, of which they had heard so much, and the value of conforming to the world about them, he spoke to the individual in each of his hearers. Popularity was for "dolls," he said; and the "bloated vanity called public opinion" should have no weight against the private will. He spoke of the "maxims of a low prudence" which they would hear every day, suggesting that the first of all their duties was to get land and money, name and place. They should turn a deaf ear to these base counsels, knowing that the search after the great was the proper occupation of youth and manhood. All young persons thirsted for a real existence, for something they could do with all their heart. And was it not true that each had his own vocation, some bias or talent or special executive skill, by feeling and obeying which alone he could rightly find his place in the world? Every man had his magnetic needle, which always pointed to his proper path, with more or less variation from other men's. He was never happy or strong until he found it, and he could only find it by trusting himself, by listening to the whisper of the voice within him. Was it not the chief disgrace in the world not to be a unit, not to be reckoned one character, not to yield that peculiar fruit which each man was created to bear, but to be reckoned in the gross, in the hundred, or the thousand, of the party or the section to which one belonged? If one paid no attention to the world's opinion, but followed one's own *proprium,* as Swedenborg called it, if one lived wholly from within, planting oneself on one's instincts and standing firm, the world would come round to one at last; for one's inner voice was the voice of the "collective psyche," as later writers called the Over-soul,—the term that Emerson used,—which imparts a common rhythm to all existence.* One would be acting in harmony with the laws of life, to which the phenomenal world is obliged to bow.

Emerson was proclaiming in these speeches and essays the doctrine which, according to William James, has marked all the periods of revival, the early Christian age and Luther's age, Rousseau's, Kant's and Goethe's, namely, that the innermost nature of things is congenial to the powers that men possess. That everything that ever was or will be, as he said in his essay, *Self-Reliance,* is here in the enveloping now, that he who obeys himself is a part of fate,—this challenged the natural faculties of his hearers. It stirred them to take life strivingly in full belief that what man had done man could do, that the world was all opportunities, strings of tension waiting to be struck, especially perhaps by thinkers and writers, to whom Emerson spoke most directly. Why were young Americans so imitative, so timid, tame, compliant? Why did they so easily lose their aims? Why did they look backward and renounce their hopes and yield to the conventions that turned them to stone? Why did they care so much for foreign opinions?

* See C. G. Jung's description of the "artist" as a type: "We see that he has drawn upon the healing and redeeming forces of the collective psyche that underlies consciousness with its isolation and its painful errors; that he has penetrated to that matrix of life in which all men are embedded, which imparts a common rhythm to all human existence, and allows the individual to communicate his feeling and his striving to mankind as a whole."—C. G. Jung, *Modern Man in Search of a Soul.*

Who bides at home, nor looks abroad,
Carries the eagles, and masters the sword.

Could they not see that the near was as great as the far,
that every drop of water was a little ocean, that the
clay with which the Persians and the Greeks moulded
their noble symbols was common lime and silex, the clay
that one held now in one's foolish hands and threw away
to go and seek in vain in sepulchres and mummy-pits in
Europe? It was the deep today that all men scorned, the
poverty that men hated, the heaving of the lungs and the
heat of the blood. All art was yet to be created, all literature yet to be written. All nature was new and undescribed.
America had listened too long to the muses of Europe. It
had met the expectations of mankind with little but the
exertions of mechanical skill. Why should not Americans
enjoy an original relation to the universe? A poetry of insight and not of tradition? A religion by revelation to
themselves? Did the discontented souls who flocked to
Europe expect to find anything essential there which they
had not found at home? Wherever they went, they could
only discover as much beauty or worth as they carried
with them. America's day of dependence, its long apprenticeship to other lands was drawing to a close. The millions who were rushing into life could not always be fed
on the sere remains of foreign harvests. Events were aris-
ing that had to be sung and that would sing themselves.
Who could doubt that poetry would revive and lead in the
continental America of the future?

The effect of these essays and lectures on the younger
people was like that of the sound of a trumpet. It was a
high and solemn music that dissolved the knots in their
minds, roused their wills, enlarged their affections, filled
them with a new illumination. It seemed to justify their
glittering dreams, even as it brought to their support the
authority of their own unconscious natures. They felt
themselves no longer "pinched in a corner," as Emerson

described their former state, but potential benefactors and redeemers, advancing on chaos and the dark. For Emerson pictured America in a way that made them feel how much the scholar counted. This careless, swaggering, shallow nation of theirs, this great avaricious America, boasting of its crops and the size of its cities, indifferent to the kind of men it bred, heedless of its liberty and other people's, gambling away the charters of the human race for a petty, selfish gain, this country needed them to calm and guide it, to see the right done, to check self-interest, to give it repose and depth. The feats it bragged about were of no great moment, telegraphs and steam, gas and ether. Its immense mechanical apparatus turned out little more than Nuremberg toys. But who doubted what the mind could do, seeing the shock given to torpid races by Mahomet, by Buddha, or by Newton or Franklin? All that was requisite, at any time, was a few superior men to give a new and noble turn to things; and Emerson summoned his hearers to the task. The path was a difficult one that lay before them. In stressing this, he won them all the more. They must be ready for bad weather, poverty, weariness, insult and repute of failure. The ease, the pleasure of treading the old paths they must surrender in making and walking their own, with the self-accusation and the faintness of heart, the uncertainty and loss of time and effort that always entangle the feet of the self-directed. Their reward would lie in exercising the highest functions of human nature, raising themselves from private considerations and breathing and living on public and illustrious thoughts. They would be the world's eye and heart, resisting the vulgar prosperity that retrograded to barbarism.

Such was the word of the Concord seer who had thought of calling his essays "Forest Essays;" for he had scarcely ever had a day-dream on which the breath of the pines had not blown.

CHAPTER XI

HAWTHORNE IN SALEM

WHILE BOSTON and little Concord were moving forward, Salem, like most of the other seaports, stricken by the War of 1812, had lapsed into quietude and decay. Beside its dilapidated wharves, where grew the fat weeds, the windlass chanty and the caulker's maul no longer broke the silence. The water-side streets were no longer thronged with sailors, "all right" for shore, with their blue jackets and checked shirts, their well-varnished hats and flowing ribbons, with bundles under their arms from the cannibal isles, or from India or China. One seldom heard the lively "Cheerily, men!" while all hands joined in the chorus. The grass choked the chinks of the cobblestones over which the drays had clattered. An occasional bark or brig discharged its hides. One saw some Nova Scotia schooner, drawn up at Derby's Wharf, unloading a cargo of firewood. A few idle seafaring men leaned against the posts, or sat on the planks, in the lee of some shabby warehouse, or lolled in the long-boats on the strand. But the great days of the port were a tale that was told, over and over, by the ancient skippers, who dozed away their mornings at the custom-house, with their chairs tilted against the wall.

Salem had an immemorial air, the air that gathers about a town which, having known a splendid hour, shrinks and settles back while its grandeurs fade. But Salem was old in spirit, aside from its faded grandeurs. The past that hovered there had much in common with that of the ancient ports of northern Europe, where the Gothic fancies of the Middle Ages have not been dispelled by modern trade. Salem was still Gothic, in a measure. In its moss-grown, many-gabled houses, panelled with worm-eaten wood and hung with half-obliterated portraits, dwelt at least the remnants of a race that retained the mental traits of a far-away past. In its isolation from the currents of world-thought and feeling, it seemed to be only a step removed from the age of the Dance of Death. In the mansions of Chestnut Street and Federal Street, one found the traces of a livelier culture, the books that were read in Boston, together with the Oriental spoils brought home by the Salem navigators. But over the quiet lanes and leafy side-streets, where the graveyards lay, brooded the hush of many generations. Queer old maids with turbaned heads peered from behind the curtains, quaint old simple-minded men hobbled along under the sweeping elms, "pixilated" creatures, many of them, as they said at Marblehead,—bewildered by the fairies,—half dead and buried in their houses, or buried in the morbid family pride that flourishes where life runs low.

There was vigour enough in Salem, there were plenty of stout merchants and politicians. One saw swarms of boys and little girls, in blue, yellow, green and crimson dresses, bursting from church and school-house, like garden-beds of zinnias or water-colours of Maurice Prendergast. It was only in comparison with Lynn and Lowell, those near-by towns whose enterprising burghers, faced with the decline of shipping, had built their factories for internal trade, that Salem seemed somehow grey and sad. The Prescotts, Story, Pickering, Choate and Bowditch, the great circle of earlier days, had long since departed. At a stone's-throw from the Essex Institute, one almost heard the silence. One caught the tinkling of the bell at the door of some little cent-shop, even the quiver of the humming-birds darting about the syringa bushes. The rattling of the butcher's cart was the only event of the day for many a household, unless perhaps one of the family hens cackled and laid an egg. Spiders abounded in these houses, eluding the vigilant spinster's eye. Indeed, there were so many cobwebs that it might have occurred to a doctor,— some old Salem doctor, as odd as the rest,—to gather the webs together and distil an elixir of life from the dusty compound. In the burying-ground in Charter Street, where the Gothic emblems flourished,—death's-heads, crossbones, scythes and hour-glasses, such as one found in Dürer's woodcuts,—the office of grave-digger passed from father to son. Just so passed the household legends, behind the bolted doors, grimmer with each generation. Beside the kitchen fires, old serving-women crouched as they turned the spit and darned the stockings, always ready to tell the children stories. Some of them seemed to remember the days of the witches. Their stories were as dusty as the cobwebs.

For Salem, like the whole New England sea-coast, bristled with old wives' tales and old men's legends. No need to invent stories there: one heard them in the taverns, from the sailors, from charcoal-burners who looked like wizards, from the good-for-nothings on the water-front. One heard of locked closets in haunted houses where skeletons had been found. One heard of walls that resounded with knocks where there had once been doorways, now bricked up. One heard of poisonous houses and blood-stained houses, old maids who lived in total darkness, misers who wallowed naked in heaps of pine-tree shillings. One even heard of Endicott's dreary times, when the stocks and the pillory were never empty. One heard of the magistrates who awoke each morning to the prospect of cropping an ear or slitting a nostril, stripping and whipping a woman at the tail of a cart, or giving her a stout hemp necklace or a brooch in the form of a scarlet letter. One heard of the grey champion who emerged from nowhere to rebuke the tyrannies of the British king, of children who had sprung from the loins of demons, of the wastrels of Merry Mount and the grizzled saints who had stamped out their light and idle mirth, clipping their curls and love-locks. Would they not have stamped out the sunshine and clipped all the flowers in the forest in order to clear a path for their psalms and sermons? In these quiet towns, where nothing happens—except an occasional murder—to agitate the surface of existence, history is ever-present, lying in visible depths under the unstirred waters; and who could have known in Salem what to believe or not? However it might have been on Chestnut Street, the fringes of Salem society were superstitious. If the ring that Queen Elizabeth gave to Essex had appeared in a collection-box on Sunday, it would not have seemed surprising to some of the people. There were plenty of old souls in the lanes and side-streets who never knew where to draw the line. They half believed the tales they told the children. Were there not hollows in the hills close by where the Devil and his subjects held communion? Were there not ill-famed men in the western mountains who were condemned to wander till the crack of doom? All these tales had their truth, and so did the Indian legends, which the farmers repeated. There was an element of fact behind them. Was there a carbuncle in the Crystal Hills that gleamed like the westering sun, as the Indians said? Or was it the sun itself? There were men still living down in Maine who had never settled the question. Carbuncle or not, they had certainly seen it. At least, they had caught its radiance, far up the valley of the Saco.

Salem was a centre for these legends. The mediæval mind had lingered there, in the absence of recent enterprise; and, while the town as a whole was sufficiently modern, there were odd corners and shadowy households where symbols and realities seemed much the same. The young men and women knew the difference, but sometimes it amused them to ignore it. They did not believe in ghosts, but mesmerism had become the fashion: they let their fancies play on the bord:r-line. They sat up at night and told tales of ghosts, larg ly in default of mundane gossip. Occasionally, they even thought they saw one. The Hawthornes, who lived in Herbert Street, under the shadow of a family curse, were often troubled by an apparition that seemed to haunt their yard. The only son of the household, Nathaniel Hawthorne, who lived like a ghost himself, haunting a little chamber under the eaves, appearing only at nightfall, could not count the times he had raised his head, or turned towards the window, with a perception that somebody was passing through the gate. He could only perceive the presence with a sidelong glance, by a certain indirection; if he looked straight at the dim thing, behold, it was not there. As no one ever passed through the Hawthornes' gate, it may have been Elizabeth, his sister, who also appeared only when dusk had fallen. In fact, one could live for two years under the same roof with this spectral sister and see her only once. That was the way with the Hawthornes. The father, a Salem skipper, had died of yellow fever, years ago, in faroff Surinam; and no mortal eye had penetrated, or was to penetrate for forty years, the Castle Dismal on the second floor where the mother of the family had taken refuge on the day she heard the news. Her meals were brought up and left outside the door, as they were at Elizabeth's door, and Louisa's door,—at least, as often as not,—and, one flight further up, at Nathaniel's door. When twilight came, one heard the sound of footsteps echoing on the stairs, and a door that must have been opened was certainly shut. Elizabeth went out for a little walk. Then Nathaniel went for a walk, alone, in another direction.

All day long, every day, or almost every day, for twelve years, he had sat in his flag-bottomed chair in his little room, beside the pine table, with a sheet of foolscap spread out before him. He was writing stories that rose in his mind as mushrooms grow in a meadow, where the roots of some old tree are buried under the earth. He had no love of secrecy or darkness, uncanny as he seemed to the handful of neighbours who knew that he existed; he was merely following the household pattern. His family, prominent once, had been almost forgotten, even in Herbert Street. No one came to see him. He had few friends, aside from the circle of his Bowdoin class-mates, with whom he had almost ceased to correspond. As a boy, he had often said he was going to sea and would never come back again; and he sometimes remarked to an acquaintance that he thought of disappearing, changing his name, escaping from the orbit of the postman, as if he had not sufficiently disappeared merely by staying at home. He had lapsed into this solitary life, half through a kind of inertia, and half,—he had always known he was going to write,—as if to protect a sensibility that was not yet ready to yield its fruits. His nickname had been Oberon at college, a reference to his shy, elusive ways. He had a massive head; his eyes were black and brilliant; he walked with the rolling gait of a sailor; he had a somewhat truculent voice and presence. Standing, he could leap shoulder-high. He liked to look at himself in the upright mirror and make up stories about the image he found reflected there. This image was dark and picturesque, tall and rather imposing. There was something vaguely foreign in its aspect.

He felt like a man under a spell, who had somehow put himself into a dungeon and could not find the key to let himself out. He had seated himself by the wayside of life, and a dense growth of shrubbery had sprung up about him, and the bushes had turned into saplings and the saplings into trees. Through the entangling depths he could find no exit. His style, his personality, his habits had been formed as far back as he could remember. At six he had read the *Pilgrim's Progress*. The first book he had bought was the *Faerie Queene*. To see the world in terms of allegory, or in the light of symbols, was second nature with him. At twelve, in a note-book his grandfather had given him, urging him to write out his thoughts,—a few every day,—he had described a child named Betty Tarbox as "flitting among the rosebushes, in and out of the arbour, like a tiny witch,"—phrases that might have occurred in the tales he was writing now. At sixteen, he had written a poem, precisely in the vein of some of these tales, about a young man dying for love of a ghost. He had certainly not acquired from Godwin's novels, however they intensified the taste, the feeling for romantic mystery that had sprung, for him, out of the Salem air. The novels of Scott had only excited further what seemed to be an inborn predilection for the history and the scenery of New England. All he knew was that these habits of mind, already formed in Salem, had been fostered in Maine, where he had spent a year, during his boyhood, on a lonely farm in a border hamlet. He had heard all sorts of stories from the farmers, tales of the supernatural, tales of ghosts, legends of the old colonial wars. He had heard the story of Father Moody of York, who had worn a black veil over his face. In summer, he had seen the Indians, on the Penobscot River, in their birch canoes, building their wigwams by the mill-dams. Round about stood the pine forests, bordering the northern lakes. He had skated all winter in the moonlight, alone and silent. He loved the black shadows cast by the frozen hills.

He might well have been thought uncanny. He was certainly "deep," as the country people said, deep as a night-scene by Albert Ryder. His mind was bathed in a kind of *chiaroscuro* that seemed to be a natural trait; and yet it was a trait that he cultivated, half by instinct, half by deliberation. He had a painter's delight in tone. He liked to throw a ghostly glimmer over scenes that he chose because they were ghostly. It was a taste like Claude Lor-

rain's for varnish. He liked to study chimneys in the rain,
choked with their own smoke, or a mountain with its base
enveloped in fog while the summit floated aloft. He liked
to see a yellow field of rye veiled in a morning mist. He
liked to think of a woman in a silvery mantle, covering her
face and figure. A man's face, with a patched eye, turning
its profile towards him; an arm and hand extended from
behind a screen; a smile that seemed to be only a part of
a smile, seen through a covering hand; a sunbeam passing through a cobweb, or lying in the corner of a dusty
floor. Dissolving and vanishing objects. Trees reflected
in a river, reversed and strangely arrayed and as if transfigured. The effects wrought by moonlight on a wall.
Moonlight in a familiar sitting-room, investing every object with an odd remoteness,—one's walking-stick or a
child's shoe or doll,—so that, instead of seeing these objects, one seemed to remember them through a lapse of
years. Hawthorne could never have said why it was that,
after spending an evening in some pleasant room, lighted
by a fire of coals, he liked to return and open the door
again, and close it and re-open it, peeping back into the
ruddy dimness that seemed so like a dream, as if he were
enacting a conscious dream. For the rest, he was well
aware why he had withdrawn to this little chamber,
where there was nothing to measure time but the progress
of the shadow across the floor. Somewhere, as it were beneath his feet, a hidden treasure lay, like Goldthwaite's
chest, brimming over with jewels and charms, goblets and
golden salvers. It was the treasure of his own genius, and
it was to find this precious treasure that he had sat at his
desk through summer and winter. The snow-flakes pelted
against the window-panes, the casement rattled in the December gusts, clouds of dust blew through the open window. Seasons and years rolled by. He had his doubts.
Was he tearing down the house of his mind in order to
find the treasure? In the end, when the house was de-

stroyed, for all he could say, there might be nothing in the chest but rubbish.

Sometimes, in summer, on a Sunday morning, he stood by the hour behind the curtain, watching the church across the way. The sunrise stole down the steeple, touching the weather-cock and gilding the dial, till the other steeples awoke and began to ring. His fancy played about this conversation carried on by all the bells of Salem. At twilight, he would still be standing there, watching the people on the steps after the second sermon. Then, as dusk set in, with a feeling of unreality, as if his heart and mind had turned to vapour, he ventured into the street. Sometimes, he was out all day, for the sake of observation. He would spend an hour at the museum, looking at the black old portraits that brought back the days of Cotton Mather. These portraits explained the books that he was reading, histories of Maine and Massachusetts, the *History of Haverhill*, Felt's *Annals of Salem*. Or he walked over to Marblehead and Swampscott, where the old salts gathered in the store, in their red baize shirts and oilcloth trousers, enthroned on mackerel barrels. He felt a natural bond with all these Yankees, fishermen, cattle-drovers, sailors, pilots. Some of them could steer with bandaged eyes into any port from Boston to Mount Desert, guided by the sound of the surf on every beach, island or line of rocks. He liked to sit with them in the bar-rooms, alive with curiosity, over a steaming hot whiskey-punch. He studied the coloured prints on the tavern walls. He noted the gateways in the crooked streets, the whales' jaw-bones set like Gothic arches, the bulging windows in the little shopfronts, filled with needles, fishhooks, pins and thimbles, gingerbread horses, picture-books and sweetmeats. He stood at the toll-house on the Beverly bridge, watching the procession of carts and sulkies that rolled over the timber ribbon under which the sea ebbed and flowed; or he strolled on to Browne's Hill and traced out the grass-

grown hollows, the cellars of Browne's Folly. Occasionally, he spent a day in Boston, haunting the public-houses
in Washington Street. He penetrated behind the sober
shop-front that masked the old Province House. Oftener,
setting out at dawn, he rambled over Endicott's Orchard
Farm, over the witchcraft ground and Gallows Hill, or
perhaps Phillips's Beach, exploring the coast from Marblehead to Gloucester. He would bathe in a cove, overhung
with maples and walnuts, pick up shells on the water's
edge, skip pebbles on the water and trail the seaweed after
him, draw names and faces in the sand. He would sit on
the top of a cliff and watch his shadow, gesturing on the
sand far below.

Occupations worthy of a poet who knew the value of
reverie. These idle, whimsical movements absorbed his
body while his mind pursued its secret operations. One
had to be bored in order to think. Passivity was Hawthorne's element, when it was not curiosity. Usually, in
the summer, dressed in his blue stuff frock, he undertook
a longer expedition, to Maine or the Berkshires, perhaps,
or to Martha's Vineyard, or along the Erie canal, as far
as Detroit, where the old Connecticut poet, John Trumbull, was spending his last years. Nothing escaped him
then; he had resumed his habit of keeping a note-book.
He would stop for commencement at some country college, at Williams, so like his own Bowdoin, and mingle
with the sheepish-looking students, half scholar-like, half
bumpkin, fidgeting in their black broadcloth coats. He
would spend a day at a cattle-fair, among the ruddy,
round-paunched country squires who, with their wonderful breadth of fundament, waddled about, whip in hand,
discoursing on the points of the sheep and oxen. He fell
in with big-bellied blacksmiths, essence-pedlars chatter-
ing about their trade, old men sitting at railway stations,
selling nuts and gingerbread, oblivious of the rush and
roar about them, wood-choppers with their jugs and axes

who had lived so long in the forest that their legs seemed
to be covered with moss, like tree-trunks, pedlars of
tobacco, walking beside their carts,—green carts with
gaily painted panels,—conjurors, tombstone-carvers,
organ-grinders, travelling surgeon-dentists, the queer con-
fraternity of the road. He would exchange a word with
a tavern-keeper, reading his Hebrew Bible, with the aid
of a lexicon and an English version. If it was a rainy day,
the toddy-stick was in active use and the faces gleamed
about the bar-room fire. He would stop at a farm for a
glass of milk or linger in the market-place at Pittsfield,
among the buckboards and the farmers' wagons, while
the stage-coach discharged its passengers. Opening his
note-book in the evening, he jotted down his observations.
Why these trivial details? He had seen a tame crow on
the peak of a barn. A half-length figure had appeared at
a window, with a light shining on the shrouded face. A
little boy had passed him on the road, lugging a basket of
custard-cups. An intrusive reader, looking over his shoulder, might have wondered why it was worth his while to
record such trifling items. To Hawthorne they were anything but trifling. Every one of these notes possessed for
him a golden aureole of associations. Traits of New England life, aspects of New England scenery: a stone wall
covered with vines and shrubs and elm-trees that had
thrust their roots beneath it, a valley like a vast bowl,
filled with yellow sunlight as with wine, the effect of the
morning sun on dewy grass, sunlight on a sloping, swelling
landscape beyond a river in the middle distance, an afternoon light on a clump of trees, evening light falling on a
lonely figure, perhaps a country doctor on his horse, with
his black leather saddle-bags behind him. Dark trees,
decaying stumps, a cave in the side of a hill, with the sunlight playing over it. How like the human heart, this cave,
with the glancing sun and the flowers about its entrance!
One stepped within and found oneself surrounded

with a terrible gloom and monsters of divers kinds. Once, before turning homeward, he pressed on to Franconia Notch. This was the artery over the mountains through which the groaning wagons from the seaports carried the goods of Europe and the Indies to northern New Hampshire and Vermont. There stood the Great Stone Face. One dined on bear's meat in these northern woods, echoing with the notes of horn and bugle. Under some avalanche an ambitious guest, a young story-teller, for example, might have been crushed at Franconia Notch. Who would ever have heard of him then, his history, his plans, his way of life? Or suppose this young writer had frozen to death on the summit of Mount Washington? The mountain would have been a pedestal, worthy of a story-teller's statue. Hawthorne roamed up and down the Connecticut Valley. He fell in with a group of vagabonds, on their way to the camp-meeting at Stamford, a book-pedlar with the usual stock,—a handful of gilded picture-books and ballads, a Life of Franklin, Byron's Minor Poems, Webster's Spelling-book, the New England Primer,—a degenerate Indian with his bow and arrows, willing to turn a penny by shooting at it, an Italian conjuror with a merry damsel attired in all the colours of the rainbow. A travelling puppet-show had joined the troupe. The grave old showman, in his snuff-coloured coat, turned the crank of the organ, and all the little people on the miniature stage broke into lively movement. The blacksmith's hammer fell on the anvil, the tailor plied his needle, the dancers whirled about on their feathery tiptoes, the soldiers wheeled in platoons, the old toper lifted his bottle, the merry-andrew shook his head and capered. Prospero entertaining his island crew! It was a masque of shadows that seemed as real as any other world that Hawthorne lived in. Would it not have been a good idea for a young story-teller to join this group and become an itinerant novelist, like the Oriental story-tellers, reciting his extemporaneous fictions at camp-meetings and cattle-fairs, wherever two or three were gathered together?

Most of Hawthorne's journeys, to be sure, were journeys *autour de sa chambre*. He was never away from Salem long. His note-books, however, filled along the road with incidents and casual observations, were precious memorabilia. They gave his ideas a local habitation. One saw this in the stories he was writing, sketches of actual life, historical tales and allegories. He thought of these as "twice-told" tales because, in several cases, he had heard them first before he had worked them out himself. How did he feel about his work? It seemed to him easier to destroy it than to court an indifferent public. He had thrown into the fire the *Seven Tales of My Native Land,* for which he had failed to find a publisher, and he had burned every available copy of his little published novel, *Fanshawe.* There was a devil in his manuscripts! He saw it laughing at him as the sparks flew upward. As for his recent stories,—the annual magazines had begun to accept them, the *Souvenir* and Peter Parley's *Token,*—they seemed to him to have an effect of tameness. They had, he felt, the pale tint of flowers that have blossomed in too retired a shade. If they were read at all, they should be read in the twilight in which they were written. They had been concocted from thin air; but it was this that gave the tales their magic. Some of them were really insubstantial, dim as ghosts basking in the starlight; in others, the apparently insubstantial was a new and original substance. In Tieck's and Hoffmann's Germany, where the Gothic mind had reawakened, in harmony with this mood of spectral Salem, even in Poe's New York, one found similar tales of the listening dead, of graves and flitting shadows and lovers knocking at each other's tombs. Processions of mourners passed with measured tread, trailing their garments on the ground.

One saw figures melting in mist. Black veils, boys with bandaged eyes, bridegrooms dressed in shrouds. Pools paved with marble and mosaic. Images shimmering in water. One heard the cries of children lost in the woods. Young men slept in the road-side shade, oblivious of the fates that might have been theirs if they had been awake; for fortune, crime and love hovered about them.

They were tales like evening moths or butterflies, light as clouds or flowers of early May, blooming in a wood-land solitude. Out of them rose, when they were gathered together, an opalescent world that was strangely old, yet fresh and unfamiliar; it was like Prospero's island, half terrestrial, half an ethereal fabric. It was a new creation, this world of Hawthorne, with a past in Merry Mount and the Province House, in Howe's Masquerade and Esther Dudley, a present in pedlars and Shakers, in vagabonds and white old maids, in sunny Connecticut valleys and forest hollows, in snowstorms and ambiguous lime-burners, a future in little puckish boys and girls at play in the flickering sunshine. All very simple, it appeared, simple as the brightly coloured leaves that drift over a sedgy stream, only that too often, before one's eyes, the stream sang its way out of the meadow and carried its bright burden into the forest, where all grew dark and baleful.

Such was Hawthorne's world, as it rose in the minds of his readers. No other American writer had revealed such a gift for finding his proper subjects; no other had so consciously pursued his ends. Hawthorne had jotted down four rules of life: to break off customs, to meditate on youth, to shake off spirits ill-disposed, to do nothing against one's genius. He had shaped a poetic personality as valid and distinct as Emerson's; but the "spirits ill-disposed" were not easily conquered. He was drifting towards a cataract, he felt. "I'm a doomed man," he wrote to a friend, "and over I must go." He was

threatened with melancholia, and he knew it. Out of this
fear had sprung, or were to spring, the themes of many
of his other stories, *Wakefield, The Man of Adamant,
Ethan Brand,* tales of the unpardonable sin that consists
in losing one's hold of the human chain. The Man of
Adamant turns to stone, Ethan Brand forfeits, in his
lonely bleakness, the key that unlocks human nature,
Wakefield, who leaves his family and lives for twenty
years in a neighbouring street, makes himself an outcast
from the world without being admitted among the dead.
Hawthorne repeated this note in twenty stories, tales of
minds and hearts like chilly caverns, hung with glittering
icicles of fancy. Tales of hyper-sensitive recluses who find
themselves in white-washed cells. Tales of diabolical in-
tellects,—*Rappaccini's Daughter* and *The Birthmark,*—
which, in the name of some insane abstraction, destroy
the life that they have ceased to feel. Tales like that of
Lady Eleanore who, wrapped in pride as in a mantle,
courts the vengeance of nature. Tales of diseased self-
contemplation, of egoists who swallow serpents and
sleepers who have missed their destiny. What traits, or,
rather, what predicament, what fears did these tales
reveal in the mind that conceived them? Hawthorne had
lived too long in this border-region, these polar solitudes
where the spirit shivered, so that the substance of the
world about him hung before his eyes like a thing of
vapour. He felt as if he had not lived at all, as if he were
an ineffectual shadow, as if, having stepped aside from
the highway of human affairs, he had lost his place forever. One night he had a dream that told him this. He
seemed to be walking in a crowded street. Three beautiful girls approached him and, seeing him, screamed and
fled. An old friend gave him a look of horror. He was
promenading in his shroud.

Luckily, Hawthorne had another self, a sensible
double-ganger. This other Hawthorne, this prosaic Haw-

thorne, the son of a Salem skipper, was interested in his
own self-preservation; and, while he would never have
taken too much trouble to keep himself afloat, he was
glad to listen to his friends in matters of worldly wisdom.
Eleven years were enough in a haunted chamber, filled
with thoughts of suicide and madness. In 1836, this other
Hawthorne entered the publishing house of "Peter Parley," wrote his *Universal History* for him and edited his
American Magazine. Then, having broken the spell and
gone to Boston, this matter-of-fact, substantial, physical
Hawthorne accepted a position at the custom-house.

To the end of Hawthorne's life, these separate personalities dominated his destiny in turn. When one of
them came to the front, as fishes, in pursuit of oxygen,
rise to the surface of the water, the other vanished or
concealed himself behind the nearest curtain. The story-
teller scarcely knew the practical man of business who
worked on the steaming docks, amid the coal-dust. Was
this resolute, forcible being really himself, or was it
someone who assumed his aspect and performed these
duties in his name? Which was the true Hawthorne,
which the phantom? The story-teller lived in a trance as
long as the automaton carried on. His writing was accomplished in the happy seasons when the automaton was
packed away, in the box where he belonged, when custom-
houses, ships and offices lay like dreams behind him.

Both these personalities, meanwhile, had focussed
themselves on a single object. Hawthorne had fallen in
love. One saw him at the Boston Athenæum, where the
ghost of Dr. Harris shadowed him, or moving silently
through the Salem streets, enveloped in the cloak with
its high-cut collar that almost concealed his features.
Vain disguise! Life had reconnoitred him and love had
tracked him out. He had become involved with the Peabody family, whose house in Salem overlooked the grave-
yard where, among so many bones, the dust of ancestral

Peabodys and Hawthornes mingled under the trees. Dr. Peabody's daughters believed they were descended from Boadicea. Whether it was true or not, the sisters possessed a store of nervous energy; and this, like youthful and impassioned nuns, they were devoting to the "higher life." Elizabeth, the oldest, the genius of the American kindergarten, was already known in Boston, where she was teaching, as the inexhaustible friend of all good causes. She was Dr. Channing's literary assistant, she was the confidante of Washington Allston, she was Bronson Alcott's aide at the Temple School. Of all these adventures of the mind she was to leave descriptions in her books.* The second sister Mary was engaged to Horace Mann. Sophia, the youngest, was Hawthorne's inamorata. A neurasthenic invalid, waiting on her couch for the magician who would command her to arise and walk, Sophia was witty and charming, as well as a clever linguist. When her sister married Horace Mann, she said that no doubt the first Peabody grandchild would open its mouth at once and utter a school-report. Her own avocations were artistic. Sometimes, while plying her needle of an afternoon, she would read a little Fénelon in French, a little Isaiah in Hebrew, a dozen pages of St. Luke in Greek and two or three scenes of Shakespeare. When she was not otherwise occupied, she spent her days modelling and painting. She had a pretty studio at the top of the house, and there she had made a medallion of one of Emerson's brothers,—for the Emersons knew the Peabodys and sometimes came to visit them,—and a bust of Laura Bridgman. Her work had been warmly praised by Allston and Channing. Meanwhile, she had passed three years in Cuba, in the hope of reëstablishing her health.

It was Elizabeth Peabody, on one of her visits from

* *Reminiscences of William Ellery Channing, Last Evening with Allston, Record of Mr. Alcott's School.*

Boston, who had disinterred Hawthorne from his living grave. With her unfailing scent for remarkable minds, she had followed his work in the magazines. A new and unique style united these often anonymous tales and sketches. Miss Peabody, who had caught this thread, wondered who the author was; and, behold, the clue led straight to a door in Salem. She drew Hawthorne out, induced him to see Sophia, inveigled him into the Transcendental circle that met on Saturday evenings at Miss Susan Burley's. Miss Burley was an amateur of antique gems and the cleverest hostess in Salem. She had even drawn Jones Very, that other Salem solitary, out of his shell. Hawthorne, caught at last in a drawing-room, stood motionless, not knowing what to do, his face pale and stricken. He picked up a knick-knack that lay on the table, to soothe his agitation. His hand trembled so that he almost dropped it.

No matter, he was "out," and out to stay, in a sort of low relief, like Sophia's medallions,—for no one was ever to see around him; and the Peabodys were determined to keep him out. The ever-active Elizabeth, who had introduced Jones Very to Emerson, called upon her friend George Bancroft, the historian-collector of the port of Boston, and obtained for him the post at the customhouse. Meanwhile, Sophia drew pictures for one of his stories, in the style of Flaxman's outlines. These delicate line-drawings of the English sculptor, so cool, so pure, so rhythmical, so graceful, were to leave long traces in American art. The Peabodys and their friends spent many an evening poring over the drawings for Dante and Homer, which they had borrowed from Professor Felton. Sophia had a passion for them, and Hawthorne's stories seemed to lend themselves to the treatment that she knew so well. It was a happy augury that Flaxman's genius, with which Hawthorne had so much in common, presided over the fate of this pair of lovers.

CHAPTER XII

ALCOTT, MARGARET FULLER, BROOK FARM

JUST AT this moment, the Peabodys moved to Boston. They rented a house at 19 West Street, which soon became a rendezvous for the younger intellectuals, those who were conscious of the "new day." In one of the rooms on the ground-floor, Dr. Peabody opened a shop for the sale of homeopathic remedies. In the front room overlooking the street, Elizabeth and her mother sold foreign books. Mrs. Peabody was herself at work translating Goethe's *Hermann und Dorothea.* "God takes care of us" was her constant motto. She saw no reason not to be high-minded "even in selling a book."

Along with *Blackwood's* and the *Edinburgh,* which everyone read religiously at the Athenæum, they sold the German and French reviews and the writings of the continental authors whose thoughts were in the air. Miss Peabody, with her multifarious interests, chiefly in the "gardening" of children, who, she felt, should be "artists from the beginning," was publishing juvenile books on her own account, among them the three little volumes of *Grandfather's Chair,* which Hawthorne contrived to write in the intervals of measuring coal at the custom-house. There Margaret Fuller was giving her Conversations; and there, on occasion, Jones Very read his sonnets aloud to a chosen few. Eager school-girls flocked into the shop and bought more pencils than they could use for a chance to see Miss Peabody or Miss Fuller. And there, on almost any afternoon, one saw some of the new illuminati, Emerson, Alcott, Frederick Hedge, who had studied in Germany with Bancroft and had settled as a minister at Bangor, John Sullivan Dwight or George Ripley. Hawthorne came often to see Sophia.

This shop, so called, though most of its frequenters were bent on "reforming out" the principle of commercial enterprise, this intellectual caravansary was the liveliest spot in Boston. As a matter of course, the literary Tories, George Ticknor's circle, for example, called it the Hospital for Incapables. It was, in fact, a nest or kindergarten where newly-born thoughts were received and fostered. Thence they emerged as books or social movements. Miss Peabody's second Bible was Gerando's essay, *On Moral Perfection and Self-Culture,* and no one was admitted to the circle who did not accept its teachings,—that life was a process of education, of which perfection was the proper aim. Miss Peabody exemplified this faith. Her sister Mary had founded a kindergarten in the very year when the German Froebel opened the first school that bore this name; and she herself wrote text-books and lectured on the history of religions. In her paper, *The Dorian Measure,* she urged the importance of dancing, not the sort that one learned from Signor Papanti but the mystical Grecian ballet, the folk-dance, the rhythmical allegory. This dancing would give the Bostonians a feeling for the customs of other nations. The Dorians had a message for enlightened Boston: severe without austerity, simple and dignified in their private relations, they yet dressed the festival of life, worshipping Apollo in the sunshine, with garlands of flowers and leaves. Perfection in all its forms was Miss Peabody's vision, and at present she busied herself in supplying wants that seemed to indicate a desire for it. The want might be Kraitsir's Lectures on Language, or Bern's Historical Chart, some of the artist's materials that she kept in stock, at Washington Allston's suggestion, a book on the new philosophy, or something more conclusive,—a plan for a desirable social system; for this was a magical shop, the kind one read about in the fairy-tales, where, in the guise of a book or a lecture-ticket, they sold Aladdin's lamps and rings of Gyges. James Freeman Clarke, another frequenter, a Unitarian minister in Louisville, who had come back to Boston for a summer visit, was astonished at the "state of fermentation" he found among his friends. "New ideas," he wrote, "are flying high and low." The centre of the whirl was the shop in West Street.

Miss Peabody was Channing's Eckermann. As a child, she had heard the doctor preach, and she had never forgotten her mother's words, "It takes genius to reach children," words she had pondered for years until she learned their meaning from Froebel's writings. She had applied for a post as Channing's secretary; and the doctor, in order to test her, read to her aloud from Plato, raising his devouring eyes to make quite sure that she understood it. All had gone well after this. She dined at Channing's table every evening; she copied his sermons for the press. He had been greatly struck by Emerson's lectures, which seemed to set the young men on fire; and almost every morning he appeared at the book-shop, sometimes bringing Washington Allston with him. He wished to keep in touch with the new ideas, although he had his doubts about socialism, the Fourieristic notions that flourished there; the trend of life, he thought, was towards individuality of expression, and individual property expressed this law,—it was the "lowest expression," but still an expression. The doctor was solicitous about the future, and the West Street shop represented the future. As for Miss Peabody's future, one could see it already. One pictured her, forty years hence, drowsing in her chair on the lecture-platform or plodding through the slush of a Boston winter, her bonnet askew, her white hair falling loose, bearing still, amid the snow and ice, the banner of education.* If, perchance, you lifted her out of a snowdrift, into which she had stumbled absent-mindedly, she would exclaim, between her gasps, "I am so glad to see you! Can you tell me which is the best Chinese grammar?" Or she would give you the news about Sarah Winnemucka. "Now Sarah Winnemucka"—this was the maligned Indian princess who was collecting money to educate her tribe. Or she would ask if you had read your Stallo. She took down every lecture she heard, although she seldom wrote what people said: most of her reports were "impressions." † She was known to have lived in Europe for two years on $200, passed on with the utmost dignity from one enlightened household to another, invariably losing the railway ticket that found itself, by a miracle, in her hands. She had mislaid the ticket in somebody's *Reminiscences,* but what conductor or purser could disbelieve her?

This was a generation later, but already Miss Peabody was the salt of Boston. With Margaret Fuller as a fellow-worker, she had been assisting Bronson Alcott, another leader of the West Street circle, the Socrates of the Temple School. Alcott, for calling in question the gods of the city, for corrupting the minds of the young with the "new ideas," had had to drink his hemlock. A tall, mild, milky, passionless man, with a singular gift for understanding children, he had had five years for his ministrations. Then

> straight a barbarous noise environed him
> Of owls and cuckoos.

* "Miss Peabody is the most dissolute woman in Boston," William James remarked in his sprightly youth. Henry James denied that he had the "grandmother of Boston" in mind in drawing Miss Birdseye in *The Bostonians,* but the likeness was unmistakable.

† "I saw it," Miss Peabody said, when she walked into a tree and bruised her nose. "I saw it, but I did not realize it."

The red-faced sheriff knocked at the Temple door. In vain, Alcott's daughter, little Louisa, striding across the room, assailed the Vandal: "Go away, bad man, you are making my father unhappy!" Down from the walls came the pictures, the maps and the blackboard, Guido's "Flight into Egypt" and the portrait of Channing; the busts came down from their pedestals, Plato, Socrates, Milton; the comely desks, the charming cast of Silence, the dozen or more of Johnson's dictionaries, all these appropriate emblems, so carefully chosen to stir and elevate the dawning mind,—down they came and vanished. And Alcott, leading a child in either hand, followed them down, with mournful steps and slow.

He might have been crushed, if anything could crush him. But the school, that Academe for nascent Boston, was only one of Alcott's paradises. Sheriffs with flaming swords might drive him forth, but who can expel a man from the Garden of Eden that exists behind his own brow? Not for nothing had he schooled himself as "one of the last of the philosophers." One of the last? He meant to be one of the first. He had, indeed, a philosophic mission, to restore the fabled innocence of man and root it in the soil of Massachusetts. He had never doubted the doctrine of pre-existence, the lapse of the soul from its primordial state, with its native creative powers, never since the days when he had first read Plato and found that Plato's cloud-land was, for him, far more solid than the United States. Coleridge had shown him clearly that the elements of the human consciousness were not to be sought in impressions of external nature, but rather in the self-existent spirit, spontaneous and outside of time and space. "Before time was, I am;" and birth was but a sleep and a forgetting. Then wherefore not awaken and remember? Why not recover what the race had lost, fatuously exiled in the realms of sense? Such were the views upon which his school was founded;

such was the faith that he had cultivated, watching over the growth of his little daughters. They had a natural pleasure in beautiful things, a happy trust and affection, free and direct as they were. In them the avenues to the Over-soul were all wide open. How dim were the perceptions of most of their elders! How cold their sympathies were, spoiled and spotted by their mundane interests! How had they fallen from their high estate! They could not become as little children. And Alcott meant to see that the little children did not become like them.

Such was Alcott's theory of education. Every great man of Greece and Rome had had a philosopher as a teacher, and his own purpose in teaching had always been, not to inculcate knowledge,—at least by the method of the pump and bucket,—but to develop genius. Was not every well-born child a genius? By the Socratic method, as it seemed to Alcott, by posing the proper questions, one could elicit from a group of children all the thoughts of Plato. He tried to reach his pupils from within. No forcing, no cramming, no rod or ferule. He had made the schoolroom gracious and attractive and devised recreations and amusements, plays, physical exercises, even a system of self-government. He encouraged the keeping of journals. Children must know themselves to become themselves and escape from the tyranny of custom. With his own little Anna, aged four, he had held intellectual conversations that seemed to him not unworthy of Plato's disciples; and Louisa had been writing her daily journal before she was able to join her letters. He had begun himself when he was twelve, making his own ink out of maple and oak-bark, steeped in alum and indigo; but he had had to fight for his education. A poor farmer's son, like Horace Mann, he had learned to write in a copy-book, forming his letters after the master's phrase, "Avoid alluring company." He had spent his youth as a pedlar, travelling through Virginia with his

horse and wagon, with his tin trunk full of Yankee notions, pins, scissors, combs, thimbles, puzzles, with a self-
respect presumably unknown to the silken sons of pride
and dissipation,—always on the lookout for a school
where he could exercise his theories. He had learned his
best lessons along the road, from some of the Southern
planters, who had taken him into their houses and taught
him manners. He had fallen in with the Philadelphia
Quakers, whose "inner light" he soon identified with the
Brahma of the Oriental Scriptures. Among them, for a
while, at Germantown, where his daughter Louisa was
born, he had conducted a school, before he opened his
great campaign in Boston.

What matter if the Temple School had failed? He
had other careers ahead, this Indra of the seven incarna-
tions. He knew that future times would vindicate him.
There were plenty of closet-philosophers: Alcott was a
philosopher in action for whom the object of life was to
be oneself. Be what you were meant to be! If you were
a crooked stick, go through the world as an oddity, to
your own merriment, at least, if not to that of your contemporaries. Character was a fact, and that was much in
a world of pretence and concession. If Boston was not
ready for such a teacher, so much the worse for Boston.
Was he going to repine and hedge and distrust the powers that always upheld the virtuous and the wise? When
a confidence-man asked him for five dollars, and Alcott
gave him ten, the groundlings laughed at his simplicity;
but the confidence-man, stricken with remorse, sent the
money back. One could trust the law of compensation.

The school was a misadventure, though more for
the children than for Alcott. So was the fate of his book, the
enlightened *Conversations on the Gospels,* most of the
copies of which had been sold to be used for trunk-linings.
This book had largely caused the trouble. It was a record
of Alcott's dialogues with the little sons and daughters

of patrician Boston, in which, in connection with the sacred story, he had tried to replace with clear ideas the fabric of traditional association. The parents were alarmed, but the children, most of them eight or nine years old, were entranced with these religious dialectics. Little Josiah Quincy spoke like an infant prophet. Rapt attention had reigned in the beautiful class-room, as the master sat in his pulpit, his pupils gathered in an arc before him, in the soft light that streamed through the Gothic windows. There were special classes for Latin, for sums and spelling, and the children of three and four had desks in the corners. They drew on their slates and learned the art of silence. Sometimes the poet Dana appeared and gave a quiet reading from Coleridge or Wordsworth, for an audience of children pleased him best. If the day was cold, the master read aloud Thomson's *Winter* and analyzed the poem on the blackboard. A dialogue might ensue on winter sports, on the nature of coasting and skating, or the master divided the words he had just been reading into their various classes, as the names of objects, qualities and relations. Or perhaps he would read one of Northcote's *Fables,* or a chapter of the *Pilgrim's Progress,* or a passage from *The Castle of Indolence.* What did it represent? There were passages that excited the moral feelings, fear, pity, courage; others called into play the intellectual faculties, reason, perception, judgment. The master followed his readings with suitable questions. Language had to be picturesque and lively to clothe these thoughts in words! What was the purpose of going to school? To learn good behaviour? What was behaviour, what was the purpose of manners? What was the purpose of the imagination? What was the meaning of a definition? One had to use one's wits at the Temple School.

Boston, hitherto so cold and formal, had begun to receive the gospel of Conversation. This was the message of the Temple School. It was the message also of Margaret Fuller, who, with Elizabeth Peabody, assisted Alcott. Miss Peabody kept the log-book of the school, reporting its operations word by word, while she was reading Greek with Dr. Channing. Margaret Fuller also assisted Channing: she spent one evening of every week reading aloud to him in German. But the doctor was too restricted to suit the impetuous Margaret. He was always looking for the moral in works of creative genius. She preferred the abandon of the poet. She liked to duck, dive and fly for truth. Besides, as an impassioned feminist, she wished to minister to the minds of women. What woman ever had a chance, among the few men who enjoyed this fortune? What were the legitimate hopes of women? Why should they all be constrained to follow employments for which only some of them were fitted? While men were called upon, from their earliest youth, to reproduce everything they learned, women never reproduced their learning except for the sake of display. It was partly the fault of society, and partly their own, because they were so unconscious, victims of domestic preoccupations. Better to have one's curtains and carpets soiled than to soil one's mind with such paltry thoughts and feelings! Better, the fragrant herb of wit, and a little cream of affability, than all the pretty tea-cups in the world! As for American men, they were tame enough, with their everlasting business, their little games of local politics, with only two or three tunes in their music-boxes. One wound them up, and they tinkled about "the office," they tinkled again about the next election, and that was the end of their music. They never added a new tune after five-and-twenty. No spirit, no variety of depth and tone! Why should American men and especially women be satisfied with the common routines of living? Why should they not be capable of such relations as those of Landor's Pericles and Aspasia? They should look for their hidden gifts. They should be satisfied with nothing less than Goethe's "extraordinary generous seeking." Genius, Margaret thought, would be as common as light if men and women trusted their higher selves. She had never questioned her own vocation, and she was just on the verge of thirty when, towards the end of 1839, she opened her Conversations in the West Street house. It was on a Saturday, at noon, her regular weekly hour. She appeared, with a regal air, with various books of reference on her arm and a huge bouquet of chrysanthemums. The lorgnette was much in evidence.

An electrical apparition, this "queen of Cambridge." She had seen men "bristle," as they frankly said,—the foolish little creatures, youths of untouched heart, shallow, as yet, in all things,—when she crossed the threshold of an evening party. She frightened them with her magnetic powers, the depth of her eye, the powerful onward motion that announced the presence of the mysterious fluid. So, at least, she felt. But most of these men had nothing to fear, the dry, cold, sordid money-getters. Margaret knew at a glance the minds that belonged to her, and she was "sagacious of her quarry." So she wrote in her journal. As the daughter of Timothy Fuller, Member of Congress, who had surrendered his income and profession in order to write a history of his country, she had lived in a great house in Cambridge, surrounded by the cleverest Harvard students, who had never seen a girl of her complexion. Her father had taught her Latin as soon as she could speak, and her infant prayers had begun, "O God, if thou art Jupiter!" Occasionally, she had prayed to Bacchus for a bunch of grapes. She thought of herself as a princess, who had been left by mistake on a Cambridge door-step. At boarding-school, at Groton, she had first revealed her insatiable will-to-power. Unable to rule by affection, she had ruled as the demon of discord, swooning at tactical moments, setting the girls

by one another's ears, striking her head against an iron
hearth, falling into fits of melancholy, until, by one
method or another, she had reduced the school to servi-
tude. As for the girls, they raved about her. She was the
"bandit's bride" of the trashy novels they read behind
their desks. No one had such hair as hers, dressed with
a tropical flower, such wild, strange, lively ways, such
flashes of the eye. There was always something odd in
the way she wore a sash or a necklace. Her simplest frock
had an air of fancy dress. The girls delighted in paying
her homage. They placed wild flowers beside her plate;
and they felt that she was born to be misunderstood by
everyone but her lover. As for the unhappy teachers, not
one of them, as Margaret said, had ever asked herself
an intelligent question about the nature of her earthly
mission. Margaret's own mission was to "grow." She
felt that her impulses were disproportioned to the persons and occasions she encountered and rightly carried
her beyond the reserves that marked the appointed lot
of women. She looked with envy at Flaxman's picture of
Hesiod sitting at the feet of the Muse. Where could she
find an intellectual guide? At fifteen, she rose at five,
walked for an hour and practised on the piano; then she
read philosophy and French. From half past nine till
noon, she studied Greek, practised again, lounged for half
an hour, read for two hours in Italian, then went for
a walk or a drive; in the evening, she played or sang and
wrote in her journal. As between Madame de Staël and
the useful Miss Edgeworth, patterns that one might follow, she had no difficulty in choosing. Over her head, as
over Madame de Staël's, had risen the sun of Goethe.
She, too, would have liked to provoke an emperor's
wrath.

    She had passed through dreams of romance, hours of
yearning and passion. She threw herself into Goethe's
life. Should he have given up his Lili? She lived through

the rapturous days of the heroines of mythology and drama, Iphigenia, Antigone, the Scandinavian world-mother Frigga, George Sand's Consuelo and Corinne, invoking them in her diary: "Antigone, Iphigenia, you were worthy to live! . . . Iphigenia, I was not born in vain, if only for the tears I have shed with thee." She saw herself as the goddess Isis, dazzling the eyes of her votaries. She might have been the Countess Emily Plater, the Polish Joan of Arc. Among her chosen men were Alfieri, the Countess of Albany's lover, and George Sand's Count de Rudolstadt, aristocratic democrats who shared the culture of the fortunate classes but longed for the welfare of all. Carlyle's was the grand method of education!—idolatrous hero-worship of genius and power. She did not expect to be happy. How could a woman of genius conform to the world about her, or find her mysterious impulses understood? She remembered how as a child she had stood at a window from which she could see an eagle chained, on one of the neighbouring balconies. She had seen people poking it with sticks, and her heart had swollen with indignation. The eagle's eye was dull, and its plumage was soiled and shabby, yet with what a mien the monarch-bird endured these paltry insults. In its form and attitude, all the king was visible, even though dethroned and degraded. Such was the fate of genius in a world of pygmies. They censured her in Boston because she filled the girls, who flocked about her, with her own romantic nonsense. She made them wish to marry Alfieris, as if State Street lawyers were not good enough,—not to mention cotton-merchants and codfish-packers with an eye on the Legislature. They laughed at her superstitions, her faith in demonology, omens, foresight. They smiled when she said that "Margaret" meant "Pearl," the gem that is cradled in slime, in disease and decay, like all that is noblest in the human soul. Only the experienced diver knows the pearl.

Who could comprehend her aspirations, the demands she made upon life, her struggles and conflicts? She would lie all day on the shore at Nahant, with the waves washing about her, looking up at the turrets and jagged cliffs bathed in prismatic light. Prometheus, or Promethea, among the rocks, or perhaps Andromeda chained, waiting for her unknown Perseus. Beethoven, at least, would have understood her. She wrote him a midnight letter. With the Boston girls, her pupils,—for she was obliged to teach, to pay for the education of her brothers and sisters, the father's death having left them in distress,— she read her beloved Goethe, Schiller and Lessing, together with Petrarch and Tasso in Italian. With her chosen friends, meanwhile, James Freeman Clarke, with whom she had first studied German, Frederick Henry Hedge, Samuel Gray Ward, and Emerson, her last and greatest conquest, to whom Harriet Martineau had introduced her as the most brilliant talker she had known, she gathered the spoils of culture,—a little meagre still in frosty Boston, but amplified by her enthusiasm,—portfolios of drawings and engravings, designs from Raphael, architectural sketches, the Athenæum casts, the Brimmer collection. In each of her friends she seemed to divine the law of his own interior growth. She gave them to themselves, or so they felt, drew out their unsuspected faculties. Many of these friends, in later years, traced to some conversation with her the moment when they had seen their way before them, when they had formed some resolution from which their careers had sprung. It was true that she had an influence in hundreds of lives. Long after her death, the painter Hunt saw on a table in Florence a copy of Mrs. Jameson's *Italian Painters*. Margaret had written on the margin, beside a passage on Correggio, "And yet all might be such." Hunt said, "These words struck out a new strength in me. They made me set my face like a flint."

She aspired to write, dry as writing seemed beside the excitement of conversation. The six historical tragedies she had planned had all come to nothing, and she could not afford the time to finish the life of Goethe for which she had gathered a mass of notes and sketches. Meanwhile, she translated the *Conversations with Eckermann,* Bettina von Arnim's *Günderode* and hundreds of pages of Uhland, Novalis and Körner, with poems of her own as commentaries. But conversation was her medium. She liked to see the effects of her mental efforts, and the Saturday classes in West Street were responsive. Half the feminine *élite* were there, Elizabeth Hoar from Concord, Lydia Maria Child, the three Peabody sisters, Mrs. Emerson, Mrs. George Bancroft, Mrs. Theodore Parker, Maria White, who was engaged to James Russell Lowell. The subjects were Greek mythology, "What is Life?", the history of art, the meaning of the various dances. Margaret had the true Boston passion for pigeon-holes and categories, for putting everything in its proper place. Wordsworth was the "poet of reflection," Jupiter stood for "the will," Bacchus for the "terrene inspiration." It was all sharp and clear, like so many definitions from a legal treatise, ready to be gathered in a note-book. Margaret's ideas had good square corners, like building-blocks that fitted at the edges. Set side by side, in just the right arrangement, they formed a solid architectural structure, a true temple of culture, as unmistakable as a Boston bank. One of the ladies kept the class in order with her unswerving eye for Christian morals, which might have been lost in aesthetic divagations. Sometimes the Gothic genius seized the reins of Margaret's fancy, and she would ride like a Valkyrie over the clouds of German metaphysics. Then, before the eyes of her worshipping hearers, the cold New England landscape melted into a dreamland of romance. One dwelt for a moment in

Valhalla, among the Scandinavian gods and heroes, as erstwhile in Athens of the violet crown.

In West Street, one could buy over the counter, in exchange for a little good will,—or a thousand dollars, in case one happened to have it,—a share in the Utopian community that was rapidly taking shape at Brook Farm. This was George Ripley's contribution to the educational movement of Massachusetts. For fourteen years, with no great zeal for the Unitarian cause, Ripley had been preaching in a Boston pulpit; and now, having resigned, he was already living at the farm, at West Roxbury, nine miles out of town. He was a cheerful, hearty, faithful soul, ready for any task, for whom the opinion of the world was but a "puff of empty air." He had always expected to be poor and rather preferred obscurity to fame. "Give me philosophy!" was all he asked. He had heard the call of "association," of the communists and Christian socialists, the Owenites and the Fourierists, followed by the Icarians and Cabet, who were establishing their communities in every corner of the young republic. Almost every month the port of New York welcomed some new boat-load of Europeans who had come to found a "Harmony" or a "North American Phalanx." Ripley, while planning the farm, was editing a work in fourteen volumes, *Specimens of Standard Foreign Literature,* translations of Cousin, Jouffroy, Goethe, Menzel, Benjamin Constant and others. He had recruited many of his translators from the West Street circle. In the winter of 1840–41, the whole group discussed Ripley's project.

It came into existence in the spring, and building was added to building, the Hive, in the shade of an ancient sycamore, the Eÿrie, the Nest, the Cottage, the Pilgrim House, and member was added to member, until, at the end of six years, there were more than a hundred and forty associates. Of the circle of the Transcendentalists, most of the ablest members remained aloof, as benevolent neutrals and visitors. "Doing things in crowds" seemed to them too youthful; they were self-sufficient. As Margaret Fuller put it, in her somewhat airy dialect, "Why bind oneself to a central or any doctrine? How much nobler stands a man entirely unpledged, unbound?" This was Emerson's feeling. For Alcott, the plan was not austere enough. All three dissented from the idea behind the association, "As the institutions, so are the men," preferring to think, with Goethe, "As the men, so are the institutions." But Hawthorne, who had no theories, hoped to find at the farm a practical basis for his married life. John Sullivan Dwight, who had translated for Ripley the *Minor Poems of Goethe and Schiller,* and Charles A. Dana, fresh from Harvard, later known as Dana of *The Sun,* were members for a longer period. So was Isaac Hecker, of the "Hecker's Flour" family of New York, the German-American priest of the future, who founded the order of the Paulist Fathers. George William Curtis and his brother Burrill and George P. Bradford were other members. Bradford, whose *Selections from Fénelon* was another volume of Ripley's series, later moved to Plymouth to realize his dreams of the simple life. In the intervals of teaching Greek, he carried on a market-garden, selling his own vegetables from the cart. This was the charming and sensitive Bradford whose New England conscience was such a nuisance. Once, during one of Webster's out-of-door speeches, he was swept up to the front of the crowd. "I have no ticket," he exclaimed, "I have no right to be here;" and, much to the discomfort of the crowd, but much to the comfort of his conscience, he shoved his way back to the outermost rim. Charles King Newcomb, another member, was an individualist of a different sort. In his high room with the French window, this young Providence mystic kept a wooden crucifix on his table, between portraits of Xavier and Loyola, with freshly gathered flowers at the foot. One often heard his voice, in the midnight hours, chanting the litany or reading Greek. Newcomb lived a strange, secret life, prolonged for half a century in Paris, devoted to the writing of a private journal, as long as Amiel's journal, or even longer, that lay unpublished in a Rhode Island attic fifty years after his death. There were farmers and artists among the members, working-men and Brahmins, girls with hazel eyes and extravagant moods, several Harvard students, an English baronet's son, a Spaniard, two Filipinos, the son of a Louisiana planter, "Omniarch" Ryckman, "Camilla" and "Sybilla," —for nicknames were in vogue,—"Chrysalis" List and "Old Solidarity" Eaton.

In the broad entry of the Hive, Ripley's library filled the shelves until, to raise more money for the venture, the master sold his books to Theodore Parker. Ripley, the ever-faithful "Archon," steered the unsteady ship with unwavering eye. He was up before the dawn, dressed in his blue tunic and cow-hide boots, milking, cleaning the stalls, blacking the shoes of some member who was going to town, carting off the vegetables to market, directing the field-operations, writing diplomatic letters, giving a Sunday lecture on Kant or Spinoza, or, on a winter evening, when the stars were bright, gathering the members about him in the snow, while he discoursed on the constellations. His wife, Sophia Ripley, Richard Henry Dana's younger sister, who was soon to join the Catholic Church, cheerfully toiled beside him, ten hours a day in the muslin-room, washing, scrubbing the floors, much to the annoyance of her kindred. The school was more than admirable. Ripley taught philosophy and mathematics. Mrs. Ripley had a class in history and a class for Dante in Italian. Charles A. Dana had classes in Greek and German. The bashful, slender, beaming little Dwight, the dictator of musical Boston in later years, carried on the classes in music. He, too, had had a Unitarian pulpit, and had had a way of forgetting to write his sermons. He had a "want of fluency in prayer," for his mind was entirely filled with Mozart and Haydn. He started his "mass clubs" at the farm. There were classes in botany and geology, carried on among the rocks and trees. All the studies were elective; the rule was to "follow one's attractions." The young men wore blouses and hunters' frocks, belted at the waist, of plain brown holland or a gayer chintz, with little tasselled caps; the girls wore muslin dresses, with flowers and ribbons. The single men lived in Attica, the garret of the Hive; and the vegetarians had a Graham table. George William Curtis trimmed the lamps; Charles A. Dana was the griddle-master. There was much sitting about on stairs and floors, and the conversation,—analytical often, bristling with the new philosophy, with "intuition" and "the analogous," the objective, the creative, the receptive,—sometimes assumed those painful forms of wit that flourish among the intelligentsia. There were many jokes about "affinities," puns of the frostier kind that make one feel so sorry for the punster, animadversions on "morbid familism," *clichés* of a dire facetiousness: "Is the butter within the sphere of your influence?" But there were merry dances every night, picnics on Cow Island or in the grove, boating parties on the Charles, close by, Shakespeare readings, Elizabethan pageants, tableaux, charades, plays, scenes from Byron's *Corsair* and Sheridan's *Pizarro*. Occasionally, in the evening, little groups walked or drove to Boston, to a Beethoven concert or an Emerson lecture,—the interest in Beethoven seemed to flourish in minds that had been quickened by Emerson,—or an anti-slavery meeting at Faneuil Hall. They filled the big farm-wagon, or Jonas Gerrish's stage, which, twice a day, plied between the Hive and Scollay Square. Their favourite rendezvous in the afternoon was Elizabeth Peabody's book-shop. At night, they gathered in Mrs. Harrington's cake-shop, and the younger men and the girls walked home under the stars.

The stage from Scollay Square brought visitors, a few, at first, those of the inner circle, then hundreds and even thousands of "civilisees," as the farmers called the rest ot the population. Margaret Fuller came to conduct a Conversation on Education, on "What can we do for ourselves and others?" Impulse was the subject on one occasion, an appropriate theme at the farm, where spontaneity was so much in order. Throwing oneself on the floor was not so bad, but yawning was a little too impulsive. Georgiana Bruce burned pastilles to perfume Margaret's room and brought the morning coffee to her bedside. For Margaret had become another Pauline Wiesel, the heroine of the German Romantics, whom Humboldt walked thirty miles to see.* Emerson often came to lead the talk; sometimes Bronson Alcott. Theodore Parker, who lived close by,—he had a church at West Roxbury,—walked over often for a chat about philosophy or farming. Orestes Brownson dropped in, shouted and pounded on the table and strolled with Isaac Hecker in the grove. They were both on the road to Rome, like Mrs. Ripley; and Brownson's coming always occasioned a talk on Catholicism, Pascal or Port Royal. This was a theme that pleased Charles Newcomb, whose favourite author was Saint Augustine. Brownson, the rustic giant from Vermont, who had passed through so many religious phases, was not a welcome guest. That there was method in his truculence, no one had any reason to suppose; and he had taken up his Greek and Latin, to satisfy his Catholic advisers, at a time when his mental bones had set. He made sad work of his spondees and dactyls, which the patient

---

* One of Pauline Wiesel's friends wrote of her, in the vein of Margaret's friends, "I look upon her in the light of a phenomenon of Greek mythology." She herself had written, much in Margaret's vein, "Every means, every possible preparation for living, and yet one must never live; I never shall, and those who dare to do so have the wretched world, the whole world, against them."—George Brandes, *The Romantic School in Germany.*

George Ripley would not have minded if Brownson had not appeared to be showing off. As for George Bradford, the ever-gentle, who had learned his Greek and Latin in the cradle, he could not sleep for the misery that Brownson caused him. False vowels and wrong measures were as painful to him as a saxophone would have been. He dreamed one night that he was a Catholic convert and that Brownson, appointed his confessor, obliged him to repeat, after himself, a Latin psalm from the Vulgate. Bradford awoke in agony.

This was a pity, for Brownson, who was honest as the day, was a man of really imposing gifts. He appeared to be unstable enough. He had passed from sect to sect, changing his ministerial coat as many times as the Vicar of Bray, although always in response to a new conviction. Every thinker he read, Lamennais, Jouffroy, Comte, Saint-Simon, Owen, overthrew all his previous views, and he rushed from one position to another, with a headlong, headstrong vehemence, telling the world each time how right he was. With a vigorous, enquiring mind that was anything but sensitive or subtle, he had a warm and generous imagination. He had founded the "Society of Union and Progress," chiefly for the advancement of the workers, and he had preached class-warfare, the death-struggle of rich and poor, as a step towards the "Church of the Future," after the Comtian pattern, of which he saw himself as a John the Baptist. He longed for a new Catholicity until he found a home in the old one. To further his ideas and reflect their changes, he carried on a quarterly review, first the *Boston Quarterly,* afterwards *Brownson's Quarterly.* In this he "aimed to startle," as he said, taking pains to be paradoxical and even as extravagant as he could be; and this method was rather accentuated after he had joined the Catholic Church. The Bishop of Boston lamented the timidity of the Catholic population, most of whom were recent immigrants, of the depressed classes, in a society that was hostile to them. The Bishop urged

Brownson not to hide his light under a bushel. As well urge a bull not to pretend to be a lamb! The rugged, fiery Brownson was happy to learn that truculence had an apostolic value. On ferry-boats between Chelsea and Boston, in barber-shops, in butcher-shops, wherever he happened to find himself, he engaged all and sundry in religious discussions. Once at an inn at Andover, where he was giving a lecture, he loudly commanded the waiter to send for the landlord. "Landlord," he exclaimed, in a voice that was meant for all the guests, "why don't you have something in your house that a Christian can eat? Why don't you have fish? No Christian eats meat on Friday."

This was one of the little things that people seldom did at Andover. They kept a special corner of hell-fire there for travellers with Brownson's views. But Brownson was a courageous man, in the Church as well as out of it, whom the Brook Farmers learned to respect in the end; for, having been too Catholic for the Yankees, he was too Yankee for the Catholics, at least for the Church as he found it, and he stormed against the Irish domination. He wished to make the Church an American Church, to counteract the powerful influence that tended to make it Irish; and no one spoke more forcefully than he against the corruptions of Tammany. He was under a cloud in Dublin as well as in Boston, and Cardinal Newman was forced to withdraw the invitation he had sent to Brownson to lecture at his new university there. He was the first lecturer that Newman invited, and he was asked to choose his own subject, geography or "opossums," if it suited him best; for Brownson's multifarious writings on history, sociology, religion, on politics, art and philosophy had given him a world-name. His standing was high in the Catholic world,* and his gifts, from the point of view

---

* "You alone can prepare us for the great controversies by founding among us a school and arming it with the principles of a sound philosophy."—Letter of Lord Acton to Brownson, 1854. See also the long correspondence with Montalembert in the *Life of Brownson* by his son.

of any school, his versatility and his breadth of knowledge, his energy and lucidity, were those of a first-rate
publicist. Something more than a journalist, something
less than a sage, Brownson was a Catholic Theodore Parker. In one book, *The Convert,* the history of his religious
life, he left the best account that has ever been written of
the spiritual cross-currents of the forties and fifties.

Of the other guests at Brook Farm, two were especially
welcome, William Henry Channing, the doctor's nephew,
a minister, albeit with many scruples, better known as a
Christian socialist, a thrillingly eloquent preacher, and the
tall, slight, graceful Christopher Cranch, with the picturesque head and curling hair, the son of a judge in
Washington, who, having ample means and mundane
tastes, had gradually "sunk the minister in the man"
and followed the call of the muses. He was a landscape
painter and a poet; he sang and played the flute and violin; he was a clever actor on occasion and the cleverest car-
icaturist in New England. In fact, he was the victim of
too many gifts, no mere Janus with a double head but a
sort of accomplished Hydra. He had taken Emerson at
his word and planted himself on his instincts, wherever
they led him. They had led him into the pulpit and out
again; they led him to Louisville, Kentucky, where he took
the place of James Freeman Clarke as editor of *The
Western Messenger.* With his flute as his constant companion, he had drawn there his comic illustrations for
some of Emerson's essays, such as the "Man expanding
like a Melon." These drawings, suggesting Thackeray's,
shocked some of the Transcendentalists. In years to come,
he was to use this talent in the pictures for his charming
books for children, *The Last of the Huggermuggers* and
Kobboltozo,—years during which he lived as a wandering
artist, in London, New York, Paris, Rome and Cambridge. What could an artist do, he would write from
New York, in a money-getting world? People rushed in

from the streets and stopped for a moment in his studio, only to hurry-scurry out again, eternally driving, driving. In Cambridge, he found a congenial circle, and there he translated the *Æneid;* but whenever he came back from Italy he was struck by the look in people's faces, the hard, weary expression about the mouth, the quick, shrewd eye, the anxious air. Everyone seemed to be worried; and back he would go to Rome, to join the circle of William Wetmore Story, write a few more poems and paint from the costume-models.

His painting was nothing out of the way, but some of his poems had a firmer touch. There are poets who survive in a single line. Cranch was destined to survive in two, from the poem called *Enosis,*—

> We are columns left alone
> Of a temple once complete,—

which hundreds of men have quoted in their latter years. At Brook Farm, where he came to visit his friend and fellow-lover of music and German, his Harvard classmate Dwight, he was the all-attractive entertainer. He drew amusing pictures of the Harvard mill grinding its grist of ministers. He performed astonishing feats of ventriloquism. William Henry Channing was more austere. He was a self-tormented creature, earnest, hypersensitive, torn by doubts, a "concave man" who was always retreating, as Henry Thoreau remarked, like a fair mask swaying from a bough. For the rest, he was a man of the world, as all the Channings were, and a preacher unexcelled when the spirit moved him. In later years, he was to live in England, where his daughter married the author of *The Light of Asia.* At the moment, he was editing in New York a magazine called *The Present,* to propagate his socialistic views. What to do for the race? was his constant question; but he was involved in metaphysics, of a sadly tenuous kind, and he was convinced, as a friend remarked, that "Christ did not understand his own religion." He had spent a season in Rome, vainly hoping to get himself converted, and the engravings on his study wall were arranged in the form of a cross. He wrote an occasional poem and various tracts and had recently translated Jouffroy's *Ethics;* but the great project of his life was a work on Vittoria Colonna, a study of the Italian Renaissance. He meditated this for many years, enthralled as he gathered his memoranda, until the enormous task of preparation became a life-work in itself. He never began the book. A mystical enthusiast, like Dr. Channing, but without his uncle's will, irresolute, introspective, the victim of innumerable intentions, a talker and taker of notes who longed to be "useful,"—such was the "evil times' sole patriot," as Emerson called him in a well-known poem. Of all the Brook Farmers, guests or members, William Henry Channing was the symbol, as later times recalled the enterprise. Whatever the facts might be, whatever happened, he could never persuade himself that the world's salvation did not lie just around the corner. He always felt, when he rose from his bed, that the "one far-off divine event" might well occur before he sat down to breakfast.

CHAPTER XIII

EMERSON: WOOD-NOTES

IN THE days of King Philip's War, the Indians had spared the town of Concord. They burned the neighbouring settlements, Sudbury, Chelmsford, Stow, but one of their chieftains said, as they glanced over Concord from a hill-top, "We shall never prosper if we go there. The Great Spirit loves that town." This was an Indian legend, and one could well believe it. Plain, low, quiet, the village had no obvious distinction. The enterprising Yankees passed it by. It had no port, no trade, no water-power, no gold, lead, coal, oil or marble. The granite was better at Fitchburg, and even the Concord ice had bubbles in it. As wood and grass were its only staples, Emerson advised his fellow-townsmen to manufacture school-teachers and make them the best in the world.* The village air favoured this, as it favoured meditation and contemplation. The hills and woods, not too exciting, afforded a gentle stimulus to genial and uninterrupted studies. One recalled in Concord the words of the old Chinese painter: "Wherein do the reasons lie that virtuous men so love *sansui*, landscape? Landscape is a place

---

* A staple for the South and West. Edward Everett Hale relates that a certain French investigator, sent by Napoleon III to study American education, found that virtually every teacher in the West and South had come from one small corner of the country, either Connecticut or Massachusetts. He asked Hale to explain this fact, which he said was unique in history. Hale, to settle the question, enquired of a leading citizen of Massachusetts how many young people of his town, when they left school, began as teachers. "He heard me," says Hale, "with some impatience, and then said, 'Why, all of them, of course.'"—E. E. Hale, *Tarry-at-Home Travels.*

where vegetation is nourished on high and low ground, where springs and rocks play about like children, a place that woodsmen and retiring scholars usually frequent, where birds cry aloud their joy in the scene."

Concord abounded in *sansui*. One found peace there and the flourishing days in which minds are high and joyous, the days that Kakki desired for the landscape-painter. There one could have good feeling and beautiful taste; one could create the *Yu,* the wonderful and mysterious. Emerson found it so, in his woodland walks. Once he had left his study, once in the fields, with the lowing cattle, the birds, the trees, the waters, the satisfying outlines of the hills and the ponds, he seemed to have come to his own and made friends with nature. He found health and affinity there,— no petulance, no fret, but eternal resource, a long tomorrow rich as yesterday. The stems of the hemlocks, pines and oaks gleamed like iron on his excited eye. The thrilling leap of the squirrel up the long bough, the softness and beauty of the summer clouds that seemed to enjoy their height and privilege of motion, the millions of sheeny fliers with green body and crape wing that overhung the grasses and the waters, the chickadees in the piny glen filled him with cheerfulness and courage. He was embosomed in beauty and wonder. The very cattle lying under the trees seemed to have great and tranquil thoughts. The songs of the birds, the sunlight full of gnats, the crickets in full cry, the goldfinches eating the seeds of the thistle, scattering the leaves in their excitement, the hedges of barberry, whitethorn, woodbine and ivy were a cornucopia of golden joys. Out upon scholars, he said to himself, with their pale, sickly, etiolated indoor thoughts! Give me the out-of-door thoughts of sound men, thoughts all fresh and blooming.

Much as the village meant to him, it was in the woods and fields that he knew the joy of the Brahmin. Concord, indeed, was a school for the study of human nature. One learned all the trades and professions by talking with the blacksmith, the grocer, the plumber. All history repeated itself in Concord. The wealth and goods of the Indies and China streamed through the village in the trucks and wagons that carried the wares of Boston to Vermont and New Hampshire. One had only to mix a little imagination with all these sights and sounds of the common life: then one found the whole world in any least corner of it, one found Asia and Europe, past and future, within the circle of one's daily walks. The large mind in small conditions, the high mind in low conditions, everything in leasts: why should not Concord be one's Rome, one's world? A tent, a little rice and asses' milk, or, say, the farmer's scale of living, plain plenty without luxury or show; for the rest, health, the south wind, books, old trees, a boat, two or three friends,—what could a poet wish that life did not shower on him there? His sunshine was Susa; Ecbatana, his shade; and he could rest assured that, if he asked them, every one of the gods would honour his feast.

It was for no private ends that Emerson sought privacy. His ends were universal, his ends were public, like those of Michael Angelo, like Dante's, who seldom dined in company. Swedenborg's best of angels, those that dwelt in the midst of heaven, did not live consociated, but separate, house and house; and Ossian's Cathmore lodged in the wood not only to avoid the voice of praise. If the seeker of truth needs solitude, and almost a going out of the body to think, should a poet apologize for the isolation that breeds Olympian thoughts? Steadily to prefer one's native choices, against all argument and all example, defending them against the multitude, even as much or more against the wise, was not this the burden of Emerson's teaching? Should everyone be busy and useful? Was it any merit in a man to make his own stove, or boil and bake his dinner, when others could do it better than he? His virtue was to carry into action his own dearest ends, to dare to do what he believed and loved, were it only the carving of a cherry-stone or the forwarding of a handful of friends. How much more was it a poet's virtue to solve his own questions, though he died, even if he died of lotus-eating! Therefore, for the poet, idleness, as others chose to think it, leisure for meditation and contemplation. He who could hope to catch the wingéd thoughts that thrilled and agitated humankind, restored youth and sanity, dissipated the dreams under which men reeled and staggered and gave heroic aims to the nations was not required to explain his means. Emerson paid his way by lecturing. For the rest, he abandoned himself to his own caprices. The writer, like the priest, had to be exempted from secular labour, for his work demanded a frolic health; he had to be at the top of his condition. Anyone who challenged Emerson's freedom would have discovered that his village mildness masked, like any woodland creature's, a sharp retractile claw.

He scarcely had a *modus vivendi*. His moods were too variable for this; and he did not wish merely to write. He wished to say only essential things, the things that could not be omitted, the things that his genius uttered,—he did not care to cultivate his talent; and his genius ebbed and flowed and ebbed again. Yesterday, Caesar had not seemed so great; today, he was a dunce. The fruit of his brain was abortive, cramped or mildewed. He was as torpid as a clod. He felt like a ship aground, and suddenly some tyrannous idea, emerging out of heaven, seized upon him. The rigid fibres relaxed; life returned to a finger, a hand, a foot. A river spread over the shoals where the ship lay aground, uplifting the timbers on its waters, and the ship put forth its sails and turned its head to the sea. Were these moods in any degree within control?—for the fruits of these moods alone were all he wished to gather. Were there any tonics for the torpid mind? The electric machine would not work, no sparks would pass; and then the world was all a cat's back, all sparkle and shock. A flash of light, a long darkness, then a flash again. Where was the Franklin with kite and rod for this celestial fluid?—he who could command it and convey it into the arts of life, inspire men and take them off their feet, withdraw them from the life of gain and trifles and make the world transparent. For to Emerson nothing seemed incredible, nothing, neither miracles nor magic, when he had experienced an insight. He longed for the consecutive, not the single glimpse but the panorama. A fuller inspiration, as it seemed to him, would cause the point to flow and become a line; it would bend the line and complete the circle.

To experience this genius and communicate it, to detect and watch the gleam of light that flashed across his mind from within, was Emerson's dream and hope; and this alone governed his method of living. Not by forethought, not by calculation, had paradise ever been gained. The "stairway of surprise" mounted thither, and this was not to be compassed by rules. To live in the hour, extempore, free as an Arab, was the only way to be ready when the gods arrived. All measures of economy were ugly: the manners of the bard should be above them. And yet was there not a kind of prudence that had its negative value? He who respected his ends had to respect his means, however he cloaked and screened them; and, if all high states of mind were transient, like every other form of inspiration, still, there were methods of inducing them, and prudence lay in making use of these. One had to have a measure of worldly wisdom in order to keep one's freedom; and no one was shrewder than Emerson, when it came to this. Well he knew what crippled and untuned him, and his stimulants and purgatives were many: the fire, as it burned in his chimney,—a kind of muse,—air, landscape, exercise, a page or two of Proclus or Plotinus. He passed into the Elysian Fields the moment he opened these authors; the grand and pleasing figures of gods and demons sailed before his eyes. These rare, brave words filled him with hilarity and spring; his heart danced, his sight was quickened, he beheld shining relations between all things; he was impelled to write and almost to sing. Proclus was his opium. But solitary converse with nature was his special *modus* of inspiration. On spring days, at summer dawns, in the October woods, by flood or field, in natural parks of oak or pine, where the ground was smooth and unencumbered, he heard sweet and dreadful words that were never uttered in libraries. The hills began to dislimn and float in the air. The atoms of his frame began to dance. He came into new circulations; the marrow of the world was in his bones; the opulence of forms poured into his intellect; he seemed to be dipping his brush into the paint-pot with which birds, flowers, the living rock, the landscape and the eternal sky were painted.

Away with prudence then! Allah never counted the days the Arab spent in the chase. The one real prudence was concentration, as the one evil was dissipation. One's work would take care of itself if one lived enough; and as long as one's genius bought the investment was safe, although one spent like a monarch. To be profligate was not to spend, but to spend off the line of one's proper life; and to fill the hour was Emerson's life, to fill the hour and own the day. Him to whom works and days were offered, no god could ever rebuke for taking works. The days came and went like veiled and muffled figures, sent from a distant friendly party; but they said nothing, and, if one did not use the gifts they brought, they carried them as silently away. What fairy or what demon possessed such power as he who used the gifts?—

Bread, kingdoms, stars, and sky that holds them all.

It was in search of this power,—call it the poet's madness,—that Emerson set out for the woods and pastures.
He was an abandoned lotus-eater. All he asked was that
the days should be, for him, as full as centuries, loaded,
fragrant. He had various favourite walks, from the
Manse down the river to Peter's Field, to the Estabrook
farm, with its straggling orchards, where the apple-trees
strove to hold their own against the encroaching forest,
to White Pond, a little Indian basin, where one could
almost see the sachem paddling his canoe in a shadowy
cove, to Walden, where he had his own pine garden and
the chickadees flitted through the branches and the
waterflies seemed full of happiness. There, as he sat on
the bank, he had read most of Goethe,—to please Carlyle,
—fifty volumes or more. Sometimes the warm south wind
drew him to the summit of the ridge above the Boston
turnpike. Sometimes he rose before the light and waited
for the dawn over the forest, sitting on a course of dark
rock that had been worn by a glacier. Often he went for
walks at night, when the moon was making amber of the
world and every cottage pane glittered with silver and
the meadows sent up the rank smell of all their ferns and
folded flowers in a nocturnal fragrance. The little harlot
fireflies of the lowlands sparkled in the grass and in the
air, and he heard the voice of the wind, so slight and
pure and deep, as if it were the sound of the stars
revolving.

How many were there who could see the charm of
close, low pine-woods in a river-town? Was Walden anything more than a "prettyish pool," as a travelling poet
remarked? One had to have musical eyes to see what
Emerson saw in these meadows and streams, in the waving rye-fields and the quiet hemlocks. He saw what others
heard: all the soothing, brisk or romantic moods that
corresponding melodies awoke in them, he found in the
carpet of the wood, in the margin of the pond, in the

shade of the pines, in the infinite variety and dance of the tree-tops. To him, a skiff on the water was a piece of fairy timber, which the light loved, the wind and the wave. When he struck the water with his paddle, he fancied he had never seen such colour, the hue of Rhine wines, jasper and verd-antique, topaz and chalcedony, gold and green and chestnut and hazel, in bewitching suc-cession and relief. In the hard clouds he saw what sculp-ture!—what an expression of immensity in the dotted and rippled rack, firm and continental, then vanishing into plumes and auroral gleams, all without crowding, bound-less, cheerful, strong. On Indian summer days, he saw the Indians under the trees in the wood. In his neighbour Edmund Hosmer's oxen, the beasts that ploughed his fields, he saw the camels of the faithful Hassan, beside whom even Tamerlane seemed a slave. The railroad at Walden, prosaic enough to others, seemed to him a shuttle, shooting across the forest, the swamp, the river, over the arms of the sea, binding city to city. In an apple-tree, he saw the sun painting itself in glowing balls and leaves,—in apples, the social fruit, in which nature had deposited every flavour. Whole zones and climates were concentrated in apples, barrels of wind and half-barrels of cider. In the oaks and pines, he saw vessels of health and vigour. They were imperfect men, groping upward, bemoaning their imprisonment, rooted in the ground. Be-side these plants, hardy in their weakness, he had a sud-den sense of relief and pleasure, observing the mighty law of vegetation.

On evenings when the moon shone, the thrifty Con-cord folk turned out the street-lamps. Emerson did not need even the moon; he could see well enough in the dark. He saw honour in scamps and justice in thieves. He could see energy in beggars and elegance of manners in a peas-ant. He could see benevolence in misers and grandeur in porters and sweeps. Why this was, he could never have told; for he who had leisure for everything else had no time for introspection. Besides, if he saw in the dark, he preferred the sunlight. None of his moments ever seemed empty in which he had given heed to some natural object, a gentian, a wild-apple-tree with fruit that hung like berries, a thorn-bush with its red fruit, the musical, streaming south wind that turned all the trees into wind-harps, the fall of snow-flakes in the still air, the blowing of sleet over a sheet of water. He felt that he was emerging from an egg-shell existence when he saw the great dome that arched above him. An everlasting Now reigned in nature, which hung the same roses on his bushes that charmed the Chaldeans in their hanging gardens.

Often, as he walked, he hummed or whistled the rhythm of some ballad, some song of Herrick's, a fragment of Taliessin, the old Welsh bard, or a strain of Persian poetry, Hafiz or Saadi. It struck him that these metres were organic, derived from the human pulse, beating with the beating of the blood, and therefore natural and universal. There was a charm in the cadences, heroic, pathetic or plaintive, that seemed to set him searching for the words to fill these vacant beats. Rhymes enchanted him, too, in a way he could not explain but had always felt. They suggested the correspondence of parts in nature, acid and alkali, body and mind, character and history, action and reaction. These iterations in the natural world, as in the world of art, had always given him pleasure: the doubling of rocks and trees reflected in water, the repetition of pillars in a colonnade, in a row of windows, or in wings, the symmetrical contrast of garden beds and walks. Rhymes to the eye, such as shadows, explained the charm of rhymes to the ear; and the inner life also had its rhymes, perception and expression, ebb and flow. Rhyme and rhythm measured for him the latitude and opulence of poets. If they were limited and unskilful, one saw it in the poverty of their chimes. But

Spenser, Marlowe and Chapman flew far and wide for their weapons: there was no manufacture in their rhymes and rhythms, but a vortex, a musical tornado that whirled the materials of their minds into the same grand order that planets and moons obeyed, and seasons, and monsoons.

He loved rhyme and return, period and musical reflection, rhyme that suggested not restraint but rather the wildest freedom. At Walden, on a winter day, he would stand on the edge of the pond and throw stones across the frozen surface. It charmed his ear as the stones fell and fell again on this crystal drum, repeating the note with just the right modulation. The rhyming and the chiming of this ice-harp filled him with exultation. Well he could understand why poetry had been called the *gaie science,* why sailors worked better for their *yo-heave-ho,* why soldiers fought better for the drum and trumpet. He could understand the building power of music, as the ancient myths described it. He could feel how the walls of Thebes had risen to the music of Amphion's harp. The excitement which the Persian bards produced exceeded that of the grape: they had driven warriors to combat, like Taileffer, who rode out at Hastings, singing the *Chanson de Roland,* challenging the Saxons. Well he could understand why bards and minstrels had been taken for makers and givers of laws, they who had stood for liberation, for courage, freedom, victory. In the myths, they restored the dead to life; they met the approbation of Allah in heaven. They made men, they added and affirmed. They set the intellectual world in action. They sang old ideas out of people's heads and sang new ideas in. They introduced fresh images and symbols that built up the world again in thought. They threw down the walls of circumstance. They awakened in other men the sense of universal relation and power.

Emerson thought of the poet as Adam in the garden

again, new-naming the beasts in the field and the gods in
the sky, calling aloud to the children of morning that all
creation was recommencing. Among partial men, he stood
for the complete man. All the forms of life were in balance in him; he saw and handled that which others
dreamed of, the whole scale of experience. He was the
representative of man, having the largest power to receive and impart. Were not most men like the shepherd
who, lost and blinded in the snow-storm, perished in a
drift outside his door? Were they not like minors who
had not come into their own and did not know what
wealth was rightly theirs? They clung to the wearinesses
of their daily life, their trivial forms and habits, their
petrified social scale of ranks and employments. They
were inferior to their proper selves and did not use the
powers they possessed. Who but the poet could redeem
them from all these routines and idolatries? Their money
was a second best, their alcohol, their politics. Which of
them would not give his lands and houses for a touch of
the perception that stirred the will? Life was a dance,
as Plotinus said, in which the bodies were moved in a
beautiful manner, as being parts of the whole. But most
men could not sustain this order. They were too lumpish
and opaque, for their souls had not been awakened. There
lay the poet's province. For him the world was always
virgin soil; for him all men had their sovereign moments,
as every clod contains its germs of life. It was the poet's
office to unfold them. He was the master of the dance of
life, who knew that every man would begin to move when
the music reached and touched his imagination.

The poets who had shown this power most clearly
were the great religious awakeners, Zoroaster and Plato,
the bards of the Vedas, of the *Vishnu Purana* and the
Bhagavad-Gita. For Emerson, these came first, or such as
these; they were never out of his mind, and he judged
other poets in the light of these commanding oracles. In

his reaction against the Church, and all that savoured of official goodness, he seldom thought of the biblical writers. But, even more than the givers of laws, he liked, or at least he liked to think of, the Norse and the Cymrian bards, Taliessin and the mythical Ossian and Merlin, together with Hafiz and Saadi, the Persian poets. It was evident that his notion of these was coloured by his reading of the Eastern scriptures; but even as they were,—as they survived in fragments,—he found them inspiring and tonic. They spoke to him of the vast, of health and courage. The rude strains of the Northern bards, struck out white-hot with love or grief, pleased him all the more in his own recoil from all that was academic in the English classics; and the cheerfulness and force of the "fortunate" Saadi were the fruits of a situation like his own. For Saadi and Hafiz, in Persia, had escaped from Mohammedan fatalism, just as he had escaped from Calvinism. Their joy was a joy of liberation. He liked to think of the Persians and Arabs. In the absence of other intoxicants, as travellers often noted, poetry and flowers were their wine and spirits: a couplet was equal to a bottle and a rose to a dram. Poetry had its highest effect among them. It was also in his wish to escape from the sway of European tradition that Emerson cultivated the Persian poets, who left so many traces in his writings. The luxuriance of their imagery, the breadth of the Eastern modes of thinking refreshed his New England imagination. The bold Oriental muse had an electric power that animated and unbound his mind.

Much as he loved poems of every kind, it was these poets of the early ages, the springtime bards and seers that he loved the best, they who spoke with authority and not as the scribes, who spoke of the morning of the world, whose words stood for things, for the simplest feelings,—not gifted men who sang, but the children of music, whose scope did not lie in exhibition, whose aim was to serve the gods. "Thus saith the Lord" began their songs. Their utterance was large and their language final, as if it came from the Eternal mind and had not been arbitrarily composed by the writer. The Greek Gnomic poets, the Persian poets, whose words might have been engraved on sword-blades, Pindar, with his grand strokes, firm as the tread of a horse,—among his own contemporaries, Landor, whose epigrams recalled the Greeks: these were his special favourites. They seemed to him the result and the justification of the ages in which they appeared: they made him think lightly of histories and statutes. In their verse, the iron lids of Reason, usually heavy with slumber, were unclosed for a moment. The individual mind became in them the vent of the mind of humanity.

In poetry, Emerson asked for the greatest. He asked that the poet should omit all but the important passages: Shakespeare was made up of such,—Shakespeare, who was like Damascus steel, hammered out of old nails. He was not interested in talent. He loved the charm and skill of execution that he found in Herrick, Collins, Gray and Landor, the elegance that suggested health, the ease that went with mastery. But for external graces he had no use. He thought with Heraclitus that "harmony latent is of greater value than that which is patent"; and Wordsworth's great design, the plan of *The Recluse,* the *Ode to Dion,* pleased him better than all the enamelled poets. None of your parlour or piano verse! None of your carpet poets, content to please! None of your sonneteering, your bookmaking and bookselling; none of your cold spying and authorship! The muse should be the counterpart of nature, exuberant and tranquil. True poetry, Emerson thought, betrayed in every word miraculous presence of mind, quickness, perception of relations. One found it seldom in current letters, even in the history of letters. In a dozen alcoves of English poets, one found

only nine or ten who were still inspirers of their race. For
literature warped away from life, and the power to
transubstantiate the world was the test and measure of
poetry. Its mark was contemporary insight, in one's own
America as in Pindar's Greece. Easy enough to repaint
the mythology of the Greeks, the mediæval Church, the
feudal castle, the martyrdoms and crusades of former
times. To point out where the same creative power
worked in one's own dwellings and public assemblies, to
convert into universal symbols the energies acting at this
hour in New York, in Chicago and San Francisco, required a subtle and commanding thought. Could one read
the poetry in affairs and fuse the circumstances of today?
Could one take the hour, with its cares and fears, and
hold it up to a divine reason, until one saw that it had a
purpose and beauty? Then one would be doing what
Pindar did, and Shakespeare and Milton in their times.
The dry twig would blossom in one's hand.

Poet that he was in all his prose, it was this other
harmony that he longed to compass. He toiled endlessly
over his verses; and, in fact, he had developed a style of
his own, as marked in his poems as in his essays, a lean,
spare, quick, intellectual style that could only have
emerged, one felt, from Concord. In his more flaccid
verses, one caught here and there glints of Shakespeare,
Collins, Gray and Wordsworth; but the Emersonian style
at its best had none of the derivative Cambridge note,
nor any of the smooth and facile charm of most of the
other American writers. In his preference of the "latent"
to the "patent," as a protest against the sort of jingles
one "put round frosted cake," as he said, Emerson sometimes purposely roughened his verses, throwing in a dis-
sonance or an ill-matched rhyme. Anything rather than
rhetoric, for himself. As a matter of fact, with others, he
was easily pleased. For all the severity of his conscious
standard, anything in rhyme was apt to catch him, pro-

vided the feeling was noble. He never took the word for
the deed, in the work of other poets, but he often took
the deed for the word. The anthology that he published,
Parnassus, a large collection of his favourite poems,
showed the inequality of his taste. In choosing his own
poems to publish, he revealed a similar weakness; for at
his own worst his work was bad as no merely talented
writer's could be. Even the *Threnody* was not really good,
and the commonplace or doggerel of much of his writing
would never have passed muster with the Cambridge
poets. One wondered at the childlike innocence that could
have led him to publish some of these verses, for his work
was only good when it was great; but he who could
write pages of artless lines, with nothing but their sincerity to redeem them, fairly shook the stars when he
wrote at his best. One turned the page of *The Adirondacks,* smiling at his ingenuousness, and caught one's
breath at his sublimity,—for *Brahma* lay on the next page.
So it was with the poet of *Merlin* and *Bacchus,* of
Uriel, Terminus and *Give All to Love.* At best, he had
an intensity like nothing else in American verse. Then, as
the Emersonian stars shone forth, over a world peopled
with gods and heroes, he seemed like the god of wealth
himself, opening power in everything he touched; and
one saw that he was one of his own immortals,—

> Olympian bards who sung
> Divine ideas below,
> Which always find us young
> And always keep us so.

Emerson's poems were *sui generis.* They were like
Poe's in this, however remote from Poe in their lonely
whiteness. Of Poe's melodious magic, Emerson had
scarcely a touch. Of colour, he had none, or next to none,
except when at moments, behind his verse, one seemed

to catch a sort of polar splendour, as of an aurora bore-
alis. There was something bleached and dry, in the best
of this verse, like that of an age-old wisdom, exposed for
thousands of years to sun and wind, and a strong, clear,
bracing mountain air seemed to have blown upon it.
Emerson's, at these moments, seemed

> the pen
> Which on the first day drew,
> Upon the tablets blue,
> The dancing Pleiads and eternal men.

CHAPTER XIV

CONCORD: 1840–1844

AT EMERSON'S house, from time to time, the so-called Transcendental Club assembled. Never a club, in the proper sense, never calling itself Transcendental, it was a group of men and women, interested in the new ideas, who met now and then to discuss them. The first meeting had taken place at Ripley's house in Boston, and Ripley, Dwight, Miss Peabody, Margaret Fuller, Alcott, Jones Very, Orestes Brownson, James Freeman Clarke and Theodore Parker were among the occasional members.

Sometimes it was called Hedge's Club, because Frederick Hedge, who lived in Bangor, where he preached to the Penobscot lumber-merchants, made sudden descents upon Boston that resulted in calls for a meeting. Hedge, with Sampson Reed, the Boston druggist, had introduced Swedenborg's writings to his friends. In his snow-bound study in the north, he smoked and read his German. He was preparing there his *Prose Writers of Germany*. Many of the members, like himself, like Emerson, Everett, Ripley, Dwight and Cranch, beginning their lives as ministers, were settling down as simple men of letters. Their vocations were fading out like daguerreotypes.* Others, ceasing to be Unitarians, had become

---

* This was a general symptom of the time. "When I lived in the West, there came a phrenologist to the town, and examining the heads of all the clergymen in the place, found us all deficient in the organ of reverence. More than that, we all admitted that the fact was so; that we were not, any of us, specially gifted with natural piety or love of worship. Then he said, 'You have all mistaken your calling. You ought not to be ministers.'"
—James Freeman Clarke, *Self-Culture.*

the same thing without the name. But James Freeman
Clarke and Theodore Parker, whatever their doubts or
deficiencies, were never to abandon the priestly calling.
Clarke's *Self-Culture,* written years later, was a characteristic expression of the West Street circle. His *Ten
Great Religions,* a standard book, also published after
the Civil War, was an example of the comparative
method that Agassiz had popularized in Cambridge. Another warrior of the pulpit who came to meetings of the
club was the hallelujah Methodist, Father Taylor. This
was the scarred old prophet who walked his quarter-deck
at the Seamen's Chapel, where the gay blue flag flew from
the roof,—"bounding like a roe over the hills of spices."
The greatest natural orator in Boston, who had adopted
all the sons of the ocean, the pleading, grieving searcher
of souls, so tender and so volcanic, whose rebukes were
like broadsides from a frigate, he was a master of unconscious style. Everyone flocked to hear him, Webster and
Channing, Dickens, Jenny Lind; for, although, as he said,
he sometimes lost his nominative case, he was always on
the way to glory.*

Father Taylor was ready for any discussion of the
lukewarm spirit of the day. This, in its hundred aspects,
was the leading topic at the club: the American genius,
the causes that hindered its growth, the indifferentism at
Harvard and the like. But the talk was often wire-drawn
and misty. What was the True, the Beautiful, the Good?
What was the Highest Aim? What could be done with
an artist who was not an artist? Could sculpture express
as well as painting the notion of immortality? Emerson
found it rather unrewarding. One did not learn to use
one's tongue in a lonely country parsonage, and the mental hinges of some of the members fairly creaked with

---

* "I have never heard but one essentially perfect orator," Walt Whitman said, referring to Father Taylor. He and his preaching are reproduced
in Father Mapple's sermon in Melville's *Moby Dick.*

rust. Not by words like these could one captivate the great American Lilliput, great in land and resources, in coal and corn, but all a village littleness, as Emerson thought. Most of the members were better at writing than talking, though this was far from true of Theodore Parker. If there was any man in the Boston pulpit,—for Parker had begun to preach in Boston,—who added cubits to the Lilliputians, it was this poet-preacher, reformer, scholar, who found fifty hours a week to spare for other than parish work.

It was for Parker's essays on manual labour, on Pharisaism, on German thought that readers bought *The Dial,* the new review with the lilac covers. This was the mouthpiece of the West Street circle, a product of Miss Peabody's shop, and Margaret Fuller was the editor.* Dr. Channing was so excited when he heard the news about *The Dial* that he lay awake for three nights. He rejoiced in all these signs of life that represented reforms on his reform; and in fact *The Dial* was a gallant venture. It rallied the younger poets and writers and gave them an adequate focus, as the *North American Review* had rallied the historical students and critics. Margaret, —for so she was called, as people said Bettina or Corinne,—was in her element as the guiding spirit; for the new illuminati were all her friends and she had correspondents all over New England, younger men and girls, aspiring students, lovers of Goethe and Schiller, most of them neophytes and shy beginners. They felt that Margaret carried a hazel twig, for she seemed to divine their hidden springs. They spread their portfolios out before her. Had some young man, who wished to write, watched Stearns Wheeler at the Athenæum transcribing the magical chapters of *Sartor Resartus?* Margaret had

* The editor's salary, which was never paid, was $200 a year. The number of subscribers never exceeded three hundred. Miss Peabody's later venture, *Æsthetic Papers,* which had only fifty subscribers, was discontinued after the first number.

seen the young man watching. She knew he had something to say for *The Dial;* and Wheeler, who had gone to Heidelberg, was glad to send her letters on German affairs. She appealed to Emerson, Alcott, Theodore Parker, Hawthorne, Cranch and Newcomb. Dwight contributed essays on music, others on archæology, Boccaccio, Shelley, notes on architecture, travel-sketches, voyages to Jamaica and Porto Rico. There were essayists of a single essay, poets of a single poem, sometimes composed at Brook Farm, where the poet plucked weeds to the rhythms of Keats and Browning. Some of the poems were obscure, for Transcendentalism had ways of its own. Others suggested Mary and her lamb. Ellen Sturgis Hooper wrote:

> I slept and dreamed that life was beauty,
> I woke and found that life was duty,—

lines that later readers recalled as embroidered on their grandmothers' pillow-shams. Little remained of *The Dial* that pleased these readers, for where it was not too simple it was often vague. Much of it was green and immature. But it stood for a moment of history. It even stood for certain frames of mind, certain ideas and convictions that were to mark Americans perhaps forever.

Meanwhile, Bronson Alcott had settled in Concord. If the world was not ready for him, be it so. It was no mean subterfuge, no ignoble surrender. He trusted in the majesty of goodness and called no man master. What did Bacon say?—"Overt and apparent virtues bring forth praise, but there be secret virtues that bring forth fortune." These were the virtues that they knew in Concord, —"certain deliveries of a man's self" that have no name or fame. Alcott was not to be embittered if the lottery went against him. A blank was as good as a prize, if one

had the equanimity to take it without whimpering or discontent.

It was true, he had no material resources, which made
it hard for his wife and the little Alcotts. The Emersons
suggested that the Alcotts should live with them, forming
a double household, even as Fichte planned to live with
the brothers Schlegel. But the wives of the brothers
Schlegel had not been congenial. Would the wives of the
Concord philosophers have been more so? The Alcotts,
at least, had plenty of apples; and a basket of pearmains
or golden russets, standing on his table, was almost all
that a sage could ask for. Snatch as one might wildness
from the woods, shrewdness from cities, compliments
from courts, one best betook oneself, for sovereign sense,
for subtlety of thought and the joy of colour, for the
graces of diction and behaviour,—

> Where on all sides the apples scattered lie,
> Each under its tree.

And, to fill the little mouths of the Alcott household, to
provide their bread and potatoes, their boiled rice and
grated cheese, Alcott resorted to the spade and saw. He
worked for his neighbours by the day, delved like any
farm-hand, chopped their wood. Wise and friendly eyes
looked on. There was something emblematic in these
labours. They suggested the annual ploughing of the
Emperor of China, and Dr. Channing, who had longed to
witness the union of labour and culture, remarked that
Alcott at the chopping-block was the most inspiring object in Massachusetts. As for Mrs. Alcott, after a good
talk and a crying spell she recovered her usual cheerfulness. Her husband's tatters, she said, were the rags of
righteousness, and there were others in a sadder plight.
Her cousins, who came for a visit, were obliged to bring
their own tea and pepper; but, as soon as the Alcotts

could count on their rice and turnips, they cut their meals down to two a day to provide for the neighbour with the drunken husband. There were those who laughed at Alcott. They said that his intemperate love of water made his mind hazy and cloudy. If he had eaten a little meat or fish, it might have had more marrow and substance. But Emerson, who knew his foibles well, loved him for his copious peacefulness and for the mountain landscape of his mind, with its darting lights and shadows.

He was preordained for the philosophic life, a life which, hospitably taken, was a very simple affair. What did he ask for his wealth and estate? A fireside and a spring, a stream to stir one's blood in the morning, the "frequent cold water" of Agathias, a web of cloth, friends and books, a chosen task, health and peace of mind. For thought, the study; for metaphors, a walk; hills for ideas; for force, a glimpse of the ocean, and over and through all the changing seasons, surcharging mind and body, rendering them primitive and elemental. Fields, streams, groves and country houses, rustic recreations, farmers to talk withal, whose wits were level with the world they worked in. Woodlots, the pleasing homestead, forest paths to foster meditation, alleys and graceful gates opening into a wood. Trees of ancient standing, vines like firm friends and royal neighbours. Orchards of Academe, suggesting the ripest learning of accomplished Greece. A garden, first of all.

> Who loves a garden still his Eden keeps,
> Perennial pleasures plants, and wholesome harvests reaps.

An occupation friendly to every virtue, the freest from covetousness and debasing cares. For the rest, a solar diet. Let the groundlings laugh as they might, they had not heard the word of the Samian sage, "A cheerful and a good heart will have a care for his meat and drink;"

and who knew better than Pythagoras how to preserve one's powers of divination, one's purity and sweetness of disposition, one's grace of form and dignity of carriage? Cherish the justice that animals claim at thy hands, nor slaughter the cow and the sheep for thy food or profit. Shun the succulent flesh that beclouds the soul. Preserve thy taste for wisdom and elegant studies. Good humour, flowing spirits, a sprightly wit, and diffidence as the flower of the rest,—these were the virtues of the Orphic life, nourished by fair water and fragrant fruit, by grains, next in the scale, and medicinal herbs, and roots as a last resort. Nor should one forget the loyal lettuce, by choosing which for a name one of the great families of ancient Rome raised itself to nobility.

The candid Alcott almost wished at times,—pleased as he was with Concord,—that he had lived in the days when groves were temples, when sylvan priests and chaste philosophers, clad in robes of linen, wise in the pastoral arts, plucked their learning from the golden bough or sauntered in the Grecian portico. Towards what was civilization tending? Had it improved upon the state of things described by the rural poets, Virgil, the sweet bucolic, the friend of every honest husbandman, Herrick, Izaak Walton? Were not the fading customs of the Yankee forbears, generous, hearty, pious, better, a hundred times, than these modern ways? What was to be the end of all this pother about steam-boats and telegraphs and railroads?—inventions that ought to be dropped or made short work of, as a squirrel dispatches a nut, that the intellect might be won to worthier occupations. For himself, he proposed to live as if the golden age had come again, or, rather, as if it had never ceased to be. Let other men follow other patterns, the English gentleman or the Roman statesman. His was another model, better drawn by Iamblicus than Plutarch. Virgilian Concord afforded a setting for it.

It was true, he had done his best, with ill success, to fabricate a more extensive Eden, the colony at Harvard village, Fruitlands. Cheering news had come to him from England, as he toiled away at the saw and the scythe. His educational theories, abhorred in Boston, had found supporters in that older world. A school had been established in his honour, Alcott House, near London. The masters had invited him for a visit, and Emerson had gladly filled his pocket with a purse of golden sovereigns. But what could anyone expect of England, choked as it was with smoke and cynicism? The school had died in its cradle; and Emerson's friend, Carlyle, had behaved like an angry peasant in the presence of the man of herbs and onions. Alcott, with potatoes for his breakfast, mixed his strawberries with them, till the juices ran together on his plate. The sage of Chelsea dropped his knife and fork and stormed about the table in disgust. Alcott, blithe as ever, had brought the "English mystics" home. One of them, Charles Lane, had a little money, enough to buy the land at Harvard village, and he brought his library with him, in all a thousand volumes, a notable collection of mystics and poets, Pindar, Alcæus, Quarlcs, Spinoza, Behmen. They planted their Eden with high hopes, to restore the Orphic life in its pristine beauty. Austerity was to be the note of Fruitlands, though not without a touch of continent mirth. Persons fit and few, twelve at the outset. At early dawn, the silent reveille. Libations, baths, morning walks alone, music,—for Lane had brought his violin,—melodies to subdue the passions, anger, despondency, complaint, dancing of a composed and Doric order, to pacify distempers of the soul, rural rites, repasts of native grains, water, herbs and fruit, to the end of edifying the healthy body. Labour, attractive labour, after the fashion of the *Works and Days,* with the spade and the glistening sickle. For raiment, canvas shoes and linen tunics. Conversation of an interior kind.

A life that knew no indurating toils, but such as Adam's family might have known, with a little advanced instruction.

Seven beautiful months, of mingled leisure, labour, recreation,—the whole of a grasshopper's lifetime, as the plodding ants made haste to say. For ants and busybodies have no love for these green isles in the sea of platitude. Then the December blasts swept through the paradise lost. Charles Lane took refuge with the Shakers. Alcott turned his face to the wall. For three days he refused to eat; then he arose, new-born, and went back to Concord. Was he going to waste his life, that fine essence housed in the handsome dust? He who possessed the richest gift of heaven, the power of contemplating eternal things? And the joys of earth as well,—the names of the herbs, for instance, that so refreshed him, mint, fennel, sweetcicely, celandine, dill, caraway, lavender, thyme? He could make poverty interesting, with Mrs. Alcott's highly skilled assistance. His journal was a resource. For income, he could count on Conversations, at Emerson's house, later perhaps in Boston. For ennobling and refining the manners and senses, there was no discipline to be compared with the Socratic dialectic, under the wise care of a thoughtful instructor. The dollars, few enough, were yet sufficient to enable him to refuse to pay his taxes,— $1.50 a year,—to a government that protected slavery and was plainly misbehaving on the Mexican border. Alcott was overseeing the children's lessons when Sam Staples, the constable, his neighbour, regretfully came to say that he would have to carry him off to jail. "Very well, Samuel," said Alcott, "if you will wait a moment till Mrs. Alcott can put some food in a basket." The prison fare was too rich for him. Mrs. Alcott brought the basket, and down they walked slowly to the jail. At the door the matron met them and said she was very sorry but Mr. Alcott's cell was not made up yet. "Very well,

Samuel," said the sage. "I will go back and resume the children's lessons, and when you want me you can come for me." In the meantime, Squire Hoar paid the taxes, with no regard for principle whatsoever.

One might have supposed that in Concord the philosophic life would be understood. But, no, these Roman fellow-citizens were as hard-headed as the other Yankees. They smiled at Cranch's drawing of the indolent magus, lying on the sofa, with a copy of *The Dial* on the floor, and his wife sitting beside him, blacking his boots. But suppose they had seen Alcott,—who did not wear boots but canvas sandals,—on the steps of the Boston Court-house, when the mob attempted to seize Anthony Burns. There he stood, at ease, cane in hand, calm as Plato in his portico, another Grey Champion, come from nowhere, to vindicate the honour of the State. No one, indeed, denied his courage, he who had been the first, with Samuel May, to shake the hand of Garrison, lodged for the night in the jail in Leverett Street, with the marks of the rope about his neck. And there were Greeks in Concord along with the Romans, who, for the rest, prized the antique virtues. For one, besides Emerson, there was Hawthorne, who had rented the old Manse from the Ripley family,—although Hawthorne had the darker temperament which Alcott regarded with suspicion. Alcott had a passion for the blond complexion worthy of those who, in times to come, were to preach the mystical virtues of the Nordic race. Blue eyes and fair hair, he thought, were signs of the angelic type, determined in a former state of existence, while the dark eye and the swarthy face betokened the demonic, a remnant of the brute in human nature. But Hawthorne, who had married his Sophia, was obviously, by disposition, friendly, the helpless victim of his twilight mood, with a tender and hesitant voice: and Alcott soon forgave his dusky air. He, too, had come to Concord by a natural

attraction that seemed to reside in the tranquil atmosphere. He was like the wise man of Plato, who resolves
to stand aside under a wall, shielded from the wind and
storms of dust, and keep still and mind his own business.

He, too, had his Eden at the Manse, under the silvery
mosses, where he was writing—living as he wrote—*The
New Adam and Eve*. Sophia, with her ever-busy paint-
brush, had worked a miracle there. The dim, dusty, dismal priestly dwelling had vanished at her touch, under
the yellow-papered walls, behind the bronze jar filled
with ferns, the gift of Margaret Fuller, the vases of
dewy rose-buds, the dishes of golden apples and purple
grapes, the floods of morning sunlight. At night, in the
soft rays of the hanging lamp, the lovers read their
Shakespeare or gave each other lessons in German; or, if
the evening was mild, ran races up and down the drive,
in the light of the moon streaming through the ash-trees.
They were up at sunrise to watch the dawn. Then Sophia
painted for an hour or two. She decorated the beds and
chairs with outlines after Flaxman,—Endymion, Venus
rising from the sea,—while Hawthorne groaned in his
study. They dined on bread and milk, with a little fruit,
and Sophia danced beside the music-box.

Now and again, Sophia went away, to spend a few days
with the Peabody household, and Hawthorne gladly took
the vow of silence. He trudged through the snow and
slush, with his rolling sailor's gait, never speaking a word
to man or dog, perhaps on his way to the village reading-
room. Sometimes the snow on the drive was untrodden
for weeks by any foot but his. He read the tales of Tieck,
Voltaire for the sceptical note, the dash of salt one's
fancy had to have, in a world so full of reformers, Rabe-
lais for a little well-fed humour. The ghosts had followed
in Hawthorne's wake and sometimes forced themselves
on his attention. He had no use for these apparitions, but
they were a part of his aura, provided for the pleasure

of his guests. It was Mrs. George Hillard, not himself, who, as they sat together on a Sunday morning, felt the touch on her shoulder, and Hillard who heard the rustle of the silken robe passing through the room. He was the ghost himself, at times. More than one caller at the Manse, charmed by the gay Sophia, saw him gliding swiftly through the entry, with his hat over his eyes. He was not unwilling to be thought uncanny. It served him as a shield and palisade.

As he went for his early swim across the meadow, beyond the flags and rushes, or strolled in the winding wood-paths, or worked among the crook-necks in the garden, admiring their graceful shapes, happy visions coursed with airy tongues through his enchanted brain. The summer days were full of bright conceptions, tinged and streaked with darker hues, gleaming in his mind like the butterflies that danced in the air about him. He was writing stories of a larger sweep than his earlier tales and sketches, and some of them were equally sombre, filled with a pervasive sense of evil, the snake that lurked even in Concord gardens. The more he had seen of reformers, and saw them still, drifting about the village, moths attracted by the Concord Pharos, the Emersonian beacon, the more aware he was of the pestilent serpent that ate the very eggs of Reform itself. The human heart,—there was the sphere wherein the original wrong subsisted of which the crime and misery of the world were merely outward types. Reform from within, in Goethe's sense: that was the only kind he understood. Was not any plan, ignoring this, destined to prove a chimera, a masquerade, like Brook Farm itself, dissolving before one's eyes like a summer cloud? Not that he was hostile to the reformers. He had joined the Brook Farmers in all good faith. He had worked at the farm in a practical way. Hawthorne was not the man who hoed up the corn and carefully formed the hills about the burdocks. It was another member,—no doubt, some executive genius,—who milked with one hand, while he held the cow's tail with the other. Hawthorne had the common sense that men of imagination usually have, when they deal with these affairs of Caesar. He had toiled like a dragon, as Ripley said, until he had begun to ask himself what part in his own economy these feats of the barn and dung-heap represented. He had not become a vulgar sceptic. He did not think that what the socialists wished was to change the ocean into lemonade. But he had brooded, brooded, sitting by himself in the hall of the Hive, after the day's work, holding a book before him, while the young people gossipped in the moonlight. He had been meditating at the picnics, under the maple-trees, watching the masques of Comus. There was a worm in the rose-bud of life, a grub, unseen by the others, at the root of the tree, as at the roots of all these touching endeavours to perfect the social man. If the human heart were purified, then, and then alone, the evil shapes that haunted the outer sphere, and seemed almost the only realities, would vanish. They would vanish of their own accord.

There was the poet's function. Who but he could reach the heart? His task was to rouse the imagination, creating magnetic images of the nobler world in which his own imagination dwelt. As for the world that lay without, the system against which the reformers protested, what could it mean to Hawthorne? No one had less faith than he in the gods that his countrymen had set up for worship. In *The Hall of Fantasy,* for instance, he ridiculed the god of machines. He pictured a great world's fair where all the new machines were shown, one for distilling heat from moonshine, one for condensing mist into building granite, one for transforming the sunset clouds into dyes for women's dresses. Hawthorne was not deceived by Feathertop, the citizen his countrymen admired, the solid

man of politics and business, living in good repute, never
seeing himself, never seen, as what he was, a scarecrow.
Hawthorne's were the eyes that satirized, in *The Procession of Life,* the shallowness and falseness of the clas-
sifications imposed on men by society, the artificiality of
the badges the world considers genuine characteristics
and that hide the true relations of human souls. No one
knew better than he the failure of a man like Everett
who, misled by vanity, acclaimed by all, had abandoned
the scholar's vocation in order to become an empty name
that brawling parties bandied to and fro. No one said
more clearly that the individual seizing of land and gold,
of benefits that all enjoy and all should have their share
in, was a trait of undeveloped intelligence. No one was
more ready than he to rid the world of its trumpery. This
was the point of his tale, *Earth's Holocaust,* retold a dozen
times by H. G. Wells. The Titan of Innovation was
Hawthorne's invention. The earth groaned under its burden of rubbish, and the titan set a match to the pile. He
threw into the bonfire all the old title-deeds, the royal
crowns and robes, the bonnets and faded finery, the guns
and battle-flags, the headsman's axe, the guillotine, the
gallows, even the marriage-certificates and the Bibles,
certain that, after the holocaust was over, everything
would be found among the ashes that really deserved to
survive.

Hawthorne was ready for any change, in social customs, politics, modes of worship, trusting that better
systems might result. He had the American taste for
innovation that characterized the reformers themselves,
as he had the American habit of restlessly moving, wandering to and fro like the palmer-worm that knows no
single diet or abode. Old houses and antiquated customs
charmed his imagination, but he dwelt on the poisonous
influences that gathered about them. That towns should
be purified by fire every fifty years was one of his fixed

opinions; and who delighted more than he in the fresh paint that covered the walls of the Manse? But of what importance, after all, were Hawthorne's views and habits? He scarcely thought of the world as real, either to be seen or touched or lived in, or, for the rest, altered or improved. It was a film on the breast of Maya, the goddess of illusion. No plummet could ever sound the depths of Hawthorne's scepticism. He felt that, in so far as the world existed, it should wish not to exist. It should recline its vast head on the first convenient pillow and take an age-long nap. For himself, he was happy enough, living as if in eternity, happy as Drowne, who made the wooden image, in this brief season of excitement, which had been kindled by love.

The music-box at the Manse belonged to Thoreau, Henry David Thoreau, the pencil-maker, Emerson's *protégé*, who had gone to Staten Island for a visit, to tutor the children of Emerson's brother William. It was a gift of Margaret Fuller's brother to the youthful poet-naturalist who, as one of his friends said, was "getting up a nose like Emerson's." Hawthorne had skated with him on the river, wrapped in his long cloak, and marvelled at Thoreau's dithyrambic dances and Dionysian leaps over the ice, while Emerson pitched along in the weary rear. Hawthorne had bought from Thoreau the fisherman's dory, green with a border of blue, the "Musketaquid," in which Henry and his brother had spent a week on the Concord and Merrimac rivers. Thoreau had changed his name. Dr. Ripley had christened him David Henry, and he had reversed these appellations, after the Concord fashion. For Emerson had altered the name of his wife from Lydia to Lidian, Alcott had revised his native Alcox, and Hawthorne, years before, had inserted the *w* in his father's "Hathorne." This practice of the Concord authors symbolized their love of independence and, better still, their love of euphony; for

all these Concordians were Pythagoreans, and the followers of Pythagoras have a taste for pleasing and musical names.

The green dory, moored among the reeds, lent itself
to other excursions. Hawthorne loved to drift in the indolent river, watching the reflections in the water. They
were composed, like pictures, far more lovely than the
stark and upright landscape. The leaves of the over-
arching boughs attuned his thoughts with their quiet
sound. Sometimes he drifted further, on a little rowing
journey with Ellery Channing,—William Ellery Channing, the poet, another of the doctor's nephews,—who
dropped in at the Manse, now and then, with an armful
of novels and reviews. For Ellery Channing, too, had
come to Concord, drawn there by Emerson's presence.
He had married Ellen Fuller, Margaret's sister, and
taken the red cottage off the turnpike, on Ponkawtassett
Hill. Ellen had opened a school for little children, and
Ellery, half in earnest,—for he was "chiefly engaged in
doing nothing,"—made shift to cultivate his acre of land.
He preferred to smoke his pipe, read his seventeenth-
century folios, stroll with his dog and write an occasional
poem; for this racy talker, this lover of landscape-
painting, this woodsman second to none, this learned
farmer, who exchanged quotations in Greek while others
did the ploughing and the planting, had sworn that he
would never desert the Muse. He was a professional
poet or nothing, and he had contributed to *The Dial*
more than anyone else. Some of his poems, *The Wood-
man*, *The Swallow is Flying Over*, the *Epithalamium* of
later years, *The Field-bird's Nest*, *The Spider*, were
among the best of the Concord school. Light in touch,
natural and lucid, with passages that were worthy of
Cowper or Wordsworth, they were touched with magic
here and there. Everyone remembered Channing's line,—

If my barque sinks, 'tis to another sea.

The Lonely Road was a fine poem. Native wood-notes wild, in every sense, these poems were the despair of Channing's friends, who felt that if he had only taken pains he might have been able to write immortal verses. Emerson edited his first collection, as he had edited Jones Very's sonnets. Channing was to be known in later years not so much for his poems as for a prose volume of the rarest charm, *Thoreau, the Poet-Naturalist.** He had struck up a friendship with Thoreau, the best Greek scholar in Concord, and had soon become his only crony. He made himself agreeable to Hawthorne.

This Ellery Channing was a moody soul, erratic as the sky in early spring, gay as a troubadour, full of salty gossip, then suddenly reserved and enigmatic. He had always been a problem, and was to be, during the sixty years he lived in Concord, with various "disappearances," outliving all the other Concord worthies. A typical Boston eccentric, quite unlike the usual crooked stick one saw in the village streets, he was perverse and unstable enough. He was a thorn in the side of the Channing clan. He had refused to take his degree at Harvard and had wandered off to the West. He lived in a log hut, which he had built, in northern Illinois, on the prairie. He had studied law and flitted East again and flitted back again to Cincinnati, where he had met and married Ellen Fuller. Margaret was much disturbed, for she had little hope that her sister would ever be happy. Why had he come to Concord? He laughed at the "gigmanity" of Boston, but he laughed still more at the rustic village ways. He would rather have settled, he said, on the icy peak of Mount Ararat. He would have liked a villa in the Euganean Hills, or in Florence, or in Malaga or Cuba. He swore at the cook and damned the butcher. He fell into

* Properly to be read in the final edition, 1902.

dark rages that lasted for days. He passed one on the
street with a stony look. Nobody dared to question him;
one had to deal with him at arm's length. He seemed to
take pleasure in hurting his friends. Then the sun would
break, and Ellery nodded and smiled again, smoking
away and joking as he smoked. He came and went like
the summer clouds, professing not to know where he had
been.

Ellery Channing and Hawthorne went fishing up the
river, sometimes turning into the Assabet. There, in a
silent cove, they drew the boat up under a leafy bower,
kindled a fire with pine-cones and driftwood, spread their
supper out on a moss-grown log and tired the sun with
talking. For Hawthorne liked to expand at times and fly
away on the wings of speculation, and Ellery's whimsical
prattle broke over the stillness of the wood like eva-
nescent spray.

CHAPTER XV

THOREAU

IN EMERSON'S white house on the Boston turnpike, Henry Thoreau had taken up his quarters. He occupied the room at the head of the stairs, a little room, but he was a little man: his nose and his thoughts were the biggest things about him. Emerson, and especially Emerson's children, had formed a warm affection for their difficult Henry, difficult, that is, for the rest of Concord but a treasure for the household of a sage. He was short, lean, frail, although nobody guessed it, he was so tough and muscular, with a meagre chest, long arms falling from the collar-bone, a workman's hands and feet, a huge Emersonian beak, rather like Julius Caesar's, bright blue eyes and flaxen hair. He walked with the swinging stride of an old campaigner. His manners were of the homespun sort, different indeed from Emerson's. But, after the first encounter, one perceived that, if Henry Thoreau was a thorn-bush, he was the kind that bears the fragrant flowers.

He was the son of the pencil-maker, who had his little house and shop on Main Street: "J. Thoreau and Sons." The Thoreaus were a mercantile family of small pretensions who had seen better days. They were well-connected in the Channel Islands, where the French Thoreaus were prosperous wine-merchants. Their maternal forbears, the Scottish Dunbars, had taken the royalist side in the Revolution. As a barefoot village boy, Henry had driven the turkeys and the cow to pasture, and Emerson had vaguely heard of him as a poor student at Harvard. He had written to President Quincy, suggesting Henry's name for a scholarship. Later, Henry walked in to Boston, eighteen miles from Concord, to hear Emerson speak, and walked home again after the lecture. Emerson, touched by this, was still more touched when, after one of his Concord lectures, his sister-in-law, who was boarding with Mrs. Thoreau, said to him, "Henry Thoreau has a thought very like that in his journal." A friendship had soon sprung up between them, and when, one day, the Emersons went on a picnic, to the Cliffs on the Concord river, they asked Henry to join them and bring his flute. The village people looked askance at him because he was so pugnacious. He had queer ideas about teaching school, refusing to use the ferule; for with children and simple folk he was always gentle. With others, he was obstinate and harsh. He liked to administer doses of moral quinine, and he never thought of sugaring his pills. He had withdrawn from Dr. Ripley's church with a thesis more defiant than Martin Luther's. He liked to speak of a cold spot as "sultry," and he had a way of calling the woods "domestic." But at boating and camping he was a master-woodsman, skilled as Ulysses, shrewd as any fox. The redskins had forgotten the arts he knew. Arrowheads and Indian fireplaces sprang from the ground when he touched it. He charmed the snakes and fishes. Wild birds perched on his shoulder. His fingers seemed to have more wisdom in them than many a scholar's head.

This young Briareus of the hundred hands was something more than Emerson's factotum. There was nothing he could not do in the matter of painting and papering, building walls, repairing chicken-houses, pruning and grafting fruit-trees, surveying, tinkering, gardening. But these were trifles in his bag of tricks, useful to pay his way in the world and justify his creed of self-reliance. He was a master of other arts that Emerson also knew, and a scholar of unusual distinction; and he wished to be a philosopher, not a mere thinker of subtle thoughts but one who, loving wisdom, lived a life that was simple, magnanimous, free. In fact, he recalled those ancient sages who, when an enemy took the town, walked out of the gate empty-handed, without a care for the morrow. Why should one be burdened with impedimenta? Henry liked the soldier's life, always on the stretch and always ready for a battle. Each of his mornings brought its strenuous sortie. He lived "for to admire and for to see." He had spoken his mind in his college themes about the "blind and unmanly love of wealth" that actuated most of his fellow-beings. The order of things, he said, should be reversed. The seventh should be man's day of toil, wherein to earn his living by the sweat of his brow; he should keep the rest of the week for his joy and wonder.

These views delighted Emerson. In fact, the two agreed on so many subjects, always with an edge of difference, that one might well have supposed the relation between them was that of master and pupil. Emerson was fourteen years the elder; and it was true that Henry had acquired some of his traits and mannerisms: his handwriting, his voice, even his nose seemed to have gone to school to Emerson. There was something contagious in Emerson's aura; everyone was affected by it, nobody seemed able to resist it. Alcott was more than a little Emersonized; and as for Ellery Channing, what did the lady say who heard him lecture?—that his gait, his inflections, the very turn of his eyebrow were Emerson to the life. Henry Thoreau had felt this influence, as he had felt the influence of Carlyle. He had his own form, none the less. Emerson and he had grown in Concord, as two flowers grow in a common bed, one of them larger and more luxuriant, the other with a much more pungent odour; but they stood in different corners of the bed, with an ample space between them, so that the breeze could blow upon each of them freely. They were different enough in temperament, as in their personalities; and Henry phrased their common points of view with a sort of acidulous accent that was never heard on Emerson's lips.

They were of one mind in a dozen matters, not least in regard to the reformers. "As for these communities," said Henry, expressing their joint opinion, "I had rather keep bachelor's hall in hell than go to board in heaven." Much as he liked Alcott, the "best-natured man" he had ever met,—"the rats and mice make their nests in him,"—he turned up his nose at Fruitlands as well as at Brook Farm. He meant to bake his own bread in heaven, and wash his own clothes there. And suppose, he said, these grievances do exist? So do you and I. And the universal soul prefers the man who sets his own house in order first. A foul thing, this "doing good," observed the contemptuous Henry, instead of looking after one's own life, which ought to be one's business, taking care to flourish, and taste and smell sweet, refreshing all mankind. He had had encounters with reformers that filled him with abhorrence. They would not keep their distance. They tried to cover him with a slimy kindness that fairly took the starch out of his clothes. These "lovers" of their kind were almost more injurious to their kind than the feeble souls that met in drawing-rooms, fabulating and paddling in the social slush, and going to their beds unashamed, to take on a new layer of sloth.

Henry had plenty of acid in his composition. He had taken a few suggestions from Zeno the Stoic,—for one, that he had two ears and a single mouth, in order to hear more and speak less,—as Alcott had followed Pythagoras and Emerson, largely, Plato. Emerson, older and riper, with a fund of sunny benevolence, the fruit of a happier culture and a fortunate bringing-up,—Emerson deplored this hedgehog's posture, the spikes, the spines, the quills

that made his Henry a John Quincy Adams of the village.
But time would certainly soothe and rectify him. Meanwhile, he was a living illustration of all his own ideas, endowed with hands and feet. Henry described himself, or
his hope for himself,—"stuttering, blundering clodhop-
per" that he said he was,—in words that seemed to have
their truth already. He was prepared for a glorious life;
he had laid out an avenue through his head, eight rods
wide; he had got the world,—much more, the flesh and
the devil,—as it were by the nape of the neck, and held
it under the tide of its own events, and let it go down
stream like a dead dog, till he heard the hollow chambers
of silence stretching away on every side and his own soul
expanded and filled them. He could not help taunting his
fellow-Yankees. Seek first the kingdom of heaven! Lay
not up for yourselves treasures on earth! What does it
profit a man! Think of this, Yankees, think twice, ye who
drone these words on the Sabbath day and spend the
other six denying them! "Doing a good business!"—
words more profane than any oath, words of death and
sin. The children should not be allowed to hear them. If
most of the merchants had not failed, and most of the
banks as well, Henry's faith in the laws of the world
would have been sadly staggered; for what was the
sweetest sight his eyes could see but a man who was
really fulfilling the ends of his being?—maintaining himself, as he could, if he wished to do so, paying the price
in terms of simplification, by a few hours a day at manual
labour. Was he a little impatient and a little narrow? If
there was anything wrong with his angle of vision, there
would always be plenty of others to correct it. For himself, he wished to live deep. He wished to suck out all
the marrow of life, to cut a broad swath and shave close,
to put to rout all that was not living. If the days and the
nights were such that he greeted them with joy, if life
emitted a fragrance like herbs and flowers, if it was more

elastic and more starry, that was his success and all he
asked for.

No use to pretend that, for Emerson, he was a balm,
however much a blessing. No, but he was medicinal,—as
a gadfly, good; as a goad for an indolent writer, who
felt that he ought to dig in his own garden, Henry was
even better. As a teacher of natural history, for a lover of
nature who, as a matter of fact, scarcely knew a robin
from a crow, Henry was better still. Best of all, as a
fellow-seeker of wisdom and a man of impeccable taste,
competent to help him with *The Dial,* which Margaret
Fuller could not wrestle with and had asked her Concord
friends to carry on. Henry was a capital editor. He had
a sharp eye for the faults of *The Dial,* the phrases,—
well one knew them,—that had to be pulled open, as one
opens the petals of a flower that cannot open itself. The
style of *The Dial* annoyed him as much as the weak and
flowing periods of the politicians. He liked to see a sentence run clear through to the end, as deep and fertile as
a well-drawn furrow. If only writers lived more earnest
lives, their minds would pass over the ground like ploughs,
pressed down to the beam, like rollers that were loaded,
not hollow and wooden, driving in the seed to germinate.
It was the height of art, in his opinion, that, on the first
perusal, plain common sense should appear,—a law that
gave short shrift to much of *The Dial;* truth on the
second perusal, beauty on the third. One had to pay for
beauty.

The two friends had much in common, in spite of all
their differences. Emerson had never built a boat, nor had
he shared the Argonautic life that Henry had enjoyed
with his brother John,—the John who had built Emerson's bluebird-box,—rounding the capes and sailing
before the wind on the Concord and Merrimac rivers, with
their cotton tents and buffalo-skins, bringing back their
unexpected news of the foreign folk who lived on the

upper reaches. Nor had he roamed over the moors and meadows, with the fishing-rod and gun that Henry loved, before he perceived that it was not for him, as a follower of the Brahmins, to "effect the transmigration of a woodchuck." He was not at home in the wilderness. He could never have whittled a wooden spoon, better than the factories made, to eat his rice with. He could not make a fork from an alder-twig, or a Wedgwood plate out of a strip of birch-bark. Nor, in the matter of teaching school, had he known such good fortune as Henry, who had kept the Concord Academy with his brother John, profiting by Bronson Alcott's methods, taking the children walking, rowing, swimming. But they both liked to lecture at the Lyceum, where Henry acted as secretary, and every citizen who had something to say was expected to give his lecture. Moreover, they loved the same authors. Henry had a preference of his own for works of a local kind, ancient gazetteers, State and county histories, histories of New England towns, farmers' almanacs, agricultural pamphlets, out-of-the-way books on birds and flowers, chronicles of old explorers, the Jesuit Relations, reports on Indian tribes. His mind bristled with antiquarian lore. But when it came to Froissart's bold beauty or Bacon's bolder terseness, to the voyages of Drake and Purchas, to Raleigh and the earlier English poets, there they were both at home. Nothing had attracted Emerson more than Henry's manifest knowledge of Drayton, Daniel, the Fletchers, Cowley, Donne, poets, little known in the eighteen-forties, whose naturalness and vigour Emerson cherished, and who, as Henry said, were as verdurous as evergreen and flowers, rooted in fact and experience, unlike so many florid modern poets who had the tints of flowers without their sap.

They agreed that in literature only the wild was attractive, and that dullness was only another name for tameness,—the wildness of the Iliad or of *Hamlet,* with

something fresh and primitive about it, something am-
brosial and fertile. All the Greek poets had this trait,
wild in their elegance, wild in their conciseness. Henry had
studied Greek with Jones Very, for a time his tutor at
Harvard, as he had studied German with Orestes Brownson, with whom he had spent a winter in a Boston suburb,
tutoring Brownson's sons. Greek was his second language.
He had translated *Prometheus Bound* and *The Seven
against Thebes,* with many pieces of the minor poets,
Anacreon, Simonides, ivory gems of an ethereal beauty
like that of summer evenings. One could perceive them
only with the flower of the mind. How still and serene life
seemed amid these classical studies! Often, walking along
the railway tracks, he listened to the harp of the telegraph-
wires, putting his ear to the posts. Every pore of the wood
was filled with music, and he could find a name for every
strain, every swell and change or inflection of tone in one
of the Greek poets. Often he heard Mimnermus, often
Menander. Emerson had the same impressions when he
listened to his ice-harp at Walden; and Henry, as much
as Emerson, delighted in the Oriental scriptures, which
he read in the French and German versions. The Bible
had lost its bloom for both; but the Vedas, the Bhagavad-
Gita came to Henry like desert winds, blown from some
Eastern summit. They fell on him like the light of the
moon when the stars are out, in the furthest reaches of
the sky,—free from particulars, simple, universal, uttered
with a morning prescience in the dawn of time. What
rhythms, what a tidal flow! Beside these ancient Asiatic
books, with their truths like fossil truths, clean and dry,
true without reference to persons, true as the truths of
science, the literatures of the European countries seemed
to him partial and clannish, presumptuous in speaking for
the world when they spoke only for corners of it. Henry
liked to remember that the barnyard cock was originally

the wild Indian pheasant, such as the poets of the Upanishads knew.

As they worked over *The Dial,* Emerson, with Henry's concurrence, took pains to include some of these Eastern writings. Emerson chose a group of passages which he called *Ethnical Scriptures.* Henry, who had translated for his own amusement *The Transmigration of the Seven Brahmins,* selected some of the Laws of Manu. Emerson also insisted on printing some of Henry's own writings, which Margaret Fuller had had doubts about. Henry was indifferent to publication. The only audience he really cared for was his own taste and judgment. He wished to write well, to warrant every statement and each remark, till the earth seemed to rest on its axle in order to back it up. Hold the bow tight! was his motto. He longed to write sentences that would lie like boulders on the page, as durable as Roman aqueducts. Sentences kinked and knotted into something hard and significant, which one might swallow like diamonds, without digesting. Sentences nervous and tough as the roots of the pine, like hardened thongs, the sinews of the deer. He wrote best when his knees were strong, when the juices of the fruits that he had eaten, ascending to the brain, gave him a heady force. Margaret Fuller had not liked *The Service,* his manual for the spiritual soldier, suggested by the talk about non-resistance of the mealier-mouthed reformers. But his essay, *The Natural History of Massachusetts,* was beyond cavil or praise. Into *The Dial* it went, with *A Winter Walk.* Henry revised and revised, until his page was a mass of blots and blackness.

Into *The Dial* went also some of his poems, the verses that he had ceased to write. These poems were of a homespun kind, well-woven, but indifferently cut, like Henry's raiment, not intended to please. They were sound and scholarly doggerel, for the most part. The smoke obscured the flame, but now and then a jet rose out of the smoke,

and Henry wrote a line or two that shivered its way up
the spinal marrow. Sometimes the smoke itself, in a
handful of lines, suggested by the Greek Anthology, suddenly turned to incense, and the incense became an Icarian
bird, melting its pinions in its upward flight. *Smoke, Mist,
Haze* were lyrics not to be forgotten. Nor could one forget *A Winter Scene,* not Greek but Anglo-Saxon,—

> The rabbit leaps,
> The mouse out-creeps,
> The flag out-peeps
> Beside the brook,—

or, for the iron strings, the lines called *Inspiration,*—

> If with light head erect I sing,—

to the end of the third stanza, or, if one insisted, to the
end of the seventh, but not a syllable further. There spoke
the poet who, for the rest, wrote his poetry in his prose
journal, in blank-books bought on those rare occasions
when he could find a book with clean white pages, not
ruled, as most of them were, for records of dollars and
cents. If his poems were often disjointed, like his prose,
it was because of this habit of journalizing. He jotted
down his paragraphs and verses, a thought or a stanza
at a time, and waited for a cooler moment to patch them
together,—a good way for epigrams, a good way for the
gnomic style, but fatal for the poetry of feeling, and none
too good for prose. He was a methodical journalizer,
much more so than Emerson. He kept his notes as his
father and his father's father, the old French merchant
from the Channel Islands, had kept their business-ledgers.
He had inherited their plodding habits, akin to the sod
as he also was, partaking largely of its dull patience. He
sometimes felt that he was in danger of living for his
journal, instead of living in it for the gods, his regular
correspondents, to whom he sent off daily bulletins. His

journal was a calendar of the ebbs and flows of the soul. It was a beach on which the waves might cast their pearls and seaweed.

These were happy months for the seekers of Brahma, not to be repeated. From Emerson's house, in 1843, Henry went to Staten Island. Later, in 1848, when Emerson went abroad again, Henry installed himself for a second visit, as counsellor and helper of the household, in the little room at the head of the stairs. But, later still, a shadow fell on the glowing intercourse of the two crusaders. Through whose fault but Henry's? His journal teemed with innuendoes against the friend who "patronized" him. Emerson was too "grand" for him. Emerson belonged to the upper classes and wore their cloak and manners. He was attracted to Plato, but he would not have cared for Socrates, whose life and associations were too humble. Emerson would never have been seen trundling a wheelbarrow through the streets. He would have thought it out of character. Henry was a commoner, as he liked to say. He thought there was something devilish in manners, —and Emerson had had no right to praise him.* "One man lies in his words," Henry wrote, "and gets a bad reputation; another in his manners, and enjoys a good one." But what about Alcott's manners, so gracious and courtly, consisting with such artlessness of soul, such frank, open, unaffected goodness? Alcott had no reputation, surely. Was there nothing in beautiful manners but foppery, prudery, starch and affectation, with false pride overtopping all? Was the noble merely the genteel? Henry's notion of the art of living was not too comprehensive. Nor his notion of friendship, either, exacting all and giving back so little.

What he gave was solid. As for the rest, the less cared he. When people spoke of the social virtues, he asked

* "Praise begins when things are seen partially. We begin to praise when we begin to see that a thing needs our assistance."—Thoreau's *Journal.*

about the virtues of pigs in a litter, lying close together
to keep one another warm. As for friends, what were
they, for the most part? Bubbles on the water, flowing
together. Very few were ever as instructive as the silence
which they shattered with their talk. When it came to
sharing his walks, Henry was rather particular. Alcott
served for a stroll, but the real art of walking was beyond
him. He always wished to perch on the nearest stump.
Hawthorne was even more annoying. One led him to one's
loveliest swamp, and Hawthorne stood on the brink, dis-
consolate. "Let us get out of this dreadful hole," he said.
He never even noticed the naked viburnum rising above
the dwarf andromeda. Besides, he said that company was
a "damnable bore." After all deductions, Emerson was
still one's best companion, best but one, Henry's only
crony, the moody, witty, generous Ellery Channing, riding his whims like broomsticks, as naturally capricious as
a cow is brindled, tender and rough by turns, another
social antinomian, even a social outlaw, by his own desire.
He was always teasing Henry about his legs, double legs,
not cork but steel, which ought to be shown at the World's
Fair, he said; and he had a Rabelaisian streak and took
pains to shock the sober Henry. There were strange, cold
pockets in the air of his mind into which one swam unwittingly. One never knew where one stood with him. But
he was crammed with poetry that glittered through the
darkness of his reserve like gems in a mine revealed by
the gleams of a lantern, or flashed, in his happier moods,
like gems in the sunlight. Some of his moods, moreover,
were much like Henry's. He wished to be let alone. "If
you go to the post-office once," he said, "you are
damned."—"No," said Henry, "you are only damned if
you get a letter." For Ellery loved solitude. He would sit
on the Cliffs by the hour, among the lichens. Then, in the
dusk of evening, one saw him flitting past on noiseless
pinion, like the barred owl, as wise as unobserved.

Henry, to be sure, had other friends, with whom he exchanged a few words, perhaps on his way to look for mud-turtles in Heywood's luxuriant meadow. There was old Haines, the fisherman, for one, wearing his patched coat of many colours, who represented the Indian still, "Polyphemus" Goodwin, of dubious fame, the one-eyed sportsman of the Concord river, and the crooked old curmudgeon Ebby Hubbard, dressed in his blue frock. There were the musquash-hunters, poets of the wild, up and out early in the wet and cold, ready for any risk at the call of their muse. They were gods of the river and woods, with sparkling faces,—late from the House of Correction, as often as not,—with mystic bottles under their oilskin jackets. How good of George Melvin to follow his bent and not spend all his days in Sunday School! Henry thanked his stars for George Melvin and thought of him with gratitude as he fell asleep. The gawky, loose-hung Melvin, dragging his feet as he walked, who was such a trial to his mother, pleased Henry like an oak-tree on the hill-side. He was one tribe, and Henry was another; and they were not at war. Henry could not deny that hunting and fishing, in spite of his brahminic preferences, were as ancient and honourable trades as the sun and the winds pursue, coeval with the faculties of man. As for his friends, he had some who were wilder than Melvin, the breams, who nibbled from his fingers, while he stroked them gently and lifted them out of the river, the muskrat that emerged from the hole in the ice. The muskrat looked at Henry, and Henry looked at the muskrat, wondering what the muskrat thought of him,—safe, low, moderate thoughts, of course. Muskrats never got on stilts, like some of the Transcendentalists. Once he conversed with a woodchuck, three feet away, over a fence. They sat for half an hour, looking into each other's eyes, until they felt mesmeric influences at work over them both. Then Henry moved closer and spoke to the woodchuck, in a quasi-forest lingo, a sort of sylvan baby-talk. The woodchuck ceased to grit his teeth. Henry, with a little stick, lifted up his paw and examined it; then he turned the woodchuck over and studied him underneath. He had a rather mild look. Henry spoke kindly to him and offered him some checkerberry-leaves. The woodchuck was one of the natives. His family had certainly lived in Concord longer than the Emersons or even the Hoars.

For the sort of friends who never hurt one's feelings, one did not have to look far. Sometimes, in the midst of a gentle rain, Henry felt an influence about him that was suddenly sweet and beneficent. Every sight and sound, the very pattering of the drops, was filled with an unaccountable friendliness. It was to seek this, and all it meant, that he went for his daily walk, with note-book and spy-glass in his pocket, and the hat with its lining gathered in the middle to make a little shelf, a botany-box. He was another Linnæus, setting out for Lapland, though he did not wish to be a "naturalist." Looking at nature straight in the eye was as fatal as to look at the head of Medusa. The man of science always turned to stone. Henry wished to look at nature sidewise, or to look through nature and beyond it. Too many observations were dissipating. One had to be the magnet, in the midst of all this dust and all these filings. Sometimes he rose at two o'clock, for a walk to the Cliffs, to wait there till sunrise, or to watch the fog on the river. He loved those valleys in the fog in which the trees appeared as if at the bottom of the sea. Sometimes he spent the whole of a moonlight night roaming the lonely pastures, where the cattle were silently feeding, to the croaking of the frogs, the intenser dream of the crickets, the half-throttled note of a cuckoo flying over. The bushes loomed, the potato-vines stood upright, the corn grew apace. One's eyes were partially closed then; the other senses took the lead. Every plant emitted its odour, the swamp-pink in the meadow, the tansy in the road. One caught the peculiar dry scent of the corn, which was just beginning to show its tassels. One heard the tinkling of rills one had never detected before. The moonlight over the village, as one stole into the street, seemed to bring antiquity back again. The church, with its fluted columns, reminded one of the Parthenon. The houses had a classical elegance.

Sometimes, even in the morning, usually sacred to reading and writing, the wind fairly blew him out of doors. The elements were so lively and active, and he felt so sympathetic with them, that he could not sit while the wind went by. His regular time was the afternoon, from two-thirty to five-thirty, the hour for a voyage to the Leaning Hemlocks, along the Assabet river, or perhaps to examine an ant-hill, nearer home. He had observed it the day before, with its little galleries, wide as a match, covered with the sluggish, crawling ants. In the early spring, the stalks and grasses, left from last year, were steeped in rain and snow, and all the brooks flowed with meadow-tea. Then came the May-days of the warm west wind, the dream-frog, leaping, willowy haze-days, when anything might happen and one thought that next year, perhaps, one might be a postman in Peru, or a South African planter, or a Greenland whaler, or a Canton merchant. Better still, a Robinson Crusoe on some far-off isle of the Pacific. Henry sometimes stood under a tree half a day at a time, in a drenching rain, prying with microscopic eyes into the swarming crevices of the bark, or studying the leaves at his feet, or the spreading fungi. He would watch for an hour a battle of ants, struggling on a chip, a black ant with two red adversaries, till the black ant severed the heads of the others, losing its own feelers and most of its legs,—a second Concord fight, no doubt with as just a cause. Or, catching sight of a fox, in some woodland clearing, he yielded to the instinct of the chase, tossed his head aloft and bounded away, snuffing

the air like a fox-hound, spurning the humanitarians and
the Brahmins. For he felt as wild, at times,—he who
preferred a vegetarian diet,—as if he lived on antelope-
marrow, devoured without benefit of fire.

The midsummer days came, when the yellow lilies
reigned in the river. The painted tortoises dropped from
the willow-stumps as he walked over the bridge. The
pickerel-weed sent up its blue and the vireo sang incessantly; the poison-sumach showed its green berries, all
unconscious of guilt, the breeze displayed the white sides
of the oak-leaves and gave the woods a fresh and flowing
look, the rush-sparrow jingled her silver change on the
broad counter of the pasture. Henry sometimes felt, on
days like this, as if he were nature itself, looking into
nature, as the blue-eyed grass in the meadow looks in
the face of the sky. He would stand for hours, up to his
chin, in some retired swamp, scenting the wild honeysuckle,
lulled by the minstrel mosquitoes: for he liked to subject
his body to rougher usage than a grenadier could endure,
and he dreamed of still remoter retirements and still
more rugged paths. He walked to Second Division Brook
and watched the yellow pebbles gleaming under the water-
cress,—the whole brook as busy as a loom, a woof and
warp of ripples, with fairy fingers throwing the shuttle,
and the long, waving stream as the fine result. Just the
place for a hut, with a footpath to the water. Or he
strolled over to Boon's Pond in Stow, when the haze
seemed to concentrate the sunlight, and he walked as if
in a halo, while the song-sparrow set the day to music, as
if the sparrow were itself the music of the mossy rail or
fence-post. Or perhaps along the Price Farm Road, with
its endless green-grass borders, with room on each side for
the berries and birches, where the walls indulged in freaks,
not bothering to run parallel with the ruts, and goldenrod
yellowed the path. On these old, meandering, uninhabited
roads, leading away from towns, these everlasting roads

where the sun played truant, one forgot what country one was in. One waved adieu to the village and travelled like a pilgrim, going whither? Whither, indeed? On the promenade deck of the world.

Days to sit in one's boat, looking over the side, when the river-bottom was covered with plants, springing up in the yellowish water, and little sparkling silvery beads of air clung to the axils of the submerged leaves. Days to watch the pout in his flurry struggling to escape from the turtle that held him. In these few inches of mud and water, what ironies, what tragedies, what growth and beauty! In one's ears sounded the roll-call of the harvest-fly, just as it sounded in Greece, in Anacreon's ode. Henry was amphibious, he felt. He could see himself swimming in the brooks and pools, with perch and bream and pout, and dozing with the stately pickerel, under the pads of the river, amid the winding aisles and corridors that were formed by the stems of the plants. And what a luxury, in a warm September, to muse by a wall-side in the sunshine, cuddling under a grey stone, to the siren-song of the cricket. He could always hear in the atmosphere a fine Æolian harp-music, like the mellow sound of distant horns in the hollow mansions of the upper air. The critics seemed to think that music was intermittent. They had to wait for a Mozart or a Paganini. Music was perpetual for Henry. He heard it in the softened air, the wind, the rain, the running water. To his expanded ear what a harp the world was!—even if another sound reached his unwilling sense in the midday stillness, a tintinnabulation from afar, the rumour of his contemporaries. It was of little moment, in these autumn days, when a young man's limbs were full of vigour, when his thoughts were like a flowing morning light, and the stream of his life stretched out before him, with long reaches of serene ripples. Thoughts like wild apples, food for walkers.

CHAPTER XVI

CAMBRIDGE: LONGFELLOW,
DANA THE YOUNGER, LOWELL

DICKENS had come and gone, with two red roses in his buttonhole. Half the households of Beacon Hill had asked him to call on Sunday, after tea, on the day of his arrival, and share their pews at the evening service. They took him in their carriages to Mount Auburn Cemetery, the favourite Boston drive; and the great Boz dinner at Papanti's Hall, presided over by President Quincy of Harvard,—for Quincy had succeeded Dr. Kirkland,—was the greatest event of the kind the town had seen.

Longfellow had returned Dickens's visit. The admiring Charles Sumner had scattered in London handfuls of *Voices of the Night,* and Longfellow found that he was an English poet, almost as renowned as Tennyson. He found that he was a German poet, too, after another summer on the Rhine, largely spent with Freiligrath, who had translated his poems, and with whom he read the *Kalevala,* the Finnish folk-epic. The Boston and Cambridge authors were multiplying their ties with the world beyond the Atlantic. They visited Maria Edgeworth in her home in Ireland, and the Nortons imported a gardener from the Edgeworth place. They had memories of moonlight evenings with Mrs. Hemans in the ruins of Melrose Abbey. They brought back roots and ivy from Miss Mitford's garden and sent her little boxes of American plants, the fringed gentian and the scarlet lily. Letters sped back and forth between Beacon Hill and Brattle Street and Edinburgh, Geneva, Bonn and Paris.

Fostered by these reciprocities, a mild haze of Europe spread over Cambridge that gradually deepened as the years went on. The customs of Brattle Street grew softer and warmer. At sewing-bees at the president's house, they still preserved the good old rustic ways, the baskets of cake, the flowing pitchers of milk that foamed as cheerfully in the Spartan air as the punch-bowls on the worldly lawns of Brookline. Cambridge was not likely to forget the Washington Elm, the blacksmith's spreading chestnut, about which Longfellow had written a poem; and good Cantabrigians liked to remember that, in the storm of 1815, the last year of the war with England, the English elms had been battered and broken, while the American elms outrode the tempest, proud and free as Commodore Perry's ships. Cambridge was a Yankee village, dyed as deeply in its proper essence as ever the indigo-bird in its native blue. But foreign streaks appeared upon its surface, blending and melting into one another. One heard Spanish songs to the guitar. There were concerts by the "Germania," fifteen young Germans; there were musical parties, with Chopin, Liszt and Schubert, balls with lamps in the trees, flowers and ices. On June evenings, scented with the new-mown hay, one caught under the moon the strains of Pergolesi's Stabat Mater. Hampers of game arrived from England, grouse and venison from the Scottish moors; and many a capacious Cambridge cellar nursed its racks of cool Johannisberger, spread the protecting cobweb over the hock and the wine that might perhaps have been Horace's Massic. Longfellow represented the changing order that blurred the lines of Norton's checker-board.

Longfellow, too, had married a merchant's daughter, fair as a Portland figurehead; and Craigie House, bought for the youthful couple, soon became the rival of "Shady

Hill." There was something Goethean in its air of ele, gant simplicity and space. Never was a poet more calmly happy. He laid out a garden behind the house, shaped like the seven-chorded lyre. Rising early, brewing his own Mocha, standing at his desk by the southern window, he opened the day by translating some lines of Dante. It was like running a ploughshare through the soil of his mind: a thousand germs of thought started up that other-wise might have lain and rotted there. Then came the lectures and the college work. In the afternoon, a horse-back ride or a stroll through Cambridgeport, to the mouth of the river, where the tide-waters spread like the sea, flashing and freshening the air; or perhaps, to slake his thirst for foreign travel, he took the stage to Boston, to the markets, where the colours and scents of the vege-tables in the carts carried him to Italy and France. Or, walking to town for exercise, he dined with Sumner and Hillard at the Parker House, a chance for a talk about Goethe and the subdued tone that he recommended, the best for artists in song as for artists in painting. Some-times he went to Newport, where the sea spoke Italian; often he went back to Portland. There the sea spoke Norse on tempestuous days. The tide gurgled under the wooden piers and softly spread its fans upon the shore, and the sails of the ships gleamed in the vapoury distance. There he recovered his youth, in the beautiful harbour. For, behind the tapestried mind of the Cambridge pro-fessor, filled with European shapes and figures, lurked the Portland boy whose longest thoughts were filled with the Atlantic, the driftwood and the seaweed, the light-house on its rocky ledge, the wings of the gulls and the whitecaps, the clattering hammers in the busy shipyards, piled with timbers of the lordly pine from the deer-haunted forests of Maine.

Now and then, at almost any moment, after a morn-ing's work on his Dante lectures, under his apple-tree, in the rustic seat, or as he rode on the beach at Newport, where *The Skeleton in Armour* had come to him, or stood with his back to the autumn fire, a poem rose in his mind, stanza by stanza, and whipped itself on paper with arrowy speed,—a song or a sonnet, a ballad of the sea-coast, suggested by some event in the morning paper. He had written his *Poems on Slavery* on shipboard, mainly to please Sumner, who had joined the Abolitionists, and much to the displeasure of most of his friends, who wished to let sleeping dogs lie; but *The Slave's Dream* and *The Slave in the Dismal Swamp* were picture-poems with a child's feeling, for indignation was not one of the chords of Longfellow's garden-lyre. Everything that passed into his mind turned into music and pictures. This was the weakness of *The Spanish Student,* the first of several poems in dramatic form without a dramatic moment; but this was the charm of the poems of cities and legends, *Nuremberg, The Belfry of Bruges,* in a generation for which "Europe," even to itself, was only a half-told tale. "Filled was the air with a dreamy and magical light," as of golden leaves and autumn afternoons, for those who, holding the book in their hands, mused over the scenes of ancient splendour that came to life again in the poet's rhymes. *Evangeline,* too, was a picture-poem. No one could forget the Acadian village, the murmuring pines and the hemlocks bearded with moss, the forest scenes, the lagoons of the Mississippi, the haunts of trappers and hunters and *coureurs de bois,* the far-away Indian lodges in sunny clearings, the swaying branches and the rushing torrents. But *Evangeline* was also a story-poem, the roundest and the ripest that Longfellow wrote. The first King Leopold of Belgium caused to be cut on a seal the word Atchafalaya, the name of the lake where the lovers passed each other, each unaware of the other's presence, because "life is like that." Longfellow felt this and conveyed the feeling. It was a feeling that will preserve a poem which has so much simplicity and grace.

Longfellow's mind was never far from the sea. Even on the hills above the valley of Grand Pré, the "sea-fogs pitched their tents." No Massachusetts mind was far from the sea. At one of Margaret Fuller's Conversations, James Freeman Clarke had spoken of the beauty of American ships. Essays, he said, should be written about them, as people wrote of the art of the Greeks, for the ship was the loveliest object in the modern world. The proof of the American search for beauty was the graceful prow and swelling hull, the tall, tapering mast, the shrouds of shredded jet, the bellying canvas and the patron saint who watched the waves from the stem. Ship-building followed the laws of fitness: to bring the form of the ship into the right relation with wind and wave was to find perfect harmony and beauty. Emerson had agreed with Clarke. What New England writer would not have agreed?* Horatio Greenough, the sculptor, when he returned from Italy a little later, exclaimed, as he looked at a clipper-ship, "There is something I should not be ashamed to show Phidias!" The group of Boston men with whom he was talking had never thought of a ship as a work of art. But Emerson and Clarke would have understood him; and so would Rufus Choate. As Choate lay dying at Halifax, looking over the harbour, he said, "If a schooner or sloop goes by, don't disturb me; but

---

* Most of the New England authors wrote well about ships and shipping. See the fine passage on ships in Harriet Beecher Stowe's *The Pearl of Orr's Island* (Chapter XXX): "Who that has seen one bound onward, with her white breasts swelling and heaving, as if with a reaching expectancy, does not feel his own heart swell with a longing impulse to go with her to the far-off shores? . . . On these romantic shores of Maine, where all is so wild and still, and the blue sea lies embraced in the arms of dark, solitary forests, the sudden incoming of a ship from a distant voyage is a sort of romance. . . . What a wonder! There comes a ship from China, drifting in like a white cloud,—the gallant creature! How the waters hiss and foam before her! With what a great, free, generous plash she throws out her anchor, as if she said a cheerful 'Well done!' to some glorious work accomplished."

if there is a square-rigged ship, wake me up." Longfellow shared these feelings, no one more so,—the author of *The Building of the Ship,*—except, perhaps, Richard Henry Dana, who was also living in Cambridge. Dana's *Two Years Before the Mast,* an Odyssey of the days of the brigs and the clippers, when half the American merchant-marine was manned by young New Englanders, was a poem about the beauty of ships. It had opened a new world for story-tellers.

This younger and bolder Dana, the son of the poet, was the boy who had almost lost an ear at school and who had so much to say on the subject of flogging. He was one of the Cambridge boys for whom the old sloop "Harvard," moored in the river, had seemed like a Viking ship. He had practised navigation on the Winthrop duck-pond and sailed away, as a Harvard junior, whose studies were interrupted by failing eye-sight, on the voyage to California that had made the brig "Pilgrim" famous. With all the positive traits that his father lacked, robust and self-reliant,—he had been one of Emerson's pupils,—he was a day-dreamer, like his father, and capable of mystical ecstasies. Returning from the voyage to finish his studies, he had assisted Professor Channing, whose lectures he edited later, and opened a law-office in 1840, the year of the publication of his book. He was already known as the sailors' lawyer, and his office smelled like a forecastle, crowded as it was with men from the ships. He battled like an avenging angel for the seamen's rights and alienated all his paying clients, for the lords of the sea, like the "lords of the loom and the lash," as Charles Sumner called them, did not like a man who called attention to the wrongs of sailors and slaves. Dana, an aristocrat in every sense, fastidious in all his tastes, excelled in the fastidiousness of conscience. He had compiled a seaman's manual to help the sailors in their fight for justice.

He had kept a journal on the voyage and written out his notes at the Law School, and he had read the manuscript aloud to his father and his uncle, Washington Allston. Horace Mann, who had also read it, offered to have it published as a tract if Dana would only add a few statistics, talk a little more about imports and exports, cut the descriptions out, make the book useful, with tables of facts, and draw a moral lesson on every page. Horace Mann preferred the "Rollo" style; but in Liverpool two thousand British sailors bought the book in a single day, and the old connoisseur, Samuel Rogers, said that it had more poetry in it than almost any modern verse. It was the real thing, as the sailors knew, the first book written about the sea, not from the bridge or the cabin, but by one of the hands, one who had shared in the humblest form of sailing. To sail for furs to the Northwest coast was a gentleman's occupation, but it was ignoble to go for hides. This was the current opinion. To say that one saw the horns sticking out of his cargo was the sharpest taunt one skipper could give another.

But a reader did not have to be a sailor to be swept along by the book. One did not even have to know the meaning of a jigger, a bunt or a knight-head, a larboard or a starboard watch, a cross-jack yard or a mizzen topsail. To small-pull a main top-gallant yard, to well it, to twig the fore might mean no more to one's etymological sense than if one were engaged in hunting the snark. The "heave ho" and the "heave and pawl," the "heave hearty ho" and the "heave with a will," the "cheerily, men," while all hands joined in the chorus, blew one's mind awake. The book, like the vessel, leaped over the seas, trembling to the keel, while the spars and masts snapped and creaked; and one felt oneself in a wholesome and bracing climate, with spray and the smell of tar and salt, scrubbed wood, glistening brass, the sunlight glancing on the bright blue waves. It was as taut as a rope from end to end, with sheer high spirits and masculine vigour, with studding-sails alow and aloft, sharp on the wind, and manned by a genius "going strong" and decidedly going somewhere. No one could fail to perceive that the ship was a symbol of life, since the first part of the voyage was spent in getting it ready for sea and the second part in getting it ready for port. The book was full of overtones and symbols, and all the details of the sailor's life were noted with the bold veracity that springs from a heightened state of consciousness, a tension, well controlled and even calm, that passed at moments into exaltation. Such were the moments when Dana, at the helm, witnessed the breaking of day over the ocean, the sighting of the iceberg, near Cape Horn,—the enormous mountain-island, with its dark cavities and valleys, its pinnacles glittering in the sun, rising and sinking at the base while its points nodded against the sky, crumbling, tumbling, thundering in the sea,—or the still, foggy night, near the Falkland Islands, when the dark silence was broken by the slow, long-drawn breathing of invisible whales, drifting to the surface or lying at full length, unseen, beside the ship.

For thirty years and more, in Harvard Square, promptly at eight o'clock every morning, one saw Dana, green bag in hand, waiting for the Boston omnibus. He was always telling tales of the sea; and everyone knew that his book had done as much for the sailors as Dickens had done for the debtors and orphans of England and *Uncle Tom's Cabin* for the slaves. The dream of his life was to make some contribution to international law. He had left far behind him the episode of his youth, with the pumps and white stockings and the white duck trousers, the blue jacket and the varnished hat and the silk handkerchief flying from the outside pocket. Once again only he wrote about the sea, in a little book, *To Cuba and Back,* which was read by tourists in Havana. But he never forgot the tropical nights, the soft trade-wind clouds under the stars, "the seas and floods in wavering morrice moving." He said that he was made for the sea and that all his life on shore was a mistake, that he should have been a traveller, with no profession or home, roaming over the world like a gypsy.

Meanwhile, the son of another Cambridge worthy, James Russell Lowell, who lived at "Elmwood,"—his father's house, the last in Tory Row,—had also appeared as a man of letters. A little younger than Dana, he had similar traits, although he was tethered to Cambridge not by conscience but by an affection for the *genius loci*. With the same animal spirits and boyish charm, he loved the soil as Dana loved the sea. He felt the thrill of the earth under his feet and soaked in the sunshine like a melon. Short, muscular, stocky, shaggy,—his friend William Page had painted him with long blond curls and a pointed beard, a black jacket and a lace collar, as if he were something more than a reader of Shakespeare,—he liked to think that his ear suggested a faun's. He had an air of the world, although he was rather self-conscious, even a little jaunty. He seemed to be pleased with himself and his early success, mercurial, impressionable, plastic; but under the romantic, susceptible surface there was something timid, hard and wooden that was to show in the grain at certain moments. There was a streak of jealousy in him, an irreducible *amour-propre,* an over-hasty zeal for "the niche and the laurel." He was much at ease in all the Zions, and there were those who even thought him shallow and found his self-confident air very provoking. In fact, he was exuberant and impulsive, and, if there was something wooden in him, there was also something rich and buoyant. His fancy was luxuriant. He was the cleverest young man in Cambridge, and even the most intelligent. He had the makings of a first-rate scholar. But his leading trait was a gift of pure enjoyment, whether of books or garden-flowers, walking, talking, smoking, drinking, reading, a gusto that was new in Brattle Street. He was a capital idler. He could lie on his back for days on end, dreaming in the fragrant air or conning some Elizabethan poet. Moreover, he, like Dana, had his trances, every year, when June, from its southern ambush, "with one great gush of blossom stormed the world."

"Elmwood" was the hub of Lowell's Cambridge, the large, square Georgian house with the tall pilasters, the old-fashioned garden, the meadows at the rear, where he liked to pitch hay on summer mornings. There, as a little boy, he had fallen asleep to the rhythms of Shakespeare and Spenser, read to him by a sister who had brought him up, Miss Mary Lowell, one of those Cambridge women who knew a dozen languages and who had learned Hungarian and Polish. He had had hallucinations as a child. Mediæval figures from the *Faerie Queene* had walked beside him on his way to school. He had burrowed among his father's books and rescued from the attic the old prints of Socrates, Plato and Seneca that had adorned his great-grandfather's study. His Latin was as fluent as his English.* To the *Natural History of Selborne,* for which his father had an old affection, he felt especially drawn; and he liked to record the events of the garden, the visits of the cross-bills, the battles of crows and robins. His father had led him out to the barn to watch the swallows on the roof, taking counsel together before their yearly migration, as Gilbert White had noted years before; and he had counted seven orioles flashing about the lawn all at once. He had studied the cedar-birds in the hawthorn-bushes and learned where to look for the king-birds, building their nests in the orchard. He had seen a cherry in full blossom, beside his study-window, covered with humming-birds that had been benumbed by a fall of rain and snow. He knew the plaintive may-be of the goldfinch when it was stealing his

* See the macaronic Latin verses in *The Biglow Papers.*

lettuce-seeds. He had listened to a pair of indigo-birds singing all day long to one another. He had heard the cuckoo strike the hour, like a Swiss clock, through the night.

Along with the birds, in much the same fashion, he had studied the English poets, observing their notes and their plumage. He could remember the time and the place when each of them had flashed into his mind, Landor, for instance, whom he had read in the old arched alcoves in Harvard Hall. He had made a collection of fragments from Rogers and Campbell, who had written of home as if they had lived at "Elmwood." He had been the member of the "band" who had copied out Tennyson's early poems and shown the manuscript-book to the other members, and he had steeped himself in Shelley and Keats,—of whom he had planned to write a life, in the days when Keats was still a morning star,*—till his mind was a music-box of impressions and rhythms. With his philological instinct, a natural Cambridge trait, he liked to trace the origins of words, the earliest use of phrases, the history of archaisms and colloquialisms; and this had led him to study the Yankee speech, which he knew as Tennyson knew the "northern farmer's." He felt that "the tongue of the people in the mouth of the scholar" was the right motto for poets, and the Yankee tongue was in his blood. He had heard it all about him in his boyhood, on muster-fields, at cattle-shows, at noonings in the hay-fields at "Elmwood," when he had sat with the hired men over their jugs of blackstrap, talking in the shadow of the ash-tree. Yankee was his mother-tongue, the tongue that some of his forbears had brought from England, while others had brought the scholar-dialect. He had revelled in the Yankee speech at Concord when, as a senior in college, he had been rusticated and packed

---

* Eighty-five years later, this project was carried out by Amy Lowell, the grand-daughter of Lowell's first cousin.

off thither, to study with the Reverend Barzillai Frost.
The people were forgetting it in Cambridge, but it throve
on the Concord farms. For Emerson, who took him on
strolls to the Cliffs, he had acquired a feeling later. In
fact, he was one of the neophytes who walked to Boston
to hear Emerson lecture and who caught the sound of
the trump in his silvery voice. He was thrilled by one of
Emerson's phrases, "The walls of the mind's chamber
are covered with scribblings, which need but the bringing
of a candle to render them legible." That one should sit
alone and meditate was almost a new idea to a college
boy whose mind was running over with animal spirits.
Emerson appealed to the *exalté* in him. But it was Mr.
Frost, the minister, who excited his fancy in Concord.
Mr. Frost, the rustic Harvard scholar, was reappearing
in *The Biglow Papers,* which Lowell was dashing off in
his usual way, with lucky hits up and down the pages.
The minister was Parson Wilbur. Concord was reproduced in some of the idyllic scenes as well as in the Yankee dialect. This was Lowell's happiest tongue in verse.

With his boyish air and his worldly air, his radical
sympathies and his Tory habits, his antiquarian tastes
and his love of nature, his sudden enthusiasms and his
constant affections, his volatility and his love of puns,—
similes made of Semele,—together with his industry and
patience, his high romantic poses and his zest for old
garrets, desks, pipes and friends, Lowell was a complicated soul who left on the mind not one but a hundred
impressions. He was compact of incongruities, like many
another humorous Yankee, and some of the readers of
his earnest poems were shocked by his inconsequence
when they met him; for, while he had a streak of the
mystic in him, he also had a pantagruelian streak. He was
warm-hearted and cold by turns, as many other men in
Cambridge were. He would rejoice in a friend and snub
him in the next breath. He had a way of setting one

gently right.* Even his spontaneity had a method, for, while he was really spontaneous, he wished to be more spontaneous than he was. He would stop, in the Yard, in the midst of some grave discussion, vault over one of the great stone columns, clap his hands and crow like a cock, and then resume the argument. If, as occasionally happened, he failed to leap the column, he was annoyed. He would keep on trying until he succeeded, saying, with a wry smile, "I commonly do that the first time." One had to be gay, or appear so, in spite of one's forbears. This note of the *voulu,* the factitious, which was marked in his personality, appeared in his poems also. His liveliest effects were often forced, and some of his sublimities as well.† The mixed impression that his poems left, the inconclusiveness of his critical thinking suggested that he had never thought anything out, and that he even felt with reservations. Had he ever found his own "average point," ‡ or made up his mind in regard to any question? There was much of the chameleon in his nature, together with much that was firm and strong. For the solid and even chunky physical frame housed a substantial Yankee, shrewd, enquiring and tenacious, with a mind which, however inconclusive, liked to coil about its acquisitions. Lowell had what the phrenologists called inhabitiveness and adhesiveness. He inhabited Cambridge, he adhered to books. No one "stayed put" better than he. He had a rare feeling for style, though his taste was less perceptive

* Said Howells, "Who in the world ever heard of the Claudian Emissary?" Said Lowell, "You are in Cambridge, Mr. Howells."—Howells, *Literary Friends and Acquaintance.*

† This was what Emerson had in mind when he refused to review Lowell's *Cathedral.* "I like Lowell," he said, "but I think he had to pump."

‡ Lowell described himself when he said, in his *Moosehead Journal:* "It is as hard for most characters to stay at their own average point in all companies, as for a thermometer to say 65° for twenty-four hours together. I like this in our friend Johannes Taurus, that he carries everywhere and maintains his insular temperature, and will have everything accommodate itself to that."

than gustatory. Where others only read, he read with passion. He had a feeling for the romance of letters that only Longfellow shared; and, if one knew his open-sesame, one found within something warm and winning. If one could rise to the charms of Mount Auburn or cap Fresh Pond with a good quotation, if one had something to say for the elms and the willows, or knew how to look at a peewee pursuing a fly, or an oriole building its nest, if one could speak with discretion of Chaucer or Dante and open an Elzevir with affectionate fingers, if one loved black-letter as one loved a meerschaum, or even understood how to be idle, one found oneself at home in Lowell's heart.

Longfellow and he had never met until, one day in 1846, they found themselves together in Lowell's study, the upstairs study at "Elmwood," discussing the anti-slavery question. Lowell was an Abolitionist. This was one of his many tinges, for he was a polychromic nature; but there were various reasons for it. His father and his grandfather had had the Boston negroes on their conscience, and Lowell's young wife, Maria White, a poet like himself,—one of the Watertown girls, a pupil of Margaret Fuller, who had belonged to the "band,"—was deep in all the democratic movements. The two young people had written for the Pennsylvania *Freeman,* and Lowell was contributing a weekly paper to the *Anti-Slavery Standard* in New York. He was full of the zeal of the convert, for all his instincts were conservative. He had ridiculed and satirized in college, like any clever boy, the uncouth ways of the reformers and the causes he was defending now, woman's rights and total abstinence, Abolition, Transcendentalism; and, if he was attacking the Mexican War, respectable Whigs like Prescott also attacked it. But he was in a state of exaltation and found it exhilarating to have an object that was outside and beyond his art. Behind his work was all the moral fervour that characterized a New England boy. His literary facility was surprising. *The Biglow Papers, A Fable for Critics,* scores of shorter pieces in verse and prose were pouring from his mind at once. Four volumes of his work appeared together, in the "year of revolutions," '48. He could hardly write slowly enough to develop his thought; he could hardly write fast enough to record his impressions. Moreover, he was a lion at twenty-nine. He was the "best launched man of his time," as N. P. Willis said. The word had gone round among the reviewers that Lowell was the poet of the future.

Of all the younger writers, he was the most adroit and the most accomplished. He seemed to be a master of all the poetic forms, ode, song, epigram and sonnet, the narrative poem, the elegy, the idyll. Everyone knew *To Perdita Singing, The Rose* and *Rosaline,* as presently *Prometheus* and *Rhœcus, The Shepherd of King Admetus* and the *Ode to France, An Indian-Summer Reverie,* with its charming scenes of Cambridge, especially *The Vision of Sir Launfal.* Longfellow and Poe alone, among the American poets, wrote with the colour and music, the skill and taste that Lowell exhibited in all these verses. His artistry was highly conscious. He had studied all the current models. He was almost as good as Keats and Shelley, as Tennyson, Landor and Hood. The question was, when Tennyson and Landor, when Keats, Shelley and Hood were better known, how much would be left to make a Lowell?—for his poetry, undoubtedly good, seemed to be largely at second hand. His titles, like his poems themselves, savoured of other poets,—so much so that one asked if Lowell's writing was not wholly prompted by his reading. Comparing him with Longfellow, Emerson, Poe, one saw that Poe, like Emerson, was unique, while Longfellow claimed little and pretended little. Longfellow's tone was humble, unlike Lowell's. He seemed to write for the joy of sharing his treasures, as if he were glad to be thought a mere translator, a simple story-teller, a nursery minstrel. This was both disarming and deceptive, for Longfellow had an original mind. He was an innovator in metres and rhythms; he introduced new modes of feeling; he touched his world with a magic that was mild but unmistakable. He had a poetic personality, an individual temperament, tame and even flat as it was at moments, scarcely ever intense. He had his own colour-box and varnish, and all the Longfellow pictures, large and small, bore the signature of the Cambridge artist.* Longfellow asked for less than his due, while it appeared that Lowell asked for more; for, with his greater energy and depth of thought, his air of accomplished maturity, one looked in his work for the signature almost in vain. Lowell took the colour of his subjects, or, rather, of the poets he had absorbed, and only a phrase here and there,—some outburst of New England moral feeling, some reference to American birds and flowers,—broke one's impression that his work was a medley of English poetry. For each and all of his poems, except *The Biglow Papers,* one found a model somewhere in England's Parnassus, in *Locksley Hall,* in *Don Juan,* in *English Bards and Scotch Reviewers,* Browning's dramatic monologues, the *Faerie Queene,* Shelley's *Prometheus,* Coleridge's *France: an Ode,* Keats's *Endymion,* Shakespeare, Gray or Spenser. In fact, to the end of his life, in Lowell's verses, lines cropped out and passages appeared that obviously belonged, in style and feeling, to Tennyson, Wordsworth or Keats.

That Lowell was a sort of shadow-poet, in spite of all his taste and cultivation, became too evident as the years went on. Even at his best, in *The Present Crisis,* that classic of radical orators, he was rewriting *Locksley Hall;* and would he have written *A Fable for Critics* if

---

* To feel the originality of Longfellow's style, one has only to see it reflected in Lowell's *The Changeling.*

Byron had not suggested the form? Tennyson gave him the model for *Sir Launfal,* a touching and popular poem, even deservedly popular, for all its jerkiness and air of haste, as a genuine expression of its time and place, the humanitarian Cambridge of the eighteen-forties. As American poets multiplied, and English poetry grew more familiar, Lowell's reputation slowly sank. Of the splendid mass of Victorian verse, the most bewildering since the age of Shakespeare, could anything be expected to survive that was not entirely fresh? "Desiring this man's art and that man's scope" seemed all too plainly Lowell's state of mind; and that his verse was good, and more than good, with its charming air of literary breeding, that his technical agility was surprising,* that his tone was often noble, all this had to face the final question, What did it add to the sum of things poetic? That it added much to other sums, local, moral, political, hardly affected the question. That the drop of Lowell's reputation implied a holocaust of lesser poets was to be taken for granted. The fact remained that one forgot his poems. One read them five times over and still forgot them, as if this excellent verse had been written in water.

Lowell was scarcely the "maker" he longed to be. He was even a little presumptuous, saying of his "kind of wingéd prose" that it "could fly if it would," when obviously the case was otherwise, since poets always fly when they can. That he was a rhetorician, according to the definition of the poet Yeats,† was closer to the truth. He deceived himself, and his contemporaries were deceived about him. In taking him for a first-rate poet, however, his contemporaries were unjust to what he was. They were no less unjust in taking him for a "radical" poet. It

---

* E.g., *An Oriental Apologue.*
† "Rhetoric is the will trying to do the work of the imagination."— *Ideas of Good and Evil.*

was observed, after his wife's death, that his radical phase rapidly passed; and those who preferred him in this aspect thought of him as a renegade. Three generations later, this view persisted. It was unfair from the first, for the shift in Lowell's point of view might have been taken for granted. Leopards do not change their spots, and Cambridge boys are Cambridge boys even when they marry Maria Whites. The radical note in Lowell's work was a kind of inverse ventriloquism, in which the voice appeared to come from the poet, while actually the speaker was his wife. It was her influence that induced his fervour, for Lowell was highly suggestible, and the influence and the fervour passed together. His radicalism was only a phase that little in his nature sustained or encouraged. It was true that this phase represented his solidest writing. Witness the poem on Garrison and *The Present Crisis,* for all its form was borrowed: witness, especially, *The Biglow Papers.* It was the glory of *The Biglow Papers,*—which made the book almost a folk-creation,—that Parson Wilbur and Hosea Biglow were brothers under their skins. That literate and illiterate in New England met on a common ground of feeling, that they were at one in essential matters, religious and political alike, that their regard for human rights, their hatred of war and false ideas of empire, sprang from their common principle,—this was the burden of *The Biglow Papers.* It was the most profound of Lowell's works because of its instinctive presentation of the folk point of view from which it sprang, for Lowell's moment of radical fervour carried him to the depths of the popular mind.

The Biglow Papers remained as a permanent landmark. No other work compared with it, either then or later, for showing the homogeneity of New England, its common stock, its common faith. But works like *The Biglow Papers* can spring from a divided mind. A heated imagination can produce them, a sudden and momentary dramatic impulse, while part of the man remains in reserve; and a large part of the man remained in reserve in all of Lowell's poetry. For Lowell as a secondary poet, much, however, remained to be said. His brooding love of country was a noble trait. If the patriotic odes of his later years, the *Ode for the Fourth of July,* the *Ode Read at Concord,* the better-known *Commemoration Ode,* seemed, in after times, too much like Websterian speeches rewritten in verse,—one felt in them, too much, the lapsed occasion, the rhetoric that required the proper moment,—passages remained that touched one still and longer passages that convinced the mind how Lowell must have touched those who heard him. *A Fable for Critics,*—at its lowest value, the classic illustration of "college humour,"—was something new under the Yankee sun. No one could know how good it was, how frank, fresh, perceptive, who had not read the critics of the eighteen-forties. Beside the New York and Boston reviewers of the "Independent Press," which Lowell satirized in *The Biglow Papers,* in the series of burlesque notices, *A Fable for Critics* had the virtue that Longfellow's poems possessed in the previous decade. Whatever Lowell promised as a critic, no one could deny that he, with Poe, had opened an era in critical practice: he and Poe were the first American critics to exercise their judgment freely. If, among Lowell's qualities, judgment was the one that developed least, if he was prejudiced and hasty, still *A Fable for Critics* marked an epoch. It formed reputations,—Lowell did not wait till they were formed. It dealt with American letters directly,—Lowell did not wait for English opinions. Aside from this, and *The Biglow Papers,* his descriptive poems were the best. A book of American verse could scarcely omit *An Indian-Summer Reverie,*—

What visionary tints the year puts on,
When falling leaves falter through motionless air
Or numbly cling and shiver to be gone!
How shimmer the low flats and pastures bare,
As with her nectar Hebe Autumn fills
The bowl between me and those distant hills,
And smiles and shakes abroad her misty, tremulous hair!

And what could be more veracious than these lines from
Pictures from Appledore, for another example?—

the blind old ocean maundering,
Raking the shingle to and fro,
Aimlessly clutching and letting go
The kelp-haired sedges of Appledore,
Slipping down with a sleepy forgetting,
And anon his ponderous shoulder setting,
With a deep, hoarse pant, against Appledore.

Everything that was rich and sunny, all that was loving,
strong and true, in Lowell's heart and talent, spoke
through his *Under the Willows* and *The Fountain of
Youth, Sunthin' in the Pastoral Line,* the "June" of *The
Vision of Sir Launfal,*—with every leaf and blade "some
happy creature's palace." The Lowell of May and June
was the joyous Lowell, the poet and the lover, off-guard
for once and all the time, transfigured with the coming
of spring and summer.

CHAPTER XVII

THE BOSTON HISTORIANS: MOTLEY

THE LAST traces of the Doric age were passing away in Boston. The antique severities were gone, along with the floridities of Gilbert Stuart, and a bland and learned elegance had taken the place of the harsh, austere or stately ways of old. The worthies who remembered the Revolution, the open-handed merchants of Stuart's portraits, who had laid down their annual pipe of Madeira, the frugal Romans who, at public dinners, perhaps to celebrate some splendid gift which they had offered to the city, departed so far from their usual rule, when the dessert was passed, as to take three almonds or a fig, the hearty old souls who, at church, sang with might and main, blowing their noses till the rafters rang,—all these types were vanishing one by one. In the old Puritan town, swept by the air of the world, one heard less of Cicero and Plutarch, more of modern Rome than of ancient Rome and much more of London than of Athens.

One by one, the faces that Stuart had painted disappeared from the Boston streets. Judge Joseph Story was dead. So was John Pickering, who had known Chinese and Cochin-Chinese, once so useful in Salem, who had studied the Polynesian dialects and collected the Yankee words and phrases that Lowell had taken up in turn. Dr. Channing had gone before them, in a country inn at Bennington. The frail little invalid's body had been placed in Mount Auburn, while the bell of the Catholic cathedral tolled, as for the passing of a saint; and every good Bostonian wrote in his journal that a generation had been buried with it. For Channing had been the father and bishop of Boston, with a truly paternal love for all that was human. The tomb of the apostle of self-culture, the friend of the slaves and the workers, the scourge of the selfish, whose name had headed all the petitions and who had fought for liberty and grace, was designed by Washington Allston; and Allston, his friend and kinsman, was the next to go. Six hours before his death, he had been working on "Belshazzar's Feast," the unfinished and unfinishable masterpiece. He was carried in the evening to the churchyard, on the edge of Harvard Square, in the flaring light of the torches borne by a crowd of students.

Of the senatorial ancients a few remained, survivors of the old three-bottle days when young men grew up on Pope's Homer, followed the Ciceronian injunctions and fell in love, by candle-light, with damsels who were singing the songs of Burns. Harvard stood firm with President Quincy, that Pharos on a rock; but John Quincy Adams, his noble kinsman, the aged statesman, the aspiring poet, had but a few more lines to write. He still rose at five on winter mornings, groped for his old-fashioned tinder-box,—for he despised the new Lucifer matches,—lighted his candle and fire and took his cold sponge, as once, in the days of his presidency, twenty years before, when he was almost sixty, he had swum across the Potomac and back and walked home under the winter moon. He still toiled over his rhymes and orations, fighting the slave-power, arousing interest in canals and roads, prompting scientific expeditions and founding institutions of research. He had laboured for weeks on a speech on astronomy; he had journeyed to Cincinnati, at seventy-seven, sleeping on the floor of a canal-boat, to lay the cornerstone of an observatory. His hope was to kindle an interest in science in the West. He rejoiced in the spread of German studies, even in Richter and Tieck, who had addled the brains of the young. During the Congressional recesses, one found him at the old house at Quincy, pruning his garden or among his books. Every day, twice a day, one saw him standing in the portico, holding his watch in his hand, timing the rising or the setting sun. And every night, kneeling beside his bed, he repeated, "Now I lay me down to sleep," which he had learned from the lips of Abigail Adams. He had said it every night of his life, in Holland, Prussia, Russia, France and England, in Washington, Boston and Quincy. "I say it out loud always," he remarked, "and I don't mumble it either."

Oratory and history were still the central interests of the Boston mind. The Bostonians had been trained to distinguish the fine points of eloquence; and, as this was still a political Age of Faith, the orators were their tribunes and standard-bearers. The commentators delighted in analyzing the styles of the various speakers,— Webster, whose vocabulary was more Teutonic than Macaulay's and far less Latinized than Burke's, Edward Everett, Webster's under-study, and Rufus Choate, who shared Webster's gift for making his clients feel like heroes and martyrs, so that they wept when he described their actions and saw themselves as Sophoclean figures. Choate was a fiery speaker, witty, weighty, plain and grand by turns, an orator for the thinking few, unlike the mellifluous Everett and the popular Webster. His wit was more than legal. Everyone had heard his phrase about Chief Justice Shaw: * "I always approach Judge Shaw as a savage approaches his fetish, knowing that he is ugly, but feeling that he is great." Thus Choate, when his learned sock was on; and, when he wore the buskin, then from his lips came noble words. Everett was the figurehead of Boston. In the years that had passed since he exclaimed, "Welcome, Lafayette!" and greeted

* The father-in-law of Herman Melville.

President Jackson at Bunker Hill,—placing two cannon-balls in the President's hands, as if this happy thought had dropped from heaven,—he had become the bust on the prow of the ship that beamed upon every passing sail. Who could present the keys of the city, or eulogize a hero or a guest, with more resplendent grace than Everett? No one, facing a crowd of mechanics or farm-ers, could picture the charms of their lot and their occupa-tions with an air that was more engaging or reassuring. He made one feel that all was going well. But Webster was still the unrivalled leader. His eyes were "catacombs of ancient wisdom," as his admirers said, even though his virtue, like stern Cato's, often warmed with wine, was also, and more often, warmed with brandy. Webster had grown sluggish with adulation, and the Fugitive Slave Bill was to drain away much of his local glory. It was not wisdom, it was prudence that dwelt in the catacombs of Webster's eyes; but prudence, after all, was a statesman's business, and Webster had done much to preserve the Union. Moreover, the second Bunker Hill oration had shown that he was still the master-speaker.

The dignity of history and its importance were con-stant themes of Everett and Webster. History was the passion of Rufus Choate, when it was not law or Massa-chusetts, and in his fine speech, *The Age of the Pilgrims,* he expressed the feeling about the past, the origins and greatness of New England, that filled the minds of the younger writers.* The stream of historical interest

---

* Another of Choate's speeches, *The Power of a State Developed by Mental Culture,* expressed the feeling of renascent Boston. Choate liked to think of the boast of Themistocles, that he knew how to make a small State a great one,—by making the State wise. How was Massachusetts to main-tain its lustre, with its young men drifting westward? Was it destined to fade as the nation grew? Massachusetts had it in its power to retain its intellectual leadership. People had thought too much of banks and cotton, and far too little of the culture that made Athens paramount in Greece, moulding the taste and opinion of Greece and Rome, then of the modern world. This was all that Massachusetts needed to hold its place, and more, in the future.

spread wider and wider. Everett's most attractive trait
was an eagerness to help his fellow-scholars, even
political enemies like Bancroft. On his journeys abroad,
he collected notes for Prescott, examining the libraries
of Paris and Florence, the Guicciardini and Medici family archives, the reports of the ambassadors of Venice,
the archives of Vienna, and interested Metternich and
the Marquis Capponi in the efforts of his Boston friend,
learning much that served himself, no doubt, in his own
diplomatic career. He exerted his influence to obtain for
Bancroft, whose history was advancing from volume to
volume, the use of collections of letters and papers in
England, although he had broken with Bancroft and
sent back his own letters, as if to put an end to their
relations. With a spirit like this prevailing in Boston, all
the historical writers advanced together. Before the end
of the forties, Sparks, Bancroft, Prescott and Ticknor
had published a dozen new volumes, Richard Hildreth
had written his *History of the United States,* John
Lothrop Motley, a younger student, had set to work on
The Rise of the Dutch Republic and Francis Parkman
had written *The Oregon Trail.* Hildreth, a prolific journalist, had shown imagination in a novel, *The Slave, or
Memoirs of Archy Moore,* which he had written in Florida, a book that thrilled the younger generation. He was
the spectre of the Athenæum, the tall, grey, silent man
who had been seen for years haunting his alcove, but who,
in truth, was very far from spectral. He was a blunt,
hard-headed hater of shams. He detested the "patriotic
rouge" of Sparks and Bancroft's pyrotechnics. His history, soberly good, was rather tame, a colourless work
in six large volumes, written in a plain business style. It
carried the story down to 1820 and pleased the conservative and the matter-of-fact. Entirely free from Bancroft's
nonsense, it also lacked Bancroft's picturesqueness, as
well as the charm of Prescott; and it lacked the original

documentation that made these other historians important.

In Beacon Street, lovely in October, overhung with
golden elms, with crimson creepers on the balconies, Prescott had built a new house, facing the Frog Pond and the
fountain. Over the drawing-room, he arranged his study,
a lofty apartment reached by a winding stairway through
a secret door behind a book-case. There he kept, over the
mantel, crossed, the swords of his father's father and his
mother's father, who had fought on opposite sides in the
Revolution, the swords that Thackeray saw, when he
visited Boston. These swords suggested to Thackeray the
idea of *The Virginians,* the story of the brother who
fought for the king and the brother who fought for
Washington. Prescott spent hours there, under the portrait of Cortez, the busts of Washington Irving and
other friends, turning over his manuscripts, the twenty
thousand folio pages, gathered from every corner of Europe, the books that had come by ship from Cadiz. He
had been idle for a while, after his first great effort. He
had earned an interlude for loafing. He played blind-
man's buff with his guests and children. He amused himself with his cats, for he often had a cat in his lap. He
visited Niagara Falls, the wonder of the world in the
eighteen-forties, where every traveller was baptized
again with a touch of Byronic emotion. In summer, he
went to Nahant and Pepperell, where he kept up the old
family farm. As much as his eyes permitted, he read
Cooper and Dumas, who refreshed his mind. He thought
for a time of writing a life of Molière.

Then plans had risen in his mind, shoots from the stock
of his Spanish studies. Why should not he, like the
Spaniards, gather gold in Mexico and the Andes? Everything combined to push him forward. His blindness, his
cheerfulness, his frankness, his youthful high spirits, his
engaging mind had caught the imagination of other

scholars. Guizot, Mignet, Thierry, Lord Holland and Milman, Humboldt in Germany, Navarrete in Spain plied him with offers of assistance. Irving, hearing that he was at work on the exploits of Cortez in Mexico, his own cherished theme for many years, on which he counted for his bread and butter, gladly gave him the right of way. With all these well-wishers working for him, there was nothing for Prescott to do but to go ahead. Much as he loved Dumas, Marcus Aurelius was his favourite author; and Alfieri's example roused the spark. No need to look for the drama in his subject. The drama of *The Conquest of Mexico* shaped itself; and to use, in building the story, he had eight thousand sheets of manuscript, beautifully copied from the Spanish archives, all the original documents, diaries, letters, never yet published, never even seen, except by a few chroniclers and amanuenses. He had Navarrete's manuscript collection, dealing with Peru and Mexico. The Spanish Academy helped him. The old Spanish families opened their chests of papers, which no other writer had asked to see. Thierry sent him books. The Spanish minister in Mexico City sent him information about the Aztecs. Four copyists in Madrid gathered materials for him. Another friend delved in the British Museum. To study the trees and the birds, the landscape and the customs of the country, which had not greatly changed since the days of Cortez, he did not have to go to Mexico. Madame Calderon de la Barca, who had lived as a governess in Concord and for whose *Life in Mexico* Prescott wrote a preface, filled the lively letters that she sent him with sketches of Mexican scenes and manners, enough to satisfy Humboldt, who knew the country, that the half-blind Prescott had also seen it. There was enough diplomacy involved in gathering the materials for his work to have founded a small republic.

No need to rope himself to his chair, as Alfieri was

obliged to do. He found it easy, in the zest of work, even to master mathematics, which had always baffled him before and which he had to know to characterize the astronomy of the Aztecs. He read various books of martial exploits, Voltaire's *Charles XII* and lives of Columbus and Hannibal. Then he set the stage with a panorama of Montezuma's empire. From the moment when Cortez, burning his boats and landing at Vera Cruz, began his march to the capital, the story moved on to its final result with the frightful inevitability of some drama of nature. The Aztecs, like the Incas, in *The Conquest of Peru,* the work that rapidly followed, were painted as the chroniclers had seen them. Their "feather-cinctured chiefs and dusky loves" were a little operatic, for no archæologist had as yet revealed the reality of these builders of civilizations that crumbled under the terrible feet of the Spaniards. But generations passed before anyone challenged the truth of the picture that Prescott drew of the conquest, grandly in the Mexican book, only less grandly in the tale of Peru,—shorter, slighter, much less unified, as the little black ruffian Pizarro was a lesser man than Cortez. Pizarro's conquest was achieved at once, and the rest of the story was an anti-climax: Prescott had to create his drama out of the sordid squabbles of the seekers of gold, who were little better than bandits. *The Conquest of Mexico* was a natural epic, while all that gave unity to the other work was that the characters were few. But everything that Prescott wrote had the same solidity, and he told these two great stories with an air of effortless ease. Massive but alive in all their parts, they were full of colour and vigorous movement. They were partly composed on horseback. Prescott mentally wrote the final chapter in a gallop through the woods at Pepperell.

While these two books were under way, Prescott and George Ticknor were always together. Ticknor was also at work on his *History of Spanish Literature,* lingering over it with such affection that he could hardly bear to part with it. Ticknor had grown more and more important, with his imposing house and his great position, of which he was by no means unaware. It was he who occasioned Longfellow's remark that "every Bostonian speaks as if he were the Pope." His large head was "full of cold brains," to quote his own phrase about William Godwin; and the more he advanced in life, the more his voice became an affront to strangers. He was a useful citizen, however, the builder of the great collection of books in the Boston Public Library, Prescott's friend and confidant, indeed the willing friend of every scholar. On his second visit to Europe, after resigning his professorship, he had been received in every quarter with the *éclat* of an ambassador. Humboldt had greeted him as an old acquaintance. He had visited Lamartine and Guizot, spent a happy evening with Sainte-Beuve, discussed philological questions with the blind Thierry, passed two days with Wordsworth, and met the youthful Ruskin, who had shown him the beautiful drawings he had made from nature. With his history constantly in mind, he had consulted countless men of letters and formed a lasting friendship with the model scholar, the Crown Prince John of Saxony, who was translating Dante into German. In Dresden, the prince had invited him to hear Tieck read aloud from his translation. The listeners followed, with the original text, and, at the end of every canto, gave their candid comments on the version. This incident was to have its consequences, for when, years later, in Cambridge, at Longfellow's instigation, the Dante Club was formed, the members, who were all friends of Ticknor and had undoubtedly heard him tell the story, followed the same procedure. Ticknor had travelled through Europe with his own coach and footman and four post-horses, very much *en prince;* and at Rome, at the Princess Borghese's, he might have joined six cardinals at whist, if a Boston man could have played on a Sunday evening.

With many of these scholars and men of letters, he kept up a regular correspondence. Milman, Hallam, Pasqual de Gayangos were always on the watch for information that might serve him in his great work. Everyone knew that he was writing it, and he could taste his glory in advance; for the universal success of Prescott's writings indicated what his own might be. But might it not be with him as it was with Gibbon, after his task was accomplished,—would he not find the days long and empty and life short and precarious? He had laboured on the work for twenty years, removing all the traces of his lectures, growing more fastidious all the time, verifying his facts again and again, weighing every authority, more and more indifferent to publication. Great was his reward when it appeared, in three handsome volumes. It was the literary event of 1849, the one book of the year that Macaulay recommended to the Queen. There were not six men living who were competent to review it, as one of the possible five remarked, and Hallam, who was another, said that it could never be superseded by any writer who was not a Spaniard, or even by any Spaniard, unless there was a radical change in Spain. Its erudition was impeccable. It was firm and clear in composition. Everything that knowledge and will could give the work possessed in overflowing measure, and edition followed edition, and translation translation, long beyond the day of Ticknor's death; for it always lay open on his study-table, ready for new revisions. He liked to remember what was said of Plato, that, even when he had passed the age of eighty, he combed and curled and braided the locks of his writings. The limitations of the work were the limitations of Ticknor himself, a lack of the spontaneity and imagination that Prescott had so amply. It was cold and hard in tone and treatment, the fruit of a carefully trained intelligence that never knew the madness of the poet.

Years later, Francis Parkman, the strenuous man of genius, a half-blind semi-invalid like Prescott, but with an explorer's or soldier's instincts, deplored the lifeless scholarship of New England,—"void of blood, bone, sinew, nerves and muscle." * It was not Prescott that he had in mind; scarcely even Ticknor. He was referring to Everett, whom he described as the most finished example of this devitalized scholarship, "with many graceful additions." He might have chosen John Gorham Palfrey, that other *North American* writer, the author of the *History of New England,* which appeared a few years later than Ticknor's work,—a man of multitudinous occupations, Everett's successor at the Brattle Square church, Andrews Norton's successor at Harvard, editor of the great review, postmaster of Boston, member of Congress, a "Christian lawyer" in his theology, a theologian in his literature. A Puritan of an earlier day, in type, without the fire that burned in the ancient settlers, unimaginative and unmagnetic, a kindly, modest, conscientious man,— recalled by Henry Adams, in his *Education,* with various pleasant phrases, as one of the members of his father's circle,—he was an active Abolitionist. Along with Dana and Sumner, he endured the sneers and snubs of Ticknor and his State Street friends. He was a thorough and trustworthy scholar, and he spent more than thirty years writing the well-known history, which long remained the authority in its field. It was a monumental work, in five large volumes. If it was almost wholly political, this was the author's intention; it was not too provincial in its point of view; it was written in the firm historical style

---

* According to Parkman, this was the result of an old New England custom. In households of small means, the privilege of going to college usually fell on the son whose feeble health unfitted him for ruder labours. The "narrow-chested hectic Benjamin" was chosen for the sedentary life, with sad results in the world of books and thought.

which all the Boston writers had developed in common. And yet the vitality of the work was low. Students were obliged to consult it, but few could have relished the adventure.

Boston, however, which had produced a Prescott, brought forth another writer in the eighteen-fifties whom readers were to enjoy for generations. John Lothrop Motley, the son of a merchant,—who wrote some of the *Jack Downing* letters, those of the second series,—had much in common with his predecessor. Born in similar surroundings, a few years later, in one of those households where Scott was the staple of reading and Irving and Channing were read as American classics, Motley was a high-spirited boy of whom the last thing to be expected was the drudgery of a scholar's life. Tall and graceful, with hyacinthine hair,—so handsome that Lady Byron, when she saw him, said that Motley looked more like her husband than any other man she had seen,— impetuous, wilful, rather vain, decidedly supercilious, he had an air that suggested a thoroughbred horse when he flung back his head and a wild look flashed in his eye. He was plastic and fickle, or appeared to be so, too clever to be industrious and too fastidious for a dull routine. He had learned to read French easily at eleven, and had studied German with Bancroft at the Round Hill school. He had entered Harvard at thirteen. Wendell Phillips and T. G. Appleton, better known in later years, had been his best friends as a boy. Every Saturday afternoon, in the garret of Motley's house, the three friends, dressed in cloaks and doublets, had acted impromptu melodramas. Pretending that they were bandits and heroes of Byron, they spouted scraps of poetry to one another.

All these three boys played later parts that had associations with the Motleys' attic. There was a strain of the actor in Wendell Phillips, T. G. Appleton was always Byronic, and Motley's love of costume and dramatic effect,—he had made and played with miniature theatres also,—appeared in his writings from first to last. Prescott, at the same age, dressed in a helmet and breastplate at the Athenæum, had shown the same romantic tendency, common enough in boys but not so common in historians. Motley had gone to Germany to study, like Ticknor, Longfellow, Bancroft and so many others. At Göttingen, where he made a translation of *Faust,* he had lived in the closest intimacy with Bismarck, whose "dear Jack" he remained for two generations, perhaps the closest of all Bismarck's friends, the one to whom he wrote with least constraint and whom he always welcomed with the warmest affection. They took their meals and exercise together. Bismarck rejoiced when Motley sat with his red slippers thrust out of the window; and Motley, in *Morton's Hope,* his first novel, left a picture of Bismarck,—peppered all over with freckles, scarred, with an eyebrow shaved, in his chaotic coat, without collar or buttons, and with his iron heels and portentous spurs,—that showed his early skill in descriptive writing. Later, in Motley's diplomatic years, when Bismarck still sang the American songs he had learned from his friend at Göttingen, the two saw much of one another, and Bismarck recalled that Motley had "never entered a drawing-room without exciting the curiosity and sympathy of the ladies." By the time he was twenty-seven, when he went to St. Petersburg as an attaché, he had met Prince John of Saxony, Ticknor's friend, the Goethe family at Weimar, Tieck, who was translating Shakespeare, and Guizot, who wrote an introduction to his *Dutch Republic,* in the French translation which he supervised. Years before, Cogswell had sent to Goethe's daughter-in-law an essay that Motley had written on Goethe while he was still in college. She had replied, "I wish to see the first book that young man will write." On Motley's second visit to Weimar, Ottilie von Goethe had heard of his

novel, but he refused to tell her the name of the book.
No one else expected much of Motley. He had studied
law, which he never practised; he had interested himself
in politics and even served a term in the Legislature. But
this had led to nothing, and *Morton's Hope,* the novel
he had published, showed little promise. It was a childish
fantasy, carelessly written, with no regard for probabili-
ties. The scene was laid half in Boston, before the Revolution, and half in the Göttingen of Motley's time,
between which the hero spent his youth. The pictures of
German student-life had a certain air of reality,—the
aesthetic tea-party, for one. They were merry enough in
tone, with happy strokes here and there; but the author
did not seem to be in earnest. In the garden of "Morton's
Hope," a Brookline house, built by an old China merchant, the lizards "shot to and fro in the patches of sunlight." Young Morton, however, was Motley himself.
He, too, burned with dreams of glory. His inflammable
nature was filled with a boundless ambition. If he had not
breakfasted with a pen behind his ear, or dined with a
folio as big as the table, he had longed to write history,
like Morton. He, too, had devoured the English poets,
from Chaucer and Gower downward. immersed himself
in Latin chronicles, read every historical work that he
could find, in German, French and Spanish, and all the
books to which the notes referred; and, whatever the
book was, on whatever subject, he had planned to write
a better one himself.

Merry Mount, Motley's second novel, was a very different affair, although no one seemed to know it, then or
later. It was a charming picture of early New England,
in its more Arcadian aspects, a fantasy of the greenwood, the story of Morton's crew at Wollaston. Hawthorne had sketched the theme in his *Twice-Told Tales,*
which Motley had refrained from reading, in order not
to confuse his own impressions; and *Merry Mount,* in

some of its scenes, might have been written by Hawthorne. It pictured the dim, unsettled time, at the dawn of Massachusetts history, when various men who seemed like apparitions, as they flitted through the early chronicles, played parts that later historians had forgotten. Who were those pale and misty figures, Blaxton, the first settler on the site of Boston, Morton and his comrades of the may-pole, wanderers from Elizabethan England whom the colony harboured in its sylvan depths? The forest scenes, the hawking scenes, the scenes in the woodland fortress, the portrait of the hermit of Beacon Hill, of Miles Standish and the giant blacksmith, of the mysterious knight, Sir Christopher Gardiner, were Motley's reply to the question. There was an element of historic fact behind every detail of the vivid picture, and it was all suffused with a glow and feeling that brought back the Shakespeare of *As You Like It*.

Meanwhile, in the middle eighteen-forties, Motley wrote a number of essays for the *North American Review*. One of these papers, on Balzac, who had begun to be widely read,—Hawthorne, for instance, had read him,—made a great stir. It was a lively defense of the artist as man of letters, the sort of defense that Poe was making and that Hawthorne might have made, but that, in fact, had not been made by any other writer in New England. Motley envied the French their freedom of speech, praising Balzac for his disregard of ordinary notions of the "nasty" in his passion for detached observation. In this he agreed with Fanny Kemble, who constantly protested, when she lived in Lenox, against the silly prudery of American women, which took the life out of novel-writing. This prudery, a recent thing, at least in circles that knew the world,—for the Boston folk of old, like other Americans of an earlier day, rejoiced in Fielding and Smollett, who spoke their own language,—was to spread like a film for generations over the work

of the novelists, to break in the end with a vengeance
that might have been foreseen. Motley had registered his
protest, and he had carried it further. He praised the
detachment of Balzac as the proper attitude of the artist
in letters, and he uttered a phrase that resounded
through New England, "Certainly the world should be
reformed, but not by novel-writing." Few readers
thought of novelists as artists, in spite of Hawthorne's
presence and example; and Motley, following Prescott,
was soon to show that history also was a form of art. For
Motley, whose early motives had been confused, had
embarked on historical writing. His essay on Peter the
Great, perhaps suggested by his year in Russia, first revealed his gifts in this direction.

The essay appeared in 1845, when the rage for Carlyle was at its height, and Peter the Great was a typical
Carlyle hero. This "strong, silent man," who had carved
a nation out of a Scythian wilderness, who had tried to
Europeanize Russia and turn it into a modern civilization, who "preferred to go to the ocean rather than wait
for the ocean to come to him" and who raised his capital
in the northern marshes, was another Oliver Cromwell,
in his way. Better still, he was an empire-builder, one of
the men who "do" things and who were doing them for
the Anglo-Saxons in all the four quarters of the globe.
He was even, one might have thought, a Russian Yankee,
an Abbott Lawrence on a larger scale, this prince who
worked as a carpenter, in his apron, in a shipbuilder's
yard at Amsterdam, learned his trade from the bottom
and laid down and built, from his own draught and model,
a sixty-gun ship. Peter was a Portland or Salem hero, the
kind they understood in the Yankee seaports, the self-
made man *nulli secundus,* the sort that makes things hum,
who had made Russia hum like another New Hampshire,
multiplied by two or three dozen Maines. Motley, like
Carlyle, admired the type, much as he disliked its brutal

aspects, those that Carlyle came to admire the most. It represented what the age called Progress. Motley did not labour the point. Perhaps he was scarcely aware of it. But, shorn of its barbarian elements, this was the type that had built his own republic.

What was the history of this type? Where had it first emerged? How had it emerged from the mediæval world that held it back? At what point in the history of Europe had the enterprising man declared himself, demanded the free institutions that gave him scope, cast off the burden of privilege? Where had the merchant, the burgher, the craftsman, the sailor, the builder of civilization in its modern form, the man who believed in freedom of thought and action, first come to grips with the old regime? In Holland, where Peter the Great had learned his trade and the Pilgrim Fathers from England had found a refuge before they sailed for America. Just why Motley chose the history of Holland none of his friends knew. When his essay on Peter the Great appeared, they felt that history was his real vocation, and one of them found him at work, soon afterward, with a huge Dutch folio and a dictionary. He had turned to another use than novel-writing his art of painting scenes and characters, but few could have seen the connection between the history of Holland and the history of the American republic. For Motley, the United Provinces, in their struggle to liberate themselves from Spain, suggested the struggle of the United States. William the Silent, for him, was a prototype of Washington. But behind this political aspect, there was another. In celebrating the rise of the Dutch Republic, Motley was celebrating the modern man, the American type in its first historic appearance.

This was the larger meaning of Motley's work, the motive, scarcely expressed, that gave him his vast popularity. It was the tendency of all his writing. American readers felt that he was defending their kind of man,

almost as much as Bancroft. For the rest, they were interested in Holland. It was a camp of the Pilgrims, it was
the battle-ground of Protestantism, it was the home of
many of their forbears; and Holland had been the
laughing-stock of Europe long before America became so.
Motley had not chosen the theme, which had become his
life-study. He felt that the theme had chosen him, before
he knew that Prescott was planning to cover almost the
same ground. Prescott, to whom he described his design,
treated him as kindly as Washington Irving had treated
himself in a similar situation; he welcomed Motley's
rivalry and even thought of giving him the manuscripts
he had gathered for himself. Motley had hoped to write
his book at home. In fact, he had begun it at Nahant, in
an old house in the village street, overhung by two great
willows, where Longfellow later spent a summer. Prescott's presence gave Nahant an atmosphere for historical
writing. Motley did not know, when he undertook *The
Rise of the Dutch Republic,* what hours of dusty labour
lay before him.

It was ten years before the book appeared, years that
were largely spent in Dresden, Berlin, the Hague and
Brussels, where Motley worked obscurely in the archives,
turning up almost as many unpublished papers as Prescott
had read for his Spanish histories. These were the
original documents, in all their native crabbedness, not
neatly copied as Prescott's were. Thousands of them had
never been read by any Dutch historian, and sometimes
they were indecipherable.* Motley felt, at times, as he
toiled in the subterranean depths of black-letter folios in
Latin and German, as if he were working in a coal-pit,
grimy, dark and cheerless. His life reminded him of a
Dutch canal, slow, silent, stagnant. But the novelist in
him never slept, as he fed upon the musty mulberry-

---

* Motley's work was instrumental in stirring the Dutch historians to publish these original documents.

leaves of which he was afterwards to spin his silk. At night, as he walked the streets of Leyden and Brussels, he lived over the scenes of the day's reading and seemed to see Egmont and Horn, Granvelle, the Duke of Alva and William of Orange in the ghosts that flitted over the moonlit squares. In one of his letters, writing of Rubens, who did not appear in the *Dutch Republic,*—one of the weaknesses of the book, in fact, was that it omitted all mention of the flowering of Dutch and Flemish art,—he showed his delight in the glowing colour that appeared in his own writing. His friendship with Bismarck, mean-while, whose career he watched with a natural interest and rather more benevolence than the case required, sharpened his understanding of the European statecraft that formed the principal theme of all his volumes.

In later life, as minister to Austria and England, Motley was immersed in politics. *The History of the United Netherlands* and *The Life and Death of John of Barneveld,* in which he continued his unfinished series,—for he planned to tell the story of the Thirty Years' War,—were all too much concerned with statesmanship. At least, they were little concerned with anything else. They were largely compilations of documents, like Bancroft's later volumes. Where was Dutch life, one might have asked, the life of the people, their art, their thought, their customs, in the history of the United Netherlands? Even in *The Rise of the Dutch Republic,* one found too little of the common scene, in its multifarious aspects, for which the battles were fought and the statesmen existed. Only the great individual interested Motley, and, generally speaking, only the man of action, although the escape of Grotius, in *Barneveld,* was one of his liveliest episodes; and his psychology was so simplified that his great men were supermen or devils. His William of Orange was a boys' hero, his Philip was a nightmare. The characters he understood the best were those whom he might have met in Boston; for the lawyers, manufacturers and bankers who founded the Dutch Republic were such as he had known in his father's circle. John of Barneveld would have felt at home with Amos and Abbott Lawrence, Webster and Choate. These were types that Motley knew, and his imagination scarcely moved outside their burgher atmosphere. His sympathies were all with oligarchies, such as the Essex Junto had represented,—a legal and commercial world. He had little feeling for the people, and less for saints, poets, artists and thinkers. But Motley was a preëminent story-teller. For sheer narrative power, the dense, moving mass of the *Dutch Republic* stood with the greatest of its kind; and some of Motley's scenes and incidents,—the executions of Egmont and Horn, the defeat of the Spanish Armada,—were destined to live with the best of Prescott and Parkman.

CHAPTER XVIII

DR. HOLMES

MEANWHILE, the son of another historian, Dr. Abiel Holmes, had made his appearance as a poet. As far back as 1830, Oliver Wendell Holmes, a young student of the Harvard Law School, who was soon to abandon law for medicine, had written a poem called *Old Ironsides*. He had composed it with a pencil, standing on one foot in the attic of his old house in Cambridge. The battle of Bunker Hill had been planned in this house, and one saw the dents of the muskets on the floor. The frigate "Constitution," in the Boston navy-yard, was about to be dismantled and abandoned. The poem, reprinted on hand-bills from a newspaper in Boston and scattered about the streets of Washington, saved the ship and made the poet famous.

He had "sneaked in," as he later said, in the same year with Tennyson and Darwin, the man of science and the man of rhymes whose natures he was to share in equal parts. His father, a moderate Calvinist, had still defended the faith of Jonathan Edwards, who said that little boys were more hateful than vipers. Against this faith the son was to fight with the diligent wit of a doctor who knew that such ideas were very harmful. But the father, kinder than his creed, a lover of books and the art of living, was also a poet in his fashion. One evening, when the children were in the parlour, he had stepped to the frost-covered window and sketched on the pane with his knife-blade a cluster of branches and stars. Above, he had written, *Per aspera ad astra*. The family had come from Connecticut, but they had Boston connections, enough to cause a boy to feel that he was one of the boys with the family portraits. Among these portraits was one of Dorothy Quincy, about whom Holmes was to write a poem. Another of his forbears was Anne Bradstreet, the old New England poetess whose blood ran in the veins of so many writers. Wendell Phillips was one of his cousins. Others were the Channings and the Danas.

To the end of his life, the rhythms of Moore and Pope, softened and sweetened in Goldsmith, were to ring through Holmes's poems, together with those of Byron, Hood and Campbell. These were the favourite poets of the Cambridge household. He had gone to the little school in Cambridgeport, where his younger cousin, Richard Henry Dana, had had so much trouble with the master. One of his fellow-pupils was Margaret Fuller, who was always reading "naw-vells," as she called them, and whose long and flexible neck looked like a swan's,—that is to say, if one liked her, for it looked like a snake if one didn't. But he had learned something from Margaret Fuller. He happened to see one of her themes, which began with the phrase, "It is a trite remark." Having learned that trite remarks existed,—for the word was entirely new to him, —he was better prepared never to make one. He found it easy to elope from school to see Revenge and Prospect on the race-course; for, although he loved learning as he loved his country, he also loved horses, observing that, wherever a trotter went, he carried in his train brisk omnibuses, lively bakers' carts, and therefore hot rolls, the jolly butcher's wagon and the cheerful gig. Every New England deacon, Holmes reflected,—the more he had occasion to study the species,—ought to see at least one Derby Day to learn what sort of a world it was he lived in.

After he had won his degree at Harvard, in the class of 1829, and having dropped the law for medicine, he

found his father eager to send him abroad,—equipped with
a good Dutch liquor-case, filled with six kinds of strong
waters,—to study for a year in Edinburgh, the favourite training-school for American doctors, and two years
in Paris. The class of 1829 included the author of "My
Country, 'Tis of Thee." Holmes had his own ideas about
this poem,* but he thought the class worthy of endless
odes, to warm and hearten its members,—other people
were not obliged to read them,—odes and odes, stretching
from decade to decade, till the poet himself had reached
three score and twenty and the first line had to begin,
" 'Tis sixty years since." As for the years in Paris, aside
from all they meant for a medical student, they sharpened
the wit of this ingenious Yankee, confirming the natural
bent of his mind as the softly romantic sentiment of the
Rhineland confirmed Longfellow's natural bent. For the
rest, the evenings at the Trois Frères, when the Chamber-
tin or the Clos Vougeot came in, and the Scotch-plaided
snuff-box went round the table, had their effect on a mind
that loved gracious living and was to claim the rights of
gracious living on behalf of his somewhat frost-bound
countrymen.

Certainly, a good slice of Paris sandwiched between
two slices of New England created a sense of contrast
that enlivened his critical spirit. With other scenes in mind,
the returning pilgrim observed the well-known vista in the
high relief that is always the fruit of comparison. He observed its lovelier aspects and other aspects that were not
so lovely,—for instance, the acidulous Yankee voice, acidulous and stridulous, bred by commercial habits, east
winds, a lean soil and too much enterprise. The young
medical student never forgot the soft and liquid inflec-

---

* "Sam Smith will live when Longfellow, Whittier and all the rest of us
have gone into oblivion. And yet what is there in those verses to make
them live? Do you remember the line 'Like *that* above'? I asked Sam what
'that' referred to. He said 'that rapture'!" And Holmes made one of his wry
little faces.—See M. A. DeW. Howe, *Memories of a Hostess.*

tions he had heard in France, so winning, so delicious, with so much woman in them. The voices of the brave Yankee girls,—too often at least, he thought,—would not be among the allurements the Enemy would put in requisition were he planning another assault on Saint Anthony's virtue. But most of his impressions were happy enough. He had said to himself, with joyous confidence, in Florence and Pisa, as in the streets of Paris, "I am a Cambridge boy!": and he was to remain a Cambridge poet. His lays were

> of one whose natal star
> Still seemed the brightest when it shone afar.

They dealt with the homeliest facts of the Yankee world, washing-day, the spinning-top, the katydid, the gale, the dinner-bell, the oysterman, the churchyard, the family portrait, the unmarried aunt, scenes and subjects touched by a fresh and original mind, however composed in forms that English and Scottish poets had made familiar. Well he knew how to dress the fable

> in which genius poured
> And warmed the shapes that later times adored.

However this genius seemed in times still later, it was a revelation in a day when foreign writers ruled the imagination. It evoked, for the Yankee ear and eye, the train of associations that made it classic.

The medical student soon became a doctor, established in a modest street in Boston. He also became a professor at the Harvard Medical School; and, as if to enlarge his field for the study of human nature, he gave Lyceum lectures in the country towns on some of the English poets, Wordsworth, Keats, Shelley, Moore. For his animal spirits superabounded,—his curiosity likewise. He kept a rattlesnake in a cage to study its manners and habits. He kept a little gold in his house, to handle now and then, in order to analyze a miser's feelings. He was known to have inhaled a dose of ether, to record his sensations and thoughts. In Springfield and Pittsfield, where he spent his summers, they liked to see the lions and hear them roar; and the doctor, who belonged to the lion family, as one of its younger members, was willing to be seen on all occasions. He was a poet laureate by avocation, always prepared to present his bouquet at a banquet or an ode at a county fair. He knew the vexations of lecturing all too well, the cold parlours, the cold apples and water, the cold beds in the cold hotel bedrooms, the cold congratulations of the committees, to whom his remarks had given "satisfaction." He was placarded and announced as a public performer and saw his name stuck up in letters so large that he scarcely dared to appear in the town by daylight. Well he knew the dangers of lecturing, too,—for he was aware of everything: one would have had to get up very early to take the doctor in,—the danger of talking down to muddier wits, the danger of shaping one's thoughts in a popular mould. How often the lecture-platform was a slippery slide down to the Avernus of the windy bores. But, if you knew yourself as your maker knew you, knew even that you had your vanities, and if you knew where to draw the line and picked out the most intelligent faces, and talked only to them, lecturing had its rewards for a student of human nature. One learned, for instance, the law of averages. Two Lyceum assemblies of five hundred each were much the same in Springfield as in Boston, and perhaps the doctor would have added Paris. And one learned to know the tribe of the Pooh-Poohs, so called from their leading expression. No doubt this tribe served a useful purpose in keeping down the noxious animals, the thinking, or rather talking and writing ones. Beyond this, they were of small value; and they were always retreating before the advance of knowledge, facing it and moving backwards, with their inextinguishable war-cry, Pooh-Pooh!

A good corrective, lecturing, for a mind a little too ready to think a little too much of its own time and place. Nor was this the only egg that was dropped into the doctor's intellect by the solemn fowl Experience, fed by so many crumbs from the lecture-platform, a fowl which, amid its idle cacklings, sometimes cackled in earnest. One of the doctor's whims was to think of all New England, and even all America, as a large and friendly boarding-house, a house with an ample breakfast-table, at which, for a number of years, he found himself appointed to preside. The role of an autocrat had been thrust upon him, for had not fate endowed him with a luminous mind, the same fate that had endowed New England with a hunger and thirst for knowledge? Well, what an opportunity these lectures gave him to study his fellow-boarders, the schoolmistress, just below the platform, whom he always found so sympathetic, the divinity student, whom he could tease a little about the One-Hoss Shay of Calvinism,—which had long since dropped to pieces, "all at once, and nothing first," in Boston, but was still a handsome carriage in these country districts,— the old gentleman opposite, who brought him down with a joke or a volley of facts if he became a little high-falutin, the landlady's daughter, lockets and ringlets and all, and Benjamin Franklin in the back row. This Benjamin Franklin, Junior, was the symbol of the rising generation, still up and coming, unversed in the *suaviter in modo* but bent on acquiring his French and science and prepared for the words of Erasmus on religion and morals. Was not the doctor himself an Erasmus or Franklin, who was planning a new *Poor Richard's Almanac* for more advanced students? There they all were, all the boarders, even the lady in black bombazine with the soul-subduing decorum, and the sad-eyed gentleman in the Spanish cloak, he of the fluted cheeks, worn by the passions of the melodrama, the symbol of the poor old Yankee theatre. What an opportunity for the doctor to take them into his confidence and plant in their minds a few well-chosen seeds,—seeds of moral etiquette, for instance, and even etiquette without the morals, Erasmian seeds, Confucian seeds, seeds of a worldly wisdom that was based on all the Commandments, and even some that Moses knew not of. When a doctor, thanks to his Creator, possesses such a store of sense and wit, and tempers it to the lambs that know not Boston, when he has learned how to approach his patients so that they swallow his pills with high good humour, when they feel better for his doses, why should not a spade be called a spade? Why should he not be called an Autocrat?

The doctor did not possess the gift of silence, and, possessing the gift of wit, he meant to use it. What would be the state of the highways of life, he said on one occasion, if we did not drive our thought-sprinklers through them, with the valves open? He enjoyed his journeys through the rural districts, where, pursuing his mission, spreading the light of the metropolis, he learned so much about his countrymen. Whether in man or tree, as he soon discovered, the provinces did not know a first-rate thing, even when they possessed it, and constantly took the second- and third-rate for nature's very best, for they had no standards of comparison; and, filled with the love of excellence as he was, he was always looking for it, and always making notes of it "when found." He carried in his pocket a measuring-tape, as Emerson carried a compass. This tape, thirty feet long, was long enough to encircle the largest brain, even Daniel Webster's; but the doctor commonly used it to measure trees. In his younger days, when he was much devoted to the young-lady population of Rhode Island, he had measured the great Johnston elm on the Providence Plantations, and with time he had formed the acquaintance of every considerable tree in New England. He knew the grand willows down in Maine, and the grand elms up the other way, the West Springfield elm, the noble Hatfield elm, the Sheffield elm, the great tree on the Colman farm at Deerfield that was living on its past reputation, the poor old Pittsfield elm, the horse-chestnut tree near the Rockport station, as well as all the elms on the Boston Common. Some of these great trees looked very meek when they saw the fatal measure begin to unreel,—like one of those politicians in the country towns who had puffed themselves up to look like Webster. They had never been measured before by a metropolitan eye when the little doctor approached them. The American elm, he observed, was tall and slender, and drooped as if from languor, while the English elm was more robust, and held its branches up, and carried its leaves longer than the native tree. Was this symbolic of the creative force on the two sides of the ocean? Did it indicate that Dr. Knox was right in thinking that Anglo-Saxons could not survive, outside the mother-country, that they were destined to die out unless they were kept up by fresh supplies? The doctor did not wish to decide a point that filled him with misgivings, although he argued stoutly the other way.

As for the "great tree" on the Boston Common, it belonged in the second rank, like the tree at Cohasset. The doctor admitted this without hesitation, for where Boston was concerned he was always candid. He had, of course, a modest pride in Boston, and, when some impertinent New Yorker asked one of his friends how he could endure the fulsome things that were constantly said of the town, he was rather inclined to agree with his friend's reply, "Because we feel that they are *true.*" Boston was the hub of the solar system: you could not pry this out of a Boston man if you had the tire of all creation straightened out for a crowbar. But how did the New Yorkers feel about New

York? Did not the axis of the earth stick visibly out through the centre of every city? Did not the smallest village of Massachusetts read, to its own advantage, Pope's well-known line, "All are but parts of one stupendous HULL"? In his weaker moments, the doctor admitted that Boston men ran a certain danger of taking their local scale for the absolute scale, an error that was natural enough, since Boston was so bright and wide-awake. But when he was his own cheerful self, he forgot these doubts and compunctions. Why not regard the Common as the unit of space, and the State House as the standard of architecture? Boston, of course, was just like other towns, except for its excellent fish-market; but one had to remember its fire-department, its admirable monthly publications, which everyone acknowledged, together with its use of the English language, which everyone ought to acknowledge. What was the real offence of Boston? One had to say this without fear or favour. It drained a watershed of intellect with which no other could be compared, and it would not let itself be drained in turn.

This was the open secret that gave the doctor's face its honest glow. This, and another secret, if it was one: the doctor loved his Boston with an affection that deepened as the wonder of it grew. Had he not, in his daily travels, bored this ancient city through and through? He knew it as an old inhabitant of a Cheshire knows his cheese; and when, with his mounting fortunes, a few years later, he moved into Beacon Street,—the last of his "justifiable domiciles,"—whence he could see Bunker Hill, from his window facing the bay, and Cambridge across the water, his cup ran over. There he could indulge his whims at last. At the Medical School, he continued to give his lectures, darting about the laboratory as nimbly as a cat, while his pupils laughed and cried as he told his stories, as often pathetic as witty, running out of the room when a rabbit had to be chloroformed, beseeching his assistant not to let it squeak. He was always tinkering at something, developing photographs or "mending things," breaking a chair or table to put it together better. He invented the best of stethoscopes and wrote a medical classic on puerperal fever, an essay that saved as many lives as Bowditch's *Practical Navigator*. He shut himself up with his violin and fiddled away industriously until he could play "Auld Lang Syne" so that anyone could recognize the tune. He never missed a horse-race and knew all the points of the favourites and winners,* as he knew the virtues of a sportsman,—to pay up, own up and shut up, that is, if you were beaten. He liked to go to the circus and the sideshows and chat with the freaks and the giants and measure their chests with his tape; for, being small himself, he had a relish for size, whether in trees or men. He knew the deeds of the prize-ring. Charles Freeman, who fought the "Tipton Slasher,"—a very superior type of American giant,—granted him confidential interviews; and the double-headed daughter of Africa allowed him to question her on the delicate subject of avoirdupois equivalents. Prudence and propriety and all the other pious P's had very little interest for the doctor; and, as only a good anatomist can, he loved to see a man prepare for boxing. Where could one find a handsomer spectacle than a fine Boston citizen resolving himself into the primitive elements of his humanity? If only the manly art of self-defense had been introduced among the reverend clergy, humankind would have had better sermons.

For the doctor never forgot that he was a doctor, even when he felt most the poet. And he never forgot that he was a poet. Sometimes, in the early morning, before the sun was up, he put out from shore in his little skiff, his "water-sulky," as he liked to call it, and glided round the

* Emerson, who admired skill, whether in men or horses, as much as Holmes, once corrected the doctor in a matter of horse-racing. It was a quarter of a second difference in the record of the trotter Flora Temple at Kalamazoo, 1859. The time was 2.19¾.

bay, up the Charles to Watertown or about the wharves, under the stern of some tall Indiaman, rubbing against the hulls of the old wood-schooners, propelling himself swiftly over the water or drifting with the tide. Only in his poems could he tell the delights of those sweet June mornings, when the bay was as smooth as a sheet of beryl-green silk, as he lay in his shell motionless over the flats, as he watched the crabs crawling in the shallows, the sculpins wavering silently under the boat, as he rustled through the long, harsh grass that led the way up some tranquil creek and paused there, moored unseen, in a loneliness so profound that the columns of Tadmor in the desert could not have seemed more remote from life. A city of idiots Boston seemed to him then, not to have covered this glorious bay with gondolas and wherries,—this bay where a poet might almost find a chambered nautilus, or at any rate might be reminded of one, brought back perhaps in that tall Indiaman, to write a poem about, one poem, at least, to make his name immortal.

For the doctor was a poet, for all he could "write so funny," a solid poet whose fruit was never green. He had observed that American poets did not commonly ripen well. They lacked severe standards; they had no sound thermometers for gauging their talents; and surely, the doctor thought, the United States furnished the greatest market in the world for the green fruit of the intellect. There were certain things, he felt, that were good for nothing until they had been kept a long while, and some that were good for nothing until they had been long kept and *used:* wine, meerschaum pipes and violins. A poem was like a violin, the parts of which were strangers to one another till they had learned to vibrate in harmony. A poem was as porous as a meerschaum,—in order to be good, it had to absorb the essence of one's own humanity. One had to keep one's poem until its sentiment harmonized with all the aspects of one's life and nature, until one had contrived to stain oneself through all its thoughts and images. That was what made poems, real poems, so much like buckwheat cakes, as the young fellow said at the breakfast-table, buckwheat being decidedly scarce and high.

So it was with the doctor's poems. Whatever else they were, they were always ripe. If they were largely occasional, and largely local, what else could be expected of a harper who could never refuse the appeal "by request of friends"? He knew his audience;

> All the gay and young
> Love the light antics of a playful tongue;

and he cheerfully plied the strings on all occasions, Commencement feasts, meetings of fellow-doctors, birthdays of eminent citizens. Would he just this once comply? Be the truth at once confessed; he wavered, yielded, did his best. And why not, when, from his nimble tongue, as from no other American tongue or pen, tripped the phrase, the epithet, on each occasion, that fired in every mind the appropriate train? These rhymes of an hour were fresh, adroit, correct. The doctor never said, in flowery language, that life was full of trials. He never said that youth was like the dewdrop. Moreover, he often glowed with intenser feeling. Well he recalled the moments when a "lyric conception" had struck him like a bullet in the forehead, when the blood dropped from his cheek and he felt himself turning as white as death. Once or twice only he had had this feeling,—as when he wrote *The Chambered Nautilus*,—a creeping as of centipedes running down the spine, a gasp, a jump of the heart, then a sudden flush, a beating in the vessels of the head, then a long sigh—and the poem was written. For the rest, his happiest vein was that which most resembled his conversation, when he felt like a jockey on the race-course, a good Yankee jockey, re-

joicing in his own vernacular, and confident, old as his
horse might be, that he would win the bet.

In this vein, he always won the bet. Had he not, in his
Rhymed Lesson, that *Essay on Man,* or rather essay on
manners, rewritten for another time and country, revealed
himself as a Yankee Pope, even as he revealed his limitations? Prickly pears are also edible, along with the other
varieties, and most of the doctor's prickles were salutary.
There were more things, it was true, even in Boston than
the doctor's philosophy dreamed of, more in the "bores"
and "earnest sages," whom Pope would have disliked as
much as he, more in Bronson Alcott,—

> groping vague and dim,
> Whose every angle was a half-starved whim;

more in Emerson, too, something he never gathered even
when he knew the "wingéd Franklin," whom he loved and
wished to comprehend and even "explained," years later,
in a patient study as good as a clever intellect could make
it. Far less could he understand those uncouth heroes,—

> such as Homer's, who, we read in Pope,
> Dined without forks and never heard of soap . . .
> Such as May to Marlborough Chapel brings,
> Lean, hungry, savage anti-everythings,
> Copies of Luther in the pasteboard style.

The reformers were not for him, any more than the
"genuine article," Luther himself, or Luther's disciples,
rather, were for his dear Erasmus. But has not history,
which Erasmus fills, a case to make also for the doctor,
whose "Reformation," though of a mundane kind, also
brought its blessings? Was he not also a reformer who,
with his ass's jawbone, slew in a thousand households the
pestilent lion that masked itself in a Geneva gown? He

was a reformer in medical matters, bent upon destroying, root and branch, the nostrums and the notions of human nature that a narrow past had bred in the Yankee mind,— even a reformer of the art of living, the lack of any real sense of which had given birth to these nostrums and notions. How many lines of reform can a man pursue without losing that fulcrum in common sense which gives his lever purchase? Great is the office of wit, ye deluded reformers, whose reforms are all in the air because your feet have no firm ground to stand on! Great is the office of wit, O optimists, who take so much for granted!—ye who will never know

> Some doubts must darken o'er the world below
> Though all the Platos of the nursery trail
> Their 'clouds of glory' at the go-cart's tail!

Because your forbears saw only the evil, can you see only the good? You must see the black squares on the checker-board, as well as the white squares, if you wish to play the game to any purpose. And you must learn to write, like men of this world, if you are going to change the world by writing, you Transcendental authors who foist upon your readers

> Mesmeric pamphlets, which to facts appeal,
> Each fact as slippery as a fresh-caught eel . . .
> Poems that shuffle with superfluous legs
> A blindfold minuet over addled eggs . . .
> Essays so dark Champollion might despair
> To guess what mummy of a thought was there,
> Where our poor English, striped with foreign phrase,
> Looks like a zebra in a parson's chaise.

What if, afflicted by these effusions, a wit should

> spread them to the smiling day
> And toss them, fluttering like the new-mown hay,
> To laughter's light, or sorrow's pitying shower?—

would it not be, for you and your readers' good, to send
you back to school where *you* might learn how to win the
bet?

No doubt, the doctor had his incomprehensions, along
with his little vanities. It was his passion to define himself,
and those who define themselves too readily are men whose
imagination has its limits. He disliked some of the friends
of progress because of their muddy brains, or because of
their Sunday frowns. Some of them he thought were moral
bullies. He also disliked them for their dingy linen, a
pardonable distaste, and yet it encroached a little on the
comic spirit, or, shall one say, the tragic spirit, of which
the imagination is all compact, and which, in minds of a
larger calibre, resolves these lesser discords. But the doctor seldom lost his sense of proportion. He never professed to see with the eye of God, and he was well aware
of his limitations. The essence of wit, he said, consists of
a partial view of whatever it touches. It throws a single
ray, separate from the rest,—yellow, red or blue,—upon
an object, never the white light: that is the province of
wisdom.

There were men wiser than he, and well he knew it; but
in all America there was none more witty. No one else
could have written *The One-Hoss Shay, The Morning
Visit, The Moral Bully,* or *How the Old Horse Won the
Bet.* That was the region where the doctor's rhymes were
safe from all rivals and invaders, where the rhymes added
a relish to the doctor's talk. For talk was his native element and his mission. Who knew, as he,—

> the little arts that please,
> Bright looks, the cheerful language of the eye,
> The neat, crisp question and the gay reply?

Who had such a festive air of finding life interesting and
full? Who liked people to speak their minds so fully?

Who opened a conversation with such a look of expecting
something good from his next-seat neighbour? He rejoiced in every kind of conversation, the kind that floated
safely over the shallows, the kind that floated over a few
fathoms, the philosophical parley, better still, that called
for a deep-sea line to reach the bottom, and best of all the
contact of two minds when they were off soundings in the
ocean of thought. The doctor was never a monopolist.
Well, hardly ever. It was his rule to talk only of subjects
he had long had in his mind, and to listen to what others
said of subjects that he had only recently studied, for
knowledge, like timber, he felt, should not be used until it
was properly seasoned. Who could have censured him if,
in later life, he talked about all subjects, and most of the
time, considering that he had had them all in mind longer
than anyone else? He never made puns, unless the occasion enjoined some very rare pun in Old Italian, the well-
known tongue invented by Andrews and Stoddard. He
considered conversation one of the arts, from which one
ought to refrain—inasmuch as listening also was an art—
unless one could match one's glass of wine with an equal
glow of light and warmth and colour. He was a master of
the art himself. At moments, when conditions favoured
him, when the candles shone in the deep mahogany, his
spirits rose like mercury under the summer sun and flashed
like the Shah's regalia. His talk was the eighth wonder of
the Boston world. In later years, on one of these occasions, Henry James the elder said to him, "Holmes, you
are intellectually the most alive man I ever knew." And
the little doctor replied, and he almost danced as he spoke,
"I am, I am! From the crown of my head to the sole of
my foot, I'm alive, I'm alive!"

CHAPTER XIX

THOREAU AT WALDEN

HENRY THOREAU had built a hut at Walden. In March, 1845, he had borrowed Alcott's axe,—which he took pains to return with a sharper edge,—and cut down some tall, arrowy pines for the timbers, studs and rafters. For the boards he bought a shanty from one of the Irish labourers on the railroad. The hut was ten feet by fifteen, shingled and plastered, with a garret and closet, a trap-door below, a brick fireplace, windows at the sides and a door facing the cove. The cost, all told, was $28.12½,—less than the annual rent of a student's room in Cambridge. There was a bean-field, close by, with a patch of potatoes, corn, peas and turnips. As a quasi-Pythagorean, Thoreau seldom indulged in beans. He exchanged his crop for rice in the village. Rice was the proper diet for one who loved so well the writings of the Oriental sages.

He had long cherished the notion of a forest-life. Ellery Channing had built himself a hut on the prairie in Illinois, and Henry's college class-mate, Stearns Wheeler, who had just died in Leipzig, had also built a rough woodland cabin, over at Flint's Pond, where he had lived for a year to save money, to buy Greek books and pay his way to Germany to study. Henry had spent six weeks in Wheeler's cabin, sharing one of his bunks of straw. There was nothing new in his own adventure, and he could not understand why his friends thought it was so peculiar. Some of them spoke as if he had gone to the woods in order to starve or freeze. Emerson had bought land on both sides of the pond, intending to build a summer-house, and Henry had carried out the project. Alcott, who liked to tinker at rustic architecture, helped him with his saw and hammer, along with the young Brook Farmer, George William Curtis of New York, who was boarding at Edmund Hosmer's in the village and working as a farm-hand. Henry felt at home in his sylvan dwelling. It made him think of some of those mountain-houses he had seen on his inland excursions, high-placed, airy, fragrant, with a fresh, auroral atmosphere about them. It was quiet, clean and cool, fit to entertain a travelling god. For company, birds flitted through his chamber, red squirrels raced over the roof, chickadees perched on the armfuls of wood he carried. There were moles living in the cellar. He had occasional visits from a hare. As he sat at his door in the evening, he remembered that he was descended from the Greeks of old. He was a wanderer, too, one of the crew of Ulysses. The shore of the cove was another Ithaca.

There was nothing about his "experiment," as his friends liked to call it, to arouse such curiosity and contempt. It was a common-sensible undertaking, and only a slight departure from Henry's usual mode of living. His average weekly outlay, for necessaries he could not supply himself, was twenty-seven cents. A few days at manual labour, building a boat or a fence, planting, grafting or surveying,—six weeks of work out of the year, when he had grown extravagant and had to have a microscope,—gave him an ample surplus. Why should anyone live by the sweat of his brow and bore his fellow-men by talking about it? Why should not everyone live with an ample margin?—as anyone could do, provided he followed the path of simplification, logically and ruthlessly enough. The mass of men led lives of quiet desperation. Why, if not to maintain a "standard of living" that every law of the universe controverted? Did they not know that the wisest had always lived, with respect to comforts and luxuries, a life more simple and meagre than the poor? Had all the philosophers, Hindu, Greek and Persian, lived and taught in vain? Had anyone measured man's capacities? Was it fair to judge by precedents, when so very little had been attempted? Who could say that if a man advanced, boldly, in the direction of his dreams, endeavouring to live the life he had imagined, he would not meet with a success that he had never expected in common hours? Henry believed, and wished to prove, that the more one simplified one's life the less complex the laws of life would seem. Why all this pother about possessions? He liked to think of the ancient Mexicans, who burned all their goods every fifty years. Hawthorne, in one of his stories, had pictured a similar holocaust; and this was the kind of reform that Henry thought was worth considering. He meant to have his furniture, actual and symbolic, as simple as an Indian's or an Arab's. There were three bits of limestone on his table. They had to be dusted every day, while the furniture of his mind was still undusted. Out of the window, quick!

If he had had the wealth of Crœsus, Henry's mode of living would not have been different. Space, air, time, a few tools, a note-book, a pen, a copy of Homer, what could he wish more than these? A bath in the pond at sunrise, a little Spartan sweeping and cleaning, then a bath for the intellect, perhaps in the *Bhagavad-Gita,* the pure water of Walden mingling in his mind with the sacred water of the Ganges. The day was his, for any wild adventure. Sometimes, on a summer morning, he would sit for hours in his sunny doorway, amid the pines and hickories and sumachs, in undisturbed solitude and stillness. The birds flitted noiselessly about him. He could feel himself growing like the corn. He knew what the Orientals meant by contemplation and the forsaking of works. He was a Yogi, too, a forest-seer, who might have composed the Upanishads. His Reality was also Brahma, not the actualities of the world, but its potentialities. What did he care for temporal interests? It was his vocation to discover God. His days were no longer days of the week, bearing the names of pagan deities, nor were they minced into hours or fretted by the ticking of a clock. He felt like a Puri Indian or a Mexican. If you had put a watch in his hand and asked him what the hour was, he might have looked at the dial and said, "Quien sabe?" The sounds of the railway rose and died in his ears like the distant drumming of a partridge.

His life here seemed to flow in its proper channels. It followed its own fresh currents, and he felt himself lurking in crystalline thought as the trout lurked under the verdurous banks. Not so much as a bubble rose to the surface. At sunset, he jumped into his boat and paddled to the middle of the pond. There he played on his flute, while the charmed perch hovered about the stern, and the moon travelled over the floor of the pond, strewn with the wrecks of the forest. The wildest imagination could not conceive the manner of life he was living, for the Concord nights were as strange as Arabian nights. He struck the side of the boat with his paddle, filling the woods with a circle of sound. What a pleasant mission it would be to go about the country in search of echoes! He knew where to find the prophetic places, the vocal, resounding, sonorous, hollow places, where oracles might be established, sites for oracles, sacred ears of Nature.

What could he say to a man who feared the woods, who shuddered at their solitude and darkness? What salvation was there for such a man? Did he not know that God was mysterious and silent? Henry could never have wearied of the woods, as long as he could visit a nighthawk on her nest. He could hardly believe his eyes when he stood within seven feet of her. There she was, sitting on her eggs, so sphinx-like, so Saturnian, so one with the earth, a relic of the reign of Saturn that Jupiter had failed to destroy, a riddle that might cause a man to go and dash his head against a stone. No living creature, surely, far less a wingéd creature of the air. A figure in stone or bronze, like a gryphon or a phœnix. With its flat, greyish, weather-beaten crown, its eyes were all but closed with stony cunning; and yet all the time this sculptured image, motionless as the earth, was watching with intense anxiety, through those narrow slits in its eyelids. Wonderful creature, sitting on its eggs, on the bare, exposed hill, through pelting storms of rain or hail, as if it were a part of the earth itself, the outside of the globe, with its eyes shut and its wings folded. It was enough to fill a man with awe. Henry thought for a moment that he had strayed into the Caucasus, and that around the hill, on the other slope, he would find Prometheus chained to the rock.

Round and round the pond, Henry followed the footpath worn by the feet of Indian hunters, old as the race of men in Massachusetts. The critics and poets were always complaining that there were no American antiquities, no ruins to remind one of the past, yet the wind could hardly blow away the surface anywhere, exposing the spotless sand, but one found the fragments of some Indian pot or the little chips of flint left by some aboriginal arrow-maker. When winter came, and the scent of the gale wafted over the naked ground, Henry tramped through the snow a dozen miles to keep an appointment with a beech-tree, or a yellow birch perhaps, or some old acquaintance among the pines. He ranged like a grey moose, winding his way through the shrub-oak patches, bending the twigs aside, guiding himself by the sun, over hills and plains and valleys, resting in the clear grassy spaces. He liked the wholesome colour of the shrub-oak leaves, well-tanned, seasoned by the sun, the colour of the cow and the deer, silvery-downy underneath, over the bleached and russet fields. He loved the shrub-oak, with its scanty raiment, rising above the snow, lowly whispering to him, akin to winter, the covert which the hare and the partridge sought. It was one of his own cousins, rigid as iron, clean as the atmosphere, hardy as all virtue, tenacious of its leaves, leaves that did not shrivel but kept their wintry life, firm shields, painted in fast colours. It loved the earth, which it over-spread, tough to support the snow, indigenous, robust. The squirrel and the rabbit knew it well, and Henry could understand why the deer-mouse had its hole in the snow by the shrub-oak's stem. Winter was his own chosen season. When, for all variety in his walks, he had only a rustling oak-leaf or the faint metallic cheep of a tree-sparrow, his life felt continent and sweet as the kernel of a nut. Alone in the distant woods or fields, in the unpretending sprout-lands or pastures tracked by rabbits, on a bleak and, to most, a cheerless day, when a villager would be thinking of his fire, he came to himself and felt himself grandly related. Cold and solitude were his dearest friends. Better a single shrub-oak leaf at the end of a wintry glade, rustling a welcome at his approach, than a ship-load of stars and garters from the kings of the earth. By poverty, if one chose to use the word, monotony, simplicity, he felt solidified and crystallized, as water and vapour are crystallized by cold.

All praise to winter, then, was Henry's feeling. Let others have their sultry luxuries. How full of creative genius was the air in which these snow-crystals were generated. He could hardly have marvelled more if real stars had fallen and lodged on his coat. What a world to live in, where myriads of these little discs, so beautiful to the most prying eye, were whirled down on every traveller's coat, on the restless squirrel's fur and on the far-stretching fields and forests, the wooded dells and mountain-tops,—these glorious spangles, the sweepings of heaven's floor. He watched the men cutting the ice on the pond. Some of this ice, stowed in the holds of ships, was going over to India; and many a seeker of Brahma in Calcutta was destined to drink from his own Walden well. If winter drove one in-doors, all the better. It compelled one to try new fields and resources. Days of merry snow-storms and cheerful winter evenings by the fire. Evenings for books of natural history, Audubon, for one. It was pleasant to read about the Florida Keys, the flowering magnolia, the warm spice-breezes, while the wind beat the snow against one's window. Days to sit at home over one's journal, in one's own nest, perhaps on a single egg, though it might prove to be an egg of chalk.

These were the days for writing, days to speak like a man in a waking moment to others in their waking moments. For Henry was hard at work. He was writing articles, which Horace Greeley placed for him. He had begun to write a book, and he wished to pay his tribute to Carlyle, who had liberated the English language, cutting away the fetters imposed upon it by the pedantic writers of the British reviews. The frigid *North American* was even worse, a venerable cobweb that had escaped the broom. He liked to think of Carlyle, on his vacations, riding on his horse "Yankee," bought from the American sale of his books. His own book, rewritten from his journal, was the *Week on the Concord and Merrimac Rivers*, the story of the journey with his brother, never to be forgotten, when they had doubled so many capes and run before the wind and brought back news of far-away men. He did not propose to crowd his day with work, even if the book had to be written. A writer, he thought, should saunter to his task surrounded by a halo of ease and leisure, and the labour of his hands should remove from his style all trace of sentimentality and palaver. One did not dance idly at one's writing when one had wood to cut and cord. As the strokes rang cheerily through the wood, so the stroke of the pen should ring on the reader's ear. Was the voyage an old story, eight or nine years old, and only a week at that? It represented a lifetime's memories. No boy who had grown up on the Mississippi recalled those floating enchantments, the river-boats, and the fabulous river-men, with more of a thrill than Henry felt, remembering the canal-boats of his childhood. The news had spread through Concord that one of these boats was stealing through the meadows, silent as a cloud, with its crew of "foreigners" from New Hampshire, and all the village boys had flocked to see it. Henry wished to write a book that would be saturated with his thought and reading, yet one that would not smell so much of the study, even the poet's cabin, as of the fields and woods. He dreamed of an unroofed book, lying open under the ether, a book that could hardly be forced to lie on a shelf.

He was not by nature a hermit. He might have frequented the bar-rooms, he thought, if he had had any business that called him thither. Almost every day he walked to the village, to trade his beans for rice, to get a boot repaired, to collect the news of the family. Sometimes he returned late at night, with a bag of rye or Indian meal, sailing back under the moon to his harbour in the woods. It was only that he was wary of gossip. He did not wish to lumber his mind with the rubbish that most men seemed to rejoice in, the details, for example, of some case in court. One day he was arrested in the village for refusing to pay his poll-tax. He felt as Alcott felt. The government supported slavery, the government was backing the Mexican War; well, he would not support the government. He did not wish to trace the course of his dollar until it bought a man, or bought a gun to shoot a Mexican. He spent the night in jail,—a fruitful night. It inspired his essay on *Civil Disobedience*. He wished to establish a principle, that one man locked up in jail for refusing to countenance slavery would be the end of slavery, or, to express it on a broader basis, "If the alternative is to keep all just men in prison, or give up war and slavery, the State will not hesitate which to choose." A foolish notion, many people thought, but some of them changed their minds, in later years, when one of Henry's Hindu readers, Gandhi, acting on the principle, disturbed the British Empire for several months. The next morning, Henry, released from jail, gathered some of the boys and girls for a huckleberry party, on a hill, whence the State was nowhere to be seen. He never fastened his door at Walden, though sometimes, in his absence, he had unwelcome visitors. How did Mrs. X happen to know that his sheets were not as clean as hers? But nothing was ever stolen, except his copy of Homer. One had to keep one's eye on bookish people.

He had other guests, especially in April, when all the world seemed to be on the move. A runaway slave appeared, then Alek Therien, the French-Canadian woodchopper, a true Homeric peasant who had learned a little Greek from his priest in the north, then Hugh Quoil, an Irish soldier, who had fought at the Battle of Waterloo. Old Quoil, with his wife and his jug, was patiently waiting for death in a hut in the woods. The shanty-Irish folk along the railroad sometimes came to see him. Henry thought them shiftless enough, with their women washing under the trees and the pigs poking about among the tubs. He eyed them with a vague hostility, as the red men had eyed the first settlers, and with as much reason; for were they not the first wave of the sea that was to sweep away so many landmarks? Among the little ragamuffins that swarmed about these cabins, there were some in whom the prophetic eye might have seen the masters of the future, the lords of Greater Boston, mayors, governors, captains of police, even, perhaps, a cardinal.

Henry had one good friend among them, little Johnny Riordan, with his quaint "old worthy" face, behind the sober visor of his cap, plodding to school through the snow in his next-to-nothing, facing and routing it like a Persian army. A great sight, Johnny, in his rags, beside the well-fed villagers, waddling about in their furs and finery. Emerson also came, of course. Henry read aloud to him some pages from his book, while they sat under an oak beside the pond. Alcott arrived one night, struggling through the snow. Ellery Channing spent a fortnight with him. When the poets and sages came, he was glad that his dwelling was so spacious. As the conversation assumed a grander and loftier tone, they shoved their chairs further and further apart, until they touched the walls in opposite corners. This left plenty of neutral ground for their sentences to deploy in martial order.

Once Henry left his house for a fortnight's excursion. He had cousins in Bangor, Maine, one of them in the lumber-trade, a good excuse to visit the northern woods. He wished to study the Indians in their forest wilderness, and he wished to climb Mount Ktaadn. He never travelled without prayer and fasting, for he did not wish to dissipate his mind. With all the industry of a busy life, how could one hope to know, really know, an area more than six miles square? Isaac Hecker had asked him to go to Rome, the two of them together, Hecker to pay the expenses, for Hecker, who had tried Brook Farm and Fruitlands, was boarding with Mrs. Thoreau for a taste of Concord. He hoped to carry Henry over to Rome, in more than one fashion. Later, another friend, an Englishman, invited him for a visit in England. In both cases, Henry said, No. If Europe was much in his mind, and became more and more to him, Concord might become less and less; and what sort of bargain would that be? He did not wish his life to lose its homely savour. If the fields and streams and woods that he loved so well, and the simple occupations of his townsmen, ever ceased to interest and surprise him, what culture or wealth could ever atone for the loss? He did not wish to go to Europe, nor did he wish to go—like the farmers—west. What could he think of this foolish American habit, going east or west to a "better land," without lifting an honest finger to till and redeem one's own New England soil? As for the rush to California, it was a disgrace to humankind,—digging gold, the merest lottery, a kind of toil, if it deserved the name, in no sense beneficial to the world. A startling development, this, of the ethics of trade and all the modes of getting a living. It filled Henry with a cold scorn. For the rest, he had his own western horizon, towards which he was always moving, pitching his tent each day nearer the Golden Gate. But the really fertile soils and luxuriant prairies lay on one's own side of the Alleghanies, wherever a man minded his own business. Were not all the essentials of life to be found in Concord, ten times found if one properly valued them?—which a man could only do if he stood his ground. Henry had something to say to the men in the covered wagons, who were running away from something besides the rocks. If the men in the covered wagons had no ears for Henry, he would be glad to wait for a few generations. The great-great-grandsons of the covered wagons would be ready to listen to him.

Nobody knew the riches of Concord. As for natural history, he had found some of the Arctic phenomena there, red snow and one or two Labrador plants. Still, a little travel now and then was not so bad to give one's mind an airing, especially if it offered him a chance to observe the ways of the Indians. For the Indians had a special charm for Henry; they suggested a simpler mode of life and a greater nearness to the earth. Were there not two eternities, one behind him, which the Indians represented, as well as one before? Wherever he went, he trod in their tracks, yet only a few poets remembered them. Here and there, one saw their lonely wigwams, on the banks of some quiet stream, like the cabins of the muskrats in the meadows,—an old squaw, perhaps, living in her solitary hut, with her dog, her only companion, making baskets and picking berries, insulted by the village boys and girls. Henry dreamed of writing a book about them; * for their memory seemed to him to harmonize with the russet hue of autumn that he loved. A race that had exhausted the secrets of nature, a race tanned with age, while the young, fair Anglo-Saxon slip, on whom the sun had shone for so short a time, was only just beginning its career. As sportsmen went in pursuit of ducks, and scholars of rare books, and all men went in pursuit of money, Henry went in search of arrowheads, when the proper season came round again. He often spent whole afternoons, especially in the spring, when the rains had washed the ground bare, pacing back and forth over a sandy field, looking for these relics. It might have rained arrow-heads. They lay all over the surface of the country, sometimes mingled with arrowheadiferous soil, ash-coloured, left by Indian fires. They were like so many fossil thoughts to Henry, forever recalling the far-away mind that shaped them.

To Maine, then!—where the Indians grew with the moose. A fortnight in the forest, the home of the bear and the caribou, the wolf, the beaver and the Penobscot redskins, where the wild fir flourished and the sprucetops, seen from an elevation, were like the odour of cake in a schoolboy's nostrils. Hemlocks and cedars, silver and yellow birches, watery maples, damp and mossgrown rocks, real woods, these, wild and bearded. One caught the whistle of ducks on solitary streams, the flicker of the darting chickadee, the loon's desolate laugh.

---

* Thoreau left eleven manuscript volumes, about 3000 pages, filled with notes about the Indians for the book he had hoped to write.

Sometimes, through the moss-clad aisles, one heard a dull, dry, rustling sound, as if smothered under the fungus-covered forest, the falling of a tree, like the shutting of a door in some distant entry of the dark and shaggy wilderness. There one could feel at home, shooting the rapids in one's birch canoe, like a bait bobbing for some river monster, darting from side to side of the stream, then gliding swift and smoothly. This was the place to sing the "Canadian boat-song," or to play on one's flute, at night, under the stars, while the wolves howled about, in the darkness of the continent. Henry watched Joe Polis, the Indian guide, glued to the bank on his stomach, talking to the muskrats in their sylvan language. Sometimes, by the fireside, Joe Polis also sang, a mild and simple nasal chant, like the dawn of civilization over the woods. The white man's brow was clear and distinct, but over the brow of the Indian lingered a haze or mist. For the Indian, the white man's noon was four o'clock in the morning.

A journey like this was only a foretaste, too rewarding not to be repeated. Henry was writing about his travels, and one of the magazines was glad to print his essay on Ktaadn. Later, on two occasions, he went to Maine again. He wished to visit Chesuncook, the Allegash and the East Branch. He was in his element in the woods, as Richard Henry Dana on the sea, as an old French-Canadian *coureur de bois*. Was he not a Frenchman as well as a Yankee, who might have run wild with Du Lhut and harried the woods for beavers? In the meantime, he had left his Walden cabin. Why? For as good a reason as he had gone there. He had other lives to live, and he had no more time to spare for this one. He wanted a change, he did not wish to stagnate. About two o'clock in the afternoon, he had felt the world's axle creaking a little, as if it needed greasing, as if the oxen laboured with the wain and could hardly get their load over the ridge of the day. Who would accept heaven on terms like this?—and a ticket for heaven had to include, for Henry, tickets for hell and purgatory also. Walden was only a bivouac in his campaign. He had other journeys in mind, to Cape Cod, for instance, with Ellery Channing, and later a jaunt to Canada, Quebec and Montreal. (Total expense, two guide-books included, $12.75.) Ellery was not a man for camping out,—that was an art one had to acquire slowly; but he shared Henry's taste for a simple equipment. And Henry would no more have thought of dressing,—dressing for a journey!—than he would have blacked his boots for fishing. Honest travelling was dirty work. A pair of overalls was the proper costume, a grey sack, corduroys perhaps; and as for this blacking of boots, he despised it on all occasions. In this, he was like some of the Harvard professors, who, as Mrs. Story was shocked to note, on one of her visits from Italy, did not have their boots blacked even for Commencement. Henry, who always carried a piece of tallow, in order to keep the water out of the leather, looked like a wood-chuck or a musquash. This was his desire, at least,—the more like a quadruped the better, tawny, russet, yellow-brown, the colour of the sands. Vermont grey was not so bad; and once he had had the perfect suit, a skilful mix-ture of browns, with light and dark cleverly proportioned, and a few threads of green. He had looked like a corner of a pasture, with patches of sweet-fern and lechea. He had been able to glide over the fields, as unperceived from the farmer's windows as a painted cruiser through a spyglass. The wild animals thought he was one of them. Ellery, who was not so systematic, shared Henry's feel-ing in the matter of hats. His own hat was old and weather-beaten and had plenty of holes around the brim. It was as rare and high as a good Stilton cheese. As for the rest of Henry's outfit, a handkerchief served for a bag, or a firm, stout sheet of brown paper, well tied up. What else? An umbrella, of course, a knapsack, with par

titions for books and papers, a music-book for pressing
flowers, a field-glass and a measuring-tape. A fish-line,
spoon and dipper, a little salt and sugar, tea, Indian
meal and a slice of fruit-cake. If anyone asked him along
the way to do a little tinkering, that was a tribute to his
common sense.

So Henry tramped to Provincetown. Having seen the
woods, he wished to see the ocean, and Cape Cod was
surely the place to see it. There, on the stretches of sand
blown clean by the wind, he could forget the towns, where
he felt so unspeakably mean and disgraced. He could forget the bar-rooms of Massachusetts, where the full-grown
were not weaned from their savage and filthy habits,
sucking cigars and guzzling whiskey-punch. On the Cape,
one saw wholesome faces, well preserved by the salty air,
faces bleached like old sails, hanging cliffs of weather-
beaten flesh. The Cape Cod boys leaped from their
leading-strings into the shrouds; it was only a bound
from their mother's laps to the masthead. They boxed
the compass in their infant day-dreams. They could hand,
reef and steer by the time they flew a kite. This was a
country almost as thrilling as Maine. Henry had three
books more or less on the stocks: *The Maine Woods,*
full of the scents of the forest, *Cape Cod,* redolent of the
sea, even *A Yankee in Canada.* The well-known publishers, Time & Co., could be trusted to see that they
were safely printed. One of his neighbours wrote about
Human Culture. Why should he not write about Cape
Cod, another name for the same thing, and hardly a
sandier phase of it? Or Canada, for that matter? He
wrote an opening paragraph, with both hands clenched:
"Read my book if you dare!"

CHAPTER XX

WEST OF BOSTON

AFTER EIGHT years of ups and downs, Brook Farm had come to an end, not without important consequences. There were not wanting well-informed observers who were to assert, in later years, that from the farm had sprung the movement of organized labour in New England and even throughout the nation. It had other results of a personal kind. Two well-known journalists of the future, Charles A. Dana of the New York *Sun* and John Sullivan Dwight of the *Journal of Music,* received their first training as editors of *The Harbinger,* the magazine published at the farm. *The Harbinger* had opened with a translation of George Sand's *Consuelo,* and almost every writer in New England contributed an essay or a poem. But the farm had not long survived the coming of the Fourierists, Owen, Horace Greeley and Albert Brisbane, who had translated Fourier's writings. Brisbane wished to turn it into a phalanstery, where all the ideas of the master were to be applied. With certain modifications, the plan was adopted, and the members were divided into "groups" and "series." But something went out of the life of the farm. Ceasing to be voluntary, it ceased to be poetic; and when disaster fell, the farm fell with it.

Dwight, the chief of the "Festal Series," was all but broken-hearted. The music-master was a pretty sight, surrounded by his class of singing children. He was happy to hoe the corn on Sundays, paying his regards to the Puritan sabbath by breaking it in every way he could; and, al-

though he did not like to hoe on week-days, he had contrived to put up with the new routine. He did not know
what to do when the sad news broke. He struggled on
for a time in Boston, trying to maintain a "combined
household" for some of the Brook Farmers. He never
lost his faith in association; he felt that a communal life was
the only life for humanity and that society must be set in
order before the individual could be himself. The organization of labour, the abolition of competition, this was the
road to the future, as Dwight conceived it. It was not until 1852 that he was able to start the *Journal of Music,*
which he was to conduct for thirty years. This was the
journal that set the musical standard of Boston. It published the musical news of Italy, Paris, Germany, England, Liszt's *Life of Chopin,* a serial life of Mozart,
hundreds of original compositions. It even led the musical thought of the country, till the editor's dislike of
Brahms and Wagner gradually destroyed its influence.
This was in the far future, when Dwight was the dictator
of music. He had made his way by lecturing and writing,
carrying on, in Boston and elsewhere in New England, the
"mass clubs" he had started at the farm.

"Archon" Ripley went to New York, with Dana, to
work on Greeley's *Tribune.* It was a sad descent, sitting
all day long in a little office, on the fourth floor of a huge,
dirty building, reached by winding, narrow, littered stairs,
with machines whizzing and clanking about him, para-
graphing and clipping for *The Tribune.* One never heard
the vireo there, and Utopia seemed very far away. Every
night he plodded home to Brooklyn. He shared a single
room with his wife in a shabby boarding-house in a dingy
street. In this room his wife died of cancer, while, Ripley,
at his table in the corner, worked away for dear life,—the
modest, laborious Ripley, too humble to collect in volume-
form the clear and scholarly essays he wrote for his paper
on Lessing, Voltaire, Rousseau, Hartmann, Spencer.

These essays, like Dwight's,—never collected either,—
deserved a place of honour in the literature of criticism.
Two decades were to pass, in this Grub-Street twilight,
while he composed, with Dana, the *New American Encyclopædia,* before the sun rose again for Ripley. He had
a brief, happy second youth, with means, a little·travel, a
brougham to drive about in Central Park. For even Brook
Farmers come to gigs at last.

Two notable women, members of Ripley's circle, had
gone to New York, at least for a while, before him. Lydia
Maria Child, the novelist, had written thence her *Letters
from New York, 1841–1844,* an unpretentious picture of
the city that was to have its interest in later years. Mrs.
Child was at home in the rural outskirts, the charming villages on the New Jersey shore, the woody banks of Wee-
hawken, a wild garden of early flowers. In the Hoboken
meadows, she found violets nestling in moss-grown stumps.
New York itself was too much in a hurry-scurry, and there
was something brutal in its life. The dog-catchers trooped
down the streets, their clothes bespattered with blood;
they had clubs over their shoulders to beat to death every
dog they found without a master. She had never seen such
sights as this in humanitarian Boston. She studied the
prisons, the care of the poor, the Swedenborgian meetings,
the meetings for the discussion of mesmerism, the popular
acclaim of Ole Bull, who had just arrived from Norway.
New York was not like Boston. It never entered the head
of a Wall Street merchant that he was himself responsible
for the evils of the town; and, although she found "Transcendental muslins" advertised in the Bowery, she never
met with the well-known cult in any other form. Was she
herself a Transcendentalist? She had certainly used the
phrase "highly gifted"; and yet she had been mystified, in
some of the Boston circles, where she had had to bite her
finger to be sure it was really solid. She felt a good deal
of sympathy with the plain man of business, and she drew

a kindly, generous, motherly picture of the town that he
had built for his habitation. But, as for his toleration of
slavery and a thousand other abuses, she did not abate a
word of her honest abhorrence.

Margaret Fuller, with her intenser mind, had also surveyed the metropolis. She had gone there in 1844 to join
the staff of *The Tribune*. She lived in Horace Greeley's
house and carried on raids of observation into the terri-
tories of the prince of darkness, Sing Sing, Blackwell's
Island, the Five Points, even the salons of the literati.
Greeley had been attracted by her books, which had appeared in *The Dial*,—the well-known feminist treatise,
Woman in the Nineteenth Century, and the notes on
Western travel, *Summer on the Lakes*. He felt that hers
was the sort of pen to make his own paper a living force;
for this female Montesquieu, as her followers thought
her, who had given her own sex its title-deeds, seemed
ready to forward every enlightened cause. She had written well of the West. With James Freeman Clarke's art-
ist-sister, she had spent the summer of 1843 in Cleveland,
Chicago and Wisconsin. She had mingled with the New
England pioneers, bent on seeking their fortunes, the
fathers and mothers of a race to come. What had been
their one preoccupation? Alas, from the oldest man to the
youngest child, they talked not of what they were going to
do but of what they were going to get, ease and money.
Could anything more be hoped of the Germans and
Swedes, who were flocking into these beautiful wilder-
nesses, amid the prairie flowers and the lowing cattle?
The scene, she knew, had a mighty meaning, and she
hoped to divine the law by which a new poetry and order
might be evoked from this chaos. She liked the outdoor
festivals of the pioneers, the huskings and the hop-gather-
ings, as merry as the Scottish harvest-home or the Italian
vintage, the groups of men and girls filling their baskets
with the gay festoons. But everywhere she saw, in germ,

the fatal spirit of imitation, a reference to European ways. She noted the fine taste the Indians showed in the sites of their clustered lodges on the lakes and streams. Let the white men blacken the Indians as they might, talk of their filth and brutality; she could well believe that an Indian brave, rambling on thesè paths, in the beams of the sun, might be mistaken for Apollo. The Indians had loved the French. How could they love the Protestant missionary, with his niggardly conceptions, his unfeeling stare? As for the general prospects of these regions, whatever the future might bring she was bound to say, "There is nothing real in the freedom of thought at the West. It is from the position of men's lives, not the state of their minds."

Now, in New York, on *The Tribune,* she was writing on current literature. She hoped to clarify American thought, in its dim and struggling state, and introduce the new European writers. She paid no attention to the magazine-stories, "written for the press, in a spirit of imitation and vanity, the paltriest offspring of the human brain." What was her criterion? "Most men, in judging another man, ask, Did he live up to our standard? To me it seems desirable to ask, Did he live up to his own?" She added that Goethe's faults fitted him all the better for the part he had to play. She interpreted the more significant writers, looking to the day "when our population shall have settled into a homogeneous national life, and we have attained vigour to walk in our own way, make our own world and leave off copying Europe." Her judgments were remarkably just,* and some of her general intuitions gave her work a measure of permanent interest. She contrasted the boyish crudity that marked so many American writers, timid and boastful at once, with the tempered, manly equipoise of the thoroughbred European; and,

---

* E.g., in regard to Longfellow, that "the ethical part of his writing has a hollow, second-hand sound," as also in regard to Emerson, that "he raised himself too early to the perpendicular and did not lie along the ground long enough."

regarding the larger aspects of civilization, she spoke for the longer time as well as the shorter. "Since the Revolution," she observed, "there has been little, in the circumstances of this country, to call out the higher sentiments. The effect of continued prosperity is the same on nations as on individuals,—it leaves the nobler faculties undeveloped. The superficial diffusion of knowledge, unless attended by a corresponding deepening of its sources, is likely to vulgarize rather than raise the thought of a nation, depriving it of another sort of education through sentiments of reverence, and leading the multitude to believe themselves capable of judging what they but dimly discern . . . . In a word, the tendency of circumstances has been to make our people superficial, irreverent and more anxious to get a living than to live mentally and morally." A statement that could hardly have been challenged ninety years later.

In 1846, Margaret Fuller set out for Europe. She had read the invisible ink in many minds and lives, in Hawthorne's, for one, the American writer whom, after Emerson, she most admired. Hawthorne had returned for three years to Salem. His friends, Horatio Bridge and Franklin Pierce had gone to Concord, to the Manse, to see him. They found him chopping wood in the shed, dressed in his old blue frock and troubled over the problem of earning a living; and they promised to use their influence with Bancroft, who had risen in the political world and was Secretary of the Navy, to find a post for him that would give him an income. Horatio Bridge himself was in the navy, and he had written a book, with Hawthorne's help, the *Journal of an African Cruiser,* a collection of lively impressions of the African Gold Coast, Liberia, Sierra Leone, the Canaries. Hawthorne went back to Salem with a heavy heart, as the new surveyor of the custom-house. A botanist who lived in the town had recently noted that the English white-thorn, the hawthorn of the poets, had slowly naturalized itself in Salem. It was otherwise with the flower of Hawthorne's mind. The mud, the dust, the east wind, the petty trickeries of the politicians, the chilliness of the social atmosphere—"Who ever heard of the Hawthornes?" one of the ladies of Chestnut Street remarked—benumbed and befogged his senses. He went about his work with the dogged and silent practicality that always characterized his mundane life, testing the rum that was sent to the Guinea Coast,—for he meant to see that the darkies had good, strong rum,—while the poet slept within him. Three years of an outward stupefaction, years in which the shipmaster's son, who might have quelled a mutiny, obliged his incompetent staff to toe the mark. In the evenings, he read De Quincey with his wife. What music, what perfection of style in the less laborious passages! How could Hawthorne talk to the Salem people? Why should he talk, indeed, when the presence of an uncongenial person caused an almost physical contraction of his great masculine frame?

At the end of the three years, he moved to Lenox. He had written *The Scarlet Letter* in Salem, the book that had won his freedom; for under his mask of insensibility the poet had been alive and brooding there. In this winter of his discontent, he had also written a few fables and sketches, worthy of one whose first American forbear had brought from England with him a copy of Sidney's *Arcadia.* The tone of *Main Street* and *The Great Stone Face,* like that of *The Snow-Image,* was of a dove-like innocence that often cloaked the wisdom of the serpent. No one else in New England had written such stories, or only one man, William Austin, the Boston lawyer, Dr. Channing's class-mate. This well-known Harvard scholar and legislator, who had studied law in London, where he had known Washington Allston and written the *Letters from London,* which all the American lawyers read because they contained such good descriptions of the British lawyers and statesmen, had published a handful of tales in the eighteen-twenties that were almost prophetic of Hawthorne. In *Martha Gardner,* Austin, a Democrat and a radical, castigated the modern corporations that fed on the miseries of the poor. Better than this was *The Man with the Cloaks,* based on a German fairy-tale. The best was *Peter Rugg, the Missing Man.* Austin had a robust, Rabelaisian humour that ran to the gigantesque, as in the story of the hungry teacher who wandered about the country drinking all the cows dry and cutting steaks out of the living oxen. *Peter Rugg* was a great invention, or one of those bold formulations of ancient inventions, the Flying Dutchman, the Wandering Jew, which, like *Rip Van Winkle* and *Peter Schlemihl,* come to the same thing. This tale of the man who disappeared from Boston and was constantly seen on the roads for fifty years, desperately whipping his horse, trying to find his way back, had all the overtones of the true folk-legend, the haunting suggestions of a symbolism that is always lending itself to some new turn of affairs. There were many Peter Ruggs, in days to come, trying to find their way back to Boston, the good old Boston of 1820; and the story was retold by later writers as if it had been a popular myth.* The ambiguous atmosphere of the tale, the mingling of the dubious and the real, the play of light and shadow suggested Hawthorne. So did the old New England setting and costumes. Hawthorne was familiar with it. Peter Rugg appeared in one of his own tales. He was the door-keeper in *A Virtuoso's Collection.*

At Lenox, the air was scented with sweet-grass and clover; and there, in the little red cottage on the lonely farm, Hawthorne had his year of wonders. There he wrote *The House of the Seven Gables* and planned *The Blithedale Romance;* and, while his wife made tracings of

* Peter Rugg was the subject of a ballad by Louise Imogen Guiney and a prose-poem by Amy Lowell.

Flaxman's outlines on the dull-yellow painted chairs and tables, he told the children stories that explained the drawings, *The Wonder Book, The Tanglewood Tales*. Tanglewood, as the children called it, was a wild spot in the woods close by where they all went for picnics in the summer and autumn. Hawthorne played the magician there. He was a great tree-climber, up in a flash to the topmost bough, showering nuts all over the floor of the forest. From old door-knobs and strips of shingle, he carved little yachts and figures, a pugilist who swung his arms in the wind. In winter, he made images of snow. The image in the tale he wrote was singularly like a man of genius, a moral that he neglected to point. The father of the children who made the image, a man of common sense and kind intentions, wished to make the image comfortable, even in spite of itself. He carried it into the warm room, where it rapidly melted away beside the fire. Alas, for the poor snow-image that loved the cold, the frosty air, the north wind! The children had known very well it could only live under the stars that glimmered in the arctic night.

Hawthorne had become a father-confessor. Letters poured in upon him from unhappy souls who had been touched by his books. Secret criminals sought him out and came to him for counsel and relief. Most of his Berkshire neighbours were less exacting. Miss Sedgwick, the aging novelist, lived at Lenox. At Mrs. Sedgwick's school, Harriet Hosmer, the merry little gnome, the sculptor of the future, was one of the pupils. Hawthorne was to meet her again in Rome; still later, he described her in *The Marble Faun*. The Sedgwicks pervaded the Berkshires. Even the grasshoppers chirped, "Sedgwick, Sedgwick!" as one of their friends remarked; and Mrs. Sedgwick said, with a measure of truth, "En France tout arrive." Everything happened at Lenox, and everyone came there. Close by lived the lovely Fanny Kemble, whose Shakespeare readings in Boston were events of the forties and who also ap-

peared in one of Hawthorne's novels.* Samuel Gray
Ward had another villa. This dearest of Emerson's
friends, not to be confused with Longfellow's friend,
Samuel Ward of New York,—Julia Ward Howe's
brother, who was later known as the "King of the
Lobby,"—was a Boston banker and patron of art. His
youth, before he entered business, had been devoted to
painting, literature and German studies. He had translated a volume of Goethe's essays and had written a paper
on Boccaccio that was one of the best in *The Dial*. His admirable essay on criticism, in Elizabeth Peabody's *Æsthetic Papers*,† contained two phrases, "creative criticism"
and "significant form," that other men in later generations
were to render more than familiar. Ward had bought
Legendre's mathematical library and had paid for the
publication of the poems of his old friend and school-mate,
Ellery Channing.‡ At Pittsfield, which had once been
Wendellboro, named after his forbears, Oliver Wendell
Holmes spent his summers. There he planted seven hun-

---

* In the character of Zenobia, in *The Blithedale Romance,* also drawn
partially from Margaret Fuller.

† A projected magazine, 1849, discontinued after the first number. In addition to Ward's essay, it contained papers by Dwight, Miss Peabody,
Emerson, Thoreau and Hawthorne. In Emerson's contribution, the essay
on War, one finds the following observation: "The manhood that has been
in war must be transferred to the cause of peace, before war can lose its
charm, and peace be venerable to men." This was perhaps the germ of
William James's later essay, *The Moral Equivalent of War.*

‡ Samuel G. Ward was the "friend" of Emerson's *Letters to a Friend,*
edited by Charles Eliot Norton. His essay on criticism contained the following observations: "Our first misfortune is, that there is a reference to a
standard from without, viz., England. As the spirit that dictates it is, from
many causes, unfair and depreciating, a natural consequence has been to
cause all our own criticism to take the opposite ground, to over-praise that
which is felt to be undervalued or invidiously regarded . . . . Although
all original literature comes from and refers to the heart of the people,
it cannot, except in a rude age, address itself to that people except through
a class capable of receiving it. If great works do not find such a class in
their own age, they wait till time and their own influence create it . . . .
We believe a conscious greatness inseparable from critical literature, and
such, therefore, we look for in this country;—a literature and art based on
thorough criticism, and thorough knowledge of what already exists in the
world."

dred trees and built himself a snug little villa on a knoll on
the old Wendell farm; and there he wrote his best bucolic
poems, *The Ploughman*, for one, for he liked to play his
part at the Berkshire agricultural fairs. At Broadhall, the
old Melville house, where Major Thomas Melville had
lived,—Holmes's "Last Leaf,"—Longfellow spent a summer, with Ex-President Tyler and Charles Sumner, for it
was now a boarding-house. Major Melville's grandson,
Herman Melville, was living at "Arrowhead," on the outskirts of Pittsfield. Melville was composing *Moby Dick*,
and the great white whale was in his flurry. He was attracted to Hawthorne and wrote an essay on his books,
and he often drove up to the little red cottage, with his big
Newfoundland dog in the buckboard beside him. He told
tales about the South Seas that were more exciting than
Dana's. Once, describing a fight there, he laid about him
as if with a club. It was so real to the Hawthornes that
when he had gone they all asked, "What became of the
club?"—which Melville had neither left nor taken with
him. Melville and Hawthorne liked to lie in the barn, on
piles of new-mown hay, discussing time and eternity.

Not far away, at Northampton, where Bancroft, at the
Round Hill school, had taught Ward, Motley and Ellery
Channing, another writer had spent his childhood, the
Hawthornesque novelist, Sylvester Judd. This hypersensitive, humble, shrinking soul, a Unitarian minister at Au-
gusta, Maine, bred in the rigours of Calvinism, had passed
through the Transcendental movement. His doubts and
ecstasies had deranged his nerves.* As a student of theology in Cambridge, he had been stirred by Goethe and Carlyle. He wished to destroy the barriers of the sects, and

---

* It was of Judd that Emerson wrote: "I once asked a clergyman in a
retired town who were his companions? What men of ability he saw? He
replied that he spent his time with the sick and dying. I said, he seemed
to me to need quite other company, and all the more that he had this;
for if people were sick and dying to any purpose, we should leave all and
go to them, but, as far as I had observed, they were as frivolous as the
rest, and sometimes much more frivolous."—*The Conduct of Life.*

exhibit the errors of false theology, war, capital punishment, the prison system. His *Margaret* was a Utopian romance, the story of the daughter of a German musician, brought up in an old New England village, who ends by transforming the village into a Mons Christi, with fountains like those of the Tuileries, belvederes and gardens, music-rooms, observatories, halls of art, where the barren lands bloom with rye and corn, and statues of Peace and Truth and marble muses line the Delectable Way, where industry, economy and love, simple fare and attractive toil create an earthly paradise and men of all nations meet as brothers. This Fourieristic fantasy, more than a little drawn from *Wilhelm Meister,* with a heroine often suggestive of Mignon, was quite in the Brook Farm spirit. It symbolized the feeling for art that was dawning in New England, the messianic socialism, the inspiration of German studies; and Judd's poem, *Philo,* a metaphysical epic, found readers who believed it would convert the world. *Margaret* was obscure and confused, but many pages and even chapters were vividly picturesque and charmingly written. Judd had studied New England. He had filled his note-books with observations of old houses, costumes and village ways, the talk of the farmers, the husking-bees, Thanksgiving, the pedlars and hawkers of ballads at country fairs. His best scenes were almost as good as Hawthorne's. There was a touch of ecstasy in some of his descriptions, the thunder-storm, the winter scenes, the snow-storm, the sunny clearing in the summer forest, the coming of the flowers in spring, the horse-tails with their storied ruffs, the fleecy mouse-ear buds, the straw-coloured blossoms of the bell-wort, the little polypods with their feathery fronds and the young mulleins, velvety, white and tender.

These were the scenes that Hawthorne knew at Lenox. Never quite at home away from the sea-shore, he still had hours there, on summer evenings, when he felt as if he could climb the sky and run a race along the Milky Way. Free at last after the leaden years he had spent at the Salem custom-house, his mind was at its fullest flood. His bones were astir, even to the marrow. Salem, the ancient seaport of his boyhood, never loved by him, shunned indeed, and yet his own so deeply, seen afresh after his life at the Manse, which had given him a standard and a measure, Salem, dust of his own dust, and with it the Boston of Puritan times, pressed against and filled his consciousness. The scarlet letter A that had haunted his mind ever since he had written the *Twice-Told Tales,* the witch, whisked up the chimney on a broomstick and flying away to a devil's communion far in the depths of the dark, still forest, the old colonial governors, the ruffed physicians, the ministers godly and of ungodly fame, the women not to be repressed, the inquisitorial deacons, the elfin children of that Gothic world, prolonged from the Middle Ages, the Boston he had imagined, the Salem he had known, the queer gabled houses and the queerer people, the cobwebs visible and invisible, cobwebs of family pride and secret fraud, bloodstains telling tales and beams of innocent sunlight piercing through: all this had waited for the dam to break, for the moment of leisure and freedom, for his dismissal from the custom-house, another of those politicians' tricks,—a score that he could repay by picturing his enemy in Judge Pyncheon,—to be written out at his desk with the secret drawers, the haunted writing-desk with the tiny panels. He had painted these little panels with impish faces, staring and smiling, while he sat in his purple writing-gown, covered with golden palm-leaves. The dam had burst, in Salem, with *The Scarlet Letter.* The overflow was *The House of the Seven Gables.*

Years before, in Hawthorne's youth, in Salem, when he had written his tales in the little chamber, there had always seemed to be a driving snow-storm on the other

side of the casement, or a cloud of dust in summer, a
film, a veil. When he had stood at the window, on Sunday mornings, studying the church across the way, watching the sunlight stealing down the steeple, he had always
stood behind the curtain. To see the world with a sidelong glance, by a certain indirection, was second nature
with him; and this was the mood his romances conveyed,
as if, in spite of all their air of daylight, he had never
looked straight at Boston or Salem, as if he had always
seen them over his shoulder. It was this that gave him his
effect of magic and made these beautiful books, with
their antique diction, something other than novels and,
if not greater, more intimate in their spell than novels
can be. They clung to the mind like music, like Gluck's
mournful strains of the land of shades or the solemn joy
of Mozart. Or, better still, like masques written for
music in the far-off days in England of which one caught
the dim reverberations in the scene of *The Scarlet Letter.*
Round about the players in the greenwood, one felt and
saw the encircling darkness gather. The deepest shade
covered *The Scarlet Letter.* But the flickering play of the
sun and the leaves set the note of *The House of the Seven
Gables.* The story moved in a soft September light, melting like a happy dream of Shakespeare.

CHAPTER XXI

THE ANTI-SLAVERY WRITERS

OUT OF the depths of the country, far from Beacon Hill and Brattle Street, one "heard as if an army muttered."

> And the muttering grew to a grumbling,
> And the grumbling grew to a mighty rumbling.

The Anti-Slavery movement was on its way. Not from the churches, not from the men of property or culture—or from them only on second thought—came the call to reform. It was the village centres that grumbled and rumbled, the back streets of the manufacturing towns, the tailors' shops and rural printing-presses, the Quaker farms and solitary homesteads. Thence came those that troubled Israel. There the *Pilgrim's Progress* and the *Book of Martyrs* were much more living facts than all the culture of the later epochs. There dwelt, unchanged, the spirit of the Puritans and the Friends, the stiff-necked sectaries of Cromwell's army who had been glad to stand in pillories and suffer their ears to be cropped rather than put bread in the mouths of priests, men who had fought for the right to wear their hats where others stood uncovered, fought for a beard as they fought for a principle and chosen the *peine forte et dure* if they were asked to surrender their opinion regarding some phrase in the Scriptures. Such were the readers of *The Liberator*. In their bones, as Garrison spoke, stirred the fires of the days of Pym and Hampden. "I am in earnest, and I will be heard!"

This was very far from the tone of Boston, far from the tone of Cambridge. It was the voice of the plough-man, the mechanic, the humble cottagers of the home-spun class whose minds were steeped in Bible and Quaker tracts. Out of these circles Garrison had come. In them he remained, in his little room with the dingy walls, bespattered with printer's ink, living on snatches of bread, fruit and milk, sleeping on his table for a bed, with his printing-press beside him. Thence had come, in minds of a similar stock, the dream of the pedlar Bronson Alcott, the vision of the Concord pencil-maker, who had built his hut at Walden. Thence came N. P. Rogers of New Hampshire, tenth in descent from the Reverend John Rogers, the first martyr of Bloody Mary's reign, and the "acts of the anti-slavery apostles," those whom neither courtesy nor money, nor hard words, eggs, blows or brickbats ever deterred from prophesying. The age of Queen Elizabeth had reawakened in the scholarly Cam-bridge mind. The age of Laud and Charles the First had reappeared in the minds of harness-makers, village bar-bers, farmers, tavern-keepers. They drove about the country in borrowed buggies, speaking at the Lyceums and meeting-houses, faring on a few cents a day, a hand-ful of biscuits and raisins, courting the lampblack and the tar and feathers. They lived among revelations and ghostly voices. An old New Hampshire Quaker farmer wrote down a vision that befell him as he stood in his field at noonday. Darkness fell upon his sight and cov-ered the whole earth. He saw the nation divided in civil war.

Under the Boston mind worked the same leaven, but much more complicated thoughts restrained it. The fears of the "cotton interest" inhibited many; so did the social ties of the merchant families, which bound them to the

families of the planters. The Whigs, who had taken
Webster for their leader, followed him in all his com-
promises. They followed Everett, who followed Webster,
and who, with his eye for the "good in everything,"
found something good in slavery: he had visited a plan-
tation in Louisiana, and he was happy to report that the
quarters of the slaves were neat and clean and the beds
were furnished with mosquito-nets. This was reassuring
to Christian souls who counted on the slaves for their
bread and butter. Beside these bread-and-butter fears,
moreover, there was a motive that deserved respect, the
fear of the disruption of the Union, which had been established against such odds. Dr. Channing had expressed
this fear, and no one suspected Channing of partisan
interests. He had shown how the Union preserved the
States from wasting and destroying one another, how the
country would be broken by disunion into restless, grasping sections, all the more hostile to one another because,
as one saw in South America, a common language multiplied jealousies; and Europe would make use of this
dissension to break the nation further for its own advantage. This was enough to sober Boston minds that had
not forgotten the Revolution.

Even in Boston, however, as in the inland regions, the
question worked like madness in the brain. Channing's
little treatise on slavery had made a measure of oppo-
sition to it almost a condition of self-respect. This book
was embarrassing to the prosperous classes, who for a
generation had nursed the illusion that, having won their
independence, they had solved the problems of the world.
The educated mind could not ignore a calm analytical
essay that set the theme in a philosophical light. It
showed, as no writer had shown before, the disastrous
effects of slavery, both on the slaves and on the masters,
and thenceforth no one who professed to think defended
the "peculiar institution" without reservations or misgiv-

ings; and the more the South advanced its claims, in the new States of the West, terrorizing the central government, and forcing the Fugitive Slave Law on the North, the more the New England mind rose against it. Officially both Church and press took sides with the merchants and the lawyers; but the Abolitionist cause made rapid progress even among those whose tastes and feelings Garrison most offended. The converts ran unpleasant risks. One might be a popular author, like Mrs. Child, but, if one published a plea for the slaves, one's fame went out like a candle. Nobody bought one's next book, one could not get a ticket for the Athenæum and a well-known lawyer might pick one's pamphlet up with a pair of tongs and fling it out of the window. One might have sixteen Boston quarterings and a gallery of Copleys and Stuarts, but, if one uttered a phrase with "colour" in it, one's cousins would cut one dead in Beacon Street. One appeared in the press as an "aristocrat," but also as a "hyena" and a "squash." In the morning mail one might receive a bulky anonymous letter from the South, containing a withered ear and a piece of rope. The ear had been cut from a slave who had tried to escape. The rope was for the Boston gentleman, in case he crossed Mason and Dixon's line.

But this was the sort of embarrassment that animated generous minds. While the bankers and politicians grew colder and colder, the poets and the literary men, always in search of a cause, a just and proper focus for their feelings, could say Ha! Ha! once more to the sound of a trumpet. Some of the lawyers joined them. Not all, as Charles Francis Adams said, were "broken in to the cotton interest." Richard Henry Dana, the sailors' lawyer, whose natural instincts and interests were all on the conservative side, threw prudence to the winds. In the name of the old Northern gentry, who had always stood for freedom, and to show how he despised the Boston cringing to the Southern oligarchy, he never lost an opportunity to act as counsel for the runaway slaves. Rockwood Hoar, the judge of later times, who had twice swum the Tiber, like Horatius, made a famous speech in the Legislature, saying that the conscience of Massachusetts had a right to be represented as well as its cotton.* Thenceforward there were two kinds of Whigs, the "cotton Whigs" and the "conscience Whigs," and most of the writers belonged to the second group. It was true that George Ticknor and his circle,—all but the tolerant Prescott,—"Hunkers" of the darkest hue, to whom all agitation was abhorrent, closed their doors to Dana and Charles Sumner, snubbed them on all occasions and cut them on the street. Ticknor grew bitter and vindictive. Sumner, he said, was outside the pale, and he even snubbed the charming Edmund Quincy, the son of the Cambridge Cato, who had betrayed his caste. But Quincy was of bluer blood than Ticknor's. He represented the oldest Boston strain, not only in its love of liberty. He had a cavalier's disregard of the interests of money and property. He scorned the cold respectabilities of the upper-bourgeoisie of Beacon Street. A man of the utmost elegance, with the easy grace of a *grand seigneur,* a lover of ancient customs, with little taste for a mercantile world, he had a paternal affection for the negroes, like that of the old Virginians of the days when they wished to free their slaves. His mind was filled with the lore of colonial times, which he had heard as a child at his father's table, stories of Boston drawing-rooms of old, tales of the Massachusetts negroes; and although, as an active Abolitionist, he wrote to further the cause, his sketches, *Lewis Herbert, Dinah Rollins, Two Nights in San Domingo* and several others, *Mount Verney, Old Houses,* were admirable from any point of view. His

* It was Rockwood Hoar who described the three stages of the too-enterprising Yankee,—"to get on, to get honour, to get honest."

short novel, *Wensley,* better known, a Thackerayan picture of New England life, with touches from *Don
Quixote,* excellent in character and setting, missed its
mark in a commonplace plot; but *The Haunted Adjutant*
was a first-rate story. Quincy, a brilliant amateur, with a
humorous eye for human traits, wrote with a dash and
colour, an ease and freshness that were later to be known
as "modern."

In this Abolitionist campaign, which was dividing
households, as the Unitarian movement had formerly
done, the orators especially had found a cause. They
were in need of a cause, for the tale of the Revolution
and the patriot fathers had grown rather stale, flat and
thin. Eulogies of Washington and Adams, profitable to
Edward Everett, rang hollow in the ears of the new generation. What was the meaning of these declamations,
this cant about the inalienable rights of men in a country
where it was known that Jefferson's nephew had chopped
a slave to pieces with an axe, where beating, branding,
mutilating slaves, selling them, kicking them, killing them
was all in the nature of the situation? * The ancient art of
oratory, the pride of ancestral Boston, had become an
abuse. It was breathing out its vacant life in words,
empty as a cloud, cold as the frozen Frog Pond; and
suddenly, as if by a blood-transfusion, its slow pulse
began to beat again. Oratory once more possessed a function. It touched the springs of action, for the voices of
Charles Sumner and Wendell Phillips were voices to
which Boston was obliged to listen. Their doctrines, their
ideas were scarcely new. What was new was their personal style, their passion, their conviction, their sense of
fact. They were members of a family of minds that had
appeared in all the Western countries, in Italy, in Germany, in France, to defend the religion of liberty, poets

* See Mrs. Stowe's incontrovertible evidence in the *Key to Uncle Tom's
Cabin;* also Mrs. Child's *Plea for that Class of Americans Called Africans.*

militant, intellectual men who were glad to fight and die for their beliefs, figures that were appearing in flesh and blood on battlefields and barricades in Europe. Brothers of Mazzini, heirs of William Tell, men of the world themselves and men of culture, they roused the indifferent minds of the thinking masses and made the American anti-slavery movement a part of the great world-struggle of darkness and light.

A century later, reading Phillips's speeches, one could still feel the moral passion that seemed to rekindle the eyes of the watching portraits when he invoked the fathers in Faneuil Hall. One could still feel the electric excitement that played about the speaker's head. It was known that the careless, courtly Phillips, so buoyant, so disdainful of the mob, the son of the first mayor of the city of Boston, was a convert to the cause. As the college friend and champion of the Southern students, with a touch of the actor in his make-up, as a brilliant and promising lawyer, he had not suggested the reformer. It was not known that at college he had made a profound study of English history at the time of the Civil War, and had read every document connected with it, every novel, play, speech and memoir, from Clarendon to the days of William Godwin. This was the arsenal of learning from which he drew when he had found his cause. With his patrician air and his flashing wit, his volleys of historical allusions, he magnetized the crowd, although he carried his life in his hands when he walked home after a stormy meeting. He seemed to say that threats were beneath contempt. There was no room for rhetoric in his fiery style. Phillips's mind was like a gatling-gun. Sumner was a siege-gun beside him, less effective in direct attack, although Sumner, his fellow-lawyer, born in the same year, had gifts that a legal world was bound to respect. Phillips, with his colloquial manner, something new in Boston that killed the Edward Everett style forever, raked the audience with his sudden sallies. Sumner obliged them to reason. Rather a lecturer than an orator, he piled his legal precedents mountain-high. His speeches were vast oral essays, bristling with quotations and citations. A little grandiloquent, compared with Phillips, but solid where Everett was hollow, he had appealed to thinking men by his speech on *The True Grandeur of Nations*. This was an attack on war, and he had shown that every warship cost as much as a college to build and keep. Each port-hole cost as much as one professor. This was an argument that impressed New England. Sumner had suggested a world-court and a League of Nations.

Many a New England schoolboy knew by heart Webster's philippic against the slave-trade, delivered in the far-off days before the great question had threatened the Union. But Phillips and Sumner had kept the "prejudices" that Webster was begging men to conquer. As they advanced, with Garrison,—Phillips as a free-lance, Sumner as leader of the "conscience Whigs,"—the movement rent society more and more, leaving wealth and power on the Southern side. One by one, however, the men of letters, the poets first of all, joined in the crusade, even those for whom "emancipation" was not a simple matter of blacks and whites, those who had other slaves to liberate, the "white slaves" of the North,* and other forms of slavery to contend with, not to be abolished by Acts of Congress, the slavery of popular indifference, timidity, sloth, stupidity, the slavery of shabby-mindedness and callous dollar-worship. What could emancipation ever mean unless there was a world worth living in? And what was a world that lacked the imagination without which freedom and slavery were empty words? Emerson was not the only writer who, when he deserted his proper studies, found that the Muse, not to be trifled

---

* "Northern gentlemen think to govern us by our black slaves; but, let me tell them, we intend to govern them by their white slaves."—John Randolph.

with, put chaos and confusion in his brain. He had his work to do, like Prescott and Hawthorne, although for him, too, the hour came,—when the Southerners seized and enslaved free-negro citizens of Massachusetts. Meanwhile, for simpler and more emotional minds, the cause was a kind of benefaction; and when volunteers from Germany, Italy, France, exiles and revolutionists, joined in the guerrilla war in Kansas, when Walter Savage Landor wrote an ode and eloquent voices rose all over the world to hearten the Abolitionists, they felt that great days had come again, like the days of '76, that America had once more become the focus of the world-old struggle for liberty. "One learns in a single day," wrote one of the New England men who were taking part in the Free-soil drama, "more about Greeks and Romans and English Puritans and Scottish Jacobites and Hungarians and all heroic peoples, than any course of history can teach. The same process is producing the same results before your eyes, and, what is most striking, the same persons whom you saw a year ago in Boston, indolent and timid, are here transformed to heroes." *

Whatever in the way of stimulus the movement afforded the poets, the poets repaid ten-fold. Even the angular Garrison wrote sonnets, in the gravest style of Milton, composing them in his midnight walks across the bridge to Cambridge; and John Greenleaf Whittier, his lieutenant, had long had cause to know that words, in times like these, had consequences. One of Whittier's anti-slavery pamphlets, *Justice and Expediency,* had caused the death of a friend. Merely for lending it to a brother-physician, Dr. Crandall of Washington had been put in prison, where his health had given way in the dampness and darkness. In fact, in the Whittier of these feverish years, there was more "deed" than "word," strangely in a Quaker non-resistant who clung to the old

* Thomas Wentworth Higginson.

Quaker ways that enabled him to get "into the quiet." But the lithe, quick Whittier, tall and eager, with his black hair and burning eyes, was anything but passive. As a child, in the "snow-bound" Haverhill farmhouse, he had seen or heard of a neighbour melting a minister's image in wax to send his soul to hell; and he himself had not read for nothing the journals of the old fighting Quakers who had wrestled with men and angels in Cromwell's day. He liked to face a mob. His black Quaker coat had been pelted with eggs, and he had seen his newspaper-office, the office of the *Pennsylvania Freeman*, burned over his head. Garibaldi was one of his heroes. Moreover, he was a skilful politician. It was Whittier who had induced Charles Sumner to stand for election to the Senate. There was no lobbyist like him at the State House, when it came to pulling wires "for righteousness' sake," in behalf of the Indians or woman's suffrage, the blind, felons, animals. This befitted the only man of his time who had read all the Utopias. Whittier had had no connection with the Brook Farm movement, but no one in America more than he longed to realize Milton's "true commonwealth."

Whittier was a shoot of the oldest New England. His family had lived in the Haverhill farmhouse since 1688, and no one had known, or was ever to know, the lore of the Merrimac Valley better than he, the legends of Essex and Middlesex and the woods of lower New Hampshire. His forbears had been farmers for six generations and had married the daughters of farmers, and his mind was steeped in local associations, tales of witches, tales of the Indian wars, the gossip of wandering farm-hands and gypsies. A Scottish farmer lived near by who wrote in the manner of Burns for the Haverhill paper. He had often stopped at the Whittier house and sung *Highland Mary* in the kitchen, over his bread and cheese and mug of cider. There were no Yankee pastorals, he had said.

The domestic life of New England had not been hallowed by tender associations. Yet how poetic was the farmer's life!—the scent of the hay-mow, the breath of the cattle, the greenery by the brookside, the huskings, berry-pickings and winter sleigh-rides. These were the days when scriptural themes and scenes had occupied the American poetasters and Jared Sparks and Bancroft had just discovered the romance of American history. Whittier was prepared for Burns and Scott. He had written his first verses in chalk and charcoal on the beam of his mother's loom and had hidden his manuscripts in the farmhouse garret. He longed to escape from farming, for exposure and over-exertion had broken his health. The rigours of the New England winter had left in Whittier's mind impressions that tougher boys would have forgotten. Then Garrison had discovered the "star of genius" who had sent a poem to his paper. He had driven out from Newburyport to find him, and, while Whittier hastened to change his clothes,—he was burrowing under the barn in search of eggs when the great man appeared at the gate,—had begged his father to give him an education. Why make war on a young man's nature?

Whittier's reputation was that of a newspaper-poet. In Cambridge, they had forgotten or scarcely known that his *Legends of New England,* published in 1831, was the first collection of poems of the young New England school. He had versified stories from Mather's *Magnalia,* anticipated Longfellow's *Hiawatha* with ballads of Indian exploits, written tales of the colony times that suggested a metrical Hawthorne. Before these writers had been heard of, Whittier had been widely known. But he had abandoned his early subjects, and there were reasons why he was not remembered outside the obscure and humble public that always cherished him most at the best of times. He had written with a reckless facility, in the well-worn metres of Scott and Campbell, with almost no distinction of language. Aside from a word here and there with a local tang and value,—lug-pole, chimney-lug,—his diction had no nap or freshness: it was a thread-bare diction, and so remained. His associations had never been literary. Among the New England poets his only friend had been Mrs. Sigourney of Hartford, where he had lived for a while. His active life had been spent with orators and reformers, editors, propagandists and politicians. He was regarded as an unlettered rhymester, an anti-slavery journalist in verse. When he asked in one of his poems—

> And wilt thou prize my poor gift less
> For simple air and rustic dress,
> And sign of haste and carelessness?—

what could one say in reply? His senses were defective. He was totally colour-blind and partially deaf. When he looked at an apple-tree, he could not distinguish the leaves from the apples, and once, in a moment of affluence, he bought a carpet that was garishly bright and showy, supposing it was a mild grey and brown, suitable for Quaker feet to walk on. His eye and ear were imperfect. His rhymes were often a scandal. Two hundred years of silence, as he put it, had "taken all the sing" out of the Quakers; and widely as he read, in later years, and carefully as he worked over his poems, he never knew when to cut them short. It was as if, having broken silence, he could not say enough. His technical methods were stereotyped. The simplest and most conventional ballad metres, the sentiments, phrases and rhythms of other poets served him to the last. He had no pride of artistry. When editors revised his manuscripts, Whittier accepted their changes without remark.

In certain aspects, he suggested a lesser Thomas Hood. But Whittier had a verve and flow as notable as

Hood's, a force of moral passion, a fund of feeling. Spirited improvisation was his special gift. Moreover, he had something to say that no one else had said, something that many others after him, true bards and simple, or bards who were merely simple, could only repeat and echo. There was even a touch of grandeur in him, the fiery zeal of a Puritan prophet, the fruit of a passionate nature that "strove in chains." The girls had led Whittier many a dance. In the days when he had longed for wealth and glory, before he became a reformer, it was the worldly girls who attracted him most. They had snubbed him for his poverty and rustic manners and teased him to the brink of suicide. No doubt, this increased his love of money, for Whittier dearly loved to turn a penny, much as he liked others to think him poor; and one of his favourite themes was the happy after-life of a high-born lady who has married a farmer's boy. The girls had made a mistake, he seemed to say, when they had jilted Whittier. For the rest, he had had his compensation, for his virginity fed his poetry. He was a philanderer all his days and could scarcely hold back the flood of "pilgrims" that threatened to engulf his later years, the lady-poets who sent him snips of their dresses, begged him for intimate souvenirs, proposed to marry him on two occasions, built houses near his own, with room for two, and popped in and almost gobbled him up, till he had to set a spring-trap at his door to warn him that they were coming and give him a chance to escape at the rear of his house. These were the days when he always put on his hat before he answered the door-bell, so that he might appear to be going out. He spent whole afternoons roaming the streets, trying to lose the curiosity-seekers. "I had hard work to lose him, but I have lost him," he would say to his sister when he reappeared. "But I can never lose a *her*." But who had encouraged the "pilgrims," the lady-poets, as if he wished to keep the fires burning? He kept the fires burning and thriftily banked them up a single chimney. Poetry was Whittier's vestal altar.

As time went on, he returned to the scenes and subjects that had characterized his early verse; and, while he continued to write for the Abolitionist cause, he became more and more the rural poet. Whittier and Longfellow, whom he scarcely knew, were rivals in popular fame, after he had published the *Lays of My Home*. Longfellow's mind was of a higher cast. Whatever it lacked in intensity, it was poetic in grain. Whittier's mind was sandy and thin beside it, though it had more spontaneity than Lowell's. It glowed with moral feeling, if only here and there with imagination. But Whittier's best work was still to come, in the early eighteen-fifties. Meanwhile, he enlarged the little cottage into which he had moved at Amesbury. He built the garden-room, always filled in season with harebells and laurel, where he liked to read his poems aloud to his friends, while his sister, Elizabeth Whittier, who was also a poet, guarded the vestal flame. In the afternoons, he sat in the village store, perched on a sugar-barrel, joining in the local gossip and putting in a word now and then to turn the vote of the farmers. No other writer had done so much to arouse public feeling for Abolition; and *Ichabod,* the poem on Webster, and *Massachusetts to Virginia* were a part of American history, as everyone felt. But he was only at home in the cause during its prophetic phase. As it entered the violent phase that preceded the war, he grew more and more quietistic and even broke with his old friend Garrison. There were limits beyond which a Quaker poet could not sincerely follow the path of action. This was the period of his prose papers, on Bunyan, Ellwood, Baxter, the notes on the Quakers of Cromwell's time, whom he defended against Carlyle's attacks. Of these the best was the essay on the old New Jersey Quaker, John Woolman, whom Lamb had urged his readers to "get by heart" and who had largely started the anti-slavery movement,—for Garrison was a disciple of one of Woolman's followers. Whittier's longest prose-piece, *Margaret Smith's Journal,* was a picture of the New England settlements in the days of the Salem witches. In a semi-archaic style, composed in tone and only less intense than Hawthorne's pictures, it conveyed the state of mind of the Pilgrim settlers with a haunting particularity. One saw the witchcraft working in the lonely cabins, the irons jumping into the pots, the tools flying about the rooms, the baskets dropping from the chimneys, the goodwives flocking to Boston to see the hangings, while the merry birds carolled in the trees and the white and yellow flowers besprinkled the banks. Through the bedevilled air, one caught the scent of the mayflower, the trailing arbutus, the symbol of a spring-time innocence.

This was Whittier's element, and more and more the "wood-thrush of Essex" sang the summer pastorals and the songs of home that had so much of New England in them:

> Along the roadside, like the flowers of gold
> The tawny Incas for their gardens wrought,
> Heavy with sunshine droops the goldenrod,
> And the red pennons of the cardinal-flowers
> Hang motionless upon their upright staves.
> The sky is hot and hazy, and the wind,
> Wing-weary with its long flight from the south,
> Unfelt; yet, closely scanned, yon maple leaf
> With faintest motion, as one stirs in dreams,
> Confesses it. The locust by the wall
> Stabs the noon-silence with his sharp alarm.
> A single hay-cart down the dusty road
> Creaks slowly, with its driver fast asleep
> On the load's top. Against the neighbouring hill,
> Huddled along the stone-wall's shady side,

The sheep show white, as if a snow-drift still
Defied the dog-star. Through the open door
A drowsy smell of flowers—grey heliotrope,
And white sweet clover, and shy mignonette—
Comes faintly in, and silent chorus lends
To the prevailing symphony of peace.

In rudely vigorous ballads, he told the old legends of the sea-coast, *Skipper Ireson's Ride, The Dead Ship of Harpswell.* In his *Songs of Labour,* recited at workingmen's meetings for three generations, he glorified the trades that he knew so well, shoemaking, lumbering, shipbuilding, droving, fishing; and his husking-poems and corn-songs, his idylls of the village and the farm, *The Old Burying-Ground, Telling the Bees, In School Days, The Barefoot Boy, My Playmate,* redolent of sweet-fern and clover and meadows ripe with corn, brought back to countless readers the world of their childhood. They saw once more the old roads winding, the gap in the wall, the stepping-stones in the brook,—

Glimpses of chimneys and gabled eaves,
Through green elm arches and maple leaves.

The night-hawk's sullen plunge in the woods of New Hampshire, the grey fort's broken wall on the coast of Maine, the rocky capes, the heavy hay-boats crawling, the salt sea-scents along the shore, the quilting-parties and the winter sleigh-rides, the pumpkins and the huckleberry-thickets lived again in the songs of the "barefoot boy."

CHAPTER XXII

NEW ENGLAND AT LARGE

UNDER a tree in front of his house at Marshfield, Daniel Webster lay in his open coffin, dressed in his blue coat with the brass buttons, his right hand over his breast, the sun full in his face. It was 1852, a warm, hazy October day. As far as one could see from the slopes of the hill, a multitude as of grasshoppers covered the land, and the fields were filled with wagons, chaises and sulkies, omnibuses and coaches. Over the silence of the vast assembly, one heard the cattle lowing in their barns.

To the remotest hamlet of the Androscoggin, New England hummed with tales of the fabulous man, how, when he knew that he was dying, he sent his faithful black servant William to hang the lantern at his shallop's mast-head and raise the colours there, saying, "I want to keep my flag flying and my light burning till I die." This was the grand style of a day that was passing, the epoch of the building of the Union, the confident young republic; and even the Abolitionists remembered that Webster, whether "Ichabod" or not, was a great New England worthy, perhaps the greatest, a masterpiece of Yankee blood and sinew whose life had been connected at every point with the interests and hopes of the people. He had thriven with their progress and their success, their farms, their mills, their schools. He symbolized their energy and triumph. Countless boys, like John Fiske, who lived at Middletown, Connecticut, felt that life had grown suddenly small and lonely and wondered how the sun could rise without Daniel Webster.

"I still live"—Webster's last phrase—was engraved on the Sheffield razors that hundreds of farmers used on Sunday mornings. New England was more alive than ever, in the towns, in the manufacturing centres, but farming life had begun to decline. The old farmers were dying out, or so it seemed to those who loved the country,—the men whose hoeing was a sleight-of-hand, who made their own ox-yokes and axe-helves, chopped their three cords of wood a day, knew every medicinal herb that grew in field or stream and knew how to select a piece of timber, chestnut or oak or walnut, that measured a given amount, cut it and score it and load it. These tamers of the wilderness were vanishing from the land. They were hewing their way to the West, along the Great Lakes, while the young men were turning to the cities, learning to pronounce their "ben" as "bin," and sometimes even "bean," and rising with the factories and the railroads.

As wealth advanced and the towns increased, the region grew more self-contemplative. Novelists were appearing here and there, picturing local manners, with an interest in social relations that was aroused by the spread of urban standards. One had to tolerate human nature first, a thing that Calvinism had scarcely encouraged, before one could find it amusing. Landscape-artists appeared in the train of the poets. Thomas Cole, Kensett, Church and others were painting up and down the coast, sketching in the Berkshires, tramping the White Hills and the Green Mountains, looking for the picturesque, catching the scent of Indian legends, following the lead of the landscape-poets; for Whittier, Longfellow, Lowell and Holmes had filled the country with associations. Every waterfall and stream and hilltop, Ossipee, Winnepesaukee, Hampton Beach, Chocorua's horn, the

Kennebec, the Saco, every ancient house and rocky ledge was the theme of some ballad or sonnet that called for the pencil. Summer visitors at Nahant noted in their journals the little scenes that pleased the landscape-painters, the cows going over the beach at sunset on their way to the cow-yards at Lynn, their red hides reflected in the wet sand and lighting up the grey of the sky and the surge. The influence of Ruskin had begun to spread, and people spoke of the beauty of rocks and the sacredness of colour. They compared the effects of changes of air in the mountains and wondered just how much of the vague and dreamy, in the matter of mist or spray, a scene had to possess to be sublime. Intervale was a favourite spot, where artists and tourists gathered. Connoisseurs of landscape from Boston or Hartford, parties from Worcester and Burlington drove on the tops of stages or in private buckboards through the Franconia Notch, observing Mount Webster and Lafayette as if they were two pictures in different styles by the hand of the same master. They scrutinized Wachusett from Monadnock; they looked at Franconia from the Pemigewassett. They studied the slopes and the cliffs, the Flume and the Profile, an older piece of sculpture than the Sphinx, climbed up to the Nose or the Chin, botanized with Asa Gray in mind and longed for a little talk with Agassiz. For Agassiz had made these scenes exciting, even more exciting than Ruskin made them. Speaking as a geologist, he had said that New England was the oldest spot on the earth's surface. They sprang out of their beds at the Mountain House when the porter, walking through the halls, rang his big bell and shouted, "Sunrise!"—assembling on the piazza to see the Franconia Mountains at earliest dawn. They tried the echo on Echo Lake and quoted Tennyson on the "horns of Elfland." They noted the yellow fields of rye and the beautiful cone of Mount Washington, yielding harvests of colour.

The more the ancient rural life receded into the background of men's lives, the more it roused their feelings of romance. The farm, the village ways, harsh enough in actuality, seemed, to the barefoot boys who had gone to New York or were making their fortunes in State Street, merry and jolly or softly sweet as Goldsmith's scenes of Auburn. They liked to remember their school-days, the wadded hoods, the knitted caps and mittens, the snow-bound evenings under the lamp, the games, the slates and pencils, rosy apples in the dish, nutting-time, coasting-time. Sawing wood in the frosty air had surely seemed less dull than adding figures. This was the theme of a hundred poems and stories that multiplied with time, as the farm became a universal symbol,—the farm, the weather-painted house and barn, the well-sweep, the orchard, the sandy field surrounded by the woods, the small blue lake at the foot of the hill. No New England boy or man could ever forget the country, the cider-making days of old, the heaps of golden apples under the trees, the cider-mill worked by the plodding horse and all agush with autumn juices. The new generation of city-dwellers longed to be reminded of these rural scenes, and the popularity of the "household poets" rose with the exodus from the "household" setting, the homestead and the farm. This was the secret of Whittier's fame. He was the emblem of Thanksgiving, when two or three New Englanders gathered together, or a houseful of scattered uncles and aunts and cousins, in far New York or on the Western plains. He brought back the painted autumn woodlands, the pumpkin pies of old, the succotash, the doughnuts and the chowder, the wild grapes, the tubs of maple sugar, the school-house, the old-fashioned winter that seemed so different from the modern winter because of the modern devices that had softened its rigours. The pioneers carried Whittier with them, as emigrant Scotsmen carried the poems of Burns. *Snow-Bound* was their image of Pallas, the safeguard of their memories. It was the touchstone of their past.

For New England men were scattering far and wide. They were sowing schools and colleges over the West. In the South Sea Islands, in China, in Burmah, they were planting Orthodox churches and mission-centres, writing their versions of the Bible in half the tongues of Asia. Some of the missionaries were learned men, two or three were great men.* They remembered Thanksgiving Day in the Himalayas and read their *Snow-Bound* on the Yang-tse River. New England seemed romantic in the distance, as Shanghai and Canton had seemed in their barefoot boyhood. The Rollo Books, to be sure, were not romantic, even to the remotest Yankee, redolent as they were of the barn-yard and pasture, the hired man, the chopping-block, early hours and earnest aspirations, nor were Elijah Kellogg's tales of boys in the good old days in the "State of Maine,"—as Maine men liked to call it, to remind the world that their State was no longer a "District." † If the fathers of Jacob Abbott's generation enjoyed the adventures of Rollo as much as their children, it was for a more substantial reason than that which drew them to the household poets; for Rollo was the model boy, in whom the model parent saw himself, the leading manufacturer in his earlier stages. Here the New England passion for self-improvement, as it was understood by the plainer folk, found its completest record. How to be dutiful, how to be conscientious, how to be genteel and well-informed, in order to be right on all occasions and able, especially, to set others right, this was

* Of the original writings of these New England missionaries,—Adoniram Judson, Hiram Bingham, S. Wells Williams, etc.,—an admirable example is *The Middle Kingdom,* a survey of the Chinese Empire. The author, S. Wells Williams, wrote two Chinese dictionaries and was later professor of Chinese at Yale.

† Kellogg's *Lion Ben of Elm Island* and other books for boys, lifeless and wooden enough, are filled with authentic details of pioneer life on the coast of Maine.

Jacob Abbott's open secret. In Rollo, the reader beheld in all its phases the shaping of one of Webster's "solid men."

No one could have doubted Rollo's future. He was destined to rise in the world, with the other factory-owners and cotton-brokers who had left their ancestral farms in Vermont and Maine, the farms that seemed idyllic in their fancy as they drowsed in their office-chairs at the end of the day. "Ik Marvel's" books, *Reveries of a Bachelor* and *Dream-Life,* appealed to this nostalgic mood. One went to the city, accepted the ways of the world, made one's pile and married for advantage, while all the while, in one's heart of hearts, one clung to the simple, wholesome dreams of childhood. Such was the burden of these romances, composed in a style that suggested Irving and Lamb. The fields, the trees, the brooks, the sweetheart whose name one had cut on the bark of the birches were much more real than the noisy, ambitious life of the changing, bustling town, the sharp transactions of the business day, all blaze and vanity. Rain in the garret, as one recalled it, school-dreams, first love, fishing, boy-romance and first ambition were the stuff of the bachelor's reveries. That the bachelor who thought of nothing but marriage was the best of advocates of the married state, that all his dreams were "pipe-dreams" added to the charm of the make-believe. That he acquiesced in what he assumed to reject, the reader quickly gathered. These aspirations and visions were only "smoke," a comforting reassurance for the practical man who had left them far behind him. For the rest, Ik Marvel's enormous vogue showed how many people desired in books the opposite of what they desired in life. It was the busiest souls, those that were eager for all the latest inventions, who most rejoiced in this philosopher, this lover of old ways who never used a watch to measure time, preferred a burning taper to a gas-jet and lighted his cigar with coal and tongs.

But Ik Marvel,—Donald G. Mitchell,—was an engaging writer. His charm of style, his gentle bookishness, the slightly archaic flavour of his mind carried these youthful romances round the world; and long after men had ceased to read them, they were to survive as books for boys, who found their vague feelings, doubts and passions reflected in the bachelor's dreams. Mitchell's later books, *My Farm at Edgewood* and *Wet Days at Edgewood,* were of a hardier quality. Written during these years when rural life was falling into decay, when the city was attracting the ambitious and many farmers were moving West, they pictured the art of husbandry, its pleasures and its benefits, as Alcott was picturing it in his Concord essays, but with more system and practical knowledge. Mitchell, a graduate of Yale, a former consul at Venice and a landscape-gardener by avocation, who had laid out the grounds of Princeton College, had retired in poor health to a farm at New Haven, where he lived among his books. His mind was filled with garden associations, the literary farmers of Greece and Rome, Hesiod, Pliny, Virgil, the old British authors and country story-tellers, from Piers Plowman to the Ettrick Shepherd; but he was a practical farmer, too, who longed to revive the dying interest in the oldest of New England occupations. He rebuked the shams of the farmer's life, the blinded front-parlour that was only entered once a month or so, to consult some gilt-bound dictionary, while it engrossed the best half of the house; and he made no false claims in regard to farming, its profits and advantages. His observations on bees and the care of cattle, on dairying, on the orchard and the garden, on the treatment of grapes, plums, apples, pears, on the dwarf trees that had to be fondled and humoured, on rural decoration, crops and markets were as shrewd and precise as

Evelyn's, or Walton's observations on the angler's art, which, with Jeremy Taylor, Browne and Bunyan, had left their traces in his style. Ik Marvel was at his best in these country essays; and Elihu Burritt, the "learned blacksmith," also wrote eloquent papers on pastoral life. Burritt, who had left his Worcester forge and made a new career for himself as a philanthropic lecturer, had organized congresses of the Friends of Peace at Brussels, Paris, Frankfort and in England, where he served as American consul at Birmingham. With his farm at New Britain, Connecticut, always in mind, he visited farms in every corner of England, making careful notes and observations, in the hope of improving rural conditions at home. His *Walk from London to Land's End,* suggesting Cobbett's *Rural Rides,* was filled with unassuming information. Burritt's account of his visit to the Queen's dairy at Windsor Castle was a more rewarding travel-sketch than most of the current essays on the Coliseum. It was a model dairy, but Burritt thought the milk-pails were too heavy. In exchange for all he had learned, he would have liked to send the Queen some of the light, white-cedar, seamless pails which the farmers used in New England.

Alcott, Burritt, Mitchell, three Connecticut men,—for Burritt was born in New Britain, as Alcott was born at Wolcott, ten miles to the west,—were the three outstanding writers of their time on pastoral life and farming. Frederick Law Olmsted, who had begun to write in the fifties, was also a Connecticut man, the son of a Hartford merchant. This local development was not surprising, for Connecticut was more rural than Massachusetts, where town-life and shipping had occupied so many minds. But even in fertile Vermont, most pastoral of all the States, factories were appearing here and there, at Burlington, especially, on Lake Champlain, where the well-known Minister to Turkey, the lawyer-scholar, George Perkins Marsh, who had been offered Sparks's chair at Harvard, carried on his studies and wrote his books. Marsh, a life-long friend of his fellow-Vermonter, the sculptor Hiram Powers, and a class-mate at Dartmouth of Rufus Choate, a stalwart, inquisitive man and a notable linguist, had published a grammar of Icelandic and was known far and wide as a Scandinavian scholar when Longfellow was studying Swedish and Finnish. The library of Scandinavian books that he kept in his Burlington house was the most complete in the world outside the Scandinavian countries; and he had printed, in 1843, an essay called *The Goths in New England,* suggested by the Northern myths and sagas, that was one of the many forerunners of the modern "Nordic" movement. With none of the animus that later writers, the Houston Stewart Chamberlains and their kind, imported into the Nordic cult, Marsh traced all the virtues of New England to the Gothic element in its forbears. What was the age of the Puritans, which had given birth to New England, but that in which the Gothic strain in England had cast out the Roman element? The Goths were the noblest of races; it was their blood that flowed at Bunker Hill. Whatever the Anglo-Saxons possessed of intellectual power and moral grandeur, they owed to the Gothic mother. Their grasping ambition, their materialism, their spirit of exclusive selfishness were due to the Roman nurse.

This represented one of those germs of feeling, innocent at the outset, like Bronson Alcott's preference for the blond complexion, that sometimes flower in sinister ways. Marsh, who had a scientific mind, would have been horrified if he had foreseen the use that later anthropologists, in the interests of tribal factions, were to make of his Gothic theory. His object was to preach the ancient virtues and simplicities, not to make invidious distinctions. Besides, *The Goths in New England* was only a pamphlet. Marsh wrote several more important works, an entertaining study of *The Camel,* filled with curious and amusing lore gathered in his Oriental travels, two philological books on the English language, based on lectures that he had delivered at Harvard, and the masterly *Man and Nature,* better described by its later title, *The Earth as Modified by Human Action.* This was to remain a classical work in the field of modern geography, for Marsh was one of the first to understand the relation between man and his physical setting. He was almost the first to protest against the wanton way in which man disturbed the harmonies of nature. It is true that, long before, a writer who remained anonymous contributed to Miss Peabody's *Æsthetic Papers* an essay, *Vegetation about Salem,* describing the reckless fashion in which the American forests were being destroyed. "Posterity must feel the consequences" was the moral of this unregarded paper, a moral that no one drew till the "conservation movement" of later years. Marsh was the prophet of this movement. No one had written with such breadth of knowledge of man as a geological agent, who can upbuild or destroy his home, the earth. No one had shown before how man had played the destroyer and what he could do to reëstablish the partnership between himself and nature.

Marsh, who died in Italy, at Vallombrosa,—he was the first American minister to the newly-established kingdom,—was the chief contributor of Vermont to the "literature of knowledge." To the "literature of power" Vermont made a modest contribution, a novel that belonged to the school of Cooper and was destined to be read as long as Cooper. Daniel Pierce Thompson, the author of *The Green Mountain Boys,* was a lawyer and judge at Montpelier, where he edited *The Green Mountain Freeman.* One saw him shuffling through the streets in his battered carpet-slippers, on his way to the newspaper-office where he had printed his book; for, although he was a local dignitary and lived in a clapboard Parthenon, he was a jolly old sloven whose greatest pleasure was to go hunting and fishing with the boys. They all knew that he had been born in Charlestown, in the shadow of Bunker Hill; but at the age of five, in 1800, he had been brought to Vermont, and there was not a worthy in the State who knew as much about it as the judge. He had grown up on a farm near Montpelier, where he had watched the building of the State House, and had seen the youthful commonwealth emerge from its old border life, which resembled that of Cooper's New York and the Scotland of some of the Waverley novels, into a thriving republic. He had gone through Middlebury College and studied law in Virginia, where he had met and talked with Jefferson on the grounds of the university he was building. As they stood together, the old President, who was almost eighty, took a chisel out of the hand of one of his Italian stone-cutters and showed him how to turn the volute of a capital; then he leaped on his horse and gallopped away. Thompson was full of these tales of the men of the Revolution. He had wandered all over Vermont, with his horse and his fishing-rod and gun, shooting wolves and catching trout, chatting at farmhouse doors, talking with the pioneer settlers, listening to yarns about Ethan Allen. A born antiquarian, like Scott, a lover of ballads and folklore, he kept careful notes of these conversations. Every client of the country lawyer gave him an anecdote or a bit of gossip.

In these little towns of Vermont, surrounded by rolling pastures and groves of maples, far from the bustling sea-coast, the eighteenth-century mind lived quietly on. The new-fangled Boston books seldom reached Montpelier, and country judges and editors read Pope and Fielding as if the good old world had never changed. Thompson, a born story-teller, although he never became a professional author, wrote his first book in the manner of Smollett. First and last, he wrote many books, all of them, save

one, surpassingly dull, and all, even the best, amateurish;
for he had few relations with other authors and scarcely
knew the meaning of criticism. Like most unprofessional
writers, he never knew where his strength lay and constantly tried his hand in directions where he was foredoomed to fail. But he had not read Scott and Cooper
for nothing, he had steeped himself in the legends of
Vermont, and, if he was a man of one book, this book,
which he largely wrote on his father's farm, sitting under
a pine-tree, was a most engaging performance. *The Green
Mountain Boys* was a home-grown product, if ever literature saw one, as unpretentious as a log-cabin, but it was
built on such a good model that no faults of style or
execution counted in the final result. It was the classic
picture of Vermont, in the days of its struggle for independence, first from New York and afterwards from
England; and the picture was undoubtedly true in its
atmosphere and feeling. One saw the beaver-hatted
mountaineers, the bold, high-hearted borderers, handsome and fearless, Seth Warner and Ethan Allen, thread-
ing their way through the greenwood, like Robin Hood
and his band, bearing the noble buck on their shoulders;
one heard their whistle echoing through the sylvan
glades. One saw the fond and spirited young ladies, im-
prisoned in block-houses and woodland cabins, ready for
brave escapes and enchanting elopements; and over all
one breathed the fragrant air of pine, spruce and balsam, a
world of sparkling lakes and flashing trout-streams,
youth, adventure, freedom and true romance.

This was a Yankee tale as brisk and wholesome as any
mountain-ballad. It was a border-song in prose, and these
were the days when the Yankee ballads throve as never
later. Catch a "real, green, live Yankee," as Father
Taylor liked to say, and you always caught a man who
could sing a song, especially on the sea-coast. In Maine,
among the old fish-houses, where they still used words

that one found only in Chaucer, there were men who could sing all night, seven score songs in succession, and count up to two or three hundred. On the Isles of Shoals, near Portsmouth, where "Old Bob," the spectre, one of Captain Kidd's men, haunted the coves and the wharves, and Celia Thaxter lived at Appledore, where her father kept the lighthouse, one might have heard an old shoaler, who had fought at New Orleans in 1815, singing by the hour, while he sat bent forward with his arms on his knees, or played on a cracked old fiddle, with his wrinkled eyelids screwed tight together. Where had his queer tunes come from? They were like the creaking and groaning of masts or the whistling of the wind in the cordage of a clipper.* *Lord Bateman* was a favourite with these singers, who added their own variations, or the deeds of "Brave Wolfe," or

> With sixteen brass nineteens the Lion did growl,
> With sixteen brass twenties the Tiger did howl.

There were minstrels and rural singers all over New England, and often a well-known poem became an anonymous ballad. Such was Walter Mitchell's *Tacking Ship off Shore*. This was adopted by the fishermen, who had never heard of the author. Dr. Holmes's *Ballad of the Oysterman* was sung up and down the coast, with hundreds of alterations and elaborations.

Aside from Thompson's tale of Vermont, few New England novels of the moment could have been described as brisk or wholesome. *The Wide, Wide World* of Susan Warner was a swamp of lachrymosity. It was a malarial book. So was *The Lamplighter*, by Maria Cummins, the story of another Cinderella, which had, however, something vigorous in it that *The Wide, Wide World* totally lacked. One felt and saw the Boston slums,—for slums

* See Celia Thaxter's *Among the Isles of Shoals*.

had appeared in Boston with a vengeance,—the street-lamps and the snow, suggesting Dickens's London. What was real in both these books, as pictures of their time, was the pervasive presence of religion.* Little Ellen was a prig, but when she was dazzled by the array of Bibles, of which her mother had promised her one, "so that her wits were ready to forsake her," and when she spent her evenings singing hymns, and "hymn succeeded hymn, with fresh and varied pleasure," she was behaving as Harriet Beecher Stowe certainly behaved at sixteen; and Mrs. Stowe had never been a prig. Her large, frank, fiery, generous nature had nothing in it of the goody-goody; and hymns, in the passionate world in which she lived, were as much a part of the atmosphere as ballads ever were in time of war. All the New England poets were writing them, following Dwight and Barlow, and the best American hymns that have ever been written appeared when Mrs. Stowe was in her heyday.† In the two hundred years that had passed since Governor Winslow refreshed himself "with singing of psalms, making joyful melody," New Englanders had exulted in hymns. Mrs. Stowe, as a child in Litchfield, had listened with ecstasy to the "fuguing tunes," those billowy compositions which they sang in church, when the four parts of the choir took up the song, and went racing round after one another, each singing a different set of words, till at length, by some inexplicable magic, they all came together again, and sailed smoothly out into a sea of harmony. She had looked with wonder from side to side when treble, tenor, counter and bass

* The religious note entirely dominated R. T. S. Lowell's *The New Priest in Conception Bay,* a novel of Newfoundland, with a few good scenes of sea-coast life. The author, an Episcopal clergyman, was a brother of James Russell Lowell.

† E.g., Holmes's "Lord of all being, throned afar," Whittier's "Dear Lord and Father of mankind," E. H. Sears's "Calm on the listening air of night" and "It came upon the midnight clear." Samuel Francis Smith, who, at twenty-four, wrote "America" in half an hour, produced almost one hundred and fifty hymns.

were thus roaring and foaming, and it verily seemed as if the psalm were about to be wrecked among the breakers. And then, to her delighted sense, every verse emerged whole and uninjured from the storm.

Harriet Beecher Stowe was one of the volcanic souls whom the Abolitionist movement brought to the front. As the daughter of Lyman Beecher, she had lived through the days of her father's "Revival." She had studied at Hartford, at her sister's school, where Catharine Beecher wrote her well-known essay refuting Jonathan Edwards on the Will, learning French and Italian there, and had answered with a "yes" her father's question, "Do you feel that, if the universe should be destroyed, you could be happy with God alone?" At twelve, however, hearing of Byron's death, she had wandered off to a lonely hillside, laid herself down in a field of daisies, looked up at the sky and wondered about Byron's soul. The vehemence and intensity of Byron's feeling fascinated all the Beechers, who felt the Calvinistic inheritance in him, and Harriet, who adored *The Corsair,* had sung "Fare thee well" with the other schoolgirls, who felt that they would never have let Byron go. Many years later, in her *Vindication of Lady Byron,* in which she turned against the poet, she showed how deep these early impressions were. Her father, who did not approve of novels, made an exception of Scott, whom his children had to read; and Harriet found the *Arabian Nights,* in the family garret, in a barrel of sermons. She dreamed of some heroic cause, some mission or crusade, that would call out her powers of devotion.

She had visited in Boston, as a girl, when Lyman Beecher, at the Park Street church, had pelted the Unitarians with his sermons, and had followed him in the rout to Cincinnati. Boston was past redemption by any Connecticut method, but the "capital of the West" received him gladly. He preached revival sermons all the way. It was there that Harriet married Calvin Stowe, a teacher in her father's seminary, "rich in Greek, Arabic and Hebrew" but as poor as other missionaries in everything else. There, during a cholera epidemic that was like the black plague of the Middle Ages,—nine thousand people in the city died in three months, and there were ten thousand cases of smallpox,—she wrote a tract that was widely read, *Earthly Care a Heavenly Discipline*. Of care she had enough herself, but there were compensations in Cincinnati. The town was half made up of New England people, with a literary club and a magazine. She began to write stories and essays, often on the kitchen table, surrounded by pots and pans, with half a dozen children asking questions. These stories, elementary enough, paler than Miss Sedgwick's, pleased a circle of readers for whom the visible world had begun to exist and the simplest observations were all-sufficient. But Dr. Stowe knew that she had a power of which these tales gave little evidence. He told her that she could form the mind of the West.

It happened that her father's seminary was an Abolitionist centre. Runaway slaves who appeared there were kept and passed along to the north, and just across the river, in Kentucky, were large slave-plantations. Mrs. Stowe spent several days on one of these plantations, which she afterwards described as Colonel Shelby's; and, although she had never lived in the South, she heard so much about it, and met so many Southern men and women, that she was prepared to picture it as no Southern writer had ever done. The moment for this came later, when she moved to Brunswick, Maine, where her husband was asked to teach in Bowdoin College. The Stowes lived there in a house where Longfellow had lodged as a student. The Fugitive Slave Law had just been passed, and letters came pouring in upon Mrs. Stowe describing its tragic consequences, the separations of husbands and wives, the scattering of mothers and their children. Her mind became suddenly incandescent. She felt she had an apostolic mission to put an end to slavery once for all; she felt that it was not herself but God who wrote the tale of *Uncle Tom's Cabin*. If this book was not the cause of the Civil War, as Lincoln said later, it was at least one of the major causes, for it blocked the operation of the Fugitive Slave Law. As a literary event, it was the greatest since Prescott's *Ferdinand and Isabella*. It was a world-event, in fact. Macaulay, Heine and George Sand reviewed it. Three Paris newspapers published it at once, and Uncle Tom's Cabins rose all over Europe, as restaurants, creameries and bazaars. It appeared in thirty-seven languages, and three times over in Welsh, into which Scott and Dickens had never been translated; and it sent Heine back to his Bible and made such an impression on Tolstoy in Russia that, when he came to write *What is Art?*, he took it as an example of the highest type, with Dostoievsky's *House of the Dead*, and much of Victor Hugo. In all the history of the printed book, the Bible alone had appeared in so many versions.

Was Tolstoy right in his opinion? On the whole, yes, ten times right; and this was not only because of the moral force that carried *Uncle Tom* around the world. Everything in Mrs. Stowe was large, her experience, her humour, her feeling for justice, her passion for the realities of human nature. Her mind had the swing and rhythm of the great story-tellers, like Dickens, Cooper, Scott and Victor Hugo, and she showed in her later novels, *The Pearl of Orr's Island* and *The Minister's Wooing*, how little she needed a moral thesis to bring all her gifts into play. "A work is great," says Mr. Joad, "when it has ceased to matter that it is bad." Dickens was great enough to be "bad," and so was Mrs. Stowe, who was also of the technically rough-and-ready, for her characters were not only real, boldly conceived and presented, but they were involved in situations of a crucial and primary kind. She had a panoramic eye and a just and truthful feeling for human relations that carried her out of the sphere of propaganda. There was no touch of cant in her moral feeling, no disposition to blame the South; she made one like the Southerners more than ever, and she chose a native Vermonter, Simon Legree, to symbolize all that was worst in a national evil. Removed from the atmosphere in which it was written, *Uncle Tom's Cabin* remained a great folk-picture of an age and a nation. For one saw the Quaker colonies in Indiana and the far-away farms of Vermont bound up with the slave-plantations and the Mississippi, the camp-meetings, the negro life; and the characters, St. Clare and Miss Ophelia, Uncle Tom, Topsy and Simon Legree, were drawn with a force that made them types and symbols. Mrs. Stowe's New England novels, written with the same rude strength, established a school and a method. It was her New England, not Hawthorne's, that gave later writers their point of departure. She set the stage for Sarah Orne Jewett. But the final proof of Mrs. Stowe's power was that she created the Southern novel,—as distinguished from the Southern romance,—and that, three generations later, Southern writers still had to reckon with her picture.

CHAPTER XXIII

CONCORD IN THE FIFTIES

EMERSON HAD revisited England in 1847. Carlyle had urged him to lecture there, and he had spent nine months, in London, Manchester and Scotland, talking and taking notes. In his pocket he carried a compass. "I like to hold the god in my hands," he said.

He had reached a solstice in his life, one of those dead points when one requires some foreign force in order to avoid stagnation. He had travelled for a whip for his top, and his top had come home spinning. Never had the "parlour Erebus" encountered so many first-rate thinkers and writers, eupeptic studying-mills, cast-iron men, whose powers of intellectual endurance compared with those of most Americans as a steam-hammer with a music-box. He had always wished to measure his valour by his ability to cope with giants, who aroused one's own central courage of insight. He wished to observe the hygiene, the gymnastic, their experience suggested and approved; and he longed to be challenged and frightened, if anyone could frighten him, to put his own thoughts to the proof. In his depressed hours, when his mind was ebbing,—

> Doomed to long gyration
> In the sea of generation,—

America seemed of a village littleness; and it was hard to go beyond one's public. Carlyle, Macaulay, De Quincey, Faraday, Tyndall, all of whom he had met and who had heard him, had roused in him anew the fire of emulation. Tyndall said that he owed to *Nature* all that he had done in the world, and Emerson found that in Oxford he had stirred and heartened Clough and Matthew Arnold, who had been bewildered by Carlyle. He had visited Wordsworth again at Rydal Mount and had spent a month with Clough in Paris, observing the first movements of the new revolution. He had come home filled with fresh ideas. Better still, the need to express himself so that a foreign audience would understand him, the challenge of so many sceptical hearers had led him to define his thoughts more closely. His style grew more and more concrete; the Franklin in his nature grew more apparent, the wisdom of the man who had dealt with men. He was preparing to write his finest books, *English Traits* and the great *Conduct of Life.* Best of all, much as he liked the English, he felt as never before the hope and faith of America. He had returned with joy to the Concord woods and pastures.

> Caesar of his leafy Rome,
> There the poet was at home.

Henry Thoreau, meanwhile, had gone to live in his father's house, the new yellow house on Concord Main Street. He had his den in the attic. There he kept his collections, the birds' nests, mosses, plants and arrowheads. His books were arranged on shelves he had built himself, using the driftwood on the river-banks. Concord was the old coat he wore, his morning-robe and study-gown, his walking-dress and suit of ceremony. If he had had to spend all his days confined to a corner of this attic, like the big spider on the rafter, he would have felt at home there. The world would have been just as large to him, as long as he had his thoughts.

He cultivated poverty like sage, the best of the garden

herbs. What poverty and obscurity meant to him, no one could ever have told,—a more than princely leisure, a poetic leisure, without care, without engagements, fancy-free. How many springs and summers he had lived, how many autumns and winters, with nothing to do but to live them, imbibing the nutriment they had to yield! Two years with the flowers, for instance, observing when they opened. He could afford to spend a whole fall watching the changing tints of the elms and the maples. He could record the drama of the month of March, when the woodchucks' holes were still choked with leaves and he saw the first bluebird two days earlier than the year before. Or had Ellery Channing seen it first? Henry Hosmer saw the first geese, honking over the Sudbury meadows, or so, at least, George Minott said, the same George Minott who was always asking, "Seen a robin?" Henry amused himself, now and then, imitating the geese. He found himself, one day, flapping his sides with his elbows and uttering *mow-ack* with a nasal twang and a sudden twist of the head.

Poverty had given him all this wealth. The leisure to spend a day, whenever he chose, walking twenty or thirty miles, or voyaging about the river in December, when the drops froze on his oars, pleased with the silvery chime of the icicles against the stems of the button-bushes. Leisure to visit his birches and tap them on an April afternoon, while he sat on a rock in the warm, sunny swamp, waiting for his vessels to be filled, watching the great black butterflies, with their buff-edged wings, dancing and fluttering about him. Leisure for a day in Gowing's swamp, where the hairy huckleberries grew and he paddled like Socrates, barefoot, in the Ilyssus; leisure to note the temperature of the springs and ponds, or look for Indian soapstone pots or mouse-holes in some hollow, or watch the flying-squirrels by the hour, skimming their way like hawks between and around the trees; leisure to stop at a grist-mill and observe the cobweb-tapestry, engaging the miller by questions while his eye sought the cobwebs on the miller's hat. Leisure for all his pursuits and contemplations, and more than amply paid for. Did some of his neighbours think that he sat on his father's shoulders? They should have seen him in the family work-shop, taking his turn, and more than his turn, at the pencils. It was he who saved the business when the German pencils threatened to drive their own out of the market. He solved the problem, bought the German clay, contrived machines for cutting the hardened paste and drilling the blocks of wood. He even supplied the Harpers of New York with their plumbago for electrotyping.

Across the way dwelt Ellery Channing. He had moved from Ponkawtassett Hill and bought an old house for himself on Main Street. He was living all alone there, with only his dog for company, to stir up the air of the room when it grew too deadly quiet,—for he experienced awful solitudes. He had fallen out with his family. He continued to write his verses, Wordsworthian meditations, winter wood-scenes, with all his old whimsical zest, and he had published his *Conversations in Rome*. This was a dialogue between an artist, a Catholic and a critic, for Ellery had visited Italy in 1845 and had almost been converted to the Roman church. He had something to say about Italian farming, as well as Salvator Rosa and Montaigne, and he was the Catholic in the "conversations." He had found himself murmuring prayers with the best of them. But for all his frequent petulance with Concord, he said the New England folk were his own flesh and blood; and he and Henry Thoreau were thicker than ever. Ellery was the rustic rhymer who had walked to Walden, after Henry deserted his hut, and hung up the verses on the wall; and Henry had actually seen a man buying a copy of Ellery's poems at Little and Brown's book-shop in Boston. Alcott was living in town, more or less, though he often came out to see his friends. The ever fresh and jubilant Alcott had built a summer-house on Emerson's lawn, rejecting the angular timber that others used, preferring the rustic branch. He had even added a second story, hung with beautiful mosses. It was a philosophic, a Euclidian structure, rather metaphysical than real, designed to exhibit the nature and value of curves. For it seemed, when Alcott walked in the woods, as if nature had looked for his coming and grown all his materials in the brush, along the lines of the fence-rows, where the young pines, bent by the snow or the axe, described, in their efforts to regain their natural rectitude, every graceful form of curve or spiral that he required for his rustic works. They lent themselves to varied combinations. Others might compose their poems and pictures. Alcott composed arbours. None knew better than he the romance of gardens. Why should not Emerson's garden have an additional touch that recalled the Garden of the Hesperides?

Henry, lending Alcott a hand, and sitting on the ridge-pole, had felt that he was "nowhere, doing nothing." Henry was a practical man, all for straight lines; he had no use for the "natural curve" in branches, men or women. No matter, Alcott also was a man who knew what nature meant him to do with her, a Virgil, a White of Selborne, a Yankee settler, wrapped in a single frame. He loved sage, too, sovereign sage, excellent for longevity, and often spoke of Pliny's good housewife who went to her herb-garden for her seasonings, instead of spending money at a spice-shop, and thus preserved the health of her family, the while she saved her purse. He had his knock-down answer for anyone who questioned his qualifications, "If Pythagoras came to Concord, whom would he ask to see?" His only faults were faults of worldly wisdom,—the truthful, candid, always magnanimous man. There were precious goods on his shelves,

as Emerson said, but he had no show-window. Were you
a child or a beggar, a lunatic or a Boston gentleman, you
got the same reply from Bronson Alcott. He had his
innocent foibles. He was much concerned with his gene-
alogy. At fifty-four, why not? He liked to think of his
old Connecticut forbears and had just revisited Wolcott.
He had copied the inscriptions on the grave-stones and
the records of fifteen towns, and he sometimes pulled out
his long note-book and read them aloud to his friends.
He had found an epitaph that he thought would interest
Henry,—one of his own forbears,—and made a copy of
it. What a preoccupation for a lover of wisdom!

But his chief preoccupations were the same as ever,
keeping the famous journal and holding his Conversations.* The journal brimmed over with his thoughts, many
of them thin, diffuse, abstract, others nutty and pregnant,
phrased in a rare, flowing, antique style, on rural affairs
and recreation, friends, books, philosophy, childhood, literary courtesy, hospitality, with a store of apt quotations.
The habit of journalizing had been for him a lesson in
the art of composition. Alcott no longer wrote in the
vague, inadequate fashion of the "Orphic Sayings." He
had learned to expand and express these tight conceits.
He had slept on his writing and reviewed it on his walks,
and *Concord Days* and *Tablets* were the fine result. Time
had ripened his life and mellowed its fruits. His Conversations in Boston were difficult still, for there he rode his
hobbies, but Emerson and Thoreau went in from Concord, Garrison sometimes came, and Theodore Parker,
Lowell, Elizabeth Peabody, James Freeman Clarke, various travelling foreigners. He spoke on "Self-knowledge"
or "The Times." He began by reading aloud a poem,
George Herbert's *Man,* or some of his own philosophical
verses, selected from the red-covered note-book. Then he

* Alcott's manuscript journal, fifty volumes or more, is still preserved in
Concord. Louisa Alcott had it bound in stout black leather.

unfolded his favourite doctrines, diet, complexion, race, the "demonic man." A real demonic man appeared one evening, with blazing eyes and swarthy face, the kind of man who lives on beef and brandy, smokes black cigars and possibly builds a railroad. This was a little embarrassing. Objectors sometimes came, as if for the purpose of throwing him off his track. Another trouble-maker was Theodore Parker, who quoted Scripture as he walked away, "The multitude separated, and no man knew wherefore they came together." What could one do with these dogmatists who take delight in shooting balloons and asking a man for proofs when revelations are his stock-in-trade? Would they catechize the sibyl in her cave? Would they ask the Delphic oracle for a demonstration? No doubt, if they lived on Beacon Street or preached in a Unitarian pulpit.

Alcott was not himself in these urban surroundings. He was at home in the country, amid the woods and waters, under the sun and stars, turning about his grounds, sauntering by a brook-side. He was a pagan after Henry's fashion, much as he loved good manners. He was very different from Margaret Fuller, who had found her soul in the world of affairs and who had just lost her life, at forty. Henry had hastened down to Fire Island, on behalf of the Concord circle, to investigate the shipwreck. Margaret had sailed with many misgivings, and the voyage from Italy had been mismanaged. The little boat had broken up at once: the hold was laden with Italian marble and Hiram Powers's statue of Calhoun. Charles Sumner had lost a brother; he had already arrived and left, with William Henry Channing. They found Margaret's desk on the beach, with some of her papers in it, a carpet-bag of the Marquis Ossoli's, the body of the child. Nothing else, no trace of the tragic lovers, no trace of the great history of the siege of Rome.

The book was a loss. The Brownings and Landor

agreed that no Italian had known Mazzini better, and
Ossoli's family connections had given Margaret the other
side of the story. No doubt, the substance of the book,
however,—*Italy in 1848–'49,*—appeared in Margaret's
letters to *The Tribune,* soon to be collected in *At Home
and Abroad,* letters that brought the siege before her
readers as if they had seen it for themselves. She was a
journalist in grain and fibre, none more brilliant, none
more sympathetic, but scarcely a historian or a critic; an
energetic, perceptive soul, not a great writer, but certainly
a great woman writing. This was the fact that her friends
wished to proclaim. Carlyle, who had been so kind to her
in London, had summed up her qualities. He had
small faith in his wife's friend Mazzini. He thought that
Italy needed an Oliver Cromwell; he would have been
delighted with Mussolini. No matter what happened in
the back parlour, provided there was "order" in the
front. But he said that Margaret's courage was "high
and clear," and that she had "a truly heroic mind, altogether unique, so far as I know, among the writing women
of this generation."

The logic of events had sent her home. Mazzini's cause
had failed, and thought and speech like hers were contra-
band in Italy. No matter, she had lived and left her record, in England, France and Rome. She had had her full
taste of the "artist life," so long and happily dreamed of.
She had found *The Dial* widely read in England. Chopin
had played for her; she had met George Sand. She had
had her say about the American artists who were flocking
to Rome and Florence, their minds filled with American
subjects, of whom she had written with understanding.
She had described the American tourists, the colonists and
foreign residents, the servile types, the parasites, the brag-
garts and "booby truants,"—"Jonathan in the sprawling
state,"—as well as the thinking Americans whom she admired; and at last she had found the cause for which she

had been waiting, to lavish all her powers of devotion,
Mazzini's "God and the People." She had met Mazzini
in London, where she told him that the best friends a man
of ideas could have were necessarily women. How could
Carlyle have comprehended him?—Carlyle, with his old
Scandinavian berserker mind, following its impulse as a
hawk its prey. Mazzini had taken Margaret at her word
and put her on her mettle. She had shared in the drama
that she had longed to witness, a heroic passage of history, a nation rising up like Milton's eagle, mewing its
mighty youth: Italy cured of its hasty boasts and meaner
adulation, learning to prize and seek realities. She had
thought of her own America, stupid with the lust of gain
and the sloth of slavery, the criminal greed of the Mexican War, the aims of its politicians petty and selfish, its
literature venal and frivolous. In Europe, a nobler spirit
struggled, a spirit that animated and cheered her own.
She had heard earnest words of faith and love and seen
the deeds of brotherhood, all that made up the America
of which she dreamed. She could not distrust her country
deeply. America was not dead, it was only sleeping. She
had thought of the Abolitionists, whom she had found
so tedious, so narrow and so rabid in their tone. They
had their lofty motives. There was something eternal in
their desire and life; and they, too, understood Mazzini.
In the end, she had had her great romance, just as it
might have occurred in the novels that once enchanted
her,—lived those high, tumultuous hours, married her
Count de Rudolstadt, played the part of Countess Emily
Plater. It had led to sorrow, anxiety, toil and death.

In Concord, as in Rome, they had understood her; and
Emerson made haste to write a memoir that would convey his feeling for her, an ode in prose outrivalling the
ode that Landor wrote in verse. She was the Ugly Duckling who had died too soon to counteract the legend of
the barnyard; but the poets and the novelists never for-

got her. The Boston Aspasia who had corrupted her sex by means of intellectual orgies lived again in Hawthorne's pages and Holmes's *Elsie Venner*.* Elizabeth Hoar, in Concord, and Sarah Ripley had many of Margaret's qualities, although without her fire of intellect. In Concord, even the farmers were writing books, Minot Pratt, for one, whose son married a daughter of Alcott. He had helped to manage Brook Farm and was carrying on botanical studies for an ambitious work on the local flora. In 1855, another writer settled in the village, the future Boswell of the Concord worthies. Frank B. Sanborn was a sophomore at Harvard when he had first walked out to call at Emerson's house. Not long afterwards, Emerson, looking about for someone to take charge of a school for the Concord children, suggested the plan to Sanborn, who was delighted with it. He rented a room from Ellery Channing and took his meals at Mrs. Thoreau's, and he spent an evening every week at the Manse, reading Greek aloud with Mrs. Ripley. No one could have said, in years to come, that the long, lank Sanborn with the rosy cheeks did not know the Concord he wrote about. He was a born antiquarian; nothing pleased him more than to pore over old family papers; and Mrs. Ripley showed him the dusty records preserved in the "prophets' chamber,"—old Dr. Ripley's memoranda about half the souls who had lived in the village. Sanborn, with his hero-worshiping instincts, soon knew more about the Concord people than most of them had ever known themselves. He was preparing himself for the many books he wrote in later years. His school became a Concord institution. He followed the methods of Alcott, in a measure, his special friend and master, taking the children for walks in the

---

* Hawthorne did not wish to admit that he had drawn his Zenobia from Margaret Fuller, with certain touches suggested by Fanny Kemble, but no one ever questioned the fact. That Dr. Holmes had Margaret Fuller in mind is evident from a passage in *Elsie Venner*. It was natural that she left some sort of trace in almost every imaginative mind of the time.

woods and fields, with picnics, plays and boating parties, and skating carnivals at Walden Pond. First or last, he had among his pupils Emerson's son, Hawthorne's son, two daughters of John Brown, Horace Mann's sons and two of Henry James's.

It was Sanborn who, a few years later, brought John Brown to Concord, where the anti-slavery cause had many friends. It was from Sanborn's house that Brown set out for Harper's Ferry. Sanborn knew his plans, of which Emerson, Alcott and Thoreau knew nothing. He was arrested after the raid. A posse came out from Boston to seize him, but he spread his arms like a windmill and braced his feet against the sides of the carriage; his sister roused the neighbours, and the church-bells rang the alarm. Judge Hoar issued a writ of *habeas corpus,* and the posse disappeared. The whole town assembled, the following morning, to protest against the outrage. Ever since 1844, when Emerson made his speech on Emancipation, and Henry Thoreau rang the bell for the meeting, Concord had been an anti-slavery centre. Emerson, Alcott and Mrs. Thoreau had special rooms in their houses for fugitive slaves, and John Brown, the Connecticut Yankee, had more friends there than he had in Kansas. When people said he had thrown his life away, "Which way have they thrown their lives?" Thoreau remarked— these figureheads on hulks, with livers in the place of hearts.

Sanborn was even a member of the Walden Pond Association. So the "Sunday walkers" were called in the village,—Emerson, Alcott, Thoreau and one or two others who never sat in pews. One had to pass a stringent test to belong to this society, severer than the Athanasian creed. There were only two or three persons with whom Thoreau, for one, felt that he could afford to walk, his hours were so precious. Was Emerson less exacting? He was only more polite. In the presence of cranks and bores,

he masked his irritation. Henry trampled on them. Two·
yards of courtesy did not make society for Henry; and
when, by chance, a bore shadowed him on one of his
walks, he took every ditch at a run, hoping to shake the
shadow off. He detested these mere strenuous pliers of
legs, these broachers of mighty arguments who spoiled
one's day and talked the bobolinks under. With his long
swinging gait, his eyes on the ground, his hands clasped
behind him, his legs like steel springs and his arms as
powerful as a moose's antlers, thrusting the brush aside,
with his wary glance, his earnest energy, as if, on the
lookout for squirrels, rabbits and foxes, he was in the
thick of a day's battle, Henry was no man to trifle with.
He was impatient even with the farmers, who were always
standing on their good behaviour, moralizing and philos·
ophizing, instead of giving a brisk report of their crops.
He preferred the sportsmen and loafers, or anyone who
had seen a painted tortoise, or taken a good look at a
flying lark, or who shared his feeling about the encroach·
ing railroad, that seventh abomination. Henry had grown
so formidable, in fact, that the village-folk had ceased to
call him Henry, especially now that he was carning a living, by lecturing, writing, surveying, by means that anyone could understand. He was Mr. Thoreau, the surveyor,
who gave you fair warning to keep your distance.

No use to attempt to join the Sunday walkers unless
you were able to meet the test. Were the woods for you
full of solicitations, were there forms and colours every·
where, powers on every hand, locked away from ordinary
Christians, to which your wit afforded you the key? The
churches on the square were ready to welcome the dry
souls whom life, as Ellery said, had put away on the
shelf like so many rinds of cheese. You had to be up to
the mark to keep pace with the Walden Society, Emerson,
twirling his stick, while he drew rhymes from the upper
air, Ellery touching off his sudden fuses, dressed in his

red flannel shirt, suggesting an indolent bandit, Thoreau with his taut mind and wound-up muscles, ready to crush you with a merciless phrase. He tied his boots in a hard lover's-knot, while Ellery, half the time, went about with his shoe-strings dangling, or even wore no laces,—just as he wrote his poems, loosely strung, to the scandal of his conscientious friends. He should have been compelled to write in Latin, Henry said and Emerson agreed. Then he would have used a dictionary and written firmly and clearly, instead of in the dangling-shoe-string style, the sublimo-slipshod style, as Henry called it. But Ellery would not pay the going-price, he would not stoop to conquer. Henry, as they walked, pulled out his note-book and jotted down his careful observations. Ellery half-heartedly followed suit, scrawled away for a moment, then drew some hasty sketch and stuffed the book in his pocket again. He had no use for the "definite" and left the "facts" to Henry. Only the "ideal" was good enough for him.

No matter, he was a virtuous walker. He had eyes for every line and every colour, for every fleet of yellow butterflies, ears for every sound, the wood-thrush pitching his notes in the pine-alleys, the oven-bird beating his brass in the heated shades of noon, the partridge's feathery roll-call, the gossiping dialogue of the brown thrashers, a comforting sound, this latter, enough to cure the heartache of a world, on one of those summer days when the sky bends over a walker with a face like Jerusalem Delivered. A fit companion, Ellery, for a dozen poets, or two, at least, Emerson and Henry, or any combination of two or three. What was the programme for the afternoon? A stroll to Conantum, perhaps, or White Pond, or to Round Hill in the Sudbury meadows. Thus the talk flowed.—We'll stop at Duganne's spring and get a drink. —Or suppose we go to Flint's.—Agreed.—That country with its high summits is good for breezy days. And we

must not forget the mountain view from the Three
Friends' Hill, beyond the pond. Across the pastures, in
any case, the broad, healthy new-springing pastures, or-
namented with apple-tree pyramids, the pastoral architecture of the cow, and the waving saxifrage and the
delicate houstonia, the dark belts of pines stalking over
the landscape.—The air is fairly spotted today with the
rigmarole of the bobolink, buttery, scattery, wittery, pit-
tery, a few yellow, a few black feathers, a summer-warm-
ing song.—Soaring over the tallest pine, the fierce hen-
harrier screams and hisses.—And see the peach-trees
yonder. Montaigne took pains to be made a citizen of
Rome. I should much prefer to have the freedom of a
peach-orchard.—Or of an accommodating trout-stream,
such as Goodwin loves, the one-eyed Ajax.—What do
you think of the farmhouse we are passing? Aren't the
clapboards needlessly stiff? Is there not too little orna-
mentation? In Italy and Switzerland and England, the
picturesque seems to spring from the soil, in the shape of
barns and buildings, as naturally as the trees and flowers.
—Moderate your words, dear Gilpin. Utility lies at the
bottom of our village architecture. The structure springs
from that. The simple edifice you see, created out of
white-pine boards, a mere casing of shingles and clapboards, as it appears to you, appears to its owner, who
built it and lives in it, anything but ugly or unpicturesque.
It fits him like a shell. Comfort, economy, use, a dry,
warm cellar, a sweet, airy milk-room, a barn with its
cellars and accommodations, all in the solidest style,—
these matters make the study of the farmer.—I say that
beauty must have an equal place with utility, if not the
first place. Your farmer shirks architecture and landscape-
gardening, with his one leg in the barn and his other in
the kitchen, and the compost-heap in the midst. And his
highest ambition is to have a patent-leather top to his
carriage.—Go to, you libel my jolly countryman. He is

no such thieving rat as this. O brother Gilpin, hearken ere you die. Those prejudices of yours for Inigo Jones have left you too little sympathy for the industrious yeoman of New England. He stands like a king in the midst of the general penury.—Have you read those old farmers Cato and Varro? "Study to have a great dung-heap. Carefully preserve the dung. Break it up fine." There speaks the New England yeoman. If you would understand him, read this manual of the Roman farmers, how they got their living, what they did from day to day.— But, come, here's the brook. Let me rest a fraction on the bridge.—I am your well-wisher in that. The manners of water are beautiful, playing its sweet games, all circles and dimples and lively gleaming motions.—The brook, the petted darling of the meadows, wild minstrel of an ancient song, poured through the vales forever.—And those eddying pools, where the old experienced trout sleeps on his oars.—Rest a little longer here.—Are not those gulls yonder, gleaming like spots of intense white light far away on the meadow?—And observe that ridiculous colt, the colour of sugar-gingerbread, set upon his four long legs and swishing a bald tail, laughing at us men-folks nibbling our crackers and herring.

Thus the talk rambled, while Peter, Ellery's dog, capered through bush and brier, plunging into the brook with his smiling tail. Peter lived as Henry aspired to live. As the Indians had amused the Jesuits by sitting all day naked on the ice, fishing through their holes, as if they were lolling on feather-beds, so Peter would sleep all night on a snow-bank in January. It was enough to make one shiver to think of, on a day like this, by Clematis Brook, when the ants, bees and millers kept open shop, when the woodchucks sat up at the mouths of their houses, when the Maryland yellow-throats and the bull-frogs and robins performed their operas all day long, and the learned advocate, the *Mephitis chinga,* probed the roads for beetles. A day for three friends to expand their fancies. Anon they took their way to the Estabrook country, or embarked on some riparial excursion, a walk along the river-bank, or a paddle in Henry's boat, leaving the boat, perhaps, for an inland stroll, at the rear of the blacksmith's house, five miles up the river. Sometimes they went for a voyage in the pinnace as far as the Port of Lilies, along the river which, in its glassy folds, laid its unswept carpet over the fragrant meadows. Anon they set forth on a wintry day, under a lead-coloured sky, to the steady, silent, windless fall of the snow, when all the pines and oak-leaves were moulded in silver. Sometimes, after dark, they dropped in to see Perez Blood, the farmer-astronomer, over towards Carlisle, sitting in his wood-shed, in his astronomical chair, with his skull-cap on his head and his short Northern figure, a Concord Tycho Brahe. They peeped through his telescope and saw Saturn's rings and the shadows of the mountains on the moon. If it was spring or summer, they reappeared in the village streets with flowers and rare insects in their hats and pockets. They might have been Linnæus and his pupils on one of their "herborizations."

Thoreau was in danger of losing his solitary habits. What with lecturing, what with surveying, what with the acclaim that followed his *Walden,* he was becoming almost a man of the world. He had had to spend ninety days surveying to pay for his *Week on the Concord,* but *Walden* was actually selling. It was finding the kind of friends that make a classic. He had had his name posted for public lectures, two or three a year, wherever—in Worcester, Nantucket, Salem, Plymouth—they absolutely required his presence. Not that he wished for "experience": one might as well have advised a bear to leave his hollow tree and run about all winter, scratching at all the hollow trees in the woods. The bear would have been leaner in the spring than if he had stayed at home and sucked his claws. But Henry was willing to go, to make a few dollars, whenever it was convenient to drop his work, provided it was clearly understood that what he said on the platform was nobody's business. It was just another chore, like surveying. Nothing one did for money was ever worth doing, but one had to pay one's way and hold one's peace. As for the surveying, it was like Haydon's portrait-painting. Haydon had wandered over England, painting the portraits of the country gentry. Henry went about in a similar fashion, to the houses of the farmers and the squires. With his staff and chain, he, too, had to paint his portraits, while his mind was filled with more important matters.

Still, he acquired thereby, and through his writings, a number of new acquaintances who were almost as rewarding as the muskrats. Agassiz, the great professor in Cambridge, was studying the American fishes. Henry was glad to send him four firkins of Concord fish, including one and probably two species that Agassiz had not seen. Agassiz, greatly pleased by this, came out to Concord and examined turtles with him. The lecturing-business also took him to Nantucket, where, as the natives said, you had to strike a whale before the girls would dance with you. This was no great news, to be sure, for Henry. That a young woman had regular features might be a reason for looking at her, but it was no reason for talking to her. Still, it was something to meet the natives; and surveying was a pleasant occupation when one had good friends to set up the staff and carry the chain. Henry was glad when Alcott offered to do so, and it was a question of surveying "Hillside," Marston Watson's country-place at Plymouth. Alcott was in his element there, for Marston Watson, having the means, had had an inspiration. On his beautiful slope overlooking the harbour, he wished to lay out a park and garden, and he proposed to build a summer-house, with front gables facing south and east,

and a lookout with winding stairs, all of rustic wood.
Alcott gathered the timbers, with plenty of knots and
sylvan ornaments, and soon constructed the bower, a riot
of natural curves, fit for a Pythagoras to talk in; and he
and Watson carried Henry's chain. As they trod the
warm, sandy Plymouth wood-roads, or lingered on the
slope, they talked over the virtues of pears and apples,
golden russets, Tolman sweetings, greenings. Pears were
too aristocratic, Henry thought. He much preferred the
democratic apples that were left to the hired man to
gather and barrel, while the land-owners plucked their
own pears and had their daughters wrap them in separate
papers. Judges and ex-judges,—Squire Hoar, for instance,
—were connoisseurs of pears and named them after emperors and kings, queens and dukes and duchesses,—
glout-morceaux, Bonne Louise. Henry thought they were
less poetic than apples, the apples that children dream
of. He meant to wait for his pears until they got American names.

But when one writes a *Walden,* one has to be prepared
for consequences. Much as Henry preferred the republican apple, Marston Watson sent him a gift of pear-trees.
Somebody else, in Brattleboro, sent him a box of may-
flowers. Another friend in Worcester sent him a hum-
ming-bird's nest. All in two days. In Worcester, they
were developing a Thoreau "cult." There Thomas Wentworth Higginson lived, the literary minister, one of the
active Abolitionists. There lived Theophilus Brown, the
literary tailor, who sent forth sparkles of wit as he bent
over his measuring-tape and scissors; and there, above
all, dwelt Harrison G. O. Blake, a terribly conscientious
Harvard man, who, as Emerson said, would even return
a borrowed umbrella and who was Henry's firmest partisan. Attracted by Henry's writings in *The Dial,*—the
essay on Persius first,—he had persuaded him to go to
Worcester, to give a sort of annual parlour-lecture, so

that his friends could really look at him. He had led Henry into a correspondence, which was conducted on the highest plane; for "Mr. Blake" was so Transcendental that Henry had to walk on stilts to please him. But he was a loyal adherent. The moment the postman arrived with a letter from Concord, he gathered his neighbours together and read the letter aloud at the breakfast-table. Blake and "Theo" Brown were also virtuous walkers. They came to Concord now and then to take walks with Henry, even as far as Wachusett.

One of Henry's expeditions took him to New Jersey, where he surveyed the two hundred acres at "Eagleswood," Perth Amboy. Marcus Spring was founding a colony there, with the Grimkés and the Welds and other Abolitionists. They wished to propagate, in combination, radical views and old-fashioned culture, and Henry laid out the streets of the village they were planning. Alcott joined him there, and they spent a night with Horace Greeley and went over to Brooklyn to see Walt Whitman, whose *Leaves of Grass* Henry had just been reading. He wished to pay his respects to the great new poet, whom Emerson had recently greeted, although he had small use for the politicians whom Whitman included in his cosmos. He meant to make his feelings clear. He had all manner of reservations in regard to this great America, and he also thought that Walt was a little rank,—although, when it came to that, if you blushed when you read the *Leaves,* at whose thoughts were you blushing, your own or Walt's? He felt that Whitman had written a great primitive poem, as wonderful in its way as the Bhagavad-Gita. It was an alarm or trumpet-note, ringing through the American camp.

Meanwhile, he had found another friend, sufficiently near home to pay him an annual visit, a Quaker and poet, like Whitman, albeit quite unknown in the world of letters. This was Daniel Ricketson, who lived at "Brooklawn," his ancestral home at New Bedford. The Quaker ship-owners in the famous whaling metropolis were shrewd, quick-witted traders. Ricketson had inherited some of their money, but none of their mercantile instincts. He was a naturalist and a man of letters, whose favourite authors were Virgil and Cowper and who had corresponded for many years with Howitt and William Barnes, the Dorset poet. A lover of Gilbert White and William Gilpin, he lectured now and then, especially on "Cowper and His Friends." He liked the ancient saying, "A spare diet and clear skies are Apollo and the Muses." He was at home with partridges, quails and rabbits, and had tramped thousands of miles through the winter woods; and he looked after his farm, his fruit-trees and garden, avoiding forms and ceremonies, seeking a simple, quiet life. A quick man, quick in heart, quick in all his movements, with a taste for free thinking and social reform, he liked to get hold of some outcast and hold him up by the chin and whisper weighty matters in his ear; and, as for the anti-slavery movement, how could he listen to the woodland songs, or look at the great clouds and the starry heavens, and not be a friend of the poor and the oppressed? In the midst of his rural pursuits, he fought for justice. He hoped to see the quarrels of nations settled by arbitration, the factory-system humanized, the prisons without tenants. He longed to see machinery, now so destructive of life, turned into safe and useful channels. An inveterate journalizer, the author of a *History of New Bedford,* a rural poet with a clear vocation, Ricketson was one of those happy readers who create for other men of letters an atmosphere in which they can breathe and work. "In proportion as we see the merits of others, we add to our own," he said. Thoreau had been touched by the word of greeting that Ricketson sent him after reading *Walden.* The modest and perceptive Ricketson had also built a shanty, like his own; and when Ellery Channing went to New Bedford, to write for one of the papers, Thoreau had a double reason for visiting the town. Where was Ellery living there? In his usual fashion, he wrote that he "did not know." Thoreau went down to bring these friends together.

They had high times in Ricketson's shanty, then and every year thereafter, especially when Alcott joined the trio. They went for walks in the neighbouring woods, and Henry found marine plants he had never seen before and an old Indian woman, living alone in her hut, the last of the Nemaskets. The shanty recalled his Walden days. It was much the same in size and style, bristling with evidences of Ricketson's hobbies, twenty rustic walking-sticks, a dozen pipes, a spyglass, Indian relics, stuffed birds, old guns and swords, slips of paper pinned on the walls with verses in praise of country life. In the surrounding woods, the quails incessantly whistled, and morning and evening one heard the strain of the bay-wing. There the happy sages sat, like so many gymnosophists of old, ready to stamp on the ground if any Alexander thrust himself in at the door. Ellery smoked his pipe and joked with Alcott, and Ricketson stood boldly up to Henry. One day, Walton Ricketson, the sculptor-son of the house, named after Izaak Walton, made a medallion of Henry, wearing the full black beard he had recently grown; and, as if to belie his beard,—on another occasion,—Henry, unable to contain his joy, jumped out of his chair and began to dance. He pranced and leaped about, like an Indian in the forest, taking pains to step on Alcott's toes.

CHAPTER XXIV

CAMBRIDGE IN THE FIFTIES

THE GREAT months in Cambridge were June and October. June was Lowell's month. When the trees were heavy with leaves and the gardens full of blossoms, when the insects chirped in the grass and the white clouds sailed aloft, Lowell, pitching his hay in the meadow at "Elmwood," felt the metres of Chaucer, Shakespeare and Keats pounding in his blood. Longfellow loved October. He always uttered the word with a curious pleasure. Every year, when the leaves turned scarlet and yellow, his mind stirred with thoughts and fancies. "Welcome, O brown October!" he wrote in his journal. "Like a monk with a drinking-horn, like a pilgrim in russet!"

At the rear of Craigie House, he had laid out a more elaborate garden, following a Gothic pattern, with borders of box. He made a little pond under the willows. It was 1854, and he had resigned from his professorship. In his brief novel, *Kavanagh,* the story of a minister in Maine, —who might have been Sylvester Judd, for his aim was to remove all prejudices and bring about a union of all the sects,—he had pictured his own predicament. Kavanagh, the youthful poet, who had been brought up on the lives of the saints, was forced to teach grammar for his living, while his mind overflowed with verses; interrupted and hampered by trivial things, he postponed his great designs from year to year and never found the courage to begin. The tale was feeble enough, for Longfellow's mind was poor and thin without its mantle of verse;

but it expressed his feeling at the moment. His college work was like a great hand laid on the strings of his lyre, stopping their vibrations. He was the Pegasus in Pound of whom he wrote in one of his poems. Still, he had written *The Golden Legend,* based on a story of the minnesingers, in form suggesting *Faust.* It was an evocation of the Middle Ages, softly melodious and picturesque, redolent of ivy and ancient ruins, with a fervent strain of religious feeling. Some of the scenes were among the best in the Longfellow picture-gallery, especially the scenes of monastic life.

The first result of Longfellow's freedom was the Indian idyll, *Hiawatha.* This was an October poem, floating in an air of Indian summer, a haze of yellow harvests and autumnal quiet and the smoke of camp-fires and far-away lodges. Ever since his boyhood in Maine, Longfellow had felt the poetry of the ancient forest people. He had seen the last of the Algonquins, stragglers in the Maine woods, and he had never forgotten the words of the Choctaw chief who said that his tribe would hear the news of his death "like the sound of the fall of a mighty oak in the stillness of the forest." He had entertained an Ojibway chief who was lecturing in Boston, and one of his students who had returned from the West and told him legends of the lodge and camp-fire had urged him to weave them into a poem. He had ploughed through Schoolcraft's collection of Indian folk-lore, and then he had remembered the *Kalevala,* the Finnish folk-epic that he had read during his summer with Freiligrath. There was much in common between these primitive peoples and their legends. Many of their metaphors were the same, and the repetitions of the *Kalevala* were characteristic of the Indian songs, so like the wind in the pine-trees. The vague myth of a sunset land, a paradise in the West, where the mountains and forests were filled with deer and the lakes swarmed with fishes, the happy hunting-ground of

the Indian braves, swept through his mind, when autumn
came, with the sighs of the south-wind, Shawondessa. He
saw it all in a wondrous light, in the mist of leaves, in
the flash of the river. The Indians that emerged in the
poem were not the warrior-stoics of flesh and blood. They
were not Indians even as Concord saw them, for Longfellow was not Thoreau. He had reshaped the legends to
suit himself, omitting all the savagery and malice. He had
softened and simplified and humanized them, picturing
the father of the lodge, the patriot, the sportsman and the
hero. There was a touch of Channing in Hiawatha,
the bringer of light, peace and the household arts, and
the elements of romance were European. The mild humanitarian glow of the poem savoured of the poet's Cambridge circle. But why not? Of what did the Indians
savour in *Atala* and *René,* if not Chateaubriand's circle
across the ocean? There was a quiet magic in the story,
a golden languor as of afternoon, of corn-fields in the
setting sun, purple vapours and the dusk of evening.

It was not for children that Longfellow wrote, although
children were his best readers always. *Hiawatha* travelled
round the world; Cardinal Newman's brother translated
it into Latin, and Freiligrath, the German translator,
amply defended Longfellow's use of the metre. He had
been accused of plagiarism, as erstwhile by the author of
The Raven, which had occasioned the lines that he wrote
in his journal,—

> In Hexameter sings serenely a Harvard professor.
> In Pentameter him damns censorious Poe.

Everybody read him, and the critical public recognized
that in his use of metres he had shown himself an original
artist. Still, the children liked him best, and Cambridge
and Craigie House were full of children. Dr. Worcester
had built the house next door, and the Longfellow boys,

perched on the fence, swooped down on the lexicographer's pears and apples. Then Dr. Worcester, roused from his studies, issued from his cave of notes and told the little boys what they were made of. Their father knew already. He had composed a jingle on the subject and also asked what little girls were made of. The Longfellow girls were more discreet. Longfellow wrote several poems about them. Brattle Street, in fact, was a garden of girls, quite in the Tennysonian vein, and Longfellow liked to go to balls in Boston, where he could see them, fair and slender, waving, like lilies on their stems, to the music as to a wind. At Craigie House, they were always reading aloud, every day at the children's hour, often by the cozy fireside, while they looked over pictures from Florence and Dresden. There were many new authors to keep up with, Hawthorne, who had gone to Liverpool, to serve as American consul there, Thackeray, Charlotte Brontë, the Brownings, Ruskin. Longfellow watched the moon, through the open window, rising in the autumnal air. Like a delicious perfume, like far-off music, floated through his mind, as through parting clouds, glimpses and visions of Tyrolean lakes.

But Europe was drifting more and more to Cambridge. Every Cunarder brought some visitor, Agassiz, Adam Gurowski, the terrible count,—the one-eyed Pole who called himself "the homeless,"—Ole Bull from Norway, Frederica Bremer from Sweden, gathering notes on the "homes of the New World," Thackeray, Clough the poet, Luigi Monti, the Italian scholar,—the Sicilian of Longfellow's *Wayside Inn,* who presently married the sister of the poet Parsons,—or Professor Sophocles, the scholar-hermit, bred in a monastery on Mount Athos, a strange Diogenes with a wild, grey beard who looked like Byron's Corsair, who lived like a monk of the Thebaid in his room in Holworthy Hall, where he did his own cooking, and whom one encountered on his lonely walks.

Felton, the great professor of Greek, Longfellow's closest friend and the friend of Dickens, the huge, hearty
old-fashioned scholar who liked to apply the epithet forci-
ble-feeble to those who simulated his own robustness,
and who often reminded his hearers that Agamemnon
had honoured Ajax with a whole sirloin after his fight
with Hector,—for he shared the Homeric enjoyment of
eating and drinking,—was lecturing at the Lowell Institute. In Zurich, on his way to Greece, he had put on a
suit of armour at the Zeughaus, to the delight of the
keeper, and laid about him with a battle-axe, for he wished
to know how the crusaders had felt, as well as the heroes
of Homer. He had made his own collection of Swiss
folk-poems and had visited Jacques Jasmin, the barber-
poet, who lived in the south of France and whose *Blind
Girl* Longfellow translated; and in Greece he had made
friends with farmers and sailors, travelled through the
mountains in search of ballads and met all the living
Greek writers, whom he brought out in a book of selections. He took the modern world-historical view in his
great courses of lectures, which later appeared as *Ancient
and Modern Greece,* a delightfully readable work. At
Harvard, everything was "comparative" now; the studies
overlapped one another. With the humorous, copious
Felton, all fire and energy and poetic feeling, with Asa
Gray, the botanist, with Peirce the mathematician and
Jeffries Wyman, with Agassiz in the chair of natural
history, the lines and angles of the checker-board had
gradually faded out. There was a genial glow in the
Cambridge air. Agassiz had brought full summer with
him.

The great Swiss professor had settled in Cambridge
in 1848. A sort of Johnny Appleseed of science, sowing
trees of learning wherever he went, he had lectured to vast
crowds from Boston to Charleston, making the great types
of the animal kingdom, articulates, radiates, molluscs, as

real and vivid as historic figures. Talking with his enchanting verve and drawing his illustrations on the blackboard, so that one saw the insects and fishes bursting from their eggs, he infected everyone with his zeal for nature. Museums rose over-night as the great showman of science passed through the country, and, as his fame grew, every strange rock that was unearthed, every queer creature that anyone caught, in pond or stream or forest, was sent to the professor for an explanation; and when he issued a circular, asking for collections of fresh-water fish, specimens came in from every quarter. He could scarcely handle his correspondence. He was never without his blackboard and his bit of chalk and was always ready to teach at a moment's notice, in camp, on the road, on the shores of lakes. All creation was his lecture-room. He carried snakes in his pockets; every room in his house was a laboratory; garret and cellar were filled with his collections. Everyone quoted his sayings. He had never known a dull hour. He had never been a dollar ahead in the world and never expected to be. He had no time to waste in making money! This made a great impression in New England; and everyone heard how he rejoiced, for science, when a book appeared that demolished a theory which he had been toiling for years to establish. It was known that, to keep his chair at Harvard, he refused the directorship of the Jardin des Plantes, offered him by Napoleon III, and a seat in the French Senate, a rank equal to Cuvier's. Nothing kept the Americans back, he said, except a consideration for the opinion in which they were held in Europe. He hated to see an American man of genius elated by some foreign recognition, taking it as a mark of honour that set him apart from his countrymen. Contemptible provinciality! America could so easily be a centre if it once discarded the foolish notion that Europeans were its proper judges.

Agassiz, with his joyous magnetism, for whom all the

species of human beings, emperors, farmers, scientists and
poets were so many bipeds and bivalves, save for his
impetuous affections, who made science a national cause
and charmed money out of the politicians with which to
found museums, as if they were asylums for the blind,
Agassiz, the Pied Piper of Cambridge, soon became Longfellow's alter ego. He took his class one summer to Nahant, where Longfellow had a cottage, not far from
Prescott's. Agassiz caught nature "in the act," while
Longfellow rejoiced in the northeast storms, the fringes
of the foam about the rocks, the wet sails struggling in
the wind, the kale, the seaweed and the waste of waters,
the scent of the wild roses about the cottage mingling with
the odour of the sea. This was Longfellow's element. He
was at home with the ocean, like Ole Bull, the Norwegian
violinist, who had come to Cambridge, where he was to
find his second wife. Ole Bull had swept through the
country, a musical Agassiz with his "storm-organ," the
whirling spray of sound in which one heard the thunder
of the northern avalanches, the wind in the pines and the
sun-flecked hollows of Norway, filled with gnomes and
elves. All the young girls had heard his music, like the
mist scattered by a fountain, and wrote about him in their
diaries. They thought he was like Adam in Paradise. He
had shared in the Norwegian national movement, working with Ibsen at the Bergen theatre. There, as in
America, a fresh, youthful spirit was in the air. Norway
had declared its independence and separated from Denmark, and the Norwegian writers were building a literature of their own, one which they hoped would express
the dreams and hidden talents of the people. P. A. Munch
was their Bancroft, and Ibsen wished to be the national
poet. He was writing odes for the May 17th celebrations,
much like the American Fourth of July, and festival
poems such as Dr. Holmes was writing for the Berkshire
cattle-fairs,—even so, Ibsen, the author of *Ghosts,* who

said that culture was "unthinkable apart from national life." He was gathering folk-tales among the fjords, as Hawthorne had gathered them on his excursions.

Ole Bull spent a winter at "Elmwood," which he had rented during Lowell's absence; for Lowell, appointed to Longfellow's vacant chair, had gone abroad for a year of study. At Craigie House, he would talk half the night about Paganini, Malibran and Liszt. He played and chanted his old Norse melodies, like one of Longfellow's gleemen of the Viking days, and spoke of his childhood in the northern forests, the flower-clad valleys, filled with singing birds, the rocky coast, the rushing cataracts, the glittering lakes of Norway, so like the woods and valleys of Maine and New Hampshire. He might have been born in Portland, as Longfellow might have been born in Bergen. Hawthorne was more like Ibsen in the sense of fate that wrapped his folk-tales in a Gothic darkness. Hawthorne, too, had appeared at Craigie House, during the years before he went abroad, coming and going like a shadow, hiding behind the curtains, where he spent whole evenings undisturbed, a Viking under a veil. Arthur Hugh Clough, the English poet, who spent a winter in Cambridge, also had a touch of the Viking in him, sadly compromised by introspection. He had written his poem, *The Bothie,* largely suggested by *Evangeline,* filled with a feeling for the out-of-doors, high-spirited youth and the wildest nature. His Scotland was another Maine or Norway. He stayed at "Shady Hill," as a friend and guest of Charles Eliot Norton, Professor Andrews Norton's only son, coaching a few young men in Greek and making a revision of Dryden's Plutarch. The calm and repose of Cambridge soothed his mind, torn and bewildered by scruples and speculation, and brought back his earlier days at Oxford.

Then suddenly who should appear but Horatio Greenough, just returned from Florence. The tall, handsome, fiery Boston sculptor, a Viking or a Greek, as one chose to see him, had come home to superintend the erection of one of his monuments at Washington. As a Boston and Cambridge boy, two of whose brothers were also artists, he had copied Roman coins in the Athenæum and a marble Phocion in his father's garden, studied anatomy under a Boston doctor, modelled in butter, wax and chalk and spent his happiest hours with Washington Allston, during his years at Harvard. In Rome, he had worked with Thorwaldsen, and Cooper had given him his first commission, for the well-known "Chanting Cherubs," the first marble group that had ever been made by an American sculptor. For twenty-three years he had lived in Florence. He had introduced Emerson to Landor, his vehement friend and fellow-republican there, and he had written to the younger Dana, "America has always acted towards her artists like a hen that has hatched ducklings. She cannot understand why they run to the water, instead of thriving on the dung-hill, which only asks to be scratched in order to feed them. She will learn better, but not yet." But he had not been able to endure the repressions of Italian life since '48. He had come in a blaze of vigour, braced by the American air, with little respect for the Tories he found about him. He made the rounds of Boston, Concord and Cambridge before he settled in Newport for the winter.

The lectures he presently gave amplified the exciting ideas which he had been spreading among his friends. They were fragments of a book that he was planning. It was he who surprised the Boston people by praising the clipper-ship as a work of art. He said that the American trotting-wagon and the bald, neutral-toned Yankee farmhouse were actually closer to Athens than the Grecian temples that people were building for banks. This seemed odd enough, but there was a method in Greenough's madness, as those who heard his lectures soon discovered. He wished to explain what was the proper basis for a native American art, and that the true way to follow the Greeks was not to transplant their forms,—a kind of impotent dilettantism,—but to accept their principles and build from the needs of one's own climate and country. This was the strength of the clipper-ship, the type of what our architecture should be. It perfectly fulfilled its natural function. All its details were organic. Would anyone retain a bellying sail, however picturesque it was, however it pleased one's sense of association, when a flat sail went closest to the wind? That was the strength of the farmhouse, too. It seemed to belong to the ground on which it stood, as a caterpillar belongs to the leaf it feeds on. The monuments of the Egyptians and the Greeks were sublime as expressions of their power and feeling, but what did a Greek temple express in State Street? Money and ostentation, nothing else, like a frock-coat on an African king. Nature provides a form for every function; and all the absurdities of modern usage were due to the fact that they were non-organic. Instead of adopting the outward shape first, for the sake of the eye or of association, without reference to the inner distribution, forcing the functions into a general form, one should begin with the heart and work outwards.

Three generations later, one was to hear much of this "functional" theory, which Greenough preached up and down the country, with a Yankee wit and a foreign culture mixed, as he said, like the matrix and pebbles in the pudding-stone of Roxbury, Massachusetts. It all came down to the doctrine that the one principle of structure was "the principle of adaptation of forms to functions." The obelisk was the simplest type of this. Its function was to signalize a spot that was memorable in history, and how completely it achieved its end! It said but a single word, "Here!"—but everyone heard this word and understood it. Greenough's "Artist's Creed" summed up his faith. There were three things he had seen in man worthy of love and thought, Beauty, Action, Character: "By beauty I mean the promise of function, by action I mean the presence of function, by character I mean the record of function." A stirring combination of New England ethics with an aesthetic point of view that was to grow in meaning.*

At "Shady Hill," Charles Eliot Norton was also preparing to preach the gospel of art. There, in the gracious house with the wide verandahs, surrounded by its rolling lawns, the beeches and the willows, filled with the clatter of crows, the Cambridge circle met, over a game of whist, for music or for conversazioni, suggesting the "Dante evenings" of the future. There old Professor Norton beguiled his leisure with Shakespeare, Pope and Scott; and there, or at the house they had built at Newport, where they passed the summer months and where Greenough suddenly died before he could finish his book, the Nortons entertained their younger friends. Among these were Clough, Rowse the artist, who was making his red-chalk portrait-drawings of literary celebrities, William J. Stillman, the painter and writer, the editor of *The Crayon,* the first American art-journal, and later the friend of the Rossettis, Thomas G. Appleton, Longfellow's brother-in-law, and Francis J. Child, the collector of ballads. Charles

---

* See Louis Sullivan's phrase, "Form follows function, function creates form," and the writings of Lewis Mumford. In the light of these recent discussions, one should read Greenough's lectures, *Æsthetics at Washington, American Architecture, Structure and Organization* and *Criticism in Search of Beauty* in H. T. Tuckerman's *Memorial of Horatio Greenough.*

See also Emerson's comment on Greenough: "His paper on Architecture, published in 1843, announced in advance the leading thoughts of Mr. Ruskin on the *morality* in architecture, notwithstanding the antagonism in their views of the history of art. I have a private letter from him—later, but respecting the same period—in which he roughly sketches his own theory: 'Here is my theory of structure: a scientific arrangement of spaces and forms to functions and to site; an emphasis of features proportioned to their *gradated* importance in function; colour and ornament to be decided and arranged and varied by strictly organic laws, having a distinct reason for each decision; the entire and immediate banishment of all makeshift and make-believe.' "—*English Traits,* I.

Eliot Norton, a young man of low vitality, always a semi-invalid, a born collector of autographs and coins, books, engravings, paintings, with ample means to satisfy his tastes, with an acute sense of his social duty, devout, fastidious, learned, a careful scholar, was cautiously feeling his way towards the world of art. He and Clough had sworn eternal friendship, and, in fact, Norton's talent for friendship was the most remarkable thing about him. He was a hero-worshipper by instinct, who only asked that his heroes should be authentic,—good museum-pieces in flesh and blood, classified and certified,—for he had an extreme distrust of anything new.* He was a born confidant. Everyone told Norton everything, for he was the soul of discretion; and one could be sure that, if he wrote one's memoirs, nothing would appear that was not in the best of taste. He had whispered to his mother, at the age of ten, in the midst of a desperate illness, "I wish I could live, so that I could edit Father's works." He was to live to edit Carlyle and Ruskin, who, like Lowell and George William Curtis, made him their literary executor. Nature had preordained him for this work, as it made other men explorers and poets. With a conscientious longing to be useful, Norton felt sure that he had a mission.

As a child, he had been taken to England, where he had met his father's friends, especially Joanna Baillie and Mrs. Hemans, the cultivated Low Church circles that read Andrews Norton's books. Wordsworth had taken him upon his knee and given him a blessing. He had had a taste of the India trade, in the counting-house of his maternal uncles, before settling down to a scholar's life. He had sailed to India as a supercargo. There he had

---

* It must be added that Lincoln and John Brown were among his heroes. Their photographs, in later days, stood on his mantelpiece at Ashfield. Norton, somewhat timid and imitative on his imaginative side, was highly independent in his moral nature. In John Brown he saw "one of those men who thought themselves commissioned to do the work of the Lord." This was the spirit of his own teaching.

found readers of his father, as well as of Everett's speeches and Longfellow's poems, and had passed much of his time with the poet Dutt and his Harvard classmate, Fitzedward Hall, the Oriental scholar.* He found good friends in several rajahs, but India struck his New England taste as "showy," and it was not till he reached Venice, travelling round the world, that his aesthetic feeling came to life. Even in Europe, on this first visit, for which he was well equipped with introductions, thanks to George Ticknor, who was one of his uncles, his social and political observations occupied him more than matters of art. Returning home, he drifted out of business, edited a volume of hymns, opened a night-school for the poor of Cambridge, busied himself with model lodging-houses, to meet the new problems of immigration, and published an anonymous book, *Considerations on Some Recent Social Theories*. This was a counterblast to the radical doctrines that interested the Concord thinkers, the theories that had come to a head in 1848, Fourierism, Kossuthism, nationalism, the "offensive declamation" of Mazzini. The British rule in India, Norton thought, was better than any native rule could be. Republicanism as such was not important; and what was the use of trying to change conditions unless the people themselves had "character"? That character was what they did not have was the evident moral of their degradation,—which gave the upper classes their Christian function. Norton was a tender-hearted man who felt that he was personally bound to rescue the world from its folly.

It was on his second visit to Europe, in 1855, that Norton's real career began. His ship-mate, James Jackson Jarves, already known as a writer on art, gave him a letter of introduction to Ruskin, who, although he was nine

---

* Professor of Sanskrit and English in the government college at Benares; later professor of Sanskrit and Hindustani in King's College, London. Hall was the first American scholar to edit a Sanskrit text, the *Vishnu Purana*.

years the elder, soon thought of Norton as his "first real tutor"; for the bright-eyed Cambridge student with the musical voice, who had steeped himself in *Modern Painters,* knew classical literature better than he, showed a surprising knowledge of Italian painting and introduced him to the *Fioretti.* Ruskin, who was still a Calvinist, might have grown up in New England, in spite of his exuberant temperament. His shrewd, sensible, prosperous merchant-father, his grim, repressive mother, who trampled on every innocent pleasure, the atmosphere of piety, thrift and culture in which he had passed his early years, his tours in a travelling-carriage over Europe, the father sympathizing with the son's ambitions, all suggested Boston. Ruskin and Norton became fast friends at once. Ruskin showed Norton his Turners and Rossettis, Norton gave Ruskin the writings of his American friends, Lowell and Dr. Holmes. They travelled together in Switzerland and climbed the mountain meadows of Sallanches. They met again in Italy. Together they stood at the fountain in Siena, under the same arches where Dante had stood, drank of it together and walked together on the hills above, as Ruskin wrote later in his memoirs, where the fireflies among the scented thickets shone fitfully in the still undarkened air, like starlight through the purple leaves.

Thus began the transatlantic friendships that gave Norton much of his later fame. His second great friendship was with Mrs. Gaskell, the Unitarian minister's wife who had described in *Cranford* a village life that also suggested New England. After Mrs. Gaskell, whom he met in Rome and to whom he recited Lowell's poems, while he gave her lessons in Italian painting, he named one of his daughters. In Paris, he met Lamartine, Vigny and Tocqueville, and he was glad to find that Ary Scheffer, like some of his acquaintances in London, thought Longfellow the greatest living poet. Ruskin, whose passion was the Middle Ages, said that Longfellow, in *The Golden Legend,* had entered into the temper of the monk more closely than any historian or theologian; and Scheffer proved to Norton's satisfaction that the most poetic imagination was always accompanied by sound sense and practical understanding. Norton was not one of those dreamers who found in Italy a romantic solace. Recalling his social interests at home, he scrutinized the Italian charities, the evening schools for boys, the work of the Misericordia. Finding Keats's grave in sad disorder, he had the stone firmly set and planted myrtles and violets around it, with the same New England instinct for tidying-up that he brought to bear on the impulsive Ruskin,—to "keep him strictly and busily at his work." Rome was falling to pieces; it was all a helpless mass of weeds and ruins. All the more reason for a Protestant grave-yard to set it a good example.* Curious about modern Rome, which seemed to him as gaudy as Calcutta, wanting in simplicity and taste, he talked with scholarly priests and architects and went to meetings of academies where cardinals sat on gilded chairs, where seminarists recited hexameters on the Sacrifice of Isaac, in excellent Latin, and charming young countesses read their poems on Dante's Beatrice and Petrarch's Laura. He took notes on the early painters, Giotto, Fra Angelico and Perugino, whom Ruskin was interpreting for the modern mind and whom the Pre-Raphaelites were imitating, with a new feeling for colour which, in England, following the Oxford Movement, represented a recoil from rationalism and Puritanism. He began his version of the *Vita Nuova,* the first of the long series of Dante translations that were to spring from Cambridge. This was more literal than Rossetti's version, and marked by the same delicate feeling; for Norton, in truth, was an exquisite scholar. He and Rossetti

* Keats's grave was tidied again, about 1874, by the daughter of W. W. Story.

met, as friends of Ruskin, and Rossetti painted a picture for him, "Dante meeting Beatrice." He also began the study of mediæval cathedral-building, the subject of his most important work. The first part of the book he was soon to publish, *Notes of Travel and Study in Italy,* dealt with the Cathedral of Orvieto. Later readers were to find this passage as good as Henry Adams on the building of Chartres.

Norton returned to Cambridge, like another Ticknor, with the same sort of apostolic fervour that had filled his uncle's mind. He was the opener of another door, the world of aesthetic studies. For half a century, as a teacher at Harvard, he was to expound the gospel of taste, the doctrines of Ruskin, Dante, Italian painting, the history of architecture, sculpture, Turner, as his father had expounded the Scriptures,—taste as a means of salvation. He who was called "Pope Charles" by his early friends was destined to outlive the days of the New England papacy; but, even in these first few years, before he became professor of the history of art, he was an autocrat in aesthetic matters. Weak in aesthetic feeling, but skilled and learned, as Ticknor, weak in literary feeling, was also skilled and learned, he had the same responsible sense of an intellectual mission. As Ticknor felt, in his heart of hearts, that all the great writers were of the past,—Ticknor, who lived out his days around the corner from Emerson, Hawthorne, Thoreau, scarcely aware of their existence,—so Norton, who made an exception of Ruskin's friends, Turner and the Pre-Raphaelites, felt that the Renaissance was the end of art. He apologized, in later years, for a Corot that hung in his hall, left him by a friend to take care of. But as Ticknor had sent boxes of his books to enquiring students in Georgia and Maine, and was always ready with counsel for every scholar, so Norton carried boxes of Turners with him, when he gave lectures in the country towns, and left them for the boys and girls to study. He was always lending his gems and precious vases, fragments of sculpture, engravings, drawings, wherever he saw a chance to spread his gospel. Hearing that someone in Portland was interested in Turner, he sent a box of his water-colours there. His tenderness and goodness to the poorer students, his constant wish to be useful and helpful soon became proverbial in Cambridge. He was an archæologist by nature who had learned the alphabet of art after his mental tissues had dried and hardened. He often seemed like a learned and elegant priest discoursing of the sacred mysteries of which he had scarcely felt the inner fire. But as a teacher, a sage, in days to come, a moralist, an expounder of manners, a master in the art of discrimination, he was the most potent of the Brahmins. No one left more of a stamp on Cambridge than Charles Eliot Norton.

CHAPTER XXV

THE ROMANTIC EXILES

AT LIVERPOOL, in his consul's office, Hawthorne spent four dull years. He had to deal with the beggars and impostors that haunt the official in foreign ports, the brutal skippers, the imbruted sailors for whom the gallant Dana was fighting at home. American claimants called upon him, "lost heirs" of English estates, usually mad or spurious, occasionally some visionary soul,—for instance, Delia Bacon,—on some phantasmal mission. One day Herman Melville came, his old friend in Lenox, wandering in a cloud, drifting to Constantinople. At the Unitarian chapel, William Henry Channing had found a pulpit. There the sunny mist of the Brook Farm doctrines mingled with the smoky fog of England.

Hawthorne plodded through the day's work with his usual mask of impassivity. Most of his troublesome visitors came and went like apparitions of smoke and fog, like figures in some romance that he would have written if he had had the energy to write. The poor, shy, proud Delia Bacon, a Hawthorne figure in real life, was a more insistent problem. As a friend of Elizabeth Peabody and Mrs. Stowe, she had written a few historical tales and novels and conducted classes in history, like Margaret Fuller, first in Connecticut, then in Boston and Cambridge, unfolding an idea that became an obsession. She had become convinced that Shakespeare's plays, actually written by a group of scholars gathered about Sir Walter Raleigh, contained a system of thought, concealed by ciphers, the deepest wisdom of the greatest epoch, a science that the world was waiting for. The question of the authorship of the plays was of the least importance in her mind. Her mission,—she was a missionary's daughter,—was to reveal their esoteric meaning. Carlyle had treated her with the utmost kindness, struck by her personality and her knowledge, and she had obtained, or thought she had, permission to unseal the tomb of Shakespeare, where she believed the final clues were buried. She had haunted the church at Stratford, at midnight, with her lantern, hovering about the grave, then lost her courage with her confidence, lost the last remnants of her reason, and shrunk into the final stage of madness.

Hawthorne might have invented the story. Later, he told it in his book on England. Without accepting Delia Bacon's theory, he had written a preface for her book, *The Philosophy of Shakespeare's Plays Unfolded*. This vast, chaotic treatise was only an introduction to the subject, but the style was impressive, here and there, in the midst of its incoherence, and some of Delia Bacon's intuitions, especially in the passages on *King Lear,* deserved a place in Shakespearean criticism.* But, as for Miss Bacon's romantic feeling for England, Hawthorne could not share it. This tendency to wander back again, to the old home of the Pilgrims, this appetite for English soil, struck him as blind and pathetic. He seemed to be thrice-armoured against the charm that more and more of his countrymen felt, proud to be at odds with it, proud of his New England prejudices, as if he had turned the tables on Mrs. Trollope and wished to see only the too-much beef, the gloom, the slums, the poverty. He was too deeply planted in his own old world across the water to suffer the beguilement of the "claimants," or so it seemed at first.

* Delia Bacon was the originator of the "Shakespeare-Bacon" movement. For a conclusive refutation of the Baconian theory, see John Fiske, *The Bacon-Shakespeare Folly,* in *A Century of Science.*

For him the Warwickshire elms could not compare with
those that had overhung his village street.

Gradually his feeling changed. His old zest for taking
notes returned. He spoke of writing an English romance
and even found a clue at Smithall's Hall, an ancient house
in Lancashire. A few stage-properties were enough to
start the machinery of his imagination, a coffer filled with
golden hair, a silver snuff-box, a bloody footstep. *Doctor
Grimshawe's Secret* began to take shape in his mind, the
novel, begun in Rome, never finished, that struck a new
note in American fiction. For was not Redclyffe, the American heir, the first of the transatlantic *revenants* that were
to fill the novels of Henry James? Irving and Longfellow,
many another, had felt the spell of the old world, but Redclyffe's nostalgia was something else than theirs: "The
thought thrilled his bosom that this was his home—-the
home of the wild Western wanderer, who had gone away
centuries ago, and encountered strange chances, and almost forgotten his origin, but still kept a clue to bring him
back . . . He began to feel the deep yearning which a sensitive American,—his mind full of English thoughts, his
imagination of English poetry, his heart of English character and sentiment,—cannot fail to be influenced by,—
the yearning of the blood within his veins for that from
which it has been estranged, the half fanciful regret that
he should ever have been separated from these woods,
these fields, these natural features of scenery, to which his
nature was moulded, from the men who are still so like
himself, from these habits of life and thought which
(though he may not have known them for two centuries)
he still perceives to have remained in some mysterious way
latent in the depths of his character, and soon to be resumed, not as a foreigner would do it, but like habits
native to him, and only suspended for a season."

In days to come, this feeling, which Hawthorne had begun to share,—a feeling that unsettled him, indeed,—was

to play a part in American culture as marked as that of the "wanderers" of Pushkin's Russia. The most exotic writers, hitherto, had had the unquestioning instinct of homing pigeons, which brought them back from every foreign journey. The great tradition of the Revolution, the feeling of the national destiny, the prevalence of the classical studies that always made the mind its "own place," had rooted them in the Western soil. They had felt that they were building a civilization; and, in fact, it was not until after the Civil War that the great diaspora began and with it the tradition of deracination. Then, as the old causes grew dimmer and dimmer, as the European peasants arrived in thousands, as wealth advanced and tourists multiplied, as the human imagination felt cramped and thwarted in the vast industrial beehive, as classical studies declined and young men forgot the Plutarchian patterns, then this yearning for an older homeland rose in people's minds and men of sensibility flocked to Europe, not to study, as in former days, and carry their spoils back, like travelling Romans, but as if they could reascend the river of time.

The mood that found expression in Hawthorne's Redclyffe was to reappear not only in Henry James but in dozens, even scores of other writers who somehow felt estranged from their native life when the thread had once been broken. The elm-scattered meadows, the hawthorn hedges, the lawns, the castle-towers, the stiles, the heavy-timbered manor-houses, the Norman churches uplifting themselves among the stately trees touched some deepest buried nature in them, as of their English progenitors, a nature that seemed to have lain unchanged under the snows and leaves of ten-score winters and summers, layers of new customs and institutions that melted away in a night. They greeted these English scenes with a sudden flash of recognition. It was like a coming home after an absence of centuries. These intimations of a previous

state, almost suggesting Plato, this sense that one had
"been there before" was partly due to the reading of English books, partly to the maintenance of English customs
in households across the Atlantic. There were thousands
of families in New England, as in New York and the
South, that had never ceased to be English, for all they
had accepted the Revolution. They had fought for English rights against the redcoats. They had defended their
country against their country because it was an English
trait to do so. Not to be patriotic was not to be English,
and they were Americans because they were English.
Meanwhile, Wordsworth and Byron, Thackeray, Dickens,
Punch and the British reviews had shaped their minds. A
thousand times, in fancy, with Dr. Johnson, they had
turned at a corner into Fleet Street. A thousand times
they had walked down Piccadilly, among the yellow
chariots of Vanity Fair. Shelley's larks were still more
real to them than all the bobolinks of their native pastures, and they saw Oliver Twist and Little Nell even
under the trees of their village lanes.

There had always been good Bostonians, like Edmund
Quincy, for whom their first pilgrimage to London was
like the Musselman's visit to the tomb of the Prophet.
They saw it as the ancient Jews beheld their holy city after
the years of bondage in a foreign land. Deep in their
minds lurked the feeling that T. G. Appleton ascribed to
the Yankee: "Europe is the home of his protoplasm, of
the long succession of forces which make him what he is."
It was against this feeling that Emerson fought, or rather
against its consequences, in everything that he said of the
"tape-worm of Europe." Those who had made England
what it was had done so by sticking where they were, regardless of their own atavistic instincts, which might have
led them back to France or Denmark. When would Americans cast out the passion for Europe by the passion for
America that would give them repose? Old and new coun-

tries were all the same to one who looked at the world with the eye of wisdom. Why this superstition for a mushroom Europe, which only had gravity and domestic rest because it lived a self-contained existence? Emerson, who travelled and believed in travel, whenever there was a reason for it, said that one should fill a place at home before one tried to find a place abroad. Who provoked pity, he remarked, like that excellent family just arriving in some foreign city, in its well-appointed travelling-carriage, as far from any honest end as ever? Each nation had asked successively, "What are they here for?" until they were all embarrassed, expecting to be asked the same question at the gates of every town. But this idle and pathetic nostalgia for Europe, which had always existed in the Yankee mind, was a minor strain before the Civil War. Two hundred years had left their stamp on almost every American, and those who had amply shared the life of their country were as self-possessed as any European. The eminent Americans of the forties and fifties confronted England with a serene aplomb. Proud of their nation, proud of themselves, proud of their own good work, objective in their point of view, contemptuous of trifles, they were eager for the welfare of the world and convinced that America had a mission.* The apologetic note of later years was wholly absent from their tone and manner. They met the Englishman as Greek met Greek, as men who spoke their minds on all occasions, as the Romans of Spain met the Romans of Rome.

The relations between America and England had reached a sort of equipoise in the eighteen-fifties. The acrimony of earlier years had largely passed away, the Civil War had not yet revived it; and English and American writers and statesmen found that they had more in

* "Why do foreign lands regard us with this intensity of interest? Is it not because the whole world looks hopefully toward America as a nation especially raised by God to advance the cause of human liberty and religion?"—Harriet Beecher Stowe, Letter of 1853.

common than at any time before or since. A dozen American authors of the moment, Prescott, Longfellow, Motley, Mrs. Stowe, Emerson, Hawthorne and others were
greeted in England with the kind of *éclat* that Dickens met
in America, the kind that English authors have always
met in America but that American authors in England
never encountered in later times. Sydney Smith had said,
before Prescott's visit, that a "Caspian sea of soap"
awaited him. The English admired his pluck and his
glorification of the life of action; but even Prescott's
triumph was a trifle beside the royal progress of Mrs.
Stowe. Hundreds of thousands, like the Queen herself,
had been stirred and moved by Uncle Tom and Dred.
They had wept over the death of Nina and shared the
Queen's annoyance that fate had not chastised Tom Gor-
don. Mrs. Stowe, like Prescott and Sumner, found her
portrait in English castles, and crowds trooped after her
carriage as if she had been a prima donna. Much of the
cordiality that united the countries was of a purely social
kind. Outside the political sphere, Sumner, Dana, Charles
Francis Adams found everything in English life congenial;
and Sumner cultivated his English connections all the more
because his political views had made him an outcast in
social Boston. His pockets were always full of letters from
duchesses and noblemen, and his diaries in England suggested Ticknor's, almost as copious and entertaining. But
behind this social interest lay another, the humanitarian
feeling that England and New England shared in common. Channing, Garrison, Whittier, Mrs. Child had
spoken the language of Wilberforce and Clarkson. Their
unaffected, intelligent goodness had touched thousands of
English hearts. Philanthropic England, the England of
the great liberal circles, busily building model dwelling-
houses, raising the condition of the poor, occupied with
popular education,—in a spirit, often pharisaical, that
was sometimes saintly,—rejoiced in these American allies,

of whom Mrs. Stowe was the largest-hearted. The Anglo-American friendships of this time, Mrs. Stowe's friendship with Lady Byron, with Mrs. Browning and George Eliot, Norton's friendship with Ruskin, Emerson's with Carlyle,—a reformer of another stripe,—were fruits of this moral solidarity. Another fruit was Emerson's *English Traits*, the best of American travel-books and one of the great and permanent works of its kind. Every candid English reader, Thackeray, Browning, Clough, felt that Emerson over-praised England; but everyone felt that the praise was the praise of a master and that Emerson spoke as befitted a sage. In point of composition, *English Traits* was Emerson's masterpiece, the only book, save one, *The Conduct of Life*, that he ever really composed. What made it sovereign, as a book on England, was its realistic grasp of essential facts, its Olympian air of detachment and self-possession. It was the work of an intellect that was always dominant and always open. One felt as if the eye of God had fallen upon England, after having refreshed its impressions of India, Egypt, Greece.* If God had a special regard for England, that was his own affair.

The romantic-pusillanimous view of England was the product of a later generation. Italy, meanwhile, was the goal of those who sought, without benefit of Argo, the golden fleece of the past. Paris, for twenty years, the years of the Second Empire,—the Paris of the Empress Eugénie's hats,—was all that London later became as a goal of American fashion, of those who never trod their native shores without a steamer-ticket in their pocket; and other Americans, on special errands, flitted all over the continent, collecting twigs for their nests at home. Lowell

---

* "England has inoculated all nations with her civilization, intelligence and tastes; and, to resist the tyranny and prepossession of the British element a serious man must aid himself by comparing with it the civilizations of the farthest east and west, the old Greek, the Oriental, and, much more, the ideal standard, if only by means of the very impatience which English forms are sure to awaken in independent minds."—*English Traits.*

Mason wrote, in 1852, his *Musical Letters from Abroad,*
—reports on the state of music in Germany and England,
—before he returned to Massachusetts with an apostolic
mission like Ticknor's and Norton's. Jacob Abbott's Rollo
and Mr. George were types of a thousand other tourists
who roamed over Europe for their improvement, visiting
silk-mills and iron-foundries, marble-quarries, mosaic-fac-
tories, gathering hints for their future in Fitchburg and
Lawrence. They did not neglect the sights, the Dying
Gladiator and the Coliseum, but they never lost their
practical sense of proportion.* They felt that their minds
should be furnished but not upholstered. If Rollo had his
doubts at times, he always saw that Mr. George's view
was reasonable and right.†

For those who were tropical by organization, who
longed for the myrtle and orange, Italy was another matter. In Rome and Florence, when Hawthorne went there,
in 1858, little bands of exiles dwelt already, grouped
about the sculptors and the painters, precursors of the
colonies to come. These were new types, lovers of the picturesque who, far from seeking another homeland, wished
to be strangers and sojourners. For them, the charm of
Italy was its strangeness, not the familiarity that one
found in England. Fugitives from the land of calculation,
from the east wind, the "whip of the sky," as T. G. Appleton called it in one of his poems, the greyness and
chilliness of coast and headland, from "cold roast Boston"
and expectant Concord, which asked them either to be
men of business or to make bread of the stones in their
native pastures, they found balm and solace in the weeds

---

* "The Coliseum may have cost the most labour," said Mr. George, "but
the Great Eastern is far above it, in my opinion, in every element of real
greatness."—*Rollo in Rome.*

† "We are travelling for improvement, not for play. We are making
a tour of Scotland for the purpose of learning all we can about Scotland,
with a view to obtain more full and correct ideas respecting it than we
could obtain by books alone. So we must attend to our duty."—*Rollo in
Scotland.*

and the ruins, the lichens and the ancient walls, the colours
and the forms that caressed the eye, the flowing life, the
*dolce far niente.**

> Nature abhors what housewives love—the clean,
> And beauty hides when pail and brush come in.

So William Wetmore Story, the sculptor, wrote,—the
son of Justice Story, who had settled in Rome,—recalling
his native Salem. All his fellow-exiles shared this feeling.
Some of them, like Story, in taking flight, had been
warned by the example of Washington Allston, whose
mind had withered away in Cambridgeport. Depressed at
home, humbled before the men who were building towns
and railroads, turning villages into factory-centres, they
revelled in a world that was tumbling to pieces. They had
heard too much about the "improvement" that seemed to
signify only money and comfort; they were weary of the
"perfectibility" that left their sensuous needs unsatisfied.
Emerson had talked too much, they thought, about the
"rococo toy of Italy." He did not understand painters and
sculptors. He had seen the case in too abstract a light, as
one of them told the sage on a visit to Concord. Nature,
he said, might be the same on the banks of the Kennebec
and the banks of the Tiber, but, however it might be with
writers, who had their books to study from, artists, whose
books were pictures, needed Europe. Concord, for them,
was another Patagonia.†

In fact, the colonists in Rome and Florence were all
painters and sculptors rather than writers, or writers
whose principal interest was painting and sculpture. James

---

* "It is this which makes Rome so admirable as a residence for an artist.
All things are easy and careless in the out-of-doors life of the common
people,—all poses unsought, all groupings accidental, all action unaffected
and unconscious. One meets nature at every turn,—not braced up in prim
forms, not conscious in manners, not made up into the fashionable or the
proper, but impulsive, free and simple."—W. W. Story, *Roba di Roma.*
† Elihu Vedder, *The Digressions of V.*

Jackson Jarves lived in Florence, where he was to remain for a generation. A man of more vigorous mind than Norton or Story, though less accomplished than either, he was producing a series of books on art that had a sort of missionary value. He had settled in Italy about 1850, after a stay in Paris and a long and adventurous youth in the South Sea Islands. The son of Deming Jarves, the glassmaker, the "Father of American Glass," who had founded the glass-works at Sandwich to utilize the fine Cape Cod sand, he had inherited a little fortune, most of which he spent in collecting pictures. He had passed several years at Honolulu and written a standard *History of the Sandwich Islands* and two amateurish novels,—with a few good pages of description, sketches of Polynesian scenes and manners,—before he happened upon his real vocation. A lively, shrewd, unworldly, honest soul, with a rare aesthetic taste, a born collector, familiar with the New England country auction, at which, as a boy, he had spent his pocket-money, buying books, especially histories,—he had a passion for Prescott,—he was engaged in a nine-years' search for his great collection of Tuscan paintings.

These were the days when the Primitives were still regarded as of dubious value, when gold-background pictures of Carlo Crivelli were burned for the sake of the gold one found in the ashes and Walter Savage Landor was called a madman for wasting a handful of silver on such rubbish. At least, if this fabulous hour had passed, largely thanks to Ruskin's eloquent writings, one still found an occasional "Muse of Cortona" used by a peasant to stop a hole in an oven, a Titian, painted over by some bungler, that sold for six dollars, a Correggio, tattered and torn, in the hands of an old-clothes dealer. The age of wild buying had begun, the forgers were busy, the couriers were swindling millionaires who proudly carried back to New York and Boston their false Murillos, Claudes and Leonardos. With no fixed standards of authentication, the art-market was a house of darkness. Jarves taught himself to see in the dark. He tramped through villas, palaces and convents, picked up a canvas here and there, cut from its frame, in a pile of earth and rubble, or tossed aside in a lumber-room, and slowly formed the collection, so famous later. It was a triumph of discrimination. It was a task of devotion, like Agassiz's, for Jarves had no thought of personal gain. He was an Agassiz of art-museums, one who found, however, that his country, ready as it was for the gospel of science, was far from ready for this other gospel. Neither New York nor Boston would accept his collection, though Norton tried to find a place for it. The critics laughed at Jarves's "wiry madonnas" and called him a scamp for all his pains; and the pictures found their dwelling-place at Yale,—where a little gallery existed, the first of its kind in America, founded in 1832,—only through a comedy of errors. But Jarves was a patient man. Italian art was the fruit of a working epoch, not unlike his own, an age of democratic energies; and he thought that the same faith was preparing his country for a similar efflorescence. He bequeathed collections of textiles and Venetian glass to the New York museum and Wellesley College. He studied the glass-making at Murano and tried to introduce the Venetian methods into the works at Sandwich.

In the books that Jarves wrote in the fifties and sixties, *Art Hints, The Art-Idea, Art Thoughts, Art Studies,*— a highly intelligent history of Italian painting, with illustrations from his own collection,—he preached like one of the missionaries with whom he had spent his youth at Honolulu. He urged the cause of art-teaching, museums, galleries, schools of design. He explained the success of the British efforts to introduce art into manufacture and asked why river-banks and public buildings, parks, shop-windows and railway-cars should not have their beauty and interest. In a strain of religious feeling that beclouded his style, for his thoughts were often wrapped in ethical phrases, he asked, in fact, more questions in his field and made more intelligent observations than any other writer of his time,—"an epoch," as he described it, "of monstrous plaster figures, daubed with crazy paint, of mammoth cast-iron wash-basins, called fountains, of cast-iron architecture and clumsy gate-ways to public parks, of shoddy portrait-statues and inane ideal ones." His writings were full of astute perceptions. Like Greenough, he praised the clipper-ship and the old-fashioned farmhouse. They were appealing and true because their style was suited to the realities behind them, the climate, the materials at hand. They were as successful in their way as the Greek temples and the Gothic churches. Why? Because the American merchants and farmers took pride in a work that really met their needs. Had any American patron of painting or sculpture shown the kind of feeling the merchant expressed in Longfellow's *The Building of the Ship?*—

> Build me straight, O worthy Master,
> Staunch and strong, a goodly vessel
> That shall laugh at all disaster,
> And with wave and whirlwind wrestle!

Well might the poet say:

> The merchant's word
> Delighted the Master heard,—

for this was the tone of Lorenzo de' Medici, in days when painting had really mattered, too. Jarves, who predicted that architecture would be the first great American art, said that it could have no healthy growth until it represented the people's life and shaped itself in conformity to local causes.*

* One of Jarves's early books contained an excellent sketch of Hokusai, who was all unknown to Ruskin. This was the first suggestion of his later handbook, *A Glimpse at the Art of Japan.* Jarves was one of the first students, with Millet, Whistler and La Farge, who, when Japan was opened in the early fifties, became aware of Japanese art.

With a somewhat forbidding style, all thumbs, too often, Jarves was an independent critic who did not spare the feelings of his friends, the American painters and sculptors in Rome and Florence. Greenough had gone home to die, but Powers lived in Florence; and, in Rome, Story, Crawford * and Harriet Hosmer, a pupil of the English sculptor Gibson, who gave her one of the rooms where Canova had worked, carried on a school of Yankee sculpture that showed what will could do, if little else. Eager workers all, anxious to justify their expatriation, they turned out busts and heroic groups, statues of American statesmen, histories in granite and romances in marble, such as the "Greek Slave" and the "Libyan Sibyl." These story-telling figures possessed every accessory and association that spoke for literature as it spoke for learning and uttered an occasional word for sculpture. Zenobia was a favourite subject, the heroine of William Ware's novel, a true New England woman born too soon. The drapery of Cleopatra, as Story conceived her, was almost a novel in itself. The school excelled in allegories, representing, for instance, the struggles of genius, a sculptor in despair, while a hand pours oil into his dying lamp. The hand was the hand of the patron, and patrons were not wanting, after all. Commissions came from Congress, from Cooper, Sumner, Ticknor, and the fame of Powers's busts had gone abroad. Thorwaldsen had said that his bust of Webster was the best work of the kind in modern times. Powers's vogue was world-wide, and travelling magnates from across the sea, manufacturers, diplomats and scholars, haunted his Florentine studio. No European journey was complete unless one carried home a bust by Powers.

To warm themselves in one another's presence, the artists in Rome met at the Caffè Greco, the dark and dirty haunt in former days of Allston, Cooper and Turner.

* Crawford's figure of Beethoven, erected in the Boston Music Hall, in 1856, is said to have been the first statue raised in America to an artist.

Little groups of aspiring students went for moonlight rambles in the Coliseum. They strolled through the Forum, singing "Hail Columbia" in chorus. They stopped at the Fountain of Trevi, where Lord Neville had talked with Corinne. They sallied forth with sketch-books for picnics on the Appian Way. They pored over one another's portfolios and wrote "Campagna bits" in their journals and letters. They gathered for musical soirées, perhaps in Charlotte Cushman's rooms, for the great Boston actress with the "thoughtful" style often spent her winters in Rome. They talked about Guido's "Aurora" and Canova, who seemed to have brought back the repose of the Greeks, and the mystery of Beatrice Cenci. They sat on ruined columns, with their colours beside them, sketching some model with dishevelled hair, a beard that suggested Moses or a well-turned arm that might have belonged to Apollo. Some of them aired their distaste for the Puritan ways that had made their life at home so drab and sober. In others, the New England strain seemed only accentuated in the foreign air. They clung to their Calvinistic views and lived in the Rome of the Popes as they had lived in Lynn or Brattleboro. Powers cultivated his Yankee speech, as if it gave him a dramatic pleasure; and he and Joel Hart abounded in mechanical shifts that would have made their fortunes in Lawrence or Lowell. The tone of the little colonies, of all the foreign artists in Rome and Florence, set by Thorwaldsen and the German painters, Overbeck and Cornelius, was rigidly moral and highly religious. One might well have found some Yankee maiden, like Hilda in *The Marble Faun,* living in her tower among the doves and trimming her evening lamp at the Virgin's shrine.

This was the little world that Hawthorne found. Story, his old acquaintance in Salem, had come to spend his life in Rome and Florence. Others came and went, Lowell to visit Story, Norton taking notes on Giotto and Dante,

Bryant the poet, George Stillman Hillard, Hawthorne's old friend and Sumner's partner, who published, in *Six Months in Italy,* a glorified and even glorious guide-book that was destined to serve a generation of tourists. Story, who took Hawthorne under his wing, a slight, wiry, nervous little man, witty, swarthily handsome, abounding in every social grace, clever at acting, singing, sketching, writing, passionately ambitious as a sculptor, had passed his earlier years as a lawyer in Boston. He had written his father's life and various legal treatises; he had shared in Margaret Fuller's Conversations and dreamed and talked of art and Rome, with Longfellow, in Lowell's study. Everything in New England annoyed and bored him, even the growing interest in German thought, for Italy had captured his imagination. His closest friends there were the Brownings and Landor, who had taken refuge with the Storys when, like King Lear, at eighty-four, he had been turned adrift by his wife and children. Browning had encountered the grand old poet, as terrible as he was grand, wandering aimlessly in the streets in Florence, under the burning sun, with a few coins in his pocket, and he had joined the Storys in Siena, where he continued to write his Latin verses attacking Napoleon III. Browning took lessons in modelling from Story, who remained his intimate friend for forty years. Once, at the Palazzo Barberini, Story's house in Rome, he recited *The Pied Piper* to the Story children; Hans Andersen read *The Ugly Duckling,* and Story, playing on his flute, headed a march of the children about the house. But, as a poet, Story followed Browning like one of the children who had heard the piper.

Hawthorne surveyed the scene of *The Marble Faun* with a certain distrust and suspicion. For strangers, he felt, the Italian air had something sinister in it. The years were empty. Postponing the realities of life, one had no present, and gradually one ceased to have a future.* The artists "linger," he wrote, "while their originality dies out of them, or is polished away as a barbarism." This was surely true in Story's case, at least in the matter of his writing. What Story might have achieved under other conditions as the poet that he always wished to be remained an open question. His first Italian poems were certainly better,—if only because he was older,—than those he had written at home, the pale Tennysonian verses, the imitations of German ballads that had given him a little name in Boston. In fact, his *Castle Palo,* his *Orestes* and some of his dramatic monologues, *A Roman Lawyer in Jerusalem, A Jewish Rabbi in Rome,* would have been surprising in their power if they had not been virtually written by Browning. Story was the cleverest of chameleons, an actor, a ventriloquist in verse, and several of these poems were brilliant sallies. But less and less one found in his work the quiet, truthful, natural note that marked such earlier verses as *The Locust;* and the same thing was true of his writing in prose. His *Roba di Roma,* the fruit of his first impressions, charmingly pictured the surface of Roman life. It was a treasury of the sort of scenes, caught by an eager artist's eye, that appeared on a thousand canvases of the eighteen-fifties, the *panem et circenses* of the streets and the markets. This was the work that Story was to live by, one that he never equalled in later years. His pretty little novel, *Fiammetta,* like some of Henry James's early tales, suggested that Story ended where James began. The *Conversations in a Studio,* filled with sophisticated schoolboy-talk,—on Shakespeare, on capping quota-

---

* "The years . . . have a kind of emptiness, when we spend too many of them on a foreign shore. We defer the reality of life, in such cases, until a future moment, when we shall again breathe our native air; but, by and by, there are no future moments; or, if we do return, we find that the native air has lost its invigorating quality,—and that life has shifted its reality to the spot where we have deemed ourselves only temporary residents. Thus, between two countries, we have none at all, or only that little space of either, in which we finally lay down our discontented bones. It is wise, therefore, to come back betimes, or never."—*The Marble Faun.*

tions, on spirit-rapping,—bespoke a mind that never found its focus, a snapper-up of trifles, not unconsidered, but without the justification of a point of view.

Was Hawthorne right in feeling that "it needs the native air" to give a writer's work reality? Rome had provided him with a fairy setting for the last of his own romances,—the last he was ever to finish,—the tale of Hilda, Miriam and Donatello, the dusky Miriam of the shrouded past, the delicate wood-anemone of the Western forest. This dance of Yankee girls and fauns and spectres was like a Pompeiian fresco or something immobilized on a Grecian urn. A bituminous light suffused it, as of an afternoon in the realm of shades. One caught in the shifting groups the magical, mythological grace of Poussin. One heard Mignon's song rising from the depths in the fitful measure of a wind-harp. Hawthorne had drawn enchantment from the Roman air; and yet, for all the spell of *The Marble Faun,* it was hardly comparable with *The Scarlet Letter* or *The House of the Seven Gables*. The orchidaceous existence of most of the exiles seemed to bear him out in his distrust. One could dream forever in these Roman gardens, under the cypress and ilex, while all one's mental muscles atrophied. Norton, with his acute social conscience, his sense of a mission at home, probed under the surface of Italian life. The repressive political system disturbed him, and he had understood, from his own observation, the sorrows of Petrarch, Dante and Alfieri, who had mourned over their country and its degradation. Norton's critical faculties were alert; he had ridiculed the old romantic guide-books and the cold and pretentious work of the German painters who were dominant in modern Rome. He had cared for the realities of Italian life, as Greenough and Margaret Fuller had cared before him. The others did not wish to care. It was to escape from the prose of existence that they had left America. If their writing lost all grip and bottom, was not this the reason and the explanation?

CHAPTER XXVI

THE AUTOCRAT

THE WELL-KNOWN house of Ticknor and Fields was the publishing centre of Boston. William D. Ticknor, the senior partner, a cousin of George Ticknor, had built up a large business with English authors by paying for their books, an act of justice that was not required by any law of copyright. He had attracted Tennyson and Browning, Coventry Patmore and others, in several cases creating a public for them when they were still unknown at home.* The younger partner, James T. Fields, a man of letters in his own right, was a big, jovial creature, always dressed in Scotch tweeds, with a full beard, abundant hair, keen, twinkling eyes and a hearty manner. The Old Corner Bookstore in Washington Street, where Fields sat behind his green curtain, laughing and manufacturing reputations, was already an institution. There was always some author in Fields's cozy nook, Longfellow, Mrs. Stowe or Emerson, sitting on the window-seat in a litter of books and papers. The shop was crowded with

---

* Many English authors of the time bore witness to the American "general gift of quicker and more subtle recognition of genius than the English public,"—as Coventry Patmore described it in talking with Hawthorne. Miss Mitford said to Fields: "It takes ten years to make a literary reputation in England, but America is wiser and bolder, and dares to say at once, 'This is fine.' "—Fields, *Yesterdays with Authors*.

See also Richard Garnett's remarks in his introduction to Lowell's *My Study Windows:* "Americans far surpass us English in the prompt recognition of excellence. Carlyle, De Quincey, Coventry Patmore, James Martineau, found their first considerable audiences across the Atlantic. Americans are quicker to discover the merits of a foreign author, more thorough in naturalizing him, and demand a higher standard of excellence in the translation of his works."

visitors, poets, historians, actors and singers, for concert and lecture-tickets were also sold there, country lawyers and ministers, on their annual journey to town, and here and there some elderly judge or merchant in search of a calf-bound set of Burke or Gibbon.

James T. Fields was a sort of liaison-officer between the European celebrities and the literati of Beacon Hill and Cambridge. He had a grand idea of the publishing business. As a Portsmouth boy, a shipmaster's son, like Hawthorne and Jones Very, a passionate lover of reading, he had watched the rise of New England letters and made up his mind to forward it. He had served his apprenticeship as a bookseller's clerk and had startled all the other clerks by guessing, whenever a customer entered the shop, the sort of book the customer presently asked for. His hero-worshipper's instinct would have pleased Carlyle. He knew the London publishers and bookmen as well as he knew New York and Boston, and he had visited all his British authors, Leigh Hunt, Miss Mitford, Wordsworth, Barry Cornwall. He had gathered together De Quincey's scattered writings and published the first collected edition of them. In rare-book rooms and auction-rooms, Fields was a familiar figure. He had read all the marginal comments in Wordsworth's little library. He had lovingly handled Lamb's own copies of Marlowe, Drummond and Drayton and the literary magnificoes at "Elmwood." There was nothing he did not know about first editions. His house, which overlooked the Back Bay, was a temple of busts and portraits, autographs and souvenirs of authors, drawings by Blake, heads of Pope and Dickens, Thackeray, Wordsworth, Hawthorne. In later years, inspired by these portraits, all of them painted from life, he was to write his *Yesterdays with Authors,* a notable memoir filled with veracious gossip. He liked a rough tramp in the Adirondacks or a camping-trip to Moosehead Lake, where one slept on the ground for a mattress with a bundle of faggots under one's head. At present, while he wrote his poems and essays,—the papers collected in *Underbrush* and various songs and ballads,—he gave most of his thoughts to business. He had a shrewd eye for the winning author that would have made the fortune of a racing-man.

The chief reader of Ticknor and Fields was Edwin P. Whipple, a self-made man of letters, like Fields himself, who had been a broker's clerk when Fields was a clerk in the bookshop. The two had been inseparable friends since the days when they had met, as fellow-bookworms, in the rooms of the Mercantile Library. Whipple was a short, slight man, always dressed in black, with a square, prim face and a manner all precision and decorum. Beside the exuberant Fields, with his overflowing air of the world, there was something ministerial in his appearance. He was extremely myopic and excessively shy, and yet this bespectacled man had a vigorous mind that often suggested Macaulay, who had praised him highly. His reputation was already brilliant, in England as well as America, and some of this reputation was deserved. As a writer for the *North American,* he had formed a method of his own, discriminating, acute and often subtle, with none of the ponderousness of his early models; and he was discussing, in his essays and lectures, such subjects as wit and humour, the ludicrous side of life, genius, intellectual health and disease, character, success and its conditions. His estimates of the early American writers were undoubtedly over-friendly, but his papers on the English dramatists and the Scottish and English critics were the best of the kind in America, by far. He had summed up Francis Jeffrey to perfection, and some of his essays, on Fielding, Thackeray, Dickens, were admirable characterizations and definitions. His only American rivals were Poe and Lowell. Whipple, at the moment, was highly regarded; his volumes went through eight and ten editions, and he was to live obscurely as one of those writers whom people rediscover with surprise.

This very intelligent, shy and modest Whipple had long been moving about in Boston and Cambridge, watching the unusual men who lived there and noting their conversation and personal traits. He had formed this habit as a boy in Salem, observing Rufus Choate in his pew at church, so strangely different from the stolid merchants, and had later followed and studied in similar fashion Webster, George Ticknor and Charles Sumner, Prescott, Agassiz, Emerson, Alcott and others. He had a way of meeting them on the street at moments that revealed their oddities, stopping to see them when some bit of news had thrown them off their guard, catching two or three of them together when something in the air satisfied his eye for character. As a bank-clerk, in the Transcendental days, he had been struck by Emerson's sound sense, as compared with the delusions of the Boston merchants. The manias that possessed the business men, who bought up waste and worthless lands and recklessly sunk their millions in hopeless railroads, convinced him that Emerson knew the laws of trade better than Amos Lawrence. And so with all these other remarkable minds. He felt he was living at a historic moment, that a group of worthies had appeared who were to be of interest in the future. Scarcely observed by them, he was the chiel among them taking notes. These notes appeared later in his liveliest book, the excellent *Recollections of Eminent Men*.

That the New England mind had crystallized, that there was a renaissance in Boston,—one of those "heats and genial periods" of which Emerson spoke in *English Traits,* "by which high tides are caused in the human spirit,"—had not escaped the firm of Ticknor and Fields. In fact, they were the practical centre of it. The publishers of Emerson, Hawthorne, Holmes, of Longfellow and Mrs. Stowe were able to feel that they were creating classics; for their authors were becoming national figures, and even international. Their little brown editions were known wherever books were read; and the day had long passed when Andrews Norton, making up a list of American writers, had placed Emerson, Longfellow and Hawthorne as minor figures in the second fifty. In Russia, even in India, even in China, all these names were favourably known, and lecturers in the West, like Whipple and Alcott, found that in St. Louis and Chicago they had an almost sovereign reputation. Seen from a distance, the New England writers appeared like fixed stars in a constellation that grew more brilliant with every decade. In fact, they were widely scattered. Aside from the groups in the capital, they rarely met. The Cambridge authors never went to Concord; the Concord authors seldom went to Boston; Whittier, Mrs. Stowe, Thoreau and others revolved in worlds of their own, and Ticknor's circle scarcely crossed the circles of Holmes and Lowell. Connecticut and Massachusetts were like different nations. Their unity was an abstraction still, largely so to remain, in fact; but Fields, the clever impresario, made a reality of it. He issued souvenir volumes of "Boston Authors," with plates of Craigie House and Lowell's "Elmwood," Webster's house at Marshfield and Ticknor's in Park Street. His "blue and gold" editions stamped his poets with authority. Willis wrote to Fields, in his flowery way, "Your press is the announcing-room of the country's Court of Poetry." From this press the English writers and the New England writers came together, and each drew something from the general glamour. Browning and Longfellow, Emerson, Tennyson, Hawthorne, Holmes, De Quincey, Mrs. Stowe presented a common front as standard authors.

One of Fields's jokes was about the Boston man who read Shakespeare late in life but found him far beyond his expectation. "There are not twenty men in Boston who could have written those plays," he said. More than twenty were engaged at present in work that Boston men were fitted for. Sparks's aspirations for the Athenæum seemed almost to have been fulfilled. There were dozens of more or less productive students in the alcoves that had once been empty; and Prince Jerome Napoleon, visiting Boston, surprised by the freedom of opinion, the absence of Puritanism that he found, remarked that the New England capital had much more intellectual movement than any other part of the country. Among the recent minor men of letters were several whose names were to be remembered. The librarian of the Athenæum, William Poole, was at work on a well-known compilation. As one of the librarians at Yale, he had started the custom of keeping on slips of paper notes on current periodicals that might be useful in student-debates, and this was developing in Boston into *Poole's Index*. Thomas Bulfinch, the architect's son, a class-mate of Prescott at Harvard and a clerk at the Merchants' Bank, whose rooms, overlooking Scollay Square, were piled high with books, published *The Age of Fable* in 1855. In this same year, another book appeared that was equally useful. "Ask John Bartlett" was the phrase in Cambridge when anyone wished to find a familiar quotation. Bartlett owned the University book-store. A notable angler, a lover of whist, who edited Izaak Walton and later wrote a concordance of Shakespeare, he made his shop a centre for literary gossip and wished to live up to his reputation. He had kept for years the voluminous commonplace-book that finally emerged as Bartlett's *Familiar Quotations*.

The founding of the *Atlantic Monthly*, in 1857, marked this high tide of the Boston mind.* In the "new

* The American mind in general reached high tide at about this time. Samuel G. Goodrich ("Peter Parley") presented in *Recollections of a Life-*

magazine," as it was called from Maine to Minnesota,
all the established writers appeared together. Lowell, the
editor, assembled for the first number contributions from
Emerson, Motley, Holmes, Longfellow, Norton, Whittier and Mrs. Stowe. It seemed, from a distance, like a
family party, in spite of the diversity of these minds, and
murmurs were heard in other regions against the self-
complacency of Boston and the mutual admiration that
flourished there. But, as Dr. Holmes remarked of his
commensals, if they had not admired one another they
would have shown a singular want of taste. It was true
that at this moment the New England mind began to
reveal signs of degeneration, traits that in later years
grieved or vexed those that knew not the Boston Zion,
and sometimes did not even wish to know it. The "breaking of the seedling tulip into high-caste colours," as Dr.
Holmes described this hour in Boston, was not without
unhappy consequences. It destroyed the noble unconscious-
ness of the past. But the note of *The Atlantic* was not
self-conscious, in spite of Lowell's tendency to be so. The
magazine was born mature. The regard of the writers
for one another sprang from an impersonal respect for
their characters and their work; and, if they over-valued
one another, they set a better example than most of the
other American writers and artists, who were all too
prone to self-depreciation. They increased the self-respect
of their fellow-craftsmen; they won for American letters
and art the respect that American letters and art had

time the following statistics of American book-manufacture: In 1820,
American authors, 30%, British authors, 70%; in 1830, American authors,
40%, British authors, 60%; in 1840, American authors, 55%, British authors, 45%; in 1850, American authors, 70%, British authors, 30%; in 1856,
American authors, about 80%, British authors, 20%. In 1800, American
school-books were wholly of English origin; by 1820, they had been ad-
justed to the needs of American readers; in 1856, they were wholly American. Goodrich added, "We produce annually more school-books than the
whole continent of Europe."

always needed.* It was observed, moreover, that, sooner
or later, almost everything *The Atlantic* published, essay,
poem and story, found its way into a book and had at
least a measure of permanent interest; and, as time went
on, and Ticknor and Fields took over the publication, and
Fields became the second editor, and the Civil War came,
and Howells followed, the scope of the magazine grew
broader and broader. It became a national institution.

Dr. Holmes had named *The Atlantic Monthly,* as
Alcott had named *The Dial;* and he was the first contributor. He had had little time for writing prose in his
active professional life, but he recalled that many years
before he had published two papers entitled *The Autocrat of the Breakfast-Table.* Nothing could be salvaged
from these old essays, but the venture had given him a
good idea, to carry a note-book with him and jot down
his own conversation. A Boswell writing out himself. Two
other contributions to the monthly, evoked by the Civil
War, were the *Battle Hymn of the Republic* and *The
Man Without a Country.* Julia Ward Howe and Edward
Everett Hale, a nephew of Edward Everett, were
destined to outlive the century and write their memories
of a hundred years. Hale, whose father was Nathan
Hale, the editor of the *Daily Advertiser,* the oldest of
New England daily journals, remembered seeing his
mother rock the cradle in which reposed his sister, the
infant Lucretia, who wrote *The Peterkin Papers* in after
years, while Webster and Justice Story dictated to her
the speeches that were to appear in her husband's paper.
To write a book, for one of the Hales, was as natural as
to breathe; the father, the mother, the sisters, Lucretia
and Susan, were all authors by instinct and almost by

---

* "We every day too easily undervalue our own artists. It is sad to say
that to a remark of Thackeray they owe some of the consideration they
enjoy. 'Never neglect or forget Trumbull,' he said, and poor America accepted the boon of praise, and thought better of her Revolutionary artist."
—T. G. Appleton, *A Sheaf of Papers.*

habit; and Edward Everett Hale, a minister, whose mind was ingenious and alert, breezy and even salty, had begun to write for the press at seventeen. He was quite outside the literary currents that had irrigated the Boston mind. His models were the familiar essayists, and his mode was evangelical journalism. But he had a "new idea" once or twice, in *My Double, and How He Undid Me,* and especially in *The Man Without a Country.* New ideas are rare in story-telling, and Hale's Philip Nolan, like Rip Van Winkle, became a folk-figure, a national myth. That the story appeared at a moment when patriotic feeling was at a pitch, when men like Thoreau, whose interests were universal, felt for the first time that they had a country, accounted for its impression on the public mind; but it was a bold and fresh conception. Julia Ward Howe, a banker's daughter from New York, a clever and charming young woman with a passion for learning, had met Dr. Howe, the teacher of the blind, on one of her visits to Boston. He was riding on a black horse, and she had straightway fallen in love with him. Miss Julia Ward's friends in New York thought that her pink stockings should have been blue, for she had herself roped to her chair, in the manner of Alfieri, during her hours of study. In Boston, they understood these matters better. As the universal reformer of the future, ready for every new crop of "causes," almost the only person who knew the New York "four hundred" as well as the Boston "forty," she was a more gracious Margaret Fuller.

Half a century later, Mrs. Howe and Dr. Hale had become folk-figures in actual life. They were almost as mythological as Philip Nolan, so many associations had gathered about them. These were the days when every child in Boston had sat on Dr. Hale's knee, when the patriarch who looked like Homer was chaplain of the Senate at Washington and the romantic old sibyl, travelling with her lecture, her cap and her laces tucked away in her hand-bag, recited the *Battle Hymn* on every occasion. They were the last leaves of the flowering thorn-bush, the Boston, historic, prehistoric, of the eighteen-forties and fifties. Dr. Holmes had fallen long before them, and Holmes had flowered late. He had outlived the life-span of Goldsmith when he appeared in prose in *The Atlantic*. No matter, the pear-trees had reassured him. Some were ripe at twenty, the Jargonelles, and one had to make the most of them when they were young, for their day was soon over. Others came into their perfect condition later. These were the autumn pears that lasted better than the summer fruit. Best of all were the Winter Nelis, hard and uninviting until all the rest of the pears had had their season. Long after the frost and snow had nipped and wrecked the orchards, the Winter Nelis got their glow and perfume. How much worm-eaten fruit, how many windfalls the doctor had seen under the boughs when the sap in his own tree was just beginning to stir!

Thus it was that, at the breakfast-table, the Autocrat resumed his seat one morning and found himself addressing his fellow-boarders, the schoolmistress, the divinity-student, the landlady's daughter, Benjamin Franklin, all the characters he had known so well, in Boston or the "huckleberry districts," during his lecture-tours. The boarding-house was a microcosm of a larger world, for what American did not find himself suggested in one of the characters? The Autocrat had earned his right to speak; he had plucked the flowers of life and come to the berries, and who could say that he was not a teacher fit for a great occasion, he who had fed with the fox in the matter of knowledge and used such Machiavellian astuteness in passing on all that he had learned? What was his mission? It was very simple: the mission of conversation. Was it not very bad to have thoughts and feelings, which ought to come out in talk, *strike in,* as people said of certain diseases? There was the great American evil, morbid introspection, class-distinctions that were unconfessed, scruples of conscience, secrets that ought to be exposed to common sense, forms of speech and phrases, ugly and distorted, the outward and visible signs of the twisted life within. Fruits of the old religion of Calvinism, fruits of isolation and provincial conditions, fruits of unconscious living. Out with them, and talk them over! The boarders knew they could trust a family doctor who read them through and through, who saw their maternal grandfathers in the way they held their tea-cups, and who would never abuse their confidence, a doctor who was used to dealing with secrets and who, without hurting their feelings, could give them the right prescription to set them on the road of mental health.

The boarders listened like a three-years' child. All America had begun to listen, and well the doctor knew it. Did people think that talk was merely a tool with which to chop a path for one's primitive wants? Did they think that absolute truth, in the form of rigidly stated propositions, was all that conversation ought to admit? Did they not see how difficult it was for two persons engaged in talk to make the most of each other's thoughts, when both had so many? (Here the boarders stirred and looked as if they wished for an explanation. They did not know they had so many thoughts, never having put them into words.) Conversation must have its partial truths, even its exaggerated truths,—the boarders stirred again, —if, as one of the fine arts, it is to serve a greater art, the art of human relations. It must not merely express the "logical mind" that builds a bridge of asses over chasms that wit leaps across.

Thus, in his diplomatic way, the Autocrat attacked all the mental habits of his hearers. What was this "logical mind," the fruit of generations of preachers and lawyers, but the One-Hoss Shay of Calvinism? The doctor had no use for Calvinism, and he knew that, while they laughed at the one-hoss shay in Boston and at Harvard, it was no laughing matter in the country. He was determined to break it up,—if laughter failed, by other means, by quoting half a dozen sciences, by the use of analogies and comparisons, by every method but controversy, since controversy equalized the foolish and the wise and no one knew this better than the fools. For what was the "logical mind" of Calvinism but the parent of all injustice, the *a priori* and the *parti pris,* narrow judgment, rigid condemnation, all those moral plagues, in other words, from which the American mind so patently suffered? Did he mean to weaken moral obligations by drawing up the blinds of this dark chamber and letting in the light? His object was merely to define them; for the light he let into the dark chamber was the light of common sense, a doctor's view of the problem of cause and effect as it really expressed itself in human nature. Was some question of crime involved? The "logical mind" spoke of original sin and anathematized the doctor. The rational mind spoke of the effect and anathematized the cause. As for the fruits of the old religion, many of the minister's patients were fools and cowards, and all too many of them were also liars. (Immense sensation at the table.)

The doctor was prepared for the sensation. The religious weeklies and monthlies, all over the country, began to throw brickbats at him. The Autocrat was imperturbable. One cannot turn over any old falsehood without a terrible squirming and scattering of the unpleasant little population that dwells under it. No one can ever say anything to make his neighbours wiser or better without being abused for doing so; and, if there is one thing that people detest, it is to have their little mistakes made fun of. The Autocrat continued, with calm good humour, always ready to talk as long as a few boarders remained at the table, twirling their knives, perhaps, balancing their spoons on

the edge of their tea-cups or tilting on their chairs against
the wall. Was he named Holmes for nothing? A holme
is a meadow surrounded by brooks; and, as long as two
or three brooks, were they only trickles, fed it with their
attention, how could a meadow run dry? Now, these
little mistakes, this tilting of chairs against walls, this
pronouncing the name of one's town as if one did not
know that it ought to be "Norridge," this calling an entry
a "hall" and a buggy a "kerridge," this saying "Yes?"
when somebody told one something,—did they think these
vulgarisms were trivial matters? Was it not plain enough
that a man with a future had to get rid of all these odious
tricks? What hope could he have when he said "How's
your health?" when people liked to hear "How do you
do?" Did not Sydney Smith say that no public man in
England ever got over a false quantity uttered in early
life? And might it not be similarly said that the woman
who "calc'lates" is lost? Worldly wisdom, merely, not at
all the wisdom of the angels; but surely the woman who
"calc'lates" is not an angel, and, since she is given to calculating, she might calculate to better purpose. And what
was one to say about those rural visitors who do not know
how to get out of a room when their visit is really over?
They wish to be off, you wish them to be off, but they do
not know how to manage it. One would think they had
been built in one's parlour and were waiting to be
launched. One had to contrive for them a sort of cere-
monial inclined plane and back them down, stern foremost, so to speak, into the great ocean of out-of-doors.
What was one to say of the "terrible smile," the smile
of those persons whose mouths, the moment they see us,
begin to twitch with an uncertain movement, conveying
the idea that they are thinking about themselves and
thinking that we are thinking that they are thinking about
themselves? What was one to say of the pretty women
who do not understand the law of the road in regard to

handsome faces? Nature and custom agree, the Autocrat remarked, in granting all males the right of at least two distinct looks at every comely female countenance, one to define the person, one as an appreciating homage. The lady of whom he approved was she who left at home her virtuous-indignation countenance, knowing that the street is a picture-gallery where pretty faces framed in pretty hats are meant to be admired, and everybody has a right to see them.

Trifles, perhaps, but not unkindly mentioned. Was not the art of living made up of trifles? And were these awkward postures and rustic phrases as merely superficial as one might think? Were they not the signs of inner dislocations, the rigidities, false reserves, distortions, torments that render human relations so difficult and make men so unhappy? Expression was the greatest need of this unexpressed New England, which almost seemed to enjoy its cold and taciturn ways, ways that concealed what tragic depths! Emotions that can shape themselves in language open the gate for themselves into the great community of human affections. That was why the Autocrat loved words, expressive words, euphonious and pleasing, just as he loved song. As long as a woman could talk, or had some musical utterance, there was nothing that she could not bear. How many a tragedy had found its outlet in a strenuous bravura or a fierce roulade on one of Jonas Chickering's pianos! Therefore the Autocrat loved to hear the all-pervading tum-tum issuing from the window of the unlovely farmhouse, with the brown stream flowing beside the door, in which Almira or Louella might have been found floating, face downward, had she not been able, in these harmless discords, to throb her wild impulses away.

The boarders listened, all America listened, as the Autocrat unfolded his amusing wisdom, unrolled that inexhaustible scroll which only those possess who have kept

their wits alive by constant use. Never had they heard
of such a man for breaking up the ice of mental habits,
for harrowing people's minds and planting in them flowers that out-shone even "Macaulay-flowers." They listened round the table, reading *The Atlantic,* drawing
virtue from it, as hot water draws the strength of tea-
leaves; for society, as the Autocrat said, is a strong solu-
tion of books. The old gentleman opposite smiled
benignly, and Benjamin Franklin gathered some valuable
hints. As for the theological remarks, the divinity-student
honoured himself by the way in which he received them:
he did not swallow them at once, neither did he reject
them, but he took them as a pickerel takes the bait. He
carried them off to his cranny upstairs to ruminate over
them at leisure. The schoolmistress pondered these things
in her heart and presently passed them on to her flock.
All Young America, sooner or later, heard her say that
"those who ask your opinion really want your praise and
will be contented with nothing less." Did she not remark,
"Sin has many tools, but a lie is the handle which fits them
all"? Did she not refer to the cubes and spheres, the little
cubes of Truth that are always white and the spheres that
have "lie" written on them but that roll so easily and so
pleasantly, although they are always rolling into the
wrong corner? One had no real excuse for mistaking the
cubes, because they always stayed where they were left;
but Timidity and Good-Nature and Polite-Behaviour insisted that Truth must roll, and they filed and polished
away the snow-white cubes till one could hardly tell them
from the spheres,—a sad mistake, since Truth is always
square. No doubt, there were members of the rising generation who did not hear this fable in their youth; but
they were not born under the Stars and Stripes.

For schoolmistresses, Dr. Holmes had a tender feeling.
He was well aware of the part they played in a nation and
generation in which the men shirked the tasks of culture.

Who but the schoolmistress, and usually the New Englander of the species, followed the pioneers wherever they went, even to the remotest corner of the Rocky Mountains, and sowed the furrows they ploughed with the seeds of education which, but for her, would have remained unsown? Well the doctor knew this heroism, and he knew it imposed on the heroine a biological handicap. "The great procession of the Unloved" filled him with compassion, for he was a match-maker on all occasions. Besides, they belonged, as often as not, to the Brahmin caste of New England, that mystical brotherhood and sisterhood in which the doctor took a special pride and which he was the first to designate. He grieved when people supposed that he meant by the Brahmins a bloated Boston aristocracy. His innocent and serviceable caste was no such thing. Its members were commonly sensitive, pallid and shy, and their only birthright was a taste for learning. Bred from races of scholars, descended from gentle souls who had stepped off the "Mayflower" or the "Arbella" with books in their hands, races that had acquired, by the repetition, generation after generation, of the same unworldly influences, a distinct organization and facial type, they took to their books at school as a pointer or a setter to his field-work. Their names were constantly rising to prominence in connection with some learned labour, and the nation owed to their devotion countless unrequited benefits. Indeed, they were a caste to which only a niggard could wish to refuse a decent homage; for, in exchange for all their lofty efforts, what were their worldly claims, their prescriptive titles?—that they wore white linen by inherited instinct, that they were able to pronounce the sacred word "view," a word not to be spelled or, by others, pronounced, the touchstone of New England Brahminism. Dr. Holmes was not to be blamed if other times brought other customs, if, in days to come, the Brahmins ceased to perform their function and, in proportion as they lost their vigour, advanced their worldly claims.

Everybody listened to the Autocrat, except a little group of thinkers who also described themselves as Humanists. Perhaps they were not in the room when he remarked: "Beware of making your moral staple consist of the negative virtues. It is good to abstain, and teach others to abstain, from all that is sinful and harmful. But making a business of it leads to emaciation of character, unless one feeds largely also on the more nutritious diet of active, sympathetic benevolence." Perhaps this little group considered the doctor frivolous, with his marked distaste for a "soul-subduing decorum." But everyone else was prepared to listen when he wrote a novel, *Elsie Venner;* for he had long believed that every intelligent man had the stuff of a novel in him, and therefore why not he? In fact, he wrote three novels, as he wrote three books about the breakfast-table, proving his theory about continuations, that they were not always justified. Good jockeying, he thought, was important for authors. One should let the public see one's horse only just enough and not too much, hold him up hard when the market was too full of him, always gently feel his mouth, never slack and never jerk the rein. He let his own horse out only when the horse grew too impatient, and sometimes with not too much success. His novels were "medicated novels"; and, as the doctor was always a talker, he strolled about from page to page, airing his views about his characters, dismissing them at times with a turn of the hand as if they were so many cases at a medical meeting. His composition was very untidy. But he always had a new story, even when it was only a ghost of a story, as in the breakfast-table series, and he always had a problem to deal with,—hysteria in a young girl, a young man's misogyny, morbid religious excitement and its effects. There were happy streaks in all his writings, and striking applications of modern science; and his essay on

Mechanism in Thought and Morals, the "underground workshop of thought,"—the unconscious,—was a brilliant anticipation of Dr. Freud. In fact, although *Elsie Venner,* of all these later books, was the only one that seriously counted, the doctor knew so much about human nature, and had such a tang of his own, that one could read him at his worst with pleasure.

He was always putting two and two together, and *Elsie Venner* stood for a large sum in this species of multiplication. He had taken one of his twos from the old medical books over which he was constantly poring, Schenckius, Andreas Baccius and Cardan, books that amused the imagination. They were full of Æsculapian gossip concerning girls who had fed on poison and who acted out the influence of the poison, gossip about men, bitten by serpents, who became the fathers of daughters whom serpents could not harm, however the daughters might mistreat the serpents. *Christabel* and Keats's *Lamia* were favourites with the doctor; and recent experiments had seemed to suggest that snake-bites might produce an influence over the moral faculties of the victim. But all these mythical and half-mythical data merely served to fertilize the doctor's fancy. He was out for larger game when he imagined the beautiful, cold girl with the glittering eyes who was destined for a tragic end, the gliding, sliding Elsie, with diamonds on her breast, and her asp-like bracelet, and the barred skirts in which she liked to dance, to the rhythm of castanets. She was still and dangerous and watchful, silent in her anger and swift in vengeance, and the village folk believed that she was able to twist herself into all sorts of shapes and tie herself in a knot. In short, she suggested the rattlesnake that Dr. Holmes kept in his cage; and the story was that a snake had bitten her mother, just before Elsie was born. Was it a case of physical cause and effect? How could any honest doctor say so, even if he liked to tease his readers? Besides, there were plenty of Elsies in New England whose mothers had not been bitten by rattle-snakes. Several of them had been hanged as witches; and who but Margaret Fuller had narrowed her lids, just as Elsie did, till her eyes were small and bright as diamonds? The doctor was interested indeed in the subject of prenatal influences, but not in quite so simple a way as this. He wished to test the doctrine of original sin, which was still raging in New England, or, to place it on a larger ground, the doctrine of human responsibility for the aberrations of a disordered will. Was Elsie "shapen in iniquity," as the farmers and the country parsons thought? Not if one saw her life as the doctor saw it and did his best to make his readers see it. Was she a subject for wrath or a subject for pity? The rattlesnake's bite was only a figure of speech for any kind of untoward circumstance,—a couple of drunken grandfathers, abuse in childhood,—that might explain anyone's aberrations of will. If one saw this clearly in Elsie's case, what about all the other unhappy creatures who were born with poison in their system?

This time the doctor cast a bombshell into the circle of his fellow-boarders. Every breakfast-table in the country resounded with *Elsie Venner*. Were you a Unitarian or a Calvinist, or any other variety of Jew or Christian, were you interested in the recent theories about heredity and environment, in medical and therapeutic questions, philosophy, criminology, education? Then *Elsie Venner* had something to say to you, and sometimes it was not a pleasant message. If, as a good Unitarian, you liked to think of the soul as an "unstained white tablet," then Elsie with her wicked little powders was an awkward nut to crack. The question whether Elsie could help herself was even more of a dose for the Orthodox. If you were a Pharisee, you fared still worse; for, if Elsie was not responsible, if she could not be accused of sin,—however one might punish her for crime,—what became of your own pretensions? Were you not obliged to see that your valour and justice, your strength, truth and virtue were merely the result of your happy fortune? What was your aristocracy but a sum that began with a one in tar and a two in tallow, and perhaps a three in whale-oil, however maintained by pluck? Your elevated type of face and figure were due not to you and your father's virtue, beyond a certain measure, but to the money made from the tar and the tallow that bought the air and sunshine, the healthy, happy summers, the good nursing and doctoring, the best cuts of the best beef and mutton, which enabled your father, and his father and his, to grow up in such a kindly fashion and, when they were grown, to afford the costly luxury of beauty and marry the finest specimens of the other sex. This train of reasoning went a long way when the valour and the truth, strength and virtue were so obviously poisoned *out* of a race by the food of the bushman in his forest, by the foul air and darkness of the tenement-houses where half one's fellow-Christians were constrained to live. Just how far it went, the doctor might not have cared to think, for the "sunny street that holds the sifted few," the "swell-fronts and south-exposure houses" had a singular charm for him, as for other mortals, and the people who lived inside these houses were not only just as good as other people but the pleasantest for a doctor to take care of. "Why not take the tops of your sparrowgrass? Somebody must have 'em,—why shouldn't you?" Such was the doctor's advice to a young disciple; and, in fact, he never pretended to be a sage, too lofty for these trifles. He knew that a certain amount of glass was mingled with the bricks in the house he lived in, a knowledge that disarmed the caster of pebbles; and meanwhile he had discharged a thunderbolt that fairly rocked the walls of Philistinism. Who, after reading *Elsie Venner*, could talk about "total depravity"? Who was to condemn? Who to judge? Or pride himself too much on his family portraits? Or think that God had given him his lands and chattels in recognition of his Christian virtue? Dr. Holmes, perhaps unwittingly, had played into the hands of Dr. Darwin. He had played into the hands of Dr. Freud. He had played into the hands of another doctor of whom he had never heard, Dr. Marx. One never knows how far a doctor's table-talk may carry him.

CHAPTER XXVII

THE SATURDAY CLUB:
LOWELL'S ESSAYS

PRESCOTT died in 1859. Almost totally blind, at the last, and racked with rheumatism, able to read only a few lines in the artificial twilight of his dark blue curtains, lying flat on the floor, with his noctograph before him, when any other posture was impossible, he had never ceased to work at the vast *History of Philip II,* of which three volumes were completed. "My spirits," he said, "are always as high as my pulse, about fifteen points above normal." He was merry and laughing as usual a day before the end. Longfellow's last remembrance of Prescott was a sunny smile at the corner of the street.

The faithful Ticknor, inconsolable, recalled the happy times at Pepperell, the drives and walks with Prescott in the "Fairy Grove" or along the Nashua river, when they had filled the woods with their laughter, the evenings when they had read *The Antiquary,* with two generations of children to share the pleasure. At Lynn, where Prescott had also had a villa, looking over the water towards Nahant, an old cherry-tree stood near the house. Round and round this tree, to protect his eyes in the shade, Prescott had walked every day until he had worn a path in the greensward. The traces of this path remained for years, worn by no foot but his, while Ticknor, touched by all these memories, slowly composed his *Life of Prescott.* This was a rare biography, picturesque and circumstantial. New England had produced no other that could be placed beside it; for Ticknor's affection for his subject had brought out all the skill, the gift for observation and characterization that made his own Journal so entertaining. The unfinished *Philip II* contained some of Prescott's most splendid writing, the Battle of Lepanto, the Siege of Malta. It was a history of Europe in the latter half of the sixteenth century, when the doctrines of the Reformation were dividing the world; and Prescott had had to spread his investigations over the whole continent. On his visit to Europe in 1850, he had spent several weeks in Belgium and Holland, studying the topography of the country, the scenes of Philip's reign, the spot where William the Silent had fallen at Delft. He had had the help of Pasqual de Gayangos, the great professor of Arabic at Madrid, who translated Ticknor into Spanish. Gayangos searched for him the manuscript collection of Sir Thomas Phillips, twelve thousand pages, gathered in boxes and closets in Phillips's house, some of them under his bed; and Prince Corsini also assisted Prescott, collecting documents in Italy. The archives of Simancas, which no historian had even seen, Philip II's own original papers, two hundred and eighty-four dusty bundles, rolled up at random, that lay like bottles of forgotten wine in the lumber-room of a Spanish castle, were sorted and scrutinized for him, along with the archives of Leyden, the Hague and Paris. In all, there were eight thousand sheets to be turned into threads for the Gobelin-loom in Boston, where the tireless Prescott wove his tapestry.

Never again perhaps were historical works to excite so much attention as at present. A generation later, Parkman's great books appeared in little editions of seven hundred copies. Only a handful of readers noticed them. Prescott's *Conquest of Mexico,* a large and expensive work in three volumes, had sold four thousand copies in four months, and *Philip II,*—like *Charles V,* Robertson's famous work, which Prescott revised and continued, to fill the gap in Spanish history between Ferdinand and Philip,—was published in England in four simultaneous editions. These splendidly printed books,—for Prescott and Ticknor took pains to appear in the grand manner, —put Peter Parley out of countenance; and the interest in history grew with the interest in public affairs, which were rapidly shaping for the Civil War. Ticknor had returned from his last European journey, with a great new collection of books for Boston. The rival Astor Library in New York, with Cogswell at its head, had filled him with apprehension. Unless something similar were done in Boston, the literary culture of New England would follow trade and capital to the rapidly-growing metropolis. Ticknor had taken the lead for the Boston Public Library, collected lists of necessary books from every interested citizen, established agencies in Florence and Leipzig and bought books in London, Paris and Rome. He had made Boston, once for all, a centre of historical research.

Prescott's example had also had its effect. He had won for Boston the interest of historians everywhere and had opened up facilities for others; and his winning personality and heroic labours made history still more attractive to younger men. Of his own generation, Bancroft, who had withdrawn for a while from public life, carried on his work from volume to volume. He had long since settled in New York, but he kept a place in New England for his household gods, a summer villa at Newport, "Roseclyff." There he planted his fruit-trees and took special pride in his roses. He corresponded with rosarians all over the world. Every evening, at Newport, he read to the ladies of his household the pages he had written during the day, asking for suggestions in regard to style; for the more the flowers grew in his garden, the more he plucked them out of his prose, which soon became monotonous and bare. Everett, who had helped both Prescott and Bancroft, had also retired from politics, adopted a coat-of-arms for a bookplate,—which he was happy to find reproduced on the china and glass of the Everett House in New York,—and withdrawn to his "temple of peace" on Summer Street. His brief term as president of Harvard had not been too agreeable, for the kindly old soul, as vain as he was kind, had grieved because the undergraduates did not touch their hats to him enough. But the aging figurehead of the Boston ship, beaten by so many storms, made of soft pine instead of oak, still Apollonian in its wrinkled beauty, was ready for another voyage. Fearing that a civil war was coming, Everett did what he could to stave it off. Washington's house at Mount Vernon was dropping to pieces. The columns of the portico were falling, the offices were in ruins, the floor of the summer-house was gone, there were pales missing from the staircase. The magnolias had been whittled away by tourists and even the tomb was in decay. Everett, who had tried in vain to save Franklin's early home in Boston, hoped to unite the North and the South in one last touch of common sentiment. He composed an oration on Washington, which he delivered in every part of the country, and helped to save Mount Vernon with the proceeds. The day had passed for Everett's oratory, but there were always crowds to applaud a speaker who held his glass of water aloft and slowly and dexterously spilled it as he spoke of the cleanliness of Washington's soul.

The wheel of time had turned again. On winter afternoons, in Beacon Street, when George Ticknor passed, strolling in the sunlight, with his air of conscious importance, one recalled the days of Gilbert Stuart. The renaissance in Boston had scarcely existed for Ticknor. It scarcely existed for the elder Dana, the author of *The Idle Man,* who had outlived his little fame and whom

one also saw, on sunny days, warming his bones in the
Common, although the Saturday Club, recently organized
by the younger writers,—touched by his charm and silvery courtesy,—elected him an honorary member. The
old guard looked askance at the reigning talents, which
were too informal to please them. Emerson's high-flown
manner offended them still. They did not like Holmes's
style, his way of referring to "Roxbury and Dorchester
boys." This made the younger people feel akin, but it
struck their elders as too familiar. It was almost as bad
as Whittier, so plain that he might have been common.
Lowell was too clever to be sound. If Burke and Johnson
were no longer read, what was more to blame than
Lowell's brilliance? * Thackeray had scandalized Boston, on his reading-tour, by driving to the lecture-hall
with his long legs thrust out of the carriage-window. His
friends had had to repress his jollity, as he ploughed
through the snow on Beacon Street with *Henry Esmond,*
just issued, under his arm. The old Bostonians knew that
Englishmen often behaved like this, but they had never
expected to see a Boston man cutting undignified capers;
and Lowell's puns and Holmes's boarding-house almost
savoured of the vulgar.

The temperature, if not the tone, had risen; and no
one from other regions ever complained that the Boston
tone was low. When Thackeray wrote to Fields, "I always consider Boston my native place," he was referring
to the temperature, the warm and genial air of the Yankee Athens in these days of its efflorescence. Agassiz's
beaming face at the Saturday Club, and Longfellow,
benign, all unconscious of the spell he wove, at the other
end of the table, set the pitch of the gatherings. If the
club had not existed, Dr. Holmes would have invented
it, for such an association, in his opinion,—a club strung

* Professor Bowen, editor of the *North American Review,* rejected
Lowell's earlier essays because they were "too brilliant."

like a harp, with a dozen ringing intelligences, each answering to some chord of the macrocosm,—was the crown of a literary centre. What would literature and art have been if Shakespeare had not had his Mermaid Tavern, and Addison and Steele their coffee-house, not to speak of Dr. Johnson, Goldsmith and Gibbon? It was one of the doctor's convictions that a handful of men, at any given moment, carry in their brains the ovarian eggs of the future, and that one should talk with them in order to seize in advance these germs of thought, not yet developed, germs that were moulded on new patterns which had to be long and closely studied. For no fresh truth ever got into a book: an egg once hatched was already old. There were jobbers of thought and retailers of thought; but he wished to know the producers of thought. That was why he loved his club so dearly. One could listen to Asa Gray on botany, Peirce on mathematics and Lowell on language, Agassiz on geology and fossils, Motley on history, Norton on cathedrals. If one followed for a dozen years any line of knowledge, every other line would intersect it; and here all the lines intersected, the doctor was happy to find,—in this carnival-shower of questions, replies and comments, axioms bowled over the table like bomb-shells from professional mortars, while wit dropped its explosive trains of many-coloured fire and pelted everyone who exposed himself. Emerson enjoyed the club for much the same reasons. Of the lonely men of Concord, he was the only member, with Judge Hoar, who drew any virtue from the meetings; for Hawthorne, who joined the club after his return from Italy, sat with his eyes fixed upon his plate. Thoreau's feeling in regard to clubs might have been described as detached.* But Emerson, who said that he fed on genius

* "As for the Parker House, I went there once, when the Club was away, but I found it hard to see through the cigar smoke; and men were deposited about in chairs over the marble floor, as thick as legs of bacon in a smoke-house. It was all smoke, and no salt, Attic or other. The only room

and who liked to see feats of every kind, feats of mathematical combination, of memory and the power of abstraction, who rejoiced in a gymnasium and a swimming-school, where one saw the power of the body, a race-course, a training-ground for horses, a laboratory, a surgeon's demonstration, who never heard of any skill or vigour without fresh resolution,—Emerson sat like a child at the meetings. Every word that was dropped set free his fancy. He talked, but rarely; he preferred to listen.* His was Goethe's gift, the "highest to which man can attain," wonder.

Lowell walked in from Cambridge to his office at *The Atlantic*. Once his hat blew into the river, as he was crossing the bridge, with a hatful of rejected manuscripts. He scarcely had to look for his contributions beyond the Boston, Cambridge and Concord circles. The Porter-house steak at the Porter House, the Parker-house rolls at the Parker House, guinea-fowl and venison on all occasions, and wine, "the grand specific against dull dinners," as Dr. Holmes called it, sped the festive enterprise; and even the abstemious author of *Snow-Bound,* who had never entered a theatre and who cared as little for dinners as the men of Concord, caught the contagion of the magazine and grew more and more the man of letters. Lowell published a series of Agassiz's essays, which spread the popular knowledge of science. A poem that

in Boston which I visit with alacrity is the gentlemen's waiting-room at the Fitchburg depot, where I wait for the cars, sometimes for two hours, to get out of town. It is a paradise to the Parker House . . . A large and respectable club of us hire it (Town and Country Club), and I am pretty sure to find someone there whose face is set the same way as my own."— Thoreau, *Familiar Letters.*

* "I sat by the side of Emerson, who always charms me with his delicious voice, his fine sense and wit, and the delicate way he steps about among the words of his vocabulary,—if you have seen a cat picking her footsteps in wet weather, you have seen the picture of Emerson's exquisite intelligence, feeling for its phrase or epithet,—sometimes I think of an anteater, singling out his insects, as I see him looking about and at last seizing his noun or adjective,—the best, the only one which would serve the need of his thought."—*Life and Letters of Oliver Wendell Holmes.*

attracted much attention, *On a Bust of Dante,* was the work of a Boston dentist, Thomas W. Parsons. It was a good poem, although notable chiefly as an expression of the *zeitgeist,* the ever-growing interest in Dante studies. Dr. Parsons, at seventeen, had spent a year in Italy, where he had formed his life-long love of Dante. He had learned the *Paradiso* by heart in Florence and had translated the *Inferno* years before Norton began his studies.* Some of his other poems were good, especially *The Shadow on the Obelisk.* They represented a kind of verse, graceful and correct, that was rapidly multiplying. Often the expression of poetic natures, of cultivated and scholarly minds, usually written with taste but almost if not quite devoid of magic, this verse, which would have seemed miraculous a generation before, was a staple of every journal in later days.† In the country towns, as in the Western cities, thousands of eager faces, by the evening lamp, scanned each new issue of *The Atlantic,* thrilled by a new poem of Whittier or Lowell, perplexed by Emerson's cryptic rhymes. "If the red slayer think he slays" was better than a hundred cross-word puzzles. A paper by Thomas Wentworth Higginson, *Letter to a Young Contributor,* fluttered a breast in Amherst that was to sing to better purpose than most of the famous poets of the eighteen-sixties. To Emily Dickinson, "moving to Cambridge" seemed "like moving to Westminster Abbey, as hallowed and as unbelieved, or moving to Ephesus with Paul for a next-door neighbour."

Cambridge still had much of the village look. A mighty elm shaded Harvard Square, and the groups of youths and maidens in summer dresses who danced on the green,

---

* A copy of Parsons's *Inferno,* translated in 1843, was placed under the cornerstone of the monument to Dante in the Piazza Santa Croce.

† American poetry has had its own "law of acceleration." Rufus W. Griswold, the anthologist, said that he had read all the American poetry published before 1850. He estimated this at about five hundred volumes. Three generations later, at least as many volumes appeared every year.

on Class Day, in front of Holworthy Hall, brought back
the May Day of merry England. Old Royal Morse, the
driver of the stage in the days of President Kirkland,
still haunted the square to tell his tales of a time when
President Kirkland had scarcely been heard of. Agassiz
strolled across the Yard, smoking his cigar, oblivious of
the university statutes. Agassiz represented all that was
new. Old Cambridge was John Holmes's special province. For Dr. Holmes's shy and modest brother, whose
occupation was friendship, the period since 1832 was
"margin" and sometimes "leavings." A "ripe local man,"
as he wished to be, he lived in a little house on Appian
Way, full of cats and birds. "I sha'n't have better quarters," he said, "till I have a better half." For a bit of
foreign travel, he went to Nantasket. He even made
three short trips to Europe, where he could find nothing
to compare with Cambridge. Every day in Venice he
repaired to a spot that reminded him of a corner of the
port, where Broadway and Cambridge Street met. Besides an occasional poem, he wrote a series of letters to
one of his nephews about Goliath Tittle, the Kennebunk
sailor. Goliath was tattooed in circles by a tribe in the
South Sea Islands, and then he was captured by another
tribe who changed all the circles into squares. John
Holmes's only ventures into print were addressed to eso-
terics in Cambridge lore, those who could answer the
following questions: "Where was the old Court House?
The old jail? The Market House? Where was the college wood-yard? Where was the old hay-scales? Where
was the little brook that ran over gravel toward the
Charles and, like the two princes, was stifled in its bed?"

In Cambridge, as in Concord, where the "little
women" and the "little men" were about to appear in
books, children filled the scene. All the New England
writers understood them and wrote about them, some-

times with exquisite feeling.* *Uncle Tom's Cabin* was composed, under the lamp, on a table surrounded by children conning their lessons, in a hum of earnest voices asking questions. Hawthorne's stories were as full of children as ever the summer woods were filled with birds; and Whittier's shy affections and Holmes's salty humours were addressed as often as not to boys and girls. Lowell, so self-conscious in most of his letters, only showed how deep his feelings were in these domestic relations. Perhaps they were deep only in these relations, like the feelings of Henry James. In later times, when boys and girls were "problems," and most of their fathers and mothers were also problems, more problematic than the children, when the old cultural forms had broken down, and literature was produced by childless rebels,—or largely so produced,—against the abuses of the older culture in the hour of its rigidity and decay, when the nation had lost much of its faith and even so much of its will-to-live that "race-suicide" was a pressing question, one found it difficult to return in fancy to Longfellow's "children's hour," when life flowed so freely between the generations. This ever-present consciousness of children, in minds so unconscious of themselves, spoke for a culture at its highest tide, a community that believed in itself, serenely sure of itself and sure of its future, eager to perpetuate its forms.

Longfellow had bought an orange-tree, with a hundred buds and blossoms. It flourished in his window beside the lemon-tree, which, for the last ten years, had kept the

---

* "Pliable as she was to all outward appearance, the child had her own still, interior world, where all her little notions and opinions stood up crisp and fresh, like flowers that grow in cool, shady places. If anybody too rudely assailed a thought or suggestion she put forth, she drew it back again into this quiet inner chamber and went on. . . . There is no independence and pertinacity like that of these seemingly soft, quiet creatures, whom it is so easy to silence, and so difficult to convince."—Harriet Beecher Stowe, *The Pearl of Orr's Island*.

See also Emerson's remarks on children, in the opening paragraphs of his essay, *Domestic Life*.

summer blooming through the winter in his white-pan-
elled study. A springtime fragrance of Italy filled the
room. On his table stood Coleridge's ink-stand, the gift
of an English admirer. A Tintoretto hung near by. One
saw an agate cup of Cellini. The folding doors opened
into the spacious library, with its two Corinthian columns. There was something large, bland and sweet,
something fresh and sunny in the atmosphere of the house
that reflected the soul of the generous poet, he whom
neither fame nor the praise of kings could ever spoil or
alter. A fathomless calm of innocent goodness brooded
in the air that spread with Longfellow's poems over the
world.* Nothing disturbed the poet's magnanimous mildness, neither the vanity that he never knew nor the fools
whom he suffered gladly. By no effort of any man could
any malicious phrase be drawn from his lips. Were you
pulling some rhymester to pieces, Longfellow had culled
and was ready to quote, in the poor bard's favour, the
only good line he had **ever** written. Did you beg him not
to waste his time on the cranks who were always beset-
ting him. "Who would be kind to him if I were not?"
was Longfellow's only possible answer. As his fame
spread like the morning sun over the English-speaking
peoples, with its notes of domestic affection and the love
of the sea, of landscape and legend, till twenty-four English publishing-houses brought out his work in competition and ten thousand copies of *The Courtship of Miles
Standish* were sold in London in a single day, as the
royalties of his poems rose till they rivalled those of
Byron and even those which, in ancient Rome, Tiberius
lavished on his poetasters,—four hundred thousand
sesterces for a dialogue,—the flood of interruptions be-

---

* "I had many things to say about the sense I have of the good you
might do this old world by staying with us a little, and giving the peaceful glow of your fancy to our cold, troubled, unpeaceful spirit. Strange,
that both you and Norton come as such *calm* influences to me and others."
—Ruskin to Longfellow.

came so great that he longed for a snow-storm to block
the door. A stranger who came to see Washington's
rooms asked him if Shakespeare did not live near by.
Some of his visitors thought he was greater than Shakespeare. An Englishman stopped to see him because there
were no American ruins to visit. Longfellow smiled when
a Frenchman asked him for *révelations intimes* regarding
his domestic life, to appear in a Paris newspaper; but he
gave a loaf of bread to every beggar, even when the
beggars, disappointed, left the loaves upright on his gate-
post. Now and then a great man came of whom Longfellow had never heard but who had heard of Longfellow,
perhaps in Russia. One day, in 1861, Bakunin arrived at
noon. He had escaped from Siberia. Longfellow asked
him to stay to lunch. "Yiss, and I will dine with you,
too," Bakunin replied, and he stayed till almost midnight. There was another Cambridge tableau.

Walking in his garden, among the birds, to the trill-
ing of the frogs in his pond, like the chorus of a Grecian
tragedy, Longfellow revolved in his mind the stories he
was telling his children, passing them on to a larger
world that was an extension of his household. He told
them with a childlike air of trust, as if he knew in advance that the listening earth shared his faith in true
love and homeland, his hatred of cruelty and his joy in
nature,—the humble sweetness of a courteous heart. He
ranged, in the *Tales of a Wayside Inn,*—the old Sudbury
tavern, on the post-road to New York, where he assembled, in fancy, in imitation of Chaucer, some of his
friends, the poet, Dr. Parsons, the Sicilian, Luigi Monti,
the landlord, Mr. Howe,—over New England, Norway,
Italy, Spain. Most of these tales were of the pretty kind
in which the romantic poets abounded. Longfellow, who
liked to say, "To stay at home is best," who had nothing
of the adventurous in him and did not like extremes or
excess, the extreme of heat, the extreme of cold, treated

the tragic in the tales with the guileless impassivity of
a Florentine monk picturing the miseries of the damned.
He, whose eye had never missed an old stone church or a
winding lane, an unusual tree, a wall, a crumbling house,
in his own American country, by which to endow the
scene with associations, paused at every page of the story-
book of history and read it again aloud with a smile of
his own. But in the New England stories, *Paul Revere's
Ride, The Courtship of Miles Standish,*—"full of the
name and the fame of the Puritan maiden Priscilla,"—
another tone appeared in his voice. He spoke with a
spirit or a tender conviction that sprang from the blood
within him. One heard this note in *My Lost Youth;* one
heard it in the sea-poems, the ballad of *The Cumberland,
The Warden of the Cinque Ports.* One heard it in *The
Saga of King Olaf,* the songs of the Norsemen. In these
runes and rhymes one heard

> the ocean's dirges,
> When the old harper heaves and rocks,
> His hoary locks
> Flowing and flashing in the surges!

Longfellow's soul was not an ocean. It was a lake,
clear, calm and cool. The great storms of the sea never
reached it. And yet this lake had its depths. Buried cities
lay under its surface. One saw the towers and domes
through the quiet water; one even seemed to catch the
sound of church-bells ringing like the bells of the city of
Is. Transparent as this mind was, there were profundities
of moral feeling beneath the forms through which it
found expression, the fruits of an old tradition of Puritan culture, and, behind this culture, all that was noble
in the Northern races. If Longfellow's poetic feeling had
had the depth of his moral feeling, he would have been
one of the major poets, instead of the "chief minor poet

of the English language,"—a phrase of Arnold Bennett's that strikes one as happy, if "minor" is understood as "popular," popular in the high sense, not the machine-made popular of later times. Longfellow's flaccidity debarred him from the front rank; but his work possessed a quality, a unity of feeling and tone, that gave him a place apart among popular poets. Of all the sons of the New England morning, save only the lonely men of Concord, he was the largest in his golden sweetness.

In Lowell, too, there was something large, or, shall one rather say, robust; for the noble unconscious New England of old had begun its decline in Lowell. The "clever" note that had appeared in his earlier verse and prose, along with Holmes's cleverness, was the first streak of decay in the "high-caste tulip"; and Lowell, unlike Holmes, was self-consciously clever. Something uneasy and insecure lurked in the depths of his soul. The serene aplomb of Longfellow, Prescott and Holmes, well-seasoned men of the world, the equipoise of Emerson and Hawthorne, citizens of the over-world, was just the thing he never knew. His judgment seemed to have no bottom. He never struck a balance between his radicalism and his Tory instincts.* His schoolmasterish pleasure in snubbing others, one of the unlovelier traits of the Cambridge mind,†—so marked that Ruskin protested against his "all-knowing attitude," ‡ was matched by his capacity for feeling snubbed by those whose superiority he recognized. Emerson, Longfellow, Hawthorne never felt, as reflecting on themselves or their

* "I would not give up a thing that had roots to it, though it might suck up its food from graveyards."

† "What a delightful, generous and human sound Dr. Holmes's letters have, especially in contrast to the self-conscious Lowell. It makes one understand father's enthusiasm for the Doctor, who, he used to say, was worth all the men in the club put together; and how indignant he used to be with Lowell's manner of snubbing him, and admiring of the perfect way the Doctor took it."—*Journal of Alice James.*

‡ "Lowell speaks of Dante as if Dante were a forward schoolboy, and Lowell his master."—Ruskin to Norton.

country, the "certain condescension in foreigners" that troubled Lowell all his life. When foreigners "condescend," the weakness lies in the foreigners, for condescension is a form of weakness; whatever else it also means, it signifies an inferior understanding. Lowell could never feel this. A sense that he had been patronized lay behind the animus that made him a "defiant American," * when he was minister to England. The English knew why he was defiant, and the Romans of Rome who had known the Romans of Spain knew that Lowell was not one of them. He was uncertain of his own values. Something in him doubted the ground he walked on, and this accounted for the painful way,—painful because it was so self-conscious,—in which, in later years, he "wore a top-hat and looked askance at the Common." † Lowell must have blushed when his eye fell on the sentence, in his essay on condescending foreigners, "I am a man of the New World and do not know precisely the present fashion of Mayfair,"—in the days when he had abandoned the "round hat and sack-coat business" and wished Howells to "feel all the honour" involved in the admiration of "some titles" who had enjoyed his books.‡

This draws the curtain of another age, the age that followed the Civil War. "One thing seems clear to me," Lowell wrote, when the new age was under way, "and that is that the Americans I remember fifty years ago had a consciousness of standing firmer on their own feet and in their own shoes than those of the newer generation. We are vulgar now precisely because we are afraid of being so." § Lowell, who was referring to Henry James, included himself in the "we" with a measure of reason. The high-caste tulip was in full decay, in these days of

* Leslie Stephen.
† John Jay Chapman.
‡ Howells, *Literary Friends and Acquaintance.*
§ Letter of Lowell, 1870.

the "furtive apology," * when people forgave the self-
conscious because it was conscious, forgetting that the
noble is only noble when it is unconscious. All that was
grand in the older America, the simple elevation, the
magnanimous faith, which Lowell had praised in his essay
on Quincy, withdrawn from the foreground of the national mind, had passed into the keeping of the Remnant,
—the Remnant that hides in its bosom the esoteric values
of the race. The soil took its revenge on the Yankee
mind, as the Yankee mind abandoned the soil. The Yankee mind ceased to be proud of its country,—that is to
say, in a measure, since all these things are relative,—for
a rootless race has no country; and, having lost its basis,
it lost its values. Then the values of England resumed
their sway, as nature abhors a vacuum. There were other
elements in the situation that became significant in later
times, when urban life spread, with its special demands,
and the old American social forms, adequate for a patri-
archal world, could not meet the new requirements. The
"problem" of Henry James was more complex than any
problem that Lowell encountered; but Lowell, whose
roots had never been deeply planted, as the roots of the
men of Concord were, whose youth had been fundamen-
tally literary, foreshadowed the beginning of the end of
the old New England culture. The weakness of his position, evident from the first, was reflected in his verse and
prose, the rhetorical factitiousness of most of his poems,
the exalted commonplace, so essentially empty, of most
of his political writings. His essays on democracy, written after the Civil War, inspired a generation of credu-
lous readers, who had lost their sense of fundamental
values. To later ears, his sentiments rang hollow. What
reality could there have been in the democratic feelings
of a man who said, when he had had a taste of England,

* Robert Grant, in reference to Henry James.

that his servants were "to do as they were bid"? * Those who do not profess to be democratic can assume this attitude with a whole-souled coolness. In Lowell's tone one feels the irritation that springs from an accusing conscience. "Harsh is he that is new at his lordship," Æschylus remarked, and he might have been speaking of a bookman who had become an ambassador. Such a phrase on the lips of a man like Lowell brings to the ground with a crash many balloons of rhetoric.

But this was only an aspect of Lowell. Lacking the largeness of the whole-souled men, he had his own ingenuousness and warmth. He had a dozen literary virtues and practised them in all sincerity. It was a pity that he went to England. He was not sufficiently mature. In this, his case resembled Motley's. The ambassadorial habit, to which American writers are prone, has spoiled many a good man of letters who was not well-seasoned enough to survive the test. Emerson or Holmes, as minister to England, would have remained the men they were before. The adventure relaxed the fibres of Motley and Lowell, who had an exaggerated sense of the value of honours and the "flattering conditions of life abroad," as Lowell described them to Howells. Neither of them wrote as well after the experience as before it. Motley might have been another Gibbon, he could certainly have been another Prescott, if, instead of spending years floating about in drawing-rooms,—"suitable for women and people of rank," in Goethe's useful phrase,—breaking his heart because he lost his post, he had buried himself in his own mind; and Lowell would have been a sounder man if he had never left his cherished Cambridge. His Cambridge sometimes irritated others, and his capacity, in Paris, for making the Rue de Rivoli a mere continuation of Brattle Street was sometimes amusing at Lowell's expense. But his Cantabrigianism was his stoutest vir-

* Howells.

tue. His way with his calves and pigs, and his melons and pears, his making hay when battles were on, even the Battle of Gettysburg, his honest bookishness and his wholesome pleasure in all who loved books like himself, —this bespoke the worthy Lowell. His worldly strain did not run deep. It was evoked by situations to which he felt unequal. There was something transparently simple in him, the boyish frankness that his friends enjoyed.* One saw the "green, live Yankee" under the cosmopolitan surface, like freckles under a coating of rouge. This was the racy Lowell who had written *The Biglow Papers;* and Lowell's bookishness was a Cambridge trait. If one smiled away the shell, or pierced the armour with a shaft of wit, if one held the key that unlocked the door, one liked and rejoiced in the man one found inside.

This was the Lowell whom everyone liked and respected, the compact little man in the velvet jacket who loved his pipe and his fire of logs and turned round *rounder* than anyone else, as Howells said in later years, when he turned to take a book off the shelf. This was the Lowell who sat in his study, winter and summer, for years on end, feeding like a silkworm on his books, only stirring abroad for his daily walk. Lowell was a bookman, pure and simple, born and bred in an alcove; and he basked and ripened in the sun of books till he grew as mellow as a meerschaum. He hardly professed to be a critic, except in textual matters, in which he was both learned and conscientious. He would spend a week, at twelve hours a day,—a fortnight, if need were,—writing a six-page notice of a dictionary. He would run through the whole of Ovid and Lucan to find a word for one of his poems. From dawn to dusk in summer, oftener in winter, in the "tumultuous privacy" of a snow-storm,—for

* "My temperament is so youthful that whenever I am addressed (I mean by mere acquaintances) as if my opinion were worth anything, I can hardly help laughing. . . . A boy of twelve behind a bearded visor."— *Letters of J. R. Lowell, I, 117.*

he drew all the virtue from Emerson's line,—he read his
Boccaccio, and his Hakluyt and Purchas, his old French
metrical romances or all he could find on the Yankee
dialect. Ever since 1855, when he had lectured on the
English poets, at the Lowell Institute in Boston, he had
been regarded as a man of letters who had no equal in
the United States, for literary knowledge and grace of
style; and all this, combined with his animal spirits, made
him a capital teacher. Ticknor and Longfellow had explored for Cambridge the foreground of the history of
letters. Lowell's task was one of interpretation; and, if
his own mind was not quite in the grand style, he still
communicated a feeling for it.* He loved his books and
he liked his students. He asked them to read with him
privately in his study.

Such was the notable Cambridge bookman, the literary
recluse and the teacher of letters. When you dropped in
and found Lowell reading a play of Calderon or a canto
of Dante, you knew you were in the presence of something real. It was not the reality of a critic and made
small pretence of being so. The critic's seat is not an
easy-chair. Its rushes are iron spikes; and he who writes
about books in relation to life, or life in relation to books,
distrusts that "precious feeling of seclusion in having a
double wall of centuries" † between himself and the
world in which Lowell revelled. The rounded curves of a
velvet coat are not for him whose proper atmosphere, as
Emerson said of the scholar, is "poverty and reproach
and danger." Lowell, as a critic, was not important, in
spite of the golden opinions he won from those who had

* "Thirty odd years ago I brought home with me from Nuremberg photographs of Peter Vischer's statuettes of the twelve apostles. These I used to
show to my pupils and ask them for a guess at their size. The invariable
answer was 'larger than life.' They were really about eighteen inches high,
and this grandiose effect was wrought by simplicity of treatment, dignity
of pose, a large unfretted sweep of drapery."—*Latest Literary Essays.*
† *Library of Old Authors.*

a right to give them,* and all his authority in other circles, wherever the English tongue was spoken.† Those who compared him with Sainte-Beuve forgot Sainte-Beuve's psychology and his feeling for life,—not to speak of his scope and massiveness,—the life that in Arnold, Taine and Renan, even in Walter Pater, served as a touchstone in the world of books. Lowell, who had no philosophy, whose general ideas were so few that only two of his essays may be said to contain them,—the essays on Rousseau and Swinburne,—had no psychology either, and wished to have none; or, rather, he had enough when the subject pleased him, when it conformed with the local proprieties, but none when it shocked the proprieties. He said it was "fortunate" that we know so little about the lives of Shakespeare and his friends, "literary bohemians, living from hand to mouth," but he could hardly know too much about the virtuous Gray and the innocent Walton. It pleased him to contemplate the latter; it shocked him to contemplate the former, the evil in whose lives his conventional mind, all too conscious of the fig-leaf, greatly exaggerated; ‡ and sometimes he was disingenuous in his suggestion that these prejudices had an objective basis.§ All this was to breed

* "I think he is altogether the best critic we have; something of what Ste. Beuve is in French."—*More Letters of Edward Fitzgerald,* 212.

† "My father, who would never accept the authority of an encyclopædia when his children got him in a corner on some debated question of fact, held James Russell Lowell as the supreme judge of letters, from whom not even he could appeal. (It is true, he had never heard of Sainte-Beuve, and regarded Matthew Arnold as a modern fad.)"—Arnold Bennett, *Your United States.*

‡ "Is it not after the discreditable particulars which excite a correspondingly discreditable curiosity that we are eager, and these that we read with greatest zest? So it would seem if we judged by the fact that biography, and especially that of men of letters, tends more and more towards these indecent exposures . . . There are certain memoirs after reading which one blushes as if he had not only been peeping through a key-hole, but had been caught in the act."—Lecture on Chapman.

§ "The so-called realist raises doubts in my mind when he assures me that he, and he alone, gives me the facts of life . . . But are they the facts? I had much rather believe them to be the accidental and transitory phenomena of our existence here."—*The Old English Dramatists.*

a reaction in later generations, when the *cache-sexe* that emphasized the sex was rudely torn away, and the spotlight fell on the sex that had fallen on the fig-leaf. Sometimes, in Lowell, a whim of taste triumphed over the *convenances,* as in a casual remark on Fielding; * but psychology and the objective were the last of his cares. Life had to be as Brattle Street desired, though the heaven of intellect fell. It had to be as nobly good as Longfellow really was, and as others wished to think it.

Conventional minds are always timid because they cannot trust their own judgment. As they never exercise their judgment, preferring to follow accepted ideas, how can they judge, indeed? Their intellectual muscles are necessarily flabby. The instability of Lowell's mind, when he had to judge for himself, was as marked as the narrowness of his understanding. His sympathies were exclusively literary, or politico-literary; and, in his rare digressions into other fields, painting, for example, or architecture, he showed an ineptitude that was almost surprising. He said that Paul Potter's "Bull" could no more be compared with Rosa Bonheur's "Horse Fair" "than a stuffed and varnished dolphin with a living one," a judgment that suggests Mark Twain; and in Rome he had "doubts about domes," which seemed to him "the goitre of architecture." † Only a Boston or a Cambridge man could ever have "doubts about domes,"—despite the shades of Bulfinch and the State House. Lowell's words on Michael Angelo,—one part truth, ten parts misapprehension, which he retracted in the sequel, indicated his want of intuition, the vacillating nature of his mind, and, more than all, his fear of the great and the

---

* "He painted vice when it came in his way (and it was more obvious in his time) as a figure in the social landscape, and in doing so he was perhaps a better moralist than those who ignore it altogether, or only when it lives in a genteel quarter of the town."—*Literary and Political Addresses.*

† *Fireside Travels.*

vital.* With the great and the vital he felt unable to cope, except when he was aware of the stream of tradition that backed him up in his authority. Hence the insinuation of a grudge in the tone with which he spoke of the great and the vital, the unconsecrated great, the newly vital. He felt that the great must be "exaggerated"; the original was original by "conscious intention." Of the stream of tradition in the plastic arts, Lowell was unaware, if only because he lived in Cambridge, the Cambridge of the pre-Nortonian era. Besides, a certain levity of judgment in regard to the plastic arts was quite in the form of his age, in London as in Cambridge. Lowell's free-and-easy way with domes and Michael Angelo was all of a piece with that of other writers who spoke the word of God where literature was concerned. Carlyle was a case in point. But Lowell's tone in literary matters, where he could not feel the stream of tradition behind him, was equally presumptuous and inconsequential. The list of his ineptitudes, in relation to all that was vital, all that was original and strong in the world of his day, where he had to think for himself, was more than surprising. His instinctive response to Whitman,† Poe ‡ and Swinburne,§ their personalities and their work alike, never corrected in regard to Whitman,‖ scarcely in regard to Poe and Swinburne, since the essay on Swinburne

* "Shall I confess it? Michael Angelo seems to me, in his angry reaction against sentimental beauty, to have mistaken bulk and brawn for the antithesis of feebleness. He is the apostle of the exaggerated, the Victor Hugo of painting and sculpture. I have a feeling that rivalry was a more powerful motive with him than love of art, that he had the conscious intention to be original, which seldom leads to anything better than the exaggerated." —*Fireside Travels.*

† "No, no, the kind of thing you describe won't do. When a man aims at originality, he acknowledges himself consciously un-original."—*Letters,* I, 242.

‡ "He probably cannot conceive of anybody's writing for anything but a newspaper reputation, or for posthumous fame."—*Letters,* I, 100.

§ "I am too old to have a painted hetaira palmed off on me for a Muse." —*Letters,* I, 377.

‖ Apropos of *Leaves of Grass:* "A book I never looked into farther than to satisfy myself that it was a solemn humbug."—*New Letters,* 115.

was non-committal and Lowell could never speak of Poe
without qualifications and disclaimers, as if he were eager
to forestall any misapprehension of his admiration, were
in keeping with his verdict on Thoreau, that "his whole
life was a search for the doctor,"—not merely false but
singularly stupid,—and his final remark on Emerson's
poems,* in which the impression left in one's mind oblit-
erated the truth that it contained. A critic who regards
the truth may well retract and qualify in order to present
his theme in all its ramifications; but a substantial critic
never leaves the reader in doubt about his final judgment.
What was Lowell's real opinion of Poe, Swinburne, Emerson, Thoreau?—since we know his opinion of Whitman. Fine pages do not make a verdict, and Lowell wrote
many fine pages about Thoreau and Emerson. But the
I-am-afraids and the *Shall-I-confesses,* the doubts, the
hesitations and the doublings, the notes of patronage and
condescension, the reluctances, the conventional phrases,
the foolish condemnations, the unworthy suspicions that
marked Lowell's critical essays concerning living men
proved that his judgment had no sure footing. He was
the father of a school of American essay-writers that
blossomed in the age that followed him. These lesser
Lowells exercised a style that shambled and wobbled self-
consciously in a welter of qualifications. One might call
this style the Indian-giver style, for it took back everything it granted. The mock-modest pretence that one does
not know, in writers of this stripe, covers a certainty that
one knows indeed. But it meets an equal certainty in
others that one knows, really knows, nothing.

Boston was to produce, as time went on, many minds
of this sort. What these minds could never see was that
their knowing humility, their treating great men as re-

---

* "As for Emerson's verse (though he has written some as exquisite as
any in the language), I suppose we must give it up."—1883, *Letters,* II, 275.

fractory children, disqualified not others but themselves. The pride of Boston gave birth to the pathos of Boston. What was real in Lowell, then? Much, if one looked for it in the right direction; and even the father of a doubt-ful brood had the importance of a father. As an editor, he played a historic role. He brought to the work his learning and his taste; and his understanding of the na-tional feeling, in the years before the Civil War, gave him a double authority. It was true that, if *The Atlantic* was full of cream, he had the top of the bottle; true, that when manuscripts came to him which could not be weighed in the scales he knew, he had a way of missing them. He thought that Rossetti was "too foggy" to be printed in his magazine. His merit was that he did not doubt the value of the men he understood and found about him. For the rest, he was a bookman beyond com-pare in literary America. How does a bookman differ from a critic? He differs in that he assumes as given the whole sphere of values. The bookman does not judge, nor is he asked to judge. He appreciates, he enjoys, he communicates pleasure. In the world of the bookman, taste is the main affair, enthusiasm, gusto, relish; and it was in these that Lowell excelled. When he felt behind him the stream of tradition, when he did not have to judge for himself, when he could follow his whims and prejudices, his preferences, his instinctive admirations, when he could let out sail, without any danger of reefs and shoals, then one saw the master. Who asks for judgments of Dante and Shakespeare, of Chaucer, Spenser, Dryden, Gray and Walton? Humanity judged these authors long ago and found them worthy of enduring fame. What one is asked to do, if one writes about them, is to evoke new aspects for appreciation. This was Lowell's gift. Here lay his glory.

"In my weaker moments," he said, "I revert with a

sigh, half deprecation, half relief, to the old notion of literature as holiday, as

'The world's sweet inn from pain and wearisome turmoil.'" *

His weaker moments were his stronger moments. When he abandoned the sphere of the critic, which called for stronger muscles than he possessed, when he gave up the attempt to judge, for which he was not mature enough, and yielded to the secondary role for which his talent equipped him, the cold, self-conscious Lowell of the world became the winning Lowell of the study. He "deprecated" it, but it "relieved" him; for his efforts as a critic were conscious efforts, while all the force of the unconscious Lowell lay behind his bookishness. His mannerisms vanished at once, all that was facetious, arch and coy in the essays where he stood on his good behaviour. In his zest for letters, miracles happened. The indecisive Lowell, the conventional Lowell, the condescending Lowell, the defiant Lowell,—all these Lowells were absorbed in the passionate lover of reading. In love, one feels the world "well lost," even when the love is the love of books. What joy, what shy delights this man revealed when he wrote of the authors he loved! And even, let us add, what judgment! He who could never judge when he had to judge judged like the best when no one was looking.

There one had the Lowell that lives and breathes, the Lowell that lives in *The Biglow Papers*. If the fresh and courageous note of the *Fable for Critics* has died out of the picture, the note of the young man who spoke his mind, regardless of what anyone thought or said, the critic hitting and missing, with the rashness of youth, often hitting well and always trusting his own opinion,— if this note has vanished, another note has taken its place.

* *Latest Literary Essays,* 148.

This later Lowell has abandoned a role for which he was ill-fitted by nature and training. He has stooped to conquer, but he conquers. Take him on his own ground! Do not remind him of his old pretensions. Do not embarrass him with questions. Forget the radical views of his earlier days. Let him rejoice in royalists and churchmen, lovers of good ale and seasoned pipes who would have had small use for Abolition. Do not trip him up with insinuations about his inconsistencies and his timid aversions. There are plenty of timid people in the world, and plenty of others who are inconsistent. But men are not born every day who can write such essays as Lowell's on Walton and Dryden.

When one takes Lowell as one finds him, yields to his tastes and preferences, then one begins to share his pleasures. His animal spirits have returned. He revels in Spenser's charms and in Chaucer's beauties as he has revelled in puns and Yankeeisms. His muscles grow springy and his lungs dilate in this atmosphere of books, as in his winter walks through the streets of Cambridge. Even his puns have a respectable meaning because his beloved Elizabethans used them. Was not Queen Elizabeth an ardent punster?—and is not Lowell's love of puns, even more extravagant than Browning's and quite in the tone of his time, a symbol of his delight in reaching back, behind his Puritan heritage, to the warm and sunny world of Shakespeare and Spenser? You would hardly know this glowing Lowell, this tipster of the library! He loses all his reserves in the joy of books. Warmed with Villon and Marlowe, he gladly admits that Poe is a genius. He is all for Emerson the man, even if he has doubts about the poet. He says the happiest things about Thoreau,—"as if all out-of-doors had kept a diary and become its own Montaigne." No doubt, he would have liked Whitman also, if he had cared for Blake. In his felicitous insights and luckier phrases,* in the tone and texture of his style, Lowell deserved his fame and still deserves it.

* On Dryden: "We always feel his epoch in him, and that he was the lock which let our language down from its point of highest poetry to its level of easiest and most gently flowing prose."

On Carlyle: "He goes about with his Diogenes dark-lantern, professing to seek a man, but inwardly resolved to find a monkey."

CHAPTER XXVIII

CONCLUSION

THE CIVIL WAR brought to a head, however inconclusively, a phase of American culture that later times described as the New England "renaissance." This movement of mind continued in the generation that followed, and many of the writers who embodied it long outlived the war. Some of them produced their best work, or work, at least, equal to their best, during this later period. But all had given their measure before the war, and several had disappeared before it. That they stood for some collective impulse, exceptional in the history of the national mind, no one questioned later or has ever questioned. Whether this impulse was a "renaissance" or only an "Indian summer," as Mr. Santayana has called it, a "golden age" or a "golden day," the impulse existed and the movement was real. The question is only one of its general meaning and what it signified in itself.

It is obvious, almost strikingly so, that this movement of mind in New England followed the typical pattern of the "culture-cycle," as Spengler has convincingly described it. Setting aside the question of scale, one finds in it the same succession of phases that one finds in the great culture-cycles,—for Spengler, in this, at least, has made a case that is so suggestive as to seem conclusive. Here we have a homogeneous people, living close to the soil, intensely religious, unconscious, unexpressed in art and letters, with a strong sense of home and fatherland. One of its towns becomes a "culture-city," for Boston, with

Cambridge and Concord considered as suburbs, answers to this name, which Spengler accords to Florence, Bruges and Weimar, as no other town has ever answered in either of the Americas. There is a springtime feeling in the air, a joyous sense of awakening, a free creativeness, an unconscious pride, expressed in the founding of institutions, intellectual, humanitarian, artistic, and—at first a little timid, cold and shy—the mind begins to shape into myths and stories the dreams of the pre-urban countryside. There is a moment of equipoise, a widespread flowering of the imagination in which the thoughts and feelings of the people, with all their faiths and hopes, find expression. The culture-city dominates the country, but only as its accepted vent and mouthpiece. Then gradually the mind, detached from the soil, grows more and more self-conscious. Contradictions arise within it, and worldlier arts supplant the large, free, ingenuous forms through which the poetic mind has taken shape. What formerly grew from the soil begins to be planned. The Hawthornes yield to the Henry Jameses. Over-intelligent, fragile, cautious and doubtful, the soul of the culture-city loses the self-confidence and joy that have marked its early development,—it is filled with a presentiment of the end; and the culture-city itself surrenders to the world-city,—Boston surrenders to New York, —which stands for cosmopolitan deracination. What has once been vital becomes provincial; and the sense that one belongs to a dying race dominates and poisons the creative mind.

Not to press a formula too far, is not this the story of New England, as the New England mind confesses it, from the days of Channing and Webster to those of Henry Adams and Barrett Wendell? In religion, the springtime faith of Channing, with its feeling of a world to create and redeem, yields to the conception of religion as hygiene in the valetudinarian Mrs. Eddy. In politics, the robust and confident Webster gives place to the querulous Lodge. The scholars and historians lose themselves among their documents; and the cheerful, unconscious, generous note of the essayists and poets of the eighteen-fifties makes way for the analytical and the precious. No doubt, the New England mind exaggerates its own decline and decay. There are times when the visitor in New England feels that it is destined for another growth that will be more vigorous than its first, and the age that followed its "golden day" is richer and fuller to the enquiring eye than its own or other historians have supposed. But that it has passed through a cycle, and some such cycle as Spengler pictures,—this grows more and more apparent.

"Men are free," said D. H. Lawrence, "when they are in a living homeland, not when they are straying and breaking away. Men are free when they are obeying some deep, inward voice of religious belief. Obeying from within. Men are free when they belong to a living, organic, believing community, active in fulfilling some unfulfilled, perhaps unrealized purpose." This was the case with the New England authors, in the epoch of the building of the nation. Perhaps it was never more truly the case with any group of authors, all question of intensity aside. They were as completely of their people as any authors of the oldest nations; and they saw, if not themselves,—for they were not self-conscious,—at least their profession as having a Promethean role to play. They were teachers, educators and bringers of light, with a deep and affectionate feeling of obligation towards the young republic their fathers had brought into being. That New England was appointed to guide the nation, to civilize it and humanize it, none of them ever doubted, a motive that was evident in all their writings, from Emerson's early addresses to the table-talk of Holmes, from Longfellow's *Hiawatha,* in which an Indian myth conveys the poet's notion of his role, to the prophecies of *Uncle Tom's Cabin*. Sometimes they suggested Miss Ophelia reforming Dinah's kitchen; but there was so little of the condescending, so much of the humble and fraternal, in their state of mind and point of view, and they threw so many ideas into circulation and wrote so sincerely and so well that they came to be accepted as fathers and sages.

What was the cause of this transfiguration? The breadth of their conscious horizon, the healthy objectivity of their minds, their absorption in large preoccupations, historical, political, religious, together with a literary feeling, a blend of the traditional and the local, that gave the local wider currency while it brought the traditional home to men's business and bosoms. They filled the New England scene with associations and set it, as it were, in three dimensions, creating the visible foreground it had never possessed. They helped to make their countrypeople conscious of the great world-movements of thought and feeling in which they played parts side by side with the intellectual leaders of the older countries. In their scholarship, their social thought, their moral passion, their artistic feeling, they spoke for the universal republic of letters, giving their own province a form and body in the consciousness of the world. Moreover, there was something in their temper that made them seem friends of the human spirit. They stood for good faith and fair play and all that was generous and hopeful in the life of their time. The hold they gained and kept over the nation possessed an extra-literary sanction, as if they were voices of the national ethos. If they found themselves "done up in spices, like so many Pharaohs," as Holmes remarked in later years, it was because they were looked upon as classics,—

In whom is plainest taught, and easiest learnt,
What makes a nation happy, and keeps it so.

This process of canonization went hand in hand with the spread of New England culture over the country. As the New England strain died out in the West, with the second and third generations of the pioneers and the growth of a native point of view, the reputations of the New England authors had to face another test. They encountered an increasing neglect and indifference, and even a widespread hostility. This was partly due to the reaction against the romantic authors in every country; but it was inevitable that the West should have turned against New England. In order to establish its independence, it was obliged to do so, as the East had turned against the mother-country. Of the popular writers, Longfellow, Whittier, Holmes, something seemed destined to survive in the general mind of the nation, when the life of all the regions, taken together, formed a final synthesis; but much of their work was ephemeral, and most of it was so bound up with regional modes of feeling and local traditions that it could only endure in the regional mind. For the rest, there are two kinds of classics, the popular and the esoteric, those that yield their meaning at the first encounter and those that we have to discover by effort and insight, the classics of the intellectual surface and the classics of the spiritual depths. The popular New England authors, whom every child could understand, remained as classics indeed, but mainly for children; while the handful of esoteric authors,— Hawthorne, with his cloudy symbols, whom one could only see through a glass, darkly, Thoreau, who "listened behind him for his wit," and Emerson, who, in life, never gave a direct answer and said that one should speak in parables,—came more and more into their own. Ironically enough, it was Boston and Cambridge that grew to seem provincial, while the local and even parochial Concord mind, which had always been universal, proved to be also national. Whatever doubts the country at large

felt regarding the other New England authors, Hawthorne, Thoreau and Emerson were clearly of the main
stream, with Emily Dickinson, Whitman, Poe and
Melville.

*

*   *

Thoreau died in 1862. He had caught cold from over-
exposure while counting the rings of some trees on a
snowy day and had fought for a year and a half with
tuberculosis. He had outlived his juvenile-braggart phase
and had grown more and more to seem the sage, whose
life and opinions might have appeared in the pages of
Diogenes Laertius. In an effort to regain his health, he
had journeyed to Minnesota and had made friends with
some of the Indians there. Then, knowing that nothing
could save him, he had settled down among his papers,
with an Indian's indifference to the future, completing
some of his lists of birds and flowers and finishing *The
Maine Woods*. No more walks to Bateman's Pond, to
Becky Stow's swamp or Nine-Acre Corner. But he said
he enjoyed existence as well as ever. His thoughts had
entertained him all his life, never so much as at present.
Fields, the second editor of *The Atlantic,* had asked him
for some of his essays, and he spent his last months
revising these.

His friends could hardly imagine Concord without
him. Solitude peered out from the dells and wood-roads,
and the bobolinks seemed to sing a minor strain. One
had thought of Henry Thoreau as a part of nature,
destined to be transformed perhaps at last into a mossy
rock or a leaf-strewn spring. At least, he was like the
hour-glass apple-shrub of which he had written in his
journal. By the end of October, when the leaves had
fallen, one saw the wild yellow fruit growing, which the

cows could not reach over the thorny hedge. It was so
with the rude, neglected genius of the Concord woods
and meadows. He had suffered many a check at first,
browsed upon by fate, springing up in a rocky pasture,
the nursery of other creatures there, and had grown up
scraggy and thorny, not like the sleek orchard-trees whose
forces had all been husbanded. When, at first, within this
rind and hedge, the man shot up, one saw the thorny
scrub of his youth about him; but, as he grew, the thorns
disappeared, and he bore golden crops of Porters and
Baldwins, apples whose fame was destined to spread
through all orchards for generations, when the thrifty
orchard-trees that had been his rivals had long since
ceased to bear their engrafted fruit. It was true that
Thoreau's fame was slow in growing. Emerson and
Ellery Channing brought out his posthumous books,—he
had published only two during his lifetime; and Emerson
collected his poems and letters. But only his friends could
imagine why anyone should wish to see his journal.
Emerson was convinced that, if it was published, it would
soon produce in New England a "plentiful crop of natu-
ralists." This was true a generation later. When volumes
of selections from the journal appeared, a school of lesser Thoreaus sprang up at once; * and

> The happy man who lived content
> With his own town and continent,

became a teacher of wisdom, even in Asia.

Two years after Thoreau, Hawthorne faded out of
the Concord picture. He had come home from Italy and
England just before the outbreak of the war and had

---

* Thoreau's manuscript journal consisted of thirty-nine blank-books of
all shapes and sizes, packed in a strong wooden box built by himself. It
was bequeathed by Sophia Thoreau to H. G. O. Blake, who brought out
four volumes of selections, 1881–1892. The complete journal was edited by
Bradford Torrey and published in fourteen volumes, 1906.

taken up his life again at "Wayside," the house he had bought from Alcott, where a man was said to have lived who believed he was never to die. Hawthorne built a tower over the house, a reminiscence of the Italian villa in which he had stayed in Florence. There he had his study, reached by a trap-door, with a standing desk fastened to the wall. With England still fresh in his mind, he composed from his note-books the beautifully rounded chapters of *Our Old Home,* a book that was somewhat unhappily named; but a sudden change seemed to have come upon him with his return to America, a blight as of winter, a deadly estrangement even from his own imagination. Had he been too old to be transplanted, so that he could never take root again? He made a few half-hearted efforts to gather up the threads of his former life. He appeared at the Saturday Club for a few of the dinners; but even Alcott and Emerson seldom saw him. Once, at Emerson's house, he picked up some photographs of Concord, the common, the court-house and the Mill-dam, which he passed in his walks every day, and asked what the pictures represented. The sight of a friend or a stranger approaching his house drove him up the hill into the woods. Along the top of the ridge, among the pines, between the huckleberry and sweetfern bushes, he walked to and fro, brooding over the novel he could not finish. He fancied that the grass and the little shrubs shrank away as he passed them because there was something in his broodings that was alien to nature. Seventy-five years later, one could still trace the path that Hawthorne's footsteps wore on the tree-covered ridge.

He had wasted away and the glow in his eyes had vanished; and, hard as he tried to write, pulling down the blinds and locking his door, he could not bring his mind into focus. The novel became two novels, and the two became four. He could not fix upon a single setting: Salem, Concord, England, "Wayside" and Smithall's

Hall drifted in confusion through his mind, their outlines melting into one another. Even his theme eluded
him. Was it the unpardonable sin, the "ancestral footstep," the man who believed he was never to die? He
made four beginnings, constantly changing his perspective, until he could scarcely bear to touch his blurred and
meaningless manuscripts. A few of the scenes took form,
with all his old perfection, with the sculptural repose of
his earlier writing and a touch of the Gothic imagination that seemed to connect America with the Middle
Ages. But life shook before his eyes, like the picture on
the surface of a pond when a stone has disturbed its
tranquil mirror. His mind had grown like Melville's in
Pierre, groping in a fog for the firm conceptions that
turned to vapour as he tried to grasp them. Then, one
day in 1864, the news reached Concord from Plymouth,
New Hampshire, that he had died in his sleep at the
village inn. For years, he had been in the habit, while
idly scribbling, of writing the number 64, which had, he
felt, some fatal meaning for him. He had not disappeared, like Septimius Felton, crushed by the failure of
his dream, but he had wandered away with as little purpose, knowing perhaps that he would not return.

The Alcotts had settled in "Orchard House," next
door to Hawthorne's. Alcott had rebuilt it, leaving the
old beams and rafters, making arched alcoves of the
ovens and ash-holes; and, over the chimney-piece in Alcott's study, Ellery Channing's lines were inscribed,—

> The hills were reared, the valleys scooped in vain,
> If Learning's altars vanish from the plain.

Alcott had been made superintendent of the public
schools in Concord. His vindication had come late, and
one could only think what he might have accomplished
if he had had this chance when he was younger. Louisa

had begun to write the stories that were to carry his name around the world. Meanwhile, now that Thoreau was gone, Emerson was the master of the Concord revels. He liked to pile the children into the haycart, which they had bedecked with flowers and mosses, and carry them off for a swim and a picnic at Walden.

Emerson was travelling, on his lecture-tours, further and further westward. He was still an impossible puzzle in the popular mind, even a national joke, a byword of the country paragraphers. No matter, there were always a few of his hearers for whom all mythology spoke in his voice, the Indian gods and the gods of the North, who felt that the beautiful and the good must also be the true, if only because Emerson had said so. He seemed to have made his own all the victories of genius, which he invited one to share, he who had never doubted the riches of nature, the gifts of the future, the wealth of the mind. Whatever one's occupation was, mechanics, law, the ministry, he broke the spell of one's routine, relating one's craft and task to the laws of the world: one felt how one's life was intertwined with the whole chain of being. He spoke for magnanimity and the power of thought. In *The Conduct of Life* he had met the objections of those who found his optimism too facile. He had fully recognized the existence of evil, the brutal and barbarous elements in the core of the world, the habits of snake and spider in human beings, the snap of the tiger, the crackle of the bones of his prey in the coils of the anaconda. Even as men rose in culture, fate continued to follow them, as Vishnu followed Maya through all her ascending changes. While their checks and limitations became finer and finer, the ring of necessity still remained perched at the top. But fate had its lord, limitation its limits. It was different seen from above and seen from below. For, if fate was immense, so was power. Man was a stupendous antagonism, and as long as he thought he was free.

It was true, there was nothing more disgusting than the crowing about liberty by slaves, as most men were, and the flippant mistaking for freedom of some statute right to vote by those who had never dared to think or act; yet men had the power to look not at fate but the other way. The practical view was the other. Well had the oracle said, "Look not on Nature, for her name is fatal!" as Hafiz described the phrase on the gate of heaven, "Woe unto him who suffers himself to be betrayed by Fate!" Instead of cringing to facts, one could use and command them. Every jet of chaos that threatened extermination, one could convert by intellect into wholesome force. The water drowned ship and sailor. But, if one learned to swim and trimmed one's bark, one clove the water with it, and the waves were obliged to carry it, like their own foam, a plume and a power.

Thus Emerson spoke to the active forces waiting in his hearers, eager for the word that would set them free. For himself, he found that the more he spent the more he had to spend, the more he communicated the results of his thinking the more new thoughts he had. His zest and curiosity grew with the years; and, for all the discomforts of his lecture-tours, he liked to get away from the Eastern sea-board, where the American current was so superficial. He learned the resources of the country, going to school to the prairies. He had no fear of the future, he did not distrust the rough, wild, incalculable road America would have to travel to find itself. As between the civil and the forcible, he had always leaned, in his sympathies, to the latter. The Hoosiers and the Badgers of the West, the hard heads of Oregon and Utah, the rough-riders and legislators in shirt-sleeves, let them drive as they might. Better than to quote English standards and miss the sovereignty of power. Out of pirates and berserkers the English race had sprung, and no strong nation could ever develop without its own strong, wild will; and the power of the buffalo-hunters, bullying the peaceable and the loyal, would bring its own antidote at last. For liberty in all its wildness bred iron conscience; the instinct of the people was right in the end, and natures with great impulses had great resources and could be trusted to return from far.

There, in the West, he thought, lay nature sleeping, too much by half for man in the picture, with its rank vegetation of swamps and forests, steeped in dews and rains. In this great sloven continent, in its high Alleghany pastures, in the sea-wide, sea-skirted prairie, the great mother still slept and murmured. Man had as yet made little impression upon it. But there, where stars and woods and hills abounded, with all things still untried, could one not foresee a social state more excellent than history had recorded, one that turned its back on musket-worship and lived by the law of love and justice? Let men but know that every day is doomsday, and let them look within, in the populous, all-loving solitude which they left for the tattle of towns; for there *he* lurked and hid, he who was reality, joy and power. So Emerson felt, in the streets of New York, or at Concord, as he strolled through grove and glen. Others, as they saw him, tall and slender, leaving the village behind him, might have said to themselves, with the Swedish poet, "The last skald walks over the meadows."

INDEX